PARTICLES AND WAVES

PARTICLES
AND
WAVES

Historical Essays in the Philosophy of Science

PETER ACHINSTEIN

THE JOHNS HOPKINS UNIVERSITY

New York   Oxford
OXFORD UNIVERSITY PRESS
1991

Oxford University Press

Oxford   New York   Toronto
Delhi   Bombay   Calcutta   Madras   Karachi
Petaling Jaya   Singapore   Hong Kong   Tokyo
Nairobi   Dar es Salaam   Cape Town
Melbourne   Auckland

and associated companies in
Berlin   Ibadan

Published by Oxford University Press
200 Madison Avenue, New York, New York 10016

Oxford is a registered trademark of Oxford University Press

Library of Congress Cataloging-in-Publication Data
Achinstein, Peter.
Particles and waves :
historical essays in the philosophy of science /
Peter Achinstein.
p. cm. ISBN 0-19-506547-6
1. Science—Philosophy—History.
2. Physics—Methodology—History.
3. Wave-particle duality—History.
I. Title. Q174.8.A24 1991
501—dc20 90-7188

2   4   6   8   9   7   5   3   1

Printed in the United States of America
on acid-free paper

For My Daughter Sharon

Contents

PARTICLES AND WAVES

General Introduction

This volume discusses methodological issues generated by three historical episodes in nineteenth-century physics: the wave-particle debate about the nature of light, the development of James Clerk Maxwell's first "particle" theory of gases, and J. J. Thomson's discovery that cathode rays are particles, not waves. The book contains three parts, each devoted to one of these topics, beginning with an essay presenting the historical background of the episode and an introduction to the methodological issues to be treated. The chosen episodes have in common the idea that unobservable entities – either particles or waves – are postulated to explain a range of observed phenomena. Unobservable waves or particles are invoked by wave and particle theorists to explain observed optical phenomena such as reflection, refraction, and diffraction of light. Maxwell introduces the idea of unobservable moving particles that exert contact forces in order to explain observed phenomena involving pressure, volume, temperature, heat conduction, and diffusion of gases. Thomson postulates the existence of unobservable charged particles, rather than waves, to explain the observed magnetic and electric deflection of cathode rays.

Various general methodological issues are raised by such postulations, of no less interest today than they were in the nineteenth century. The most important concerns the legitimacy of introducing hypotheses that invoke "unobservables." If science is to be empirical, can such hypotheses be employed? How, if at all, is it possible to confirm them? A number of the scientists who participated in these episodes held strong methodological views regarding the proper answers to these questions. So did methodologists of the period, as well as ones today, commenting on these episodes. Two of these views are particularly important.

One espouses the "method of hypothesis," or hypothetico-deductivism, which permits hypotheses about unobservables provided that from them observational predictions are derivable. The second, inductivism, permits hy-

3

potheses only if they are inductively inferred from observable phenomena. Indeed, it has been claimed by a number of contemporary writers that the debate between particle and wave theorists of light in the nineteenth century stemmed from fundamental differences over scientific methodology. The particle theorists in the nineteenth century, it is alleged, not only defended Newton's corpuscular theory of the early eighteenth century, but did so on Newtonian inductive grounds. By contrast, it is said, nineteenth-century wave theorists defended their theory using the antithetical method of hypothesis.

Essays in Part I of this volume are devoted to these methodological disputes in connection with theories of light. Since particle theorists were strongly influenced not only by Newton's physics but also by his methodological views, Essay 2 discusses Newton's general methodological position regarding "hypotheses" and then considers to what extent it is put into practice in defense of his own corpuscular theory of light. Essay 3 analyzes the methodology actually practiced by nineteenth-century wave and particle theorists in order to determine whether this debate rested on a division between supporters of the method of hypothesis and inductivists. Essay 4 considers the philosophical basis for the nineteenth-century dispute between John Stuart Mill and William Whewell over the legitimacy of the method of hypothesis. Various probabilistic formulations of this dispute are constructed, and, using these, the opposing positions of Mill and Whewell are assessed. Both men applied their views to the wave theory. This essay analyzes the actual strategy of the nineteenth-century wave theorists in terms of the probabilistic formulations introduced.

In Part II, I turn to Maxwell's development of the kinetic theory of gases in the middle of the nineteenth century. Maxwell himself held methodological views about the postulation of unobservables; a number of these views are discussed in the essays in this Part. For example, in 1855, in his first major electrical work, he advocates what he calls the method of physical analogies as one that enables him to avoid hypotheses about unobservables. He also speaks in terms of an analogy in his first work on kinetic theory. Essay 7 considers to what extent he is employing a method of analogy when he develops his kinetic theory, and why and how he does and must go beyond analogies and introduce hypotheses about unobservables. In later work Maxwell explicitly rejects the method of hypothesis in favor of what he calls the "method of physical speculation." Unlike the former, the latter requires that a hypothesis have independent warrant. In Essay 8 I consider whether Maxwell had such warrant for the fundamental assumptions of his 1860 kinetic theory. For some he did, for others not. By appeal to Maxwell's actual practice, I develop a general position that explains why various hypotheses about unobservables that he introduced were worth considering, despite their lack of independent warrant. In this respect, I suggest, the method of hypothesis is correct, even if other claims it makes are questionable.

One of Maxwell's most important contributions was his derivation of a distribution law for molecular velocities that bears his name. Essay 6 raises the question of what role such derivations play in theoretical physics. It challenges a basic assumption in the method of hypothesis, inductivism, and other methodologies that the only or at least the principal role of a derivation is to provide an empirical test for a theory or to explain some known empirical fact. By examining the specific historical context, roles for Maxwell's derivation quite different from this are discovered.

Part III of the volume discusses J. J. Thomson's postulation of the electron as a result of a series of experiments he conducted on cathode rays at the end of the nineteenth century. The main methodological question raised concerns the relationship between the particle theory of cathode rays defended by Thomson (against the wave theory) and the experiments he performed to support the theory. Were the latter somehow derived from the former, or is the reverse true? More generally, how are theories postulating unobservable entities related to the experiments to which they lead and that are alleged to confirm them? I defend a series of theses about this relationship and draw conclusions concerning the hypothetico-deductive method as well as standard philosophical theories about what constitutes scientific evidence for hypotheses about unobservables.

One theme appearing in various essays concerns a strategy frequently employed to argue for theories invoking "unobservables." Because this strategy is of particular importance, and because its full development and philosophical justification take place over the course of several essays, it may prove useful at the outset to bring together various strands. The strategy contains both an explanatory part and what I call "independent warrant." The latter is usually established by some form of inductive or causal-inductive reasoning. Schematically, in the simplest case, we have some "substance" S (e.g., light, gases, cathode rays) that exhibits some observed property P. In other known cases when something X exhibits P this is always or usually caused by X's having some components (or structure) Q. It is inferred that probably S's exhibiting P is caused by its having Q as well, even though Q in the case of S is too small to be observed (e.g., light particles, gas molecules, electrons).

Frequently, this reasoning is more complex due to the fact that more than one known cause can produce property P. A typical nineteenth-century argument for the wave theory of light begins by noting that light exhibits the property of moving from one point to another in a finite time. In other known cases finite motion is produced by the transference of some body or bodies from one point to another or by the transmission of a wave disturbance through a medium. It is concluded with some probability that the motion of light is produced by either particles or waves.

Now in this case wave theorists need some further argument to show why it is unlikely to be particles. This they provide in one of two ways, each of which also involves inductive reasoning from observed cases. One is direct. If light consists of particles emanating from luminous bodies, then light should exhibit some property P, since observed particles generally exhibit that property. (For example, light from massive bodies such as the sun should be decelerated by gravitational forces exerted by such bodies.) Since light is not observed to have P, it is concluded that it is unlikely that light consists of particles. There is also an indirect method of argument. In order to explain certain observed phenomena (e.g., diffraction), those who support the opposing particle theory of light introduce certain auxiliary assumptions (e.g., that diffraction at the edges of an aperture is caused by attractive and repulsive forces that act at a distance and have certain features). Although such forces are probable, given the assumption that light consists of particles, wave theorists argue that the forces are very improbable without such an assumption. And these improbabilities are established by induction from observed properties of known forces. (See Essay 3 for the development of this argument.) By contrast, it is claimed, the wave theory introduces no auxiliary assumptions with this feature.

Whether the reasoning is direct or indirect, and whether it supports its conclusion by an explicit consideration of contrary hypotheses, an essential element involves inductive or causal-inductive reasoning from observed properties. Such reasoning yields high probability for a theory about "unobservables" based on observed properties together with known regularities involving such properties in other cases. Let T be the theory in question, O the fact that the substance S exhibits certain observed properties (which form the basis for the induction), and b (for background information) the observed regularities in other cases (b may include other established facts as well). Then the inductive reasoning is claimed to show that $p(T/O\&b) > k$, i.e., the probability of T on O and b is "high" — greater than some threshold k of high probability. This is what I call the "independent warrant" for theory T.

Now for the explanatory part of the strategy. Typically a scientist developing a theory postulating unobservables will spend much of his time showing how the theory can explain various observed phenomena — ones in addition to those in O above. The wave theorist will use his theory to try to explain rectilinear propagation, reflection, refraction, diffraction, interference, etc. Frequently these explanations take the form of deductive derivations from basic assumptions of the theory expressed quantitatively. The scientist regards these as important not only because he wishes to explain the phenomena in question in some unified way, but also because he regards a theory of light that can do so as more likely to be true than one that cannot. In short, where $O_1, \ldots, O_n$ are observed properties of light in addition to those in O, a scientist wants to determine not just whether his theory T has high probability given O and b — the "independent warrant" — but whether it has high probability given this together with the other observed properties of light, i.e., given $O_1, \ldots, O_n\&O\&b$. If the former probability is high, and if he can show that T can explain the remaining observed optical phenomena $O_1, \ldots, O_n$ in such a way that they follow deductively from T together possibly with b, then the latter probability—$p(T/O_1 \ldots O_n \& O \& b)$—must be at least as high. This is an important role played by such explanations in the assessment of the probability of a theory. Such a role is possible even when no inductive arguments can be constructed from the explained phenomena to the theory.

Can the fact that $O_1, \ldots, O_n$ are explainable by derivation from theory T *by itself* guarantee high probability for T? It cannot, since the same phenomena may be explainable by derivation from a conflicting theory T'. If the probability of such a conflicting theory T' on the basis of the background information b alone is at least as great as that of T on b, then the probability of T cannot rise above 1/2 no matter how many observable phenomena are explained by derivation from T (see Essay 4). Suppose we require not just that the observations be derivable from the theory T but what Whewell in the nineteenth century called "consilience" and "coherence." Consilience is the demand that T explain a range of phenomena including ones of a kind different from those that prompted the theory in the first place. Coherence is the demand that the assumptions in T "run together," that they be "mutually supporting." Both consilience and coherence are somewhat vague notions. Can they be given sufficiently precise interpretations so as to enable us to determine whether a theory that explains known phenomena and that satisfies these criteria is guaranteed high probability? In Essay 4 various interpretations are proposed. These are precise, they capture some intuitive ideas underlying "consilience" and "coherence," but they fail to guarantee high probability. I am dubious that interpretations exist that accomplish all three.

One additional argument is considered in Essay 9. Suppose that theory T explains phenomena $O_1, \ldots, O_n$, and that it is the only theory known by the experts to do so, or else it is regarded by the experts as far more plausible than any other theory they can think of that explains these phenomena. Under such conditions we may say that it is "the only game in town." If it is, doesn't this fact mean that it has high probability? Or, more guardedly, doesn't this fact at least increase T's probability? Or even more weakly, doesn't it make T worth pursuing? The answer given in Essay 9 to each of these three questions is: not necessarily.

In the last two paragraphs I have noted conditions some methodologists want to impose on theories to guarantee high probability for the theory when it explains the phenomena. In point of fact, in each of the three historical episodes discussed in the volume when high probability is claimed for (some of) the assumptions of the theory, the basis for this claim is not just the explanatory virtue of the theory, or this together with its consilience, or coherence, or the fact that it is "the only game in town." In each case, in addition, there is "independent warrant" of the sorts described earlier. There are known regularities involving the same or similar properties in other cases that form the basis for a (causal-) inductive inference to assumptions of the theory. In short, the strategy actually employed involves reasoning that is not just explanatory, or explanatory-plus-coherence (or other conditions sometimes mentioned by supporters of the method of hypothesis). Nor is it simply inductive. Rather, it combines elements of both.

This is a philosophical work that treats methodological issues generated in actual scientific episodes—issues that influenced the participants and concerning which they often held views of their own. Each episode involves the postulation of unobservable entities, and each raises general philosophical questions of interest to contemporary as well as past thinkers concerning what scientific method is appropriate in such cases. My aim is to present the history as well as the philosophy in sufficient depth to make the result enlightening to philosophers and historians of science as well as to others who relish methodological pursuits.

Of the eight nonintroductory essays, two (7 and 11) are unpublished, and six have been published elsewhere. (Essay 2 appears in Phillip Bricker and R. I. G. Hughes, eds., *Philosophical Perspectives on Newtonian Science* (M.I.T., 1990); 3 in *Studies in History and Philosophy of Science* 18 (1987); 4 in *British Journal for the Philosophy of Science* 41 (1990); 6 in *Studies in History and Philosophy of Science* 17 (1986); 8 in *Philosophy of Science* 54 (1987); 9 in *Philosophical Studies* 58 (1990).) The essays resemble their original self-contained forms, and so they may be read independently of each other. Voracious readers with short memories will no doubt benefit from the fact that some arguments and examples appear more than once. Others may wish to read more selectively.

I am indebted to the National Endowment for the Humanities for a three-year research grant to study methodological problems in nineteenth-century physics. Many of the essays were written or planned during this period. Various individuals share responsibility for this volume. David Sachs and Fred Suppe both suggested the idea to compile my recent essays on topics in the history and philosophy of science. Robert Rynasiewicz read practically all the material and made devastating comments. Would that I could saddle him with the remaining errors! Laura J.S. Mlawer made very helpful suggestions in the case of a number of the essays. She also ably assisted with the proofs, as did Alan Penczek and Sara Radcliffe. My wife Merle Ann provided valuable advice and encouragement throughout this project.

PART I

Theories of Light:
Particles versus Waves

PARTICLE THEORISTS

Isaac Newton.

Henry Lord Brougham.
(Courtesy National Portrait Gallery, London.)

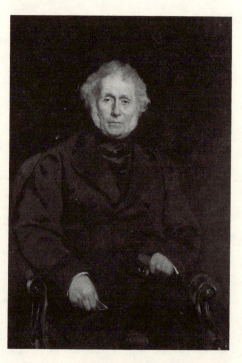

David Brewster.
(Courtesy National Portrait Gallery, London.)

WAVE THEORISTS

Thomas Young.

Augustin Fresnel.

John Herschel.
(Courtesy National Portrait Gallery, London.)

ESSAY 1

Introduction

"Sometimes I think I would let them imprison me in a place a thousand feet beneath the earth, where no light could reach me, if in exchange I could find out what stuff that is: 'Light'."

BERTOLT BRECHT, *"Galileo"*

1. HISTORICAL BACKGROUND[1]

In 1704 Isaac Newton published the first edition of the *Opticks*. Book III of this edition contains 16 queries concerning the nature of light. Later editions expanded this number to 31. Query 29 begins as follows:

> *Qu.* 29. Are not the Rays of Light very small Bodies emitted from shining Substances? For such Bodies will pass through uniform Mediums in right Lines without bending into the Shadow, which is the Nature of the Rays of Light. They will also be capable of several Properties, and be able to conserve their Properties unchanged in passing through several Mediums, which is another Condition of the Rays of Light.[2]

The theory that Newton is introducing in this query—known as either the particle, corpuscular, emission, or projectile theory—makes three fundamental assumptions: first, that light consists of material particles projected from luminous bodies; second, that these particles obey Newton's three laws of motion; third, that they are subject to short-range forces of attraction and repulsion, although, unlike the case with gravitation, Newton supplies no special force law for light. In Query 29 Newton proceeds to show how these assumptions, together with some supplementary ones, can explain various observed properties of light. In the passage just quoted he assumes that no

---

1. I have benefited very substantially from the historical account in G. N. Cantor, *Optics after Newton* (Manchester, 1983). Also worthy of mention here is Jed Z. Buchwald, *The Rise of the Wave Theory of Light* (Chicago, 1989).

2. Isaac Newton, *Opticks* (New York, 1979), p. 370.

forces act on the light particles in uniform media, so that, in accordance with his first law of motion, the light particles will move in straight lines (the so-called rectilinear propagation of light). Following this he asserts that if refraction of light is produced by a force of attraction exerted on the light particles by the refracting medium, then Snell's law relating the sines of the angles of incidence and refraction follows, as he demonstrated in Book I of the *Principia* (Proposition 94).

In addition, Newton shows how various other known properties of light can be explained by the particle theory. Different colors, for example, are associated with different degrees of refrangibility of the light rays that can be observed when the rays are dispersed by a prism. The latter phenomenon is explained on the particle theory by assuming that light consists of particles of different sizes, those associated with red being the largest and with violet the smallest. Forces on these particles in dispersion produce the least dispersion in the heaviest particles and the greatest dispersion in the lightest ones. Another optical phenomenon involves the alternating dark and bright rings (called *Newton's rings*) produced by light traveling through a thin film of air between two lenses. Some of the light is reflected, producing the bright rings, and some is transmitted, producing the dark ones. Newton speaks of a ray as alternatively in a disposition to be reflected or transmitted (its "fits of easy reflection and transmission"). He explains these fits by supposing that the particles of light produce a vibration in the surrounding medium that is swifter than the rays of light and would "overtake them successively, and agitate them so as by turns to increase and decrease their Velocities, and thereby put them into those Fits."[3]

Finally, the phenomenon of double refraction might be mentioned. When light falls on the surface of certain crystals, including Iceland spar, two refracted rays are produced. One, called the ordinary ray, obeys the standard law of refraction; the other, the extraordinary ray, does not, but continues at an angle to the former. To explain phenomena associated with double refraction, in Query 26 Newton introduces the idea that rays of light have "sides." Whether a ray is refracted by the crystal in the usual manner, or in the unusual one, will depend on the position of its sides with respect to the crystal. In Query 29 Newton returns to double refraction, suggesting that only if rays of light are bodies can they "have a permanent Virtue in two of their Sides which is not in their other Sides, and this without any regard to their Position to the Space or Medium through which they pass."[4]

Newton's Query 29, in which he shows how the particle theory can account for various observed properties of light, is preceded by Query 28, which begins as follows:

---

3. *Ibid.*, p. 373.
4. *Ibid.*, p. 374.

Qu. 28. Are not all Hypotheses erroneous, in which Light is supposed to consist in Pression or Motion, propagated through a fluid Medium?

In this query, Newton attacks a theory—or better, perhaps, a group of theories—according to which light is not a physical substance, but some type of pressure or impulse or motion propagated through a medium or ether. Various physicists had espoused a view of this sort. Descartes, for example, held that light is not itself a motion of bodies but rather a tendency to motion that is transmitted instantaneously through a medium. Hooke associated light with the motion of the parts of luminous bodies that is transferred through a medium, though probably not instantaneously. Huygens, who developed the most sophisticated view of this sort in the seventeenth century, conceived of light as a series of irregular pulses in an ethereal medium produced by the motions of the particles of the luminous bodies. The transmission of the pulses occurs in a finite time, not instantaneously, and

is propagated, as that of sound, by surfaces and spherical waves. I call these *waves* because of their resemblance to those which are formed when one throws a pebble into water and which represent gradual propagation in circles, although produced by a different cause and confined to a plane surface.[5]

Huygens introduced a principle, which came to bear his name, according to which

each particle of the medium through which the wave spreads does not communicate its motion only to that neighbor which lies in the straight line drawn from the luminous point, but shares it with all the particles which touch it and resist its motion. Each particle is thus to be considered the center of a wave.[6]

Huygens used this idea in offering explanations of various observed optical phenomena, including reflection, refraction, and the rectilinear propagation of light.

In Query 28 Newton proposes a host of objections to wave theories of these types. For example, he argues—presumably referring to Descartes' theory—that if light were only the communication of a pression without actual motion, then it would be incapable of heating objects. If light involved the communication of actual motion *instantaneously*, it would require an infinite force. One of his most powerful objections is that if any of the versions of the wave theory were correct, then light hitting some obstacle should bend into

---

5. Christian Huygens, *Treatise on Light*, reprinted in part in Henry Crew, ed., *The Wave Theory of Light* (New York, 1900); quotation on p. 11.

6. *Ibid.*, p. 21.

the shadow (should be diffracted). Newton observed that this is so with water waves and sound waves:

> The Waves on the Surface of stagnating Water, passing by the sides of a broad Obstacle which stops part of them, bend afterwards and dilate themselves gradually into the quiet Water behind the Obstacle. The Waves, Pulses or Vibrations of the Air, wherein Sounds consist, bend manifestly, though not so much as the Waves of Water.[7]

But Newton concludes: "Light is never known to follow crooked Passages nor to bend into the Shadow."[8]

The only wave-theoretic explanation for double refraction of which Newton was aware was one by Huygens. This explanation postulates two different vibrating media or ethers for light. In one, standard spherical waves appear yielding the ordinary ray. The other, in which the velocity depends on the direction of the pulse, is responsible for the extraordinary ray. In objecting to this, Newton points to results of experiments he has described in Query 25 involving two crystals with planes of perpendicular refraction at right angles to each other. In such cases rays that are refracted in the ordinary way in the first crystal are refracted in the extraordinary way in the second one. Newton observes that Huygens admitted being unable to explain such experiments. Indeed, Newton adds, pulses or motions propagated from a source through a uniform medium should be "on all sides alike; whereas by those Experiments it appears, that the Rays of Light have different Properties in their different Sides" (p. 363).

Newton's particle theory was accepted without question by many physicists until the mid-eighteenth century, when problems with it came to be recognized by its defenders as well as by a few who espoused a wave theory, such as Leonhard Euler and Benjamin Franklin. Wave theorists regarded these problems as undermining the particle theory, while particle theorists viewed them as an incentive to revise, refine, or augment the assumptions of their theory. Let me mention just two of these problems.[9]

Gravitation. If light is composed of particles, then light rays from massive bodies such as the sun and the stars should be decelerated by gravitational forces exerted by such bodies. Accordingly, contrary to what was generally thought, the velocity of light would depend on the mass of the body emitting the light. Particle theorists proposed various possible remedies, including the hypothesis that the gravitational force from the sun and stars is so small

---

7. Newton, *Opticks*, p. 362.

8. *Ibid.*, p. 363. Newton admits that there is some diffraction, but it is away from the shadow, never into it.

9. For detailed accounts of these and various other problems, and of who raised and responded to them, see Cantor, *op. cit.*, ch. 3.

compared with the force ejecting the light particles that decelerations are difficult if not impossible to detect.

Short-range forces. Following Newton, particle theorists invoked the existence of short-range forces, both attractive and repulsive, to explain various optical phenomena. For example, to explain the refraction that occurs when light passes from one medium to another of different density, Newton invoked an attractive force with a direction perpendicular to the surface of the denser medium. Newton attributed the diffraction of light by an obstacle away from the shadow to a repulsive force. Particle theorists required different forces for different optical phenomena, without producing any quantitative laws governing such forces or any unification of the forces postulated. This was regarded by many as the most serious deficiency of the particle theory.

Despite these and other problems, most physicists at the end of the eighteenth century clung to the particle theory for two reasons.[10] First, it seemed capable of explaining more optical phenomena in less objectionable ways than any rival.[11] Second, it was part of a general program, so successful in celestial mechanics, to explain phenomena in terms of material bodies subject to forces obeying Newtonian laws.

In 1800 Thomas Young, a British physician and scientist, published a paper entitled "Outlines of Experiments and Inquiries Respecting Sound and Light."[12] In Section 10 of the paper ("Of the Analogy between Light and Sound"), Young, noting the controversy between wave and particle theorists, proposes to bring forward considerations that will mitigate objections to the wave theory and to present some difficulties for the particle theory that he claims "have been little observed." The first difficulty Young mentions derives from the observed fact that in a uniform medium light travels with the same velocity no matter what its source. But Young finds it difficult to believe that "whether the projecting force is the slightest transmission of electricity, the friction of 2 pebbles, the lowest degree of visible ignition, the white heat of a wind furnace, or the intense heat of the sun itself, these wonderful corpuscles are always propelled with one uniform velocity" (p. 613). A second difficulty, which Young regards as even more serious than the first, concerns partial reflection (the fact that at a refracting surface some light rays are reflected and others are transmitted). If the light is monochromatic and consists of particles of exactly the same kind, why should some be reflected and others refracted? (He obviously rejects Newton's proposal that the particles set up

---

10. See Cantor, *op. cit.*, p. 89.

11. Besides the wave theory there was a fluid theory, held by a small minority, according to which light is produced by rectilinear motion rather than vibration of a fluid ether. The theory was associated particularly with certain doctrines in chemistry and theology rather than physics. See Cantor, *op. cit.*, ch. 4.

12. Thomas Young, *Philosophical Transactions of the Royal Society* 90 (1800), pp. 106–150.

swifter vibrations than the surrounding medium.) By contrast, Young believes, these two phenomena are readily explainable by the wave theory. For example, the latter postulates an elastic ether, and vibrations "are known to be transmitted through an elastic fluid with the same velocity" (p. 614). Young claims that to explain partial reflection, as well as the phenomena of refraction and diffraction, one need only suppose that denser refracting media contain greater quantities of ether without an increase in elasticity, and that light "is a propagation of an impulse communicated to this ether by luminous bodies" (p. 614).

In 1802 Young published "On the Theory of Light and Colours" (a Bakerian lecture given in 1801).[13] He writes:

> The object of the present dissertation is not so much to propose any opinions which are absolutely new, as to refer some theories, which have been already advanced, to their original inventors, to support them by additional evidence, and to apply them to a great number of diversified facts, which have hitherto been buried in obscurity. Nor is it absolutely necessary in this instance to produce a single new experiment; for of experiments there is already an ample store. (p. 47)

There follow four propositions, which Young labels "hypotheses," that express basic assumptions of the wave theory: first, that a rare and highly elastic luminiferous ether pervades the universe; second, that a luminous body excites undulations in this ether; third, that the different color sensations depend on the frequency of vibrations excited by light in the retina; and fourth, that material bodies attract the ethereal medium so that the latter accumulates within them and around them for a small distance. Young claims that, contrary to what has usually been supposed, the first three hypotheses can be found in Newton's writings. And he defends these by appeal to passages from Newton. The fourth hypothesis, which was contrary to Newton's assumption that ordinary matter repels the ether, Young holds to be less fundamental than the others, but "the simplest and best of any that have occurred" to him.

Following this are nine "propositions" that develop the wave theory in a qualitative way by indicating various properties of the undulations and how certain observed optical phenomena are to be explained by reference to them. (For example, the first states that impulses are propagated through a homogeneous elastic medium with uniform velocity.) These propositions are defended by invoking experiments and observations, analogies with sound, deductive argumentation, and appeals to authority. Historically the most important of the propositions is the eighth, which is an early formulation of the principle

---

13. Thomas Young, *Philosophical Transactions of the Royal Society* 92 (1802), pp. 12–48. Reprinted in part in Crew, *op. cit.*, pp. 47–61.

of interference, Young's most famous single contribution to optics. Proposition 8 is this: "When two undulations, from different origins, coincide, either perfectly or very nearly in direction, their joint effect is a combination of the motions belonging to each" (p. 60). This is the case when undulations are in the same phase, and is called *constructive interference*. In the discussion that follows this proposition, Young also speaks of the case when the undulations are 180 degrees out of phase, as a result of which they are destroyed (*destructive interference*). (He makes it clear he is speaking of undulations of the same frequency.)

In 1807 Young published a two-volume work on natural philosophy.[14] Lecture XXXIX, entitled "On the Nature of Light and Colours" is a defense of the wave theory.[15] Young begins by noting that "it is allowed on all sides that light either consists of the emission of very minute particles from luminous substances, . . . or in the excitation of an undulatory motion, analogous to that which constitutes sound, in a highly light and elastic medium pervading the universe . . . " (p. 359). He shows how both theories attempt to explain various optical phenomena. With regard to a significant number of them, including diffraction, uniform velocity of light, partial reflection, double refraction, and so on, he claims that the particle theory but not the wave theory introduces improbable auxiliary explanatory hypotheses. Of major interest in this lecture is his first description of the double-slit experiment demonstrating interference — his most famous experiment. It involves a beam of homogeneous light falling on a screen in which there are two small slits that produce diffraction of the light. This results in an image consisting of light or dark stripes (the interference pattern) on a surface placed beyond the screen.

Young's work did not succeed in convincing particle theorists to mend their ways. Some regarded it simply as a defense, albeit with some new wrinkles, of an already discredited theory. Other particularly empirically minded scientists rejected it primarily on the grounds that it postulated a luminiferous ether — an hypothesis that was entirely speculative. Among the latter, Henry Brougham, one of the founders of the *Edinburgh Review* and later Lord Chancellor of England, was particularly virulent. Characterizing Young's 1802 paper as "destitute of every species of merit," Brougham objected to Young's claim to be able to defend the wave theory without producing a single new experiment. Brougham, a champion of the Newtonian particle theory, argued that the particle theory, by contrast to the wave theory, is legitimate because it is inferable by induction from experiments.

The most important contributor to the wave theory in the early nineteenth century, and the one who turned the tide in its favor, was the French engineer Augustin Jean Fresnel. Instead of relying heavily on qualitative accounts

---

14. Thomas Young, *A Course of Lectures on Natural Philosophy and the Mechanical Arts* (London, 1807).

15. *Ibid.*, pp. 358–372.

often appealing to analogies between light and sound, as Young had done, Fresnel introduced quantitative mathematical analyses into wave theoretical explanations of various optical phenomena. His most important contribution was a mathematical analysis of diffraction, for which he received a prize from the Paris Academy in 1819.

Fresnel's prize essay begins with a comparison between wave and particle theory explanations of several optical phenomena, including the diversity of colors, Newton's rings (fits of easy reflection and transmission), and diffraction. Fresnel argues that these are readily explained by the assumptions of the wave theory, whereas to explain them on the particle theory requires invoking additional, highly improbable assumptions. In the case of diffraction, for example, the particle theory invokes an attractive force to explain diffraction bands formed inside the shadow of the diffracting obstacle and a repulsive force to explain those produced outside the shadow. In one type of diffraction experiment, a beam of light passes through a narrow aperture and, according to the particle theory, is diffracted by attractive and repulsive forces with their origin at the edges of the aperture. But if this is so, Fresnel argues, then forces should vary with the mass and shape of the edges of the aperture, and thus affect the shape of the observable diffraction fringes produced. In experiments using two edges of different mass and shape, however, Fresnel observed no changes in the diffraction bands produced.[16] Fresnel concludes that the phenomenon of diffraction does not depend on the mass or shape of the body intercepting the light but only on its size or on the size of the aperture. He adds

> We must, therefore, reject any hypothesis which assigns these phenomena to attractive and repulsive forces whose action extends to a distance from the body as great as that at which rays are inflected [diffracted]. (pp. 98–99)

Similarly he rejects another possible particle explanation that attributes diffraction to the existence of a "shallow atmosphere which has the same thickness as the sphere of activity of these forces, and whose refractive index differs from that of the neighboring medium" (p. 99). This assumption, like the former, yields the conclusion that diffraction should vary with the shape and mass of the edges. Fresnel thus concludes: *"The phenomena of diffraction cannot be explained on the emission-theory."*[17]

Turning to the positive side of the argument, Fresnel writes:

> I now propose to show that we may find a satisfactory explanation [of diffraction] and a general theory in terms of waves, without recourse to any auxiliary hypothesis, by basing everything upon the principle of Huygens and upon that of interference, both of which are inferences from the fundamental hypothesis. (p. 99)

---

16. A. Fresnel, "Memoir on the Diffraction of Light," reprinted in part in Crew, *op. cit.*, pp. 81–155; see pp. 96–97.

17. *Ibid.*, p. 99. Italics Fresnel's.

He appeals to Huygens' idea that from each point on a wave front secondary waves emanate, and, in accordance with the idea of interference, these secondary waves either constructively or destructively interfere, depending on the phase relationships. What Fresnel attempts to determine quantitatively is the resultant vibration at any point behind the diffracting device. His account is much more sophisticated than Young's, not only because it is quantitative, but also because in determining the resulting vibration it considers wave contributions from all points on a wave front and because it considers all cases of interference, not just the limiting ones involving a maximum or minimum. Fresnel derives mathematical expressions for the amplitude of the vibration at any point behind the diffractor, and for the light intensity at that point. From these he infers the positions and intensities of the diffraction bands—inferences that were confirmed experimentally. One striking confirmation occurred with respect to a consequence noted not by Fresnel himself but by Simeon-Denis Poisson, one of the judges for the prize. It follows from Fresnel's assumptions that when a circular disk is used as a diffractor, then at the center of the shadow a bright spot should appear. This prediction was also established experimentally.

Fresnel also made substantial contributions to a wave-theoretic understanding of the polarization of light. Certain phenomena, including double refraction, illustrate asymmetrical properties of light, which led Newton, for example, to postulate sides for light rays. A set of light rays with sides oriented in the same direction was polarized, one with sides in different directions was unpolarized. Jed Buchwald has suggested that prior to the work of Fresnel, physicists thought of rays of light as countable physical objects comprising a beam whose intensity is determined by the number of rays it contains.[18] To characterize asymmetries among the rays, Buchwald invokes the analogy of a stick with a crosspiece at right angles to it. If the crosspieces are oriented in the same direction, the light is polarized. Now in experiments conducted by Fresnel together with Arago in 1819 it was discovered that while unpolarized rays exhibit interference effects, those polarized at right angles to each other do not. This cast doubt on the traditional assumption of wave theorists that light waves, like those of sound, are longitudinal (i.e., their direction of vibration is parallel to the direction of propagation). In 1821, as a result of this and other polarization phenomena, Fresnel concluded that these phenomena required forces acting in a direction perpendicular to the rays, and therefore that light consisted of transverse, not longitudinal, waves. (A transverse wave is one whose direction of vibration is perpendicular to that of its propagation.)

Prior to Fresnel, even wave theorists frequently discussed optical phenomena by reference to *rays* of light. For example, Young most often spoke of

---

18. Buchwald, *op. cit.*, p. xv.

constructive and destructive interference at a point produced by the interference of two rays. With Fresnel, optical phenomena are analyzed entirely in wave-theoretic terms. A ray of light is no longer construed as something physical, but as a mathematical abstraction representing a line drawn in the direction of motion of a wave perpendicular to the wave front. The ether, however, in which the waves are present was to be thought of as physical and not as a mathematical tool or abstraction. According to Fresnel it consists of mutually repelling molecules of material points that fill space and that satisfy Newtonian mechanics.

By the 1830s, as a result of Fresnel's work, the wave theory was much more widely accepted. During this period two major review articles appeared. The first, a 246-page article by John Herschel,[19] was completed in 1827. Herschel presents detailed mathematical treatments of the wave and particle theories of light. He admits that "neither the corpuscular nor the undulatory, nor any other system which has yet been devised, will furnish that complete and satisfactory explanation of *all* the phenomena of light which is desirable" (p. 450). Nevertheless he argues for the superiority of the wave theory with respect to numbers of phenomena. In many cases, interference being just one example, the particle theory offers either no explanation or one based on improbable or purely ad hoc speculative assumptions, whereas the explanation provided by the wave theory follows from its basic principles alone and introduces no such questionable assumptions. And for at least some phenomena — such as Newton's rings and the velocity of light in denser and rarer media — the two theories make different predictions that can be experimentally tested. In the case of Newton's rings, for example, Herschel notes that the wave theory predicts that the intervals between the rings produced by the perpendicular incidence of light should be black, whereas this should not be the case for the particle theory. He writes: "M. Fresnel describes an experiment made for this purpose and states the result to be unequivocally in favour of that of undulations."[20]

The second review article, 119 pages in length, was published by Humphrey Lloyd in 1835.[21] Like Herschel, Lloyd proceeds by taking various known optical phenomena and showing how, if at all, the two major rival theories propose to explain each. He argues that the wave theory is superior to the particle theory on the grounds that, unlike the wave theory, the particle theory is either unable to explain various phenomena in a precise quantitative way or can do so only by the introduction of complex assumptions that, given established facts, are highly improbable or yield conclusions that are.

---

19. John Herschel, "Light," in *Encyclopedia Metropolitana* (1845).
20. *Ibid.*, p. 473.
21. Humphrey Lloyd, "Report on the Progress and Present State of Physical Optics," *Reports of the British Association for the Advancement of Science* 4 (1835), pp. 295–413.

There were a number of phenomena, including dispersion and selective absorption, that had not been adequately explained by the wave theory, and during the 1830s these were investigated from a wave-theoretic perspective. Some physicists, including Brougham, David Brewster, and Richard Potter, continued to defend the particle theory even beyond 1850. Brewster, for example, appealed to absorption phenomena in criticism of the wave theory. How is it possible, he asked, for two rays with small differences in wavelength to be such that one is absorbed and one transmitted by the same medium?[22] However, despite the fact that several known phenomena remained to be given satisfactory wave-theoretic explanations, by the 1830s and 1840s most physicists concerned with optics came to support the wave theory. In 1833 one such physicist, Baden Powell, constructed the table reproduced in Figure 1. This table lists 23 optical phenomena and evaluates the explanations offered by the wave and particle theories as "perfect," "imperfect," or "none." In the last category there are 12 entries for the particle theory and only 2 for the wave theory, while in the "perfect explanations" category there are 18 for the wave theory and only 5 for the particle theory. Even the remaining particle theorists agreed that as the wave theory had come to be developed in a quantitative manner, it generally offered more satisfactory explanations of a range of phenomena than did the particle theory. Because of this, Brewster, while refusing to admit the truth of the wave theory, was willing to consider it a useful instrument of analysis and prediction.

2. METHODOLOGICAL ISSUES

A fundamental methodological question suggested by the wave-particle debate is this: Under what conditions, if any, can scientists legitimately introduce and claim support for hypotheses that invoke "unobservables" such as light waves or particles? Light waves are not visible in the manner of water waves, nor can light particles be seen the way larger projectiles can. How, then, can either theory be defended empirically, and how is one to choose between them? Various physicists who participated in the wave-particle debate, as well as historical and philosophical commentators, expressed strongly held views on these questions.

Two general methodologies loom particularly important. One is the so-called method of hypothesis, or *hypothetico-deductivism*, which claims that if an hypothesis explains and predicts a variety of phenomena, this fact is sufficient to confirm the hypothesis or render it probable. A second methodology — *inductivism* — insists that an explanatory and predictive connection

22. David Brewster, "Observations on the Absorption of Specific Rays in Reference to the Undulatory Theory of Light," *Philosophical Magazine* 2 (1833), pp. 360–363.

Phenomena	Corpuscular explanation	Undulatory explanation
Reflection	Perfect	Perfect
Ditto at boundary of transparent medium	Imperfect	Perfect
Refraction (light homogeneous)	Perfect	Perfect
Dispersion	Imperfect	Imperfect (?Cauchy)
Absorption	Imperfect	Imperfect
Colours of thin plates (in general)	Perfect (with subsidiary theory of fits)	Perfect
Central spot	None	Perfect (Imperfect according to Mr. Potter)
Airy's modification	None	Perfect
Thick plates	Perfect	Perfect
Coloured fringes of apertures and shadows in simple cases	Imperfect (with subsidiary theory of inflection)	Perfect (Imperfect according to Mr. Barton)
——in more complex cases	None	None
Stripes in mixed light	None	Perfect
Shifting by interposed plate	None	Perfect (Imperfect according to Mr. Potter)
Colours of gratings	None	Perfect
Double refraction	Perfect	Perfect
Polarization	Imperfect (with subsidiary theory of polarity)	Perfect (with subsidiary theory of transverse vibrations)
Connexion with double refraction	None	Perfect
Law of tangents	None	Perfect
Interferences of polarized light	None	Perfect
Polarized rings	Imperfect (with subsidiary theory of moveable polarization)	Perfect
Circular and elliptic polarization: at internal reflection	None	Imperfect
at metallic surfaces	None (? Sir D. Brewster)	None
Conical refraction	None	Perfect

FIG. 1 Baden Powell's 1833 Comparison of Particle and Wave Explanations

between hypothesis and phenomena is not sufficient. There must also be some *independent warrant*, which consists of an inductive connection (that is not simply explanatory or predictive) between the phenomena explained or others and the hypothesis. In the essays that follow we will see how such methodologies are developed and defended by participants in the wave–particle debate, and we will consider the extent to which they are employed in actual arguments given in favor of one theory or another. Do particle theorists champion one of these methodologies and wave theorists another? Is this reflected in their actual practice? Is the methodology they do in fact employ legitimate?

Newton's methodology, which is a type of inductivism and a rejection of the method of hypothesis, is explicitly formulated in various passages in the *Principia* (particularly in the "Rules of Reasoning in Philosophy" at the beginning of Part III, and in the General Scholium at the end), in a passage at the end of the *Opticks* (pp. 404–405), in various letters, and in some unpublished material.

At the end of the *Principia* Newton confesses that although he has established that the force of gravity exists and has the various properties he attributes to it (e.g., it varies with the quantity of matter contained in bodies), he has

> not been able to discover the cause of those properties of gravity from phenomena, and I frame no hypotheses [*hypotheses non fingo*]; for whatever is not deduced from the phenomena is to be called an hypothesis; and hypotheses, whether metaphysical or physical, whether of occult qualities or mechanical, have no place in experimental philosophy. In this philosophy particular propositions are inferred from the phenomena, and afterwards rendered general by induction.[23]

This passage, although brief, makes a number of important claims. It defines an hypothesis as "whatever is not deduced from the phenomena." It claims that hypotheses "have no place" in empirical science. And it tells us that particular propositions in empirical science must be inferred from the phenomena and then inductively generalized. The questions that need answering, then, are what Newton means by "phenomena," by "deduction," and by "induction."

These questions are discussed in detail in Essay 2. Very briefly, to anticipate, by a "phenomenon" Newton means a fact established by observations and acceptable by anyone making the appropriate observations. (In the *Principia*, following the "Rules of Reasoning in Philosophy," Newton lists six propositions as describing phenomena, including the proposition that the five primary planets revolve about the sun—Phenomenon 3.) By "induction" I

---

23. Isaac Newton, *Principia* (*Mathematical Principles of Natural Philosophy*) (Berkeley, Calif., 1966), p. 547.

take Newton to mean an inference from some property found to hold for all observed members of a class to the claim that it holds for all members of the class or for some members not yet observed. To cite one of Newton's own examples, "the bodies which we handle we find impenetrable, and thence conclude impenetrability to be a universal property of all bodies whatsoever" (*Principia*, p. 399). "Deduction" for Newton is a term that includes both induction, as just defined, and (ordinary) deductions or demonstrations of the sort produced in mathematical proofs. It also includes certain forms of reasoning from observed effects to causes (e.g., from the fact that the moons of Jupiter and Saturn obey Kepler's laws to the proposition that the motions of these moons have the same causes). An hypothesis, then, for Newton is any proposition that has not been derived from accepted observational facts by ordinary deduction, inductive generalization, inference from similar effects to similar causes, or any combination of these. Newton believes that the aim of the scientist should be to provide the highest certainty possible in an empirical endeavor, and that "deductions from phenomena," and only these, will do so. Furthermore, he explicitly rejects the idea that the method of hypothesis can provide such certainty. You cannot infer an hypothesis on the grounds that it explains or entails the phenomena, no matter how many and varied these are, since there may be conflicting hypotheses that will do so as well.

Now the fundamental assumptions of Newton's particle theory—that light consists of material bodies that obey the laws of motion and are subject to short-range forces of attraction and repulsion—are not "deduced from the phenomena" by Newton in the queries of the *Opticks*. Accordingly, they are "hypotheses" in the Newtonian sense. If we are to take seriously Newton's remarks at the end of the *Principia*, they have no place in empirical science. Yet clearly Newton does propose and consider them in the *Opticks*. Is he violating his own methodology in doing so?

Obviously he is if one focuses only on his dictum that hypotheses have no place in experimental philosophy. In the queries, and indeed in other parts of his writings, Newton considers various propositions that are not deduced from the phenomena. (Indeed, in the *Principia* there is a proposition even called an hypothesis, viz., that the center of the system of the world is immovable—Book III, p. 341.) Granted, then, that in practice he at least considers hypotheses, the question is whether Newton makes any inferences to them that are of a kind precluded by his inductive methodology. Does he, for example, infer the truth of his particle hypotheses on the ground that they explain various optical phenomena?

One possibility is that he does not violate this part of his methodology at all since he makes no inferences concerning the particle hypotheses. He is simply raising the question of whether such hypotheses might be true.[24] An-

---

24. This interpretation of Newton is suggested by A. I. Sabra, *Theories of Light from Descartes to Newton* (London, 1967), p. 312.

other possibility is that Newton is indeed violating his own methodology by using the method of hypothesis to argue from the explanatory success of the particle theory to its truth. The first interpretation does not seem to be a fair reading of Newton, since the queries are formulated rhetorically ("Are not the Rays of Light very small Bodies emitted from shining Substances?") so as to suggest strongly the answer: Of course! Moreover, Query 29 is followed by a lengthy discussion that offers arguments in favor of the particle theory, and is preceded by a substantial discussion giving arguments against the rival wave theory. Newton does indeed seem to be making inferences. If he is, must these be construed in accordance with the second possibility as instances of the method of hypothesis, that is, as inferences of a type that Newton clearly and explicitly rejects in his methodological remarks? In Essay 2 this question is answered in the negative. An attempt is made to reconstruct Newton's reasoning in favor of the particle theory so as to take into account Queries 28 and 29 of the *Opticks*, together with the general methodological views he expresses in various writings. This form of reasoning is then reconstructed in probabilistic terms and critically evaluated, and the question is raised as to how, if at all, it differs from "deduction from the phenomena."

As noted, Newton's influence in optical theory was dominant for more than 100 years after Queries 28 and 29 were written. When Young attempted to revive the wave theory at the beginning of the nineteenth century, he was met either with indifference or scorn. Henry Brougham attacked him not only for daring to question the authority of Newton in physics, but for failing to follow Newton's methodological precepts requiring deductions from phenomena and the rejection of the method of hypothesis. Some commentators on the history of the wave–particle debate have taken this fact together with others as suggesting that the debate involved not just differences over physical commitments but, equally important, differences over methodologies. Cantor, for example, writes that nineteenth-century particle theorists considered "induction to be the proper scientific method," while "supporters of the wave theory, unlike its objectors, championed the method of hypothesis."[25] Larry Laudan also claims that nineteenth-century wave theorists employed a form of the method of hypothesis, by contrast to the eighteenth-century inductivist critics of the wave theory and of the imperceptible ether it postulates.[26]

In Essay 3, these historical claims about methodologies are examined and found wanting. A typical argument strategy used by many nineteenth-century wave theorists involves the following steps:

---

25. Geoffrey Cantor, "The Reception of the Wave Theory of Light in Britain: A Case Study Illustrating the Role of Methodology in Scientific Debate," *Historical Studies in the Physical Sciences* 6 (1975), pp. 109–132; quotations on pp. 111, 114.

26. Larry Laudan, "The Medium and Its Message," in G. N. Cantor and M. J. Hodge, eds., *Conceptions of the Ether* (Cambridge, 1981).

1. Start with the assumption that light is either a wave phenomenon or a stream of particles.

2. Show how each theory explains various observed optical phenomena.

3. Show that the particle theory in explaining one or more of these phenomena introduces improbable hypotheses, whereas the wave theory does not.

4. Conclude that the wave theory is very probably true and the particle theory is not.

Step 2 does involve the idea of explaining a range of phenomena, which is central to the method of hypothesis. But in steps 1 and 3 wave theorists typically introduce considerations of a different sort. For example, in step 1 Lloyd bases the assumption that light is either a wave or a particle phenomenon, among other things, on the fact that light travels from one point to another in a finite time, and that in nature one observes such motion occurring by the transference of particles or by a wave movement. Again, in step 3 part of the argument against a particle theory explanation of some optical phenomenon is that this explanation introduces a cause that is very improbable, given other observed phenomena. For example, to explain diffraction bands both inside and outside the shadow, particle theorists introduce attractive and repulsive forces exerted by the edges of the aperture. But Fresnel, for example, argues that in the case of other known forces the intensity of the force varies with the mass and shape of the edges of the aperture. Yet experiments show that with diffraction no such variation exists. Accordingly, the existence of such forces is improbable.

In both of these cases there is *inductive* reasoning from a property found in observed instances of a certain type to the assumption that it probably holds for unobserved ones of that type—an inference that Newton himself could accept. More generally, a typical argument strategy of wave theorists contains two components: (a) show that the wave theory can explain a variety of optical phenomena and (b) show that the wave theory has independent warrant. The second is accomplished using an eliminative argument that depends on inductive reasoning at crucial points. While the first component is present in the method of hypothesis, the second is not. In Essay 3 the steps of the wave theorist's argument are analyzed in detail, and the view that the argument is a form of the method of hypothesis is criticized. In addition, it is argued that the wave theorists did not support the method of hypothesis even in philosophical reflections about their own practice. The question is then raised concerning the extent to which the methodologies both practiced and preached by *particle* theorists—including Newton in the eighteenth century and Brougham and Brewster in the nineteenth—were different in kind from that employed by nineteenth-century wave theorists. I argue that strong similarities exist between these methodologies.

In the 1840s the philosopher John Stuart Mill and the scientist, historian, and philosopher of science William Whewell debated the issue of the proper methodology to be used in science. Central to this debate was the question of whether, and if so how, scientific hypotheses, particularly those postulating "unobservables," can be verified. Whewell defends a version of the method of hypothesis requiring that, in addition to an hypothesis explaining known phenomena, it should satisfy three conditions: (i) it should *predict* new phenomena; (ii) it should explain (and/or predict) phenomena different in kind from those it was initially proposed to explain; (iii) it should render the system into which it is introduced more "coherent." Whewell calls requirement (ii) the *consilience of inductions*. (In Essay 4 I follow the practice of some Whewellian commentators and lump (i) and (ii) together under *consilience*.) If an hypothesis that explains known phenomena also satisfies (i), (ii), and (iii), then, says Whewell, it is established. By contrast, Mill rejects the method of hypothesis, explicitly denying that an hypothesis is even probable under the conditions Whewell espouses. In place of the method of hypothesis Mill proposes what he called the *deductive method*, which requires not simply an explanatory or predictive connection between the hypothesis and the phenomena, but that an inductive generalization be possible from those phenomena or others to the hypothesis in question. For the hypothesis to be proved or even probable, this last condition, which the method of hypothesis omits, must be satisfied.

Whewell and Mill applied their opposing methodological views to the controversy between wave and particle theorists of light. Whewell defended the wave theory on the grounds that, unlike the particle theory, it not only explained known facts but was also *consilient* and *coherent*. Mill attacked the wave theory, particularly the unobservable ether it postulated, by rejecting the method of hypothesis — even Whewell's more sophisticated version of it — that he thought was being used to support it.

Essay 4 constructs various probabilistic formulations of the Whewellian method of hypothesis and assesses the methodological debate in terms of these. It argues that although both Mill and Whewell were correct in certain judgments and mistaken in others, Mill's criticisms of the method of hypothesis should be given the edge over Whewell's defense of it. However, contrary to the claims of both Whewell and Mill, nineteenth-century wave theorists typically did not employ a method of hypothesis. They were attempting to provide not only explanations of phenomena — whether or not consilience and coherence were satisfied — but also independent warrant for their theory. This they did by using an eliminative strategy. Essay 4 provides a very general analysis of this strategy in probabilistic terms and applies the analysis to the specific argument that wave theorists used to defend their theory.

ESSAY 2

Newton's Corpuscular Query and Experimental Philosophy

The most controversial part of Newton's *Opticks* is the set of queries in Book III. Here Newton introduces numerous unproved hypotheses. This seems strikingly incompatible with his methodological views about empirical science or "experimental philosophy" (as he calls it), as well as with his actual practice in earlier parts of the *Opticks* and in the *Principia*. One such hypothesis— on which I shall concentrate in what follows—is the subject of Query 29. It states that light consists of particles. More precisely, it asks the question: "Are not the Rays of Light very small Bodies emitted from Shining Substances?"[1] Following this question there is a substantial discussion of the particle theory. And immediately prior there is a discussion for several pages of the rival wave theory, or more precisely, of the hypothesis that "Light is supposed to consist in Pression or Motion, propagated through a fluid Medium."

In this essay I consider various interpretations of Newton's procedures in those queries in the *Opticks* that pertain to the corpuscular hypothesis. My aim is to see whether, and if so to what extent, these procedures violate Newton's fundamental ideas about experimental philosophy. To determine this some review of these ideas is necessary. Later I will assess part of the Newtonian methodology.

PART I: NEWTON'S IDEAS ABOUT HYPOTHESES
AND EXPERIMENTAL PHILOSOPHY

My aim here is to focus on Newton's views about the proper procedures in experimental philosophy, and on some examples in his work where he seems

---

1. Isaac Newton, *Opticks* (New York, 1979), p. 370.

to be following such procedures. (I do not claim that he always does.) Newton's methodological views have been widely discussed, and some of what I shall say is not new, although I make certain claims here that I have not found in the literature.

I begin not with the *Opticks* but with a celebrated methodological passage at the end of Newton's *Principia*, immediately following "*hypotheses non fingo*":

> Whatever is not deduced from the phenomena is to be called an hypothesis; and hypotheses, whether metaphysical or physical, whether of occult qualities or mechanical, have no place in experimental philosophy. In this philosophy particular propositions are inferred from the phenomena, and afterwards rendered general by induction. Thus it was that the impenetrability, the mobility, and impulsive force of bodies, and the laws of motion and of gravitation, were discovered.[2]

Again in a letter to Cotes in 1713 Newton writes:

> . . . as in geometry, the word "hypothesis" is not taken in so large a sense as to include the axioms and postulates; so in experimental philosophy, it is not to be taken in so large a sense as to include the first principles or axioms, which I call the laws of motion. These principles are deduced from phenomena and made general by induction, which is the highest evidence a proposition can have in this philosophy. And the word "hypothesis" is here used by me to signify only such a proposition as is not a phenomenon nor deduced from any phenomena, but assumed or supposed — without any experimental proof.[3]

In these two passages Newton speaks of "deducing" or "inferring" propositions from phenomena and then making them general by induction. In Rule 4 of the "Rules of Reasoning in Philosophy" in Book III of the *Principia*, he combines these locutions and speaks of "propositions inferred by general induction from phenomena." In a letter to Oldenburg, July 1672, he omits a reference to induction, saying simply that "the proper method for inquiring after the properties of things is to deduce them from experiments."[4] In the *Opticks* a reference to induction is also omitted and the words "deduction" and "inference" are replaced by "proof." Newton begins the *Opticks* thus: "My design in this Book is not to explain the properties of Light by Hypotheses, but to propose and prove them by Reason and Experiments. . . . "[5] And the propositions that follow, which he also calls theorems, he defends by providing "proof by experiments." However, at the end of the *Opticks* the term *induction* reappears:

---

2. Isaac Newton, *Principia* (Berkeley, 1966), p. 547.
3. H. S. Thayer, ed., *Newton's Philosophy of Nature* (New York, 1953), p. 6.
4. *Ibid.*, p. 7.
5. Newton, *Opticks*, p. 7.

As in Mathematicks so in Natural Philosophy, the Investigation of difficult Things by the Method of Analysis, ought ever to precede the Method of Composition. This Analysis consists in making Experiments and Observations, and in drawing general Conclusions from them by Induction, and admitting of no Objections against the Conclusions, but such as are taken from Experiments, or other certain Truths.[6]

Let me try to provide accounts of some of the Newtonian concepts.

1. PHENOMENA

In the *Principia* immediately following the "Rules of Reasoning in Philosophy" Newton lists six "Phenomena." They concern the orbits of the satellites of Jupiter and Saturn, the five primary planets, and the moon. Newton offers no published definition of the term *phenomenon*. The following definition intended for the second edition of the *Principia* was never published:

Definition 1. Phenomena I call *whatever can be seen and is perceptible* whatever things can be perceived, either things external which become known by the five senses, or things internal which we contemplate in our minds by thinking. As fire is hot and water is wet, *and gold is heavy*, and *sun is light*, I am and I think. All these are sensible things and can be called phenomena in a wider sense; but those things are *properly called* phenomena which can be seen, but I understand the word in a wider sense.[7]

Although Newton here defines phenomena as "whatever can be seen and is perceptible" by the external senses or "internally"—which would seem to allow physical objects such as the sun to count as phenomena—the examples he gives in this definition are all facts rather than objects (fire is hot, water is wet). And this is true as well of the six phenomena listed as such in the *Principia*.[8] For example, the first phenomenon is that the satellites of Jupiter describe areas proportional to the times of description and their periods are proportional to the $3/2$th power of their distance from Jupiter. The third phenomenon is that the five primary planets revolve about the sun.

As suggested by the unpublished definition, Newton regards these facts as

---

6. *Ibid.*, p. 404.

7. From a manuscript sheet translated by J. E. McGuire, "Body and Void in Newton's De Mundi Systemate: Some New Sources," *Archive for History of Exact Sciences* 3 (1966), pp. 238–239. There are two other unpublished definitions of phenomena that are substantially the same as this. In addition to this definition there is an unpublished Rule 5 that contains a brief discussion of phenomena that conforms to the unpublished definition. See I. Bernard Cohen, *Introduction to Newton's Principia* (Cambridge, Mass., 1978), p. 30.

8. They are so listed in the second and third editions, but not in the first, where they are called "hypotheses." For a comment on Newton's terminological change see note 30.

"perceptible." But more than this, in the *Principia* he treats the phenomena as facts whose existence not only can be *but has been* established by observations. Concerning Phenomenon 1 Newton writes: "This we know from astronomical observations." That phenomena are established by observation does not necessarily preclude the need for inferences to them. Perhaps some of the examples of phenomena he lists in his unpublished definition can be established directly without inference (especially the "internal" ones: I am, I think). But the six phenomena of the *Principia* are pretty clearly inferred from what is observed. That the five primary planets revolve about the sun (Phenomenon 3) is not determined to be so simply by seeing the planets revolve. Rather Newton infers that they do revolve "from their moon like appearances" (in the case of Mercury and Venus). Similarly Phenomenon 1 is inferred from astronomical data Newton cites (pertaining to the periods of Jupiter's four satellites and the distances of the satellites from Jupiter's center) by using mathematical calculations. Newton does not say what sorts of inferences to the phenomena are allowable. The important point seems to be that whatever the nature of such inferences they are "from observations" and they are sufficiently strong to establish the facts in question.

There is another respect in which the discussion of the six phenomena in the *Principia* goes beyond the simple unpublished definition. Newton treats the phenomena of the *Principia* as noncontroversial, or potentially so. They are not facts that, although observed by some scientists, are disputed by others. They are facts that scientists aware of the results of observations that have been made do agree on, or would if they came to be aware of them. In the case of Phenomenon 1 Newton gives the results of observations by three different astronomers which establish this phenomenon. And he writes that Phenomenon 4 (Kepler's third law) "is now received by all astronomers."[9]

In the *Opticks*, phenomena are not listed as such. Nor does the word appear when Newton gives a "proof by experiment." Yet there is something here that corresponds to Newton's notion of a phenomenon in the *Principia*, namely, an established fact about the result of the (type of) experiment that anyone who performed the experiment would agree to on the basis of observation. For example, Proposition 2 of Book I of the *Opticks* states that the light of the sun consists of rays differently refrangible. To prove this Newton describes a series of experiments, the first of which involves the passage of sunlight through a single prism and the formation of the solar image on a sheet of paper. This image, writes Newton, is "oblong and not oval [as might otherwise be expected], but terminated with two Rectilinear and Parallel Sides, and two Semicircular Ends." Newton's description of the results of this experiment is, I suggest, the description of a "phenomenon." It is a fact—one that Newton has determined to be so by observation and that can be so determined by anyone performing this type of experiment—that an oblong

---

9. Newton, *Principia*, p. 404.

image is produced in such an experiment. This fact would be agreed to by all, even if there were doubts about whether it proves that light is composed of rays of different refrangibility.

2. DEDUCING PROPOSITIONS FROM PHENOMENA

Following the six phenomena in Book III of the *Principia* is a set of what Newton calls *propositions* (as well as theorems). These propositions are inferred from one or more of the phenomena and from earlier propositions in the *Principia*. In some cases the inference is deductive in a sense that any contemporary philosopher or logician could acknowledge. For example, the first part of Proposition 1 of Book III states that Jupiter's satellites are continually drawn off from rectilinear motion and retained in their orbits by a centripetal force directed to Jupiter's center. This follows deductively from Phenomenon 1 (given above) and from Proposition 2, Book I, "Every body that moves in any curved line described in a plane, and by a radius drawn to a point either immovable, or moving forwards with a uniform rectilinear motion, describes about that point areas proportional to the times, is urged by a centripetal force directed to that point."

Accordingly, when Newton speaks of "deducing" propositions from phenomena he means to include at least ordinary deductions—deductions of a type that would be found in mathematical proofs. However, Newton also includes inductions.[10] I shall follow McMullin and Mandelbaum in supposing that by induction Newton has in mind an inference from some property found to hold for all observed members of a class to the claim that this property holds for some members of that class that have not been observed, or for all members.[11] The inferences he cites in his Rules of Reasoning are of this type. Here are two examples:

---

10. In a letter to Cotes in 1713, written as the second edition of the *Principia* was being prepared for publication, Newton explicitly counts induction as a method of deduction (indeed, in this passage, as the only method): " . . . experimental philosophy proceeds only upon phenomena and deduces general propositions from them only by induction." However, it is difficult to believe that for Newton the only deductions from phenomena are inductions. Recall that at the end of the *Principia* he writes that "particular propositions are inferred from the phenomena and *afterwards* rendered general by induction," which suggests that there are noninductive inferences to begin with and then inductive ones to generalize from these. Newton's remarks to Cotes in the previous passage pertain to "general" propositions. So perhaps he is thinking here only of those propositions (such as the laws of motion, which he mentions) that do require generalization by induction.

Descartes also uses "deduction" to include induction as well as deduction. See Desmond Clarke, *Descartes' Philosophy of Science* (University Park, Pa., 1982), ch. 3.

11. Ernan McMullin, *Newton on Matter and Activity* (Notre Dame, 1978); see pp. 13ff; Maurice Mandelbaum, *Philosophy, Science, and Sense Perception* (Baltimore, 1964); see pp. 74ff.

The bodies which we handle we find impenetrable, and thence conclude impenetrability to be a universal property of all bodies whatsoever. That all bodies are movable, and endowed with certain powers (which we call the inertia) of persevering in their motion, or in their rest, we only infer from the like properties observed in the bodies which we have seen.[12]

Although Newton does not explicitly use the term "induction" here, he does use it later in the General Scholium in Book III when referring to such inferences concerning impenetrability, mobility, and so on. (See the first quotation in the present essay.)

Does Newton impose any conditions on induction? He imposes none on the number of members of the class that needs to be observed. But in his Third Rule of Reasoning he introduces a condition that might be interpreted as affecting the kinds of properties subject to induction. The Third Rule says:

The qualities of bodies, which admit neither intensification nor remission of degrees, and which are found to belong to all bodies within the reach of our experiments, are to be esteemed the universal qualities of all bodies whatsoever.

For present purposes three questions need to be asked. First, what does Newton mean by qualities that "admit neither intensification nor remission of degrees"? Second, is he committed to the view that where bodies are concerned inductions are possible only where qualities are of this sort? Third, is Rule 3 to be construed as governing all inferences whether or not they involve bodies?

The phrase "admit neither intensification nor remission of degrees" (or in another translation, "admit neither intension nor remission") is a scholastic one that Newton probably used in his own special way. McGuire suggests that for Newton a quality subject to "intension and remission" is one that "can manifest continuous and successive degrees of intensity: as can the pitch of a sound or the depth of a color."[13] Even more generally, McGuire takes such qualities to be those that admit of "more or less" (pp. 245–246) or of differences of degree. In his discussion following Rule 3 Newton does use the expression "not liable to diminution" to refer to the qualities he has in mind. And his examples of qualities to which the rule applies (and hence presumably qualities that "admit neither intensification nor remission of degrees") are extension, hardness, impenetrability, mobility, and inertia. Newton's discussion contains no examples of qualities that can be "intended and remitted,"

---

12. Newton, *Principia*, p. 399.

13. J. E. McGuire, "The Origins of Newton's Doctrine of Essential Qualities," *Centaurus* 12 (1968), pp. 233–260; see p. 244. McGuire argues that Newton held that qualities not subject to "intension and remission" are *essential* qualities of bodies.

but in an earlier draft of this rule he lists heat and cold, wet and dry, light and darkness, color and blackness, among others.[14]

Is Newton committed to the view that, where bodies are concerned, inductions can involve only properties that cannot be "intended and remitted"? This is doubtful. In the discussion following Rule 3 he admits that the *gravity* of bodies "is diminished as they recede from the earth." Accordingly, it should be a property with "intension and remission," and hence not subject to Rule 3. Yet in this passage, as well as in Corollary 2 of Proposition 6, Newton explicitly says that the property of gravitating toward the earth is subject to Rule 3. Moreover, hardness and impenetrability, which Newton cites in his discussion of Rule 3, might be said to admit of degrees. Yet these properties are supposed to be subject to the rule. McMullin has suggested that perhaps by "hardness" here Newton did not mean the property that admits of degrees, but the property of possessing (some degree of) hardness (impenetrability, gravity, etc.).[15] But then, as McMullin notes, the same could be said for qualities such as color and heat (possessing some degree or intensity of color and heat); yet Newton explicitly classifies color and heat as being subject to "intension and remission." McMullin concludes that Newton "could have omitted the troublesome intensity criterion from the published version of Rule 3, without in the least affecting the manner of applying the Rule to concrete cases."[16] I tend to agree.[17]

Finally, it is even more dubious to suppose that Newton meant that where bodies are not concerned inductions are restricted to qualities that cannot be "intended and remitted." In the *Opticks* (as we shall see) Newton needs to make inductions involving the property of refrangibility, which by his own admission is subject to degrees. These inductions concern light rays, which Newton does not want to have to assume at the outset to be bodies. Accordingly, in what follows I shall not construe Newton as requiring that the properties subject to induction be those that cannot be "intended and remitted."[18]

---

14. See McGuire, "Origins," p. 237.

15. McMullin, *op. cit.*, pp. 11–12.

16. *Ibid.*, pp. 12–13.

17. Indeed, in his first version of the rule Newton omits the "intension and remission" clause and writes simply: "The laws (and properties) of all bodies on which it is possible to institute experiments, are laws (and properties) of all bodies whatsoever." (See McGuire, "Origins," p. 236.)

18. A somewhat different interpretation of Newton might be given as follows. By "induction" Newton means an inference from observed members of a class to unobserved but observable members. Where induction is concerned there is no restriction to properties that do not admit of "intension and remission." Rule 3, however, is not a (straightforward) inductive rule but a more powerful one. It sanctions inferences from observed members of a class to all members of that class, including the unobservable ones. And when one makes an inference from the observed to the unobservable, a restriction is required to properties that cannot be "intended and remitted." Such an interpretation seems to be the one, or at least close to the one, offered by McGuire in

When Newton speaks of "deductions from phenomena," does he mean to include more than inductions and (ordinary) deductions? In addition to his Rules 3 and 4,[19] which involve *induction*, there are Rules 1 and 2, which pertain to *causes*. From considerations of simplicity, we should admit no more causes of natural things than are true and sufficient to explain the appearances (Rule 1); and therefore, to the same natural effects we should, so far as possible, assign the same causes (Rule 2). As examples of the latter, Newton cites the cause of the descent of stones in Europe and in America, and the cause of the reflection of light in the earth and in the planets. Newton does not relate the first two (causal) rules to the last two (inductive) ones. (He does not claim, for example, that the causal rules are special cases of the inductive ones.) Moreover, he uses all four rules in the early parts of Book III in a series of arguments leading to his law of universal gravitation. Both facts suggest that he thought of his causal rules and his inductive ones as distinct.

What sorts of inferences are Rules 1 and 2 supposed to generate, and how might the difference between these and inductions be expressed? Newton may well have several types of inferences in mind that are sanctioned by his first two rules. Let me note two that he explicitly uses. He begins the argument for Proposition 5, Book III, as follows:

> For the revolutions of the circumjovial planets around Jupiter, of the circumsaturnal about Saturn, and of Mercury and Venus, and the other circumsolar planets, about the sun, are appearances of the same sort with the revolutions of the moon about the earth; and therefore, by Rule 2, must be owing to the same sort of causes. . . . (p. 410)

Newton seems to be arguing from facts about the observed Keplerian motions of the moons of Jupiter, Saturn, and so on, described in his six phenomena, to the proposition that these motions have the same causes. The form of the inference is this:

"Atoms and the 'Analogy of Nature': Newton's Third Rule of Philosophizing," *Studies in History and Philosophy of Science* 1 (1970), pp. 3–58; see p. 12. It is in conflict with interpretations of Mandelbaum (*op. cit.*, p. 62) and McMullin (*op. cit.*, p. 15), both of whom construe Rule 3 as an inductive rule that permits inferences from the observed to the unobservable. I take the latter position in what follows. Newton does not explicitly say that inductions are restricted to the observable. And, as noted earlier, he does use the term "induction" in referring to the sorts of inferences he illustrates in Rule 3. In any event, on both the interpretation suggested by McGuire, and on the one I shall adopt, Newton is not to be construed as restricting inductions to cases involving properties that cannot be "intended and remitted."

19. Rule 4: In experimental philosophy we are to look upon propositions inferred by general induction from phenomena as accurately or very nearly true, notwithstanding any contrary hypotheses that may be imagined, till such time as other phenomena occur by which they may either be made more accurate or liable to exceptions.

C_1:   Effects $E_1, \ldots, E_n$ are the same in systems $S_1, \ldots, S_k$.
      Therefore (by Rule 2)
These effects have the same causes in all these systems.

Here, as well as in the examples he gives following the introduction of Rule 2, Newton simply infers that these effects in different systems are produced by the same cause, without identifying that cause. Perhaps he believes that an induction will permit an inference from the fact (phenomenon) that various known planets and their satellites satisfy Kepler's laws to the proposition that all the planets and their satellites do; whereas it will not permit an inference from the similar motions of these bodies to the claim that their causes are similar as well.

A second use of Rules 1 and 2 is illustrated by parts of Newton's discussion of Proposition 4. Here these rules are explicitly invoked in sanctioning an inference from the fact that the force keeping the moon in its orbit and the force of gravity on the earth both have features in common—they are both responsible for motions of bodies, they are both centripetal forces, and they are both inverse-square forces—to the claim that they are one and the same (type of) force, namely, gravity. (In saying that they are one and the same force Newton seems to mean that not only do they obey all the same laws but also that, were they both to act on a body, the total force exerted would be the same as that exerted by either.)

This second type of argument might be given the following general form:

C_2:   The cause of effects E (e.g., motion of a certain type) in system 1 is an x (a type, e.g., a force) with properties $P_1, \ldots, P_n$.
      The cause of the same or similar effects E in system 2 is an x with properties $P_1, \ldots, P_n$.
      Therefore (by Rules 1 and 2)
The cause of effects E in system 1 is the same x (e.g., the same force) as that which causes E in system 2.

Here, by contrast with the previous inference, information about the cause is provided.

How is C_2 different from induction? From the first two premises in C_2, induction would allow us to conclude:

The cause of effect E in every similar system (or in some unobserved one) is an x with properties $P_1, \ldots, P_n$.

But, on this interpretation, induction would not allow us to conclude that the cause is the *same* (type of) x. Thus, from the fact that the force retaining Mercury and Venus in their orbits around the sun is centripetal and varies inversely as the square of the distance, induction permits Newton to conclude that the force retaining the other planets in their orbits is also centripetal and inverse-square. But Newton seems to believe he needs additional rules to infer that these inverse-square centripetal forces are the same, namely, gravity. He seems to believe that while induction allows generalizing that a cause with the features in question will operate in other cases, it will not permit an inference that we are dealing with one (type of) cause here, not many.

In addition to C_1 and C_2 there may well be other types of causal inferences Newton regards as sanctioned by Rules 1 and 2. For example:

C_3:   Effects $E_1, \ldots ,E_n$ in system 1 are caused by C.
     Effects $E_1, \ldots ,E_n$ are also present in system 2.
        Therefore (by Rules 1 and 2)
     Effects $E_1, \ldots ,E_n$ are caused by C in system 2.

Let me call inferences C_1 through C_3—and any others Newton would regard as generated by the first two rules—examples of *causal simplification*. The reason for choosing this name is that Newton explicitly justifies Rule 1 (and Rule 2, which he seems to think follows from it) by an appeal to simplicity ("Nature is pleased with simplicity"). In the introduction to the *Principia*, and especially in an unpublished preface to the *Opticks*,[20] Newton stresses the idea of deriving everything in physics from a *few* general principles rather than inventing a new one for each phenomenon. Perhaps his thinking is that induction will yield principles that are general but not necessarily few in number. By induction we may arrive at the generalization that the cause which keeps each of the planets in its path around the sun is some centripetal inverse-square force. But this is compatible with the idea that these forces are different in other respects, thus requiring a separate law for each. To simplify and unify the situation, Newton's Rules 1 and 2 permit him to say that, until new phenomena show otherwise, from the fact that these forces have the same observed effects, we may infer that they are one and the same force.[21]

In the case of induction Newton imposes no restrictions on the numbers of observations, and (arguably) none on properties or classes. The same is true of causal simplification. He offers no restrictions on the types or numbers of effects that must be observed for one to infer identical causes. What does seem reasonably clear is that Newton treats these principles differently—both in the Rules and in the arguments for early propositions in Book III. Moreover, if we are to construe those arguments as being or containing "deductions from the phenomena," then the latter category will include ordinary deduc-

20. Reprinted in J. E. McGuire, "Newton's 'Principles of Philosophy': An Intended Preface for the 1704 *Opticks* and a Related Draft Fragment," *British Journal for the History of Science* 18 (1970), pp. 178–186.

21. William Harper (in a draft ms "Newton's Unification of Heaven and Earth") emphasizes the idea of unification here rather than simplicity. He thinks of Newton's first two rules as endorsing a policy of unifying natural-kind conceptions wherever possible.

tions, inductions, and causal simplification. There are propositions (such as Propositions 1 and 2 of Book III) that he derives from the phenomena and previous propositions by (ordinary) deduction alone without inductive generalization or causal simplification. There are also propositions (such as Proposition 4) which he derives using inferences of all three types. (See, in particular, the alternative "demonstration" that Newton offers for Proposition 4 in the Scholium, page 409.)[22]

Accordingly, I suggest that for Newton, "deduction from the phenomena" is a certain form of reasoning from facts regarded as established by observation. Such reasoning can be deductive in the ordinary sense; it can be inductive in the sense of inferring properties of all or some members of a class from properties of all the observed members; it can be causal simplification; or it can be a combination of these. (In what follows I shall use "deduction" in quotes, either by itself or in "deduction from phenomena," when speaking of it in Newton's sense, and without quotes when speaking of it in the ordinary sense.)

Two points concerning this definition deserve note. First, Newton regards a proposition "deduced from phenomena" as being established "beyond reasonable doubt" (my expression), or as having the "highest evidence that a proposition can have in this [experimental] philosophy" (Newton's expression). This does not make such a proposition *incorrigible* for Newton. A proposition "deduced from phenomena" may be false, but only further phenomena can show this. Merely imagining a "contrary hypothesis" (in the style of Descartes' method of doubt) is not sufficient to diminish the extent of its believability on the basis of the phenomena. This is clear from Newton's Rule 4 in the *Principia* (see note 19).

Second, in his discussion of the Third Rule of Reasoning Newton allows inferences from some observed members of a class to other members of the class even if the latter are not only not observed but unobservable in principle:

> The extension, hardness, impenetrability, mobility, and inertia of the whole result from the extension, hardness, impenetrability, mobility, and inertia of the parts [this presumably Newton has inferred from observations]; and hence we conclude the least parts of all bodies [which we have not seen and which may not be observable] to be also all extended, and hard and impenetrable, and movable, and endowed with their proper inertia.[23]

---

22. McGuire ("Atoms") thinks that after 1690 Newton regarded only his laws of motion and the eight axioms in Book I of the *Opticks* as deduced from phenomena. This strikes me as too strong. In that same 1713 letter to Cotes (note 10), Newton does cite the laws of motion as examples of propositions deduced from phenomena by induction; but he also cites the law of gravitation and the proposition that bodies are impenetrable, mobile, and exerters of force.

23. Newton, *Principia*, p. 399.

This form of reasoning allows Newton to claim that if all observed members of a certain class have a property, then this property can be ascribed to all members of the class, even if some are unobservable. The rule itself, however, does not commit him to postulating unobservable members of the class.[24] In the preceding passage I take Newton to be saying that extension, hardness, and so on are applicable to the least parts of bodies, if such there be, even if these parts are unobservable in principle. He admits that

> In the particles that remain undivided, our minds are able to distinguish yet lesser parts, as is mathematically demonstrated. But whether the parts so distinguished, and not yet divided, may by the powers of Nature, be actually divided and separated from one another, we cannot certainly determine.[25]

So Rule 3 does not commit Newton to a belief in atoms (i.e., physically indivisible parts), but only to the position that if they exist, then they are extended, hard, impenetrable, and so on.

As previously noted, in the *Opticks*, by contrast to the *Principia*, Newton does not write down "phenomena" as such. Instead he describes a series of experiments. Nor does he use the expression "deduction from the phenomena." Instead he speaks of "proof by experiment." Whether these expressions had the same meaning in Newton's mind,[26] "proofs" Newton offers in the *Opticks* do, or can readily be made to, conform to the previously noted criteria of "deductions from phenomena." Consider the first proposition in the *Opticks* and the experiment Newton suggests to prove it.

Proposition 1 states, "Lights which differ in Colour differ also in Degrees of Refrangibility." In the first experiment Newton obtains a black oblong stiff paper which he divides into two equal parts, painting one part red and the other blue. He then views the paper through a prism and finds that when the refracting angle of the prism is turned upward, so that the paper seems to be displaced upward by the prism, its blue half is displaced upward further than its red half. Similarly, when the refracting angle of the prism is turned downward, the blue half is displaced downward further than the red half. From this Newton draws the following conclusion:

---

24. McGuire ("Atoms") calls inferences that proceed from "what is observable to what is in principle unobservable," *transductions* (p. 3), which (by contrast to Mandelbaum and McMullin), he wants to distinguish from inductions. My claim is that Rule 3 allows Newton to make inferences to properties of all members of a class, even if some members and their properties are unobservable. By itself it does not allow Newton to infer that unobservable members of the class exist (just because observable ones do).

25. Newton, *Principia*, p. 399.

26. In a 1713 letter to Cotes Newton uses the expression "experimental proof" in such a way as to suggest that it has the same meaning as "deduction from phenomena." See the second quote at the beginning of this essay.

Wherefore in both cases the Light which comes from the blue half of the Paper through the Prism to the Eye, does in like Circumstances suffer a greater Refraction than the Light which comes from the red half, and by consequence is more refrangible.[27]

As a "proof" this is somewhat incomplete. But I suggest that it can be reconstructed in a more complete way, using one of Newton's previous axioms in the *Opticks*, as follows:

1. We begin with the following result of Newton's first experiment, which we can call a phenomenon, since it is a fact that Newton himself has established by observation and he thinks will readily be accepted by anyone performing the experiment: when the paper, one half of which is red and the other half blue, is viewed through a prism, the blue half is more displaced than the red half.

2. From Axiom 8 and the discussion following it (pp. 18–19): when an object is seen through a prism the rays of light from that object are refracted, and the object is seen not in its "proper" position but in some displaced position as a result of this refraction.

3. From points 1 and 2, by (ordinary) deduction, the blue rays coming from the colored paper are more refracted by the prism than the red.

4. From point 3, by induction, blue rays are more refrangible than red (or even more generally: rays of different colors are differently refrangible).

So reconstructed, we have an (ordinary) deduction of the proposition in point 3 from the phenomena (plus previous propositions). And in point 4 we make this general by induction. The last step is crucial, because Newton is obviously generalizing from his experiments with the type of prism he uses to other prisms, indeed, to any case in which there is refraction of light from objects painted blue and red, whether or not a prism is involved. Even more generally, to arrive at the proposition he is trying to prove he needs to infer that such differences in refrangibility are present in all colors, not just red and blue. Whether the argument is sufficiently strong to establish this conclusion I will not explore here (see section 6). My claim is only that if the preceding argument, or something like it, is a reasonable reconstruction of what Newton is doing here, then his first "proof" in the *Opticks* is a perfectly good example of what in the *Principia* and other writings he would classify as

---

27. Newton, *Opticks*, p. 21.

"deducing propositions from the phenomena and making them general by induction."[28]

It is not my claim that each of Newton's "proofs" in the *Opticks* is successful. In some (perhaps even in the proof just given), the inductive generalization might be considered too sweeping if based only on the experiments mentioned. In others a proposition is introduced as a premise that is not "deduced from the phenomena" in the sense indicated previously, and is indeed controversial.[29] Whatever the validity or persuasiveness of the "proofs

---

28. In *The Newtonian Revolution* (Cambridge, 1980), I. B. Cohen claims that Newtonian methodology in the *Opticks* is significantly different from that in the *Principia* (see pp. 13ff). Cohen points out that although Newton includes axioms and definitions in both, he makes use of these only in the *Principia*, not in the *Opticks*, where the proof is "by experiments." Moreover, Cohen claims that Newton's methodology in the *Principia* (which Cohen calls the "Newtonian style") involves a process of mathematical idealization and simplification foreign to the *Opticks*. This process begins with a set of idealized physical entities and conditions that can be expressed mathematically; deductions are made and compared with data and observations. This leads to a modification of the original assumptions to form a more complex mathematical system and to further deductions and comparisons with nature (see pp. 62–68). "In the *Principia*," writes Cohen, "the role of induction is minimal" (p. 16). I have three comments on this.

1. Cohen is certainly correct when he points out that in the *Opticks*, when Newton "proves" his propositions, he does not make explicit reference to the axioms and definitions, as he does in the *Principia*. The work is considerably less formal and precise. But the proofs work, that is, they demonstrate what they are supposed to, only if the definitions and axioms are implicitly assumed. For example, to infer Proposition 1 in the *Opticks* from the facts reported in Experiment 1, Newton is making at least implicit use of his definition of "refrangibility" as the disposition of rays to be refracted or turned out of their way in passing out of one transparent body or medium into another (p. 2). And unless he relates refraction to how a refracted body appears—as he does in Axiom 8 and in the discussion that follows—in his proof of Proposition 1 he will not be able to infer anything about differences in degrees of refrangibility from differences in the displacements of the observed positions of the red and blue colors on the paper.

2. Newton himself regarded his axioms of motion in the *Principia* as "deduced from the phenomena and made general by induction." That is, he regarded induction as crucial for generating his three most basic laws. Moreover, he makes explicit reference to induction in the proofs of various propositions in Book III. As far as mathematical idealizations go, it is true that many of the propositions in the *Principia* are concerned with systems that do not exactly correspond to any known in nature. For example, Proposition 1 in Book I deals with one body subject to a single central force. But Newton derives this proposition by deduction from his laws of motion plus their corollaries. He does not begin in this case with an *actual* system such as a planet and the sun which he then idealizes by ignoring forces on the planet exerted by other planets. The question is simply: What would happen if a body were subject to a central force? The answer is supplied by deduction from other propositions.

3. Finally, as McGuire has emphasized ("Intended Preface," p. 182), if we examine Newton's intended preface for the *Opticks*, we will conclude that Newton himself "did not see any dichotomy in method between that used in the *Principia* and that found in the *Opticks*."

29. For example, in his discussion of Proposition 6 of Book I, Newton offers a demonstration of the sine law that involves introducing what he himself calls a "supposition," that is, that bodies refract light by acting upon its rays in lines perpendicular to their surfaces. Newton makes clear in what follows that he means that a *force* is exerted by the refracting medium on the rays of light. Now for Newton a force can only act upon a *body*. (In the *Principia*, Newton's definition

by experiment" in the *Opticks*, I suggest that Newton treated them as "deductions from phenomena." He thought of them as demonstrating the truth of the propositions beyond reasonable doubt from facts themselves established by observing the results of experiments—facts that anyone capable of performing the experiments could agree on.

3. HYPOTHESES AND THEIR REJECTION

Newton used the word *hypothesis* in different senses in his writings.[30] But I shall focus on one use in what follows, since it is, I think, central for understanding Newton's professed methodology. This is the use of "hypothesis" contained in the first two quotations at the beginning of the present essay:

> Whatever is not deduced from the phenomena is to be called an hypothesis.[31]

> And the word "hypothesis" is here and used by me to signify only such a proposition as is not a phenomenon nor deduced from any phenomena, but assumed or supposed—without any experimental proof.[32]

An hypothesis is any proposition that is not "deduced from phenomena" in the sense of this expression explicated above. Newton allows that hypotheses (in this sense) may be "metaphysical or physical . . . , of occult qualities or mechanical."[33] However, presumably he does not include purely mathematical propositions even though they are not "deduced from phenomena."[34] When a proposition is "deduced" from phenomena it has "the highest evidence that a

---

of an impressed force begins with the phrase "an action exerted *upon a body.* . . . ") So it seems that here Newton is treating the rays of light as bodies. Yet the claim that the rays are bodies (which strongly suggests the corpuscular theory) is not something that Newton "deduces from the phenomena." Despite this, Newton does not seem to regard the "supposition" as a mere supposition, since he takes the resulting demonstration "to be a very convincing Argument of the full truth" of the sine law (p. 82).

30. See I. B. Cohen, *Franklin and Newton* (Philadelphia, 1956), pp. 138–40, and "Hypotheses in Newton's Philosophy," *Physis* 8 (1966), pp. 163–184; Alexander Koyré, *Newtonian Studies* (Chicago, 1965), pp. 261–272; N. R. Hanson, "Hypotheses Fingo," in Robert E. Butts and John W. Davis, eds., *The Methodological Heritage of Newton* (Toronto, 1970), pp. 14–33. We need only be reminded that what in the second and third editions of the *Principia* are called "phenomena" are called "hypotheses" in the first edition. According to Koyré (*op. cit.*, p. 31), in the first edition by contrast to later ones Newton means by "hypothesis" any fundamental assumption of the theory (so that the laws of motion would be hypotheses, in this sense, even though, according to Newton, they are "deduced from phenomena").

31. Newton, *Principia*, p. 547.

32. Thayer, *op. cit.*, p. 6.

33. Newton, *Principia*, p. 547.

34. See Hanson, *op. cit.*, p. 14.

proposition can have in this [experimental] philosophy."[35] Hypotheses do not have such evidence. Whether Newton thought that hypotheses can have some evidence in their favor, just not the "highest," or whether he meant by an hypothesis a proposition for which no evidence at all has been proposed, is not clear. (The second quote just given might suggest the latter interpretation, except that Newton here speaks of "experimental *proof*" rather than "evidence.") In what follows I will use "hypothesis" in the broader sense in which a proposition is an hypothesis if it is not "deduced" from phenomena, even if there is some evidence in its favor. Accordingly, an hypothesis does not have the highest evidence achievable in experimental philosophy; it is not established beyond reasonable doubt, though there may be some reason to believe it.

One potential ambiguity must be cleared up. When Newton says that an hypothesis is a proposition that is "not deduced from phenomena," does he mean (i) that it has not actually been derived (in the way suggested above), or (ii) that it is not deriv*able* from phenomena, or perhaps even (iii) that it is not derivable from phenomena or from any facts that will become phenomena? I shall understand him to be asserting (i), which is of course entailed by both (ii) and (iii), though not conversely. Newton's primary concern in experimental philosophy is to provide reasons for believing propositions that are as strong as possible in this philosophy. Such reasons have not been provided for a proposition that is deducible from phenomena but not yet deduced. Propositions of this sort do not have the highest evidence possible. Accordingly, a proposition might be an hypothesis at one time not at another. Further observations and experiments could change its status.[36]

Now in some sense or other Newton professes to reject hypotheses, though in what sense is not perfectly clear. For example, in the last paragraph of the *Principia*, which immediately follows the paragraph in which he writes "hypotheses non fingo," Newton introduces what is clearly an hypothesis "concerning a certain most subtle spirit which pervades and lies hid in all gross bodies; by the force and action of which spirit the particles of bodies attract one another at near distances, and cohere if contiguous. . . . "[37] Newton seems to recognize that this is an hypothesis since he writes that we are not "furnished with that sufficiency of experiments which is required to an accurate determination and demonstration of the laws by which this electric and elastic spirit operates."[38] How, then, can Newton be said to reject hypotheses?

---

35. Thayer, *op. cit.*, p. 6.

36. Here I disagree with Koyré (*op. cit.*, pp. 36–37), who says that "hypothesis" (in the sense under discussion) "means for Newton something that cannot be proved." Whether Koyré means this in sense (ii) or (iii) is not clear.

37. Newton, *Principia*, p. 547.

38. In a letter to Boyle of February 1678 (*Opera*, vol. 4, pp. 385–394), Newton speculates a great deal more about this subtle spirit or ether, even offering an hypothesis about the cause of

One thing he pretty clearly rejects is a certain version of the so-called "method of hypothesis." In a letter to Oldenburg of June 2, 1672, he writes,

> If any one offers conjectures about the truth of things from the mere possibility of hypotheses, I do not see how anything certain can be determined in any science; for it is always possible to contrive hypotheses, one after another, which are found rich in new tribulations.[39]

Newton rejects inferences to the truth of an hypothesis from its "mere possibility," that is, from its ability to explain some observed phenomena or from the fact it entails these phenomena. I take Newton to be rejecting inference forms such as these:

Phenomena $p_1, \ldots, p_n$ are established by observation.
Hypothesis h if true would explain $p_1, \ldots, p_n$.
Therefore, h is true.

Phenomena $p_1, \ldots, p_n$ are established by observation.
$p_1, \ldots, p_n$ are derivable from hypothesis h.
Therefore, h is true.

Newton's objection is that numerous hypotheses can be contrived on the basis of which the phenomena can be derived and explained. Such forms of reasoning do not establish the truth of hypotheses. They do not confer on hypotheses the highest certainty possible in experimental philosophy. Accordingly, such inferences are rejected in this philosophy.

Even if this is clearly a part of Newton's position on hypotheses, still the rest of that position is not so clear. Here are two possibilities:

1. In experimental philosophy you can introduce hypotheses for various purposes, *so long as you do not infer their truth*. For example, in the passage from which the last quotation was taken, Newton allows one to construct explanations of observations by means of hypotheses, and also to use hypotheses "as an aid to experiments" (perhaps to suggest new experiments). But from the fact that the hypothesis does explain the observations and even predict the results of new experiments, you cannot infer its truth. Such an inference will not yield the highest certainty possible in experimental philosophy; in that philosophy only inferences that do yield such certainty—only "deductions from phenomena"—are permitted.

---

gravity: "I shall set down one conjecture more, which came into my mind now as I was writing this letter: it is about the cause of gravity. For this end I will suppose aether to consist of parts differing from one another in subtlety by indefinite degrees . . . " (p. 394). Newton indicates considerable hesitation in proposing hypotheses to Boyle, and he is clearly not saying that such hypotheses are established. Yet equally clearly he is not avoiding them.

39. Newton, *Principia*, appendix, p. 673.

2. In experimental philosophy you should avoid not only inferring the truth of hypotheses but introducing them for any purposes. In the same passage in which Newton seems to allow hypotheses to be introduced to explain observations and to serve as "an aid to experiments" he also writes: " . . . wherefore I judged that one should abstain from considering hypotheses as from a fallacious argument. . . . "[40] And, of course, in the *Principia* itself Newton writes "hypotheses . . . have no place in experimental philosophy" (p. 547).

Newton's *pronouncements* about hypotheses in experimental philosophy do not clearly favor one or the other of these interpretations. In actual practice, as already noted, he in fact does introduce (what even he would regard as) hypotheses. So perhaps (1) reflects his position more accurately than does (2). However, there is another possibility, as follows.

3. The highest aim in experimental philosophy is to establish propositions with certainty, or at least with as much certainty as is possible for a science that is based on experience. The most certainty possible in experimental philosophy is achieved when propositions are "deduced from phenomena." Since, by definition, hypotheses are not "deduced from phenomena," they do not have the most certainty possible in empirical science. Accordingly, the highest aim here is not achieved by inferences to hypotheses. If there is some proposition of interest to us that we think is or might be true and it is possible to "deduce" it from the phenomena, or if it is possible to construct new experiments that will yield new phenomena from which it can be "deduced," then the "deduction" should be made. However, there may be some proposition of interest to us for which we have found no "deduction from phenomena." In such a case we are not entitled to infer that it is true on the grounds that it explains or predicts phenomena. But we are entitled to consider it, to determine what sorts of explanations and predictions it yields. Moreover, we may be able to give some reasons, some evidence, in its favor, even if this is not the highest possible evidence. If we can give such reasons, we should. (What these might be will be discussed in Part II when I turn to Queries 28 and 29 in the *Opticks*.) Yet we must recognize that whatever their nature, these reasons are not the strongest, and we should continue to search for better ones.

Indeed, the last clause in the previous paragraph may reflect another sense in which Newton means to reject hypotheses. He rejects the idea (which he may be attributing to Hobbes and Descartes) that once you have introduced an hypothesis (or a set of them) to explain the phenomena, and have shown that the phenomena are consistent with your hypothesis, *there is nothing more to do.*[41] On the contrary, although it can be perfectly legitimate to

---

40. *Ibid.*
41. See Robert Hugh Kargon, *Atomism in England from Harriot to Newton* (Oxford, 1966), pp. 107,108,124.

introduce an hypothesis to explain phenomena, this is only the beginning. You must try to "deduce" the hypothesis from these or other phenomena. You must try to rid the hypothesis of its hypothetical nature.

Newton's pronouncements about hypotheses do not form a consistent set, since both (1) and (2) can be found in them. However, if one also takes into account Newton's actual practice, then perhaps his overall position on hypotheses is best represented by (3). Admittedly, (3) is incompatible with some of his pronouncements (e.g., "hypotheses . . . have no place in experimental philosophy"), as well as with some of his practice (e.g., in the *Opticks* the introduction of the supposition that a force acts on light rays to produce refraction—a supposition not "deduced from phenomena" but treated with the certainty of something that is. See note 29). However, if we want to attribute a consistent view to Newton that reflects a good deal, though by no means all, of his pronouncements and his practice, then I think (3) is superior to (1) or (2).[42]

Interpretation (3) allows us to view the queries in the *Opticks* in a way that does not violate Newtonian methodology. Indeed, as I will show, (3) is suggested by some remarks Newton makes about his methodology in Book III of the *Opticks*. Finally, as noted, (3) admits the possibility of providing reasons for hypotheses, even though these do not generate the certainty of "deductions from phenomena." There are occasions in Newton's actual practice when he provides such reasons, *and explicitly recognizes this*. Thus, in a letter to Oldenburg in July 1672, Newton responds to a criticism by Hooke who accuses Newton of assuming as an hypothesis that light is composed of bodies. He writes:

> It is true that from my theory I argue the corporeity of light, but I do it without any absolute positiveness, as the word *perhaps* intimates, and make at most but a very plausible consequence of the doctrine, and not a fundamental supposition, nor so much as any part of it which was wholly comprehended in the precedent propositions.[43]

Again in a letter to Boyle of February 1678, after proposing various hypotheses about the ether (including one concerning the cause of gravity), Newton writes: " . . . by what has been said, you will easily discern whether,

---

42. Even if (3) is more adequate than other interpretations, one must not assume that it best reflects Newton's overall views and practice *throughout his professional career*. It is quite possible that by the later 1690s, in response to criticisms of the first edition of the *Principia*, not only did Newton's use of the term "hypothesis" change but also his ideas about hypotheses (in the sense in question) became more sharply articulated. See Cohen, "Hypotheses in Newton's Philosophy," *op. cit.*, p. 179.

43. Newton, *Opera* IV, p. 324.

in these conjectures, there be any degree of probability; which is all I aim at."[44]

I believe that Newton was proposing such nonconclusive probabilistic reasons for at least some of the hypotheses in the queries; in Part II I will attempt to analyze such reasoning. Newton says that "deduction from the phenomena" is the highest evidence that a proposition can have in experimental philosophy; he does not say that it is the *only* evidence.

4. ANALYSIS AND SYNTHESIS

At the end of the *Opticks* Newton offers the following methodological remarks:

> As in Mathematicks, so in Natural Philosophy, the Investigation of difficult Things by the Method of Analysis, ought ever to precede the Method of Composition. This Analysis consists in making Experiments and Observations, and in drawing general Conclusions from them by Induction, and admitting of no Objections against the Conclusions, but such as are taken from Experiments, or other certain Truths. For Hypotheses are not to be regarded in experimental Philosophy. And although the arguing from Experiments and Observations by Induction be no Demonstration of general Conclusions; yet it is the best way of arguing which the Nature of Things admits of, and may be looked upon as so much the stronger, by how much the Induction is more general. . . . By this way of Analysis we may proceed from Compounds to Ingredients, and from Motions to the Forces producing them; and in general, from Effects to their Causes, and from particular Causes to more general ones, till the Argument end in the most general. This is the Method of Analysis: And the Synthesis consists in assuming the Causes discover'd, and establish'd as Principles, and by them explaining the Phenomena proceeding from them, and proving the Explanations.[45]

Although Newton does not use the phrase "deduction from phenomena" in this passage, I take it that in analysis one provides such "deductions." From the results of experiments and observations one proceeds to draw general conclusions by induction; and " . . . it is the best way of arguing which the Nature of Things admits of." However, Newton also speaks of the method of composition or synthesis. His idea seems to be that once we have "deduced" some proposition from the phenomena we can then use that proposition in explaining phenomena "proceeding from" it. He also speaks of "proving the Explanations," although he does not say what this means or how it is to be done.[46]

---

44. *Ibid.*, p. 394.

45. Newton, *Opticks*, pp. 404–405.

46. In the nineteenth century, Henry Brougham, a follower of Newton in both professed methodology and in his defense of the particle theory of light, also speaks of analysis and

Following this general methodological passage, Newton writes that in the first two books of the *Opticks* he has proceeded by means of "Analysis to discover and prove the original Differences of the Rays of Light in respect of Refrangibility, Reflexibility, and Colour. And these Discoveries being proved may be assumed in the Method of Composition for explaining the Phenomena arising from them." However, Newton has something different to say about his procedure in the third book:

> In this third Book I have only begun the Analysis of what remains to be discover'd about Light and its Effects upon the Frame of Nature, hinting several things about it, and leaving the Hints to be examin'd and improv'd by the farther Experiments and Observations of such as are inquisitive.[47]

Newton seems to be referring to the queries in Book III rather than to the eleven "Observations" with which the third book begins.[48] But these queries contain propositions that are not deduced from phenomena. The analysis has only begun, and further experiments and observations will be necessary to complete it. Nevertheless, Newton obviously believes it is of value to introduce such hypotheses. And what he has done (the "hints" he has given) may provide some reasons, albeit not conclusive ones, for believing the hypotheses introduced. This conforms with the foregoing interpretation (3).

PART II: LIGHT

5. THE CORPUSCULAR HYPOTHESIS OF LIGHT

The final 67 pages of the *Opticks* contain a set of 31 queries, most of which are followed by discussions, some fairly extensive. What will be of particular concern here is Query 29, in which Newton asks whether rays of light are not very small bodies emitted from shining substances. There follows a discussion in which Newton points out that such very small bodies will have various observed features of light. For example, they will pass through a uniform medium in straight lines without bending into the shadow. They will be subject to certain forces that will permit them to satisfy the laws of reflection and refraction. Their different sizes will produce the different observed colors and degrees of refrangibility. By the forces they exert they can cause vibrations

---

synthesis. (See Essay 3.) Brougham insists that the phenomena explained in synthesis must be such as to provide a sufficient basis for an inductive argument to the explanatory proposition. Perhaps this is what is meant, or part of what is meant, by "proving the explanation." However, Newton in the passage quoted does not explicitly require what Brougham does.

47. Newton, *Opticks*, p. 405.
48. Cohen, *Franklin and Newton*, p. 184, so interprets Newton.

that produce fits of easy reflection and transmission observable in the phenomenon known as Newton's rings. And so forth.

Whatever Newton is supposing about the proposition that light consists of
small bodies or particles (and the ancillary proposition that these particles
can exert, and be acted on by, forces subject to his laws of motion), he is not
supposing that this proposition is "deduced from phenomena." Accordingly,
it is an *hypothesis*, and one that he invites us to seriously consider. In doing so
is he violating his methodology? Yes, if that methodology is to be construed
in accordance with interpretation (2), of section 3, which forbids the introduction of hypotheses in experimental philosophy for any purposes. But (2) is
a fairly radical interpretation of Newton's methodology. What about (1) and
(3)? He would be violating both of these if from the fact that the particle
hypothesis, if true, can explain a variety of phenomena he is inferring the
truth of that hypothesis. For then he would be employing a version of the
method of hypothesis that he rejects and that both (1) and (3) preclude.
However, Newton does not at least explicitly claim that the particle hypothesis
is true. And before we saddle him with such a view, let us consider alternatives.

One is that all he is doing is *considering* the hypothesis—seeing what
follows from it and what it can explain; he is not claiming that the fact that it
can explain such phenomena provides a reason to believe it true. In short, the
query is to be construed as just that—a question—which makes no commitment to the hypothesis in the question. Such an interpretation seems to be the
one offered by A. I. Sabra when he writes:

> These are *hypotheses* advanced by Newton without consideration of their truth or
> falsity. The fact that they appear in the *Opticks* as Queries and not as Propositions
> means that they do not form part of the *asserted* doctrine of light and refraction.[49]

This interpretation is compatible with both (1) and (3), which allow one to
introduce hypotheses for various purposes, so long as one does not infer that
they are true.

There is another interpretation, one particularly suggested by (3). On this
interpretation Newton is doing more than simply considering the hypothesis
by seeing what follows from it and what it can explain. He is providing some
grounds for believing it to be true, or at least he is attempting to do so,
although not the "highest evidence" possible. What grounds are these?

Is he perhaps saying that the fact that the particle hypothesis (together with
ancillary assumptions) *can explain a variety of observed optical phenomena*
provides some grounds for believing that hypothesis? That is, is he accepting
an inference of the following type:

---

49. A. I. Sabra, *Theories of Light from Descartes to Newton* (London, 1967), p. 312. Italics
in original.

Phenomena $p_1, \ldots, p_n$ are established by observation.
Hypothesis h if true would correctly explain $p_1, \ldots, p_n$ (or $p_1, \ldots, p_n$ are deducible from h).
   Therefore (probably)
h

Such an inference is a version of the method of hypothesis, though not the one rejected earlier. In the present case, as opposed to the previous one, h is inferred only with probability. On this interpretation Newton would allow us to use the method of hypothesis so long as we recognize that the conclusion is not drawn with certainty (or with the highest certainty possible in experimental philosophy). This interpretation is compatible with both (1) and (3), since h here is inferred only with probability, not certainty. Indeed, (3) speaks explicitly of a form of reasoning to an hypothesis that provides some reason for believing it, but not the highest evidence possible.

Let us call an inference to a proposition that furnishes that proposition with the highest evidence possible in experimental philosophy a *strong* inference. Let us call an inference to a proposition that provides some evidence for that proposition, but not the highest possible in experimental philosophy, a *weak* inference. For Newton in experimental philosophy, all and only strong inferences are "deductions from phenomena." Now, on the present interpretation, Newton is proposing a weak inference to the hypothesis that light rays are corpuscular.

If so it is dubious that the inference above is what he has in mind. For one thing, the fundamental objection he raises against the earlier version of the method of hypothesis is applicable to this one as well. The objection is that numerous hypotheses can explain the same phenomena. We cannot infer each of these hypotheses with probability.

Second, to say that Newton's inference to the corpuscular hypothesis involves reasoning only of the type above would be to ignore completely his discussion in Query 28, the one that immediately precedes the query in which the corpuscular hypothesis is introduced. In Query 28 Newton considers the wave theory, which he takes to contain "all Hypotheses . . . in which Light is supposed to consist in Pression or Motion, propagated through a fluid Medium."[50] In the ensuing nine-page discussion Newton offers numerous objections to the wave theory (or rather wave theories). For example, in explaining various observed optical phenomena (such as refraction), wave theories suppose that these phenomena arise from the modification of light rays. (To explain the different degrees of refraction produced by a prism, wave theories claim that the prism modifies the homogeneous rays of light rather than separating heterogeneous rays). But Newton believes he has refuted "modifi-

---

50. Newton, *Opticks*, p. 362.

cation" theories by a series of experiments reported in Book I. Among Newton's other objections to the wave theory, perhaps the most famous is that if light "consisted in Pression or Motion either in an instant or in time, it would bend into the Shadow,"[51] as with water waves and sound waves. But no such bending (no diffraction) had been observed.

The wave theory, various forms of which were supported by Newton's critics Hooke and Huygens, was the rival to Newton's corpuscular theory. That there are objections to such theories seems to be at least part of Newton's reason for favoring a particle theory. Putting Queries 28 and 29 together, then, we might say that Newton is proposing a weak inference to a particle theory from two sets of considerations: the explanatory success of the particle theory (Query 29) and the objections to wave theories (Query 28). But how exactly is this inference supposed to proceed? What form does it take?

If Newton is making such an inference—and I think it is plausible to suppose that he is—he does not spell it out. On the basis of the discussions in Queries 28 and 29 it is, I think, reasonable to say that Newton is arguing in some such way as this:

> The hypothesis that light is corpuscular explains a range of observed optical phenomena.
> The rival wave hypothesis has such and such difficulties.
>   Therefore (probably)
> Light is corpuscular.

The inference is intended to be weak, not strong. But even so, *exactly* how it is supposed to go and whether it is reasonable even as a weak inference is not at all clear.

In what follows I will construct an idealized version of this argument, which, although I cannot claim it to be Newton's, may nevertheless reflect some features of his thought. (See Essay 3.) The argument will have two essential components: objections to the wave theory, and an appeal to the explanatory power of the particle theory. Moreover, it will be an argument whose conclusion is drawn with probability. This probability will be reasonably high but not high enough to achieve the certainty, or virtual certainty, of a "deduction from phenomena." In constructing the argument I will assume that the usual axioms of the probability calculus are satisfied. Probability can be construed here as representing rational degrees of belief.

Let us assume to begin with that light is either a particle phenomenon or a wave phenomenon. Newton himself offers no explicit argument for such an assumption, although here is one that he was in a position to offer (and that is very similar to one in fact offered by his wave-theoretic opponents in the nineteenth century; see Essay 3):

---

51. *Ibid.*

Light is observed to travel in straight lines with uniform speed.
In other cases, when something travels with uniform speed in a straight line this motion is always observed to be caused by a series of bodies or by a series of wave .pulses produced in a medium (e.g., sound waves, water waves).
Therefore
Light is either a particle or a wave phenomenon.

Let us assume that the premises are true, that they report "phenomena," and that this is a "deduction from phenomena," so that the conclusion has the highest certainty possible in experimental philosophy. Such an inference, a type of causal simplification, would be permitted by Newton's Rule 2 requiring that like causes be assigned to like effects, as far as possible. If in other cases motion is caused by particles or waves, then, unless there is evidence to the contrary, we should infer like causes in the case of the motion of light.

Let T_1 be the hypothesis that light consists of particles, T_2 the hypothesis that light consists of waves, O the observed fact that light travels in straight lines with uniform speed, and b the accepted background information, which includes the information in the second premise above. We might express the results of this argument probabilistically, as follows:

(1) $$p(T_1 \text{ or } T_2/O\&b) = 1$$

That is, the probability that either T_1 or T_2 is true, given O and b, is equal to 1. (With minor alterations an argument similar to that which follows can be made if equation (1) is changed to say that the probability in question is close to 1; see Essay 3.)

Let us suppose that by appeal to certain other observed facts about light — call them O' — we can show that the probability of the wave theory is low, say less than 1/2. Which facts these are, and how this is to be shown, will be taken up in a moment. For the present let us simply write

(2) $$p(T_2/O\&O'\&b) < 1/2$$

Now if $p(T_1 \text{ or } T_2/O\&b) = 1$, then $p(T_1 \text{ or } T_2/O\&O'\&b) = 1$. Therefore from (1) and (2), since T_1 and T_2 are incompatible, we can infer

(3) $$p(T_1/O\&O'\&b) > 1/2$$

Let $O_1, \ldots, O_n$ be various observed facts about light (e.g., reflection, refraction, variety of colors, fits of easy reflection and transmission, etc.) other than those in O and O'. We would like to know how probable T_1 is when these facts are considered in addition to $O\&O'\&b$. Is $p(T_1/O_1, \ldots, O_n\&O'\&b)$ also high? Suppose that explanations of $O_1, \ldots, O_n$ by theory T_1 can be constructed in such a way that $O_1, \ldots, O_n$ follow deductively (in the ordinary sense) from T_1 together possibly with the background information b. But if the particle theory T_1 (together possibly with b) deductively entails $O_1, \ldots, O_n$, then it follows from the probability calculus that $p(T_1/O_1, \ldots, O_n \& O \& O' \& b) \geq p(T_1/O \& O' \& b)$. So from (3), given the existence of such explanations, we derive

(4) $p(T_1/O_1, \ldots, O_n \& O \& O' \& b) > 1/2$

which can be construed as the conclusion of the argument. It says that the particle theory is probable (more probable than not) given not just a few chosen optical phenomena but a range of them, including ones explained by that theory.

The explanations of $O_1, \ldots, O_n$ provided by the particle theory do not create the high probability for that theory, but they do sustain it. (In Essay 4 I argue that, in general, derivational explanations, even those subject to certain further conditions, will not by themselves suffice to guarantee high probability, although they can increase it.) These explanations permit an inference from (3) to (4). In an attempt to establish high probability for the particle theory on the basis of a range of optical phenomena, this is an essential role played by such explanations. To create high probability in the first place, a type of eliminative argument is used in which the wave and particle theories exhaust the probability but the probability of the wave theory is low. How is the latter to be established?

Newton offers arguments of two types, one direct, the other indirect. An argument appealing to diffraction is an example of the former. In the case of other wave motions such as sound waves and water waves, diffraction into the shadow of an obstacle is observed, but no such diffraction into the shadow had been observed by Newton or others in the case of light (though Newton had observed diffraction away from the shadow).[52] So if we include in the background information the fact of observed diffraction with other wave phenomena and the absence of such observations in the case of light, then the probability of the wave theory, given b, is low.

Second, Newton offers a more indirect type of argument. He points out that to explain certain observed optical phenomena, the wave theory introduces auxiliary assumptions that are either refuted by, or made very improbable by, observations. For example, to explain differences in refrangibility of rays emerging from a prism, wave theories introduce the auxiliary hypothesis that the prism modifies rather than separates the rays. Newton argues that this modification assumption is refuted or at least made extremely unlikely by further refraction experiments. (See Experiment 5, Book I, pp. 34ff.) Can we

---

52. See Roger H. Stuewer, "A Critical Analysis of Newton's Work on Diffraction," *Isis* 61 (1970), pp. 188–205.

infer from this that the wave theory is improbable? We can if we suppose that the probability of the modification assumption, *given the wave theory* and the observations, is close to 1. Letting M be the modification assumption, T_2 the wave theory, and O' the results of various of Newton's refraction experiments, if $p(M/O\&O'\&b)$ is close to zero and $p(M/T_2\&O\&O'\&b)$ is close to 1, then $p(T_2/O\&O'\&b)$ is close to zero. Even more generally, we get the same result if we suppose simply that $p(M/T_2\&O\&O'\&b)$ is much, much larger than $p(M/O\&O'\&b)$, without needing to suppose that the former probability is close to 1. (See Essay 3.)

Accordingly, there are two sorts of arguments to show that the probability of the wave theory is low, that is, (2). Once this is shown, we can infer the high probability of the particle theory (3), and its continued high probability in light of the various observed facts that it explains, that is, (4).

How "Newtonian" is the previous argument? In one respect, quite un-Newtonian, since it explicitly invokes numerical probabilities and the probability calculus, neither of which, of course, Newton does. However, in certain other respects it reflects what Newton seems to be doing in Queries 28 and 29. Assuming, as I have been, that Newton intends to provide some reasons for believing the particle theory, albeit "weak" ones, it gives a basis for inferring that theory with probability rather than certainty. Moreover, in doing so it takes into account Newton's criticisms of the wave theory and the explanatory virtues of the particle theory (each of which Newton himself emphasizes), showing how both contribute to the probability of the particle theory.

One objection that might be offered is that this argument is a type of *eliminative* one, whereas Newton at one point rejects (a certain form of) eliminative reasoning. In a letter to Oldenburg of July 1672 he writes:

> I cannot think it effectual for determining truth to examine the several ways by which phenomena may be explained, unless there can be a perfect enumeration of those ways. You know, the proper method for inquiring after the properties of things is to deduce them from experiments. And I told you that the theory, which I propounded [the theory of the heterogeneity of light rays] was evinced to me, not by inferring 'tis thus because not otherwise, that is, not by deducing it only from a confutation of contrary suppositions, but by deriving it from experiments concluding positively and directly.[53]

Newton here seems to be rejecting eliminative arguments of this form:

E: Each of the hypotheses $h_1, \ldots, h_n$, if true, will correctly explain phenomenon p.
But hypotheses $h_2, \ldots, h_n$ are false.
Therefore, hypothesis h_1 is true.

---

53. I. B. Cohen, ed., *Newton's Papers and Letters* (Cambridge, Mass., 1978), p. 93.

Such arguments, which infer the truth of an hypothesis from the falsity of competitors, are fallacious, unless a complete enumeration can be made of all the competitors. Newton appears to be thinking of deductive interpretations of E in which if the premises are true the conclusion must also be true. And he is correct in saying that arguments of form E, thus construed, are fallacious unless a complete enumeration of hypotheses is given. They are also fallacious if construed nondeductively, that is, as being such that the premises make the conclusion probable without entailing it. Unless some suitable assumption is made about the probability of the disjunction of hypotheses that are mentioned in the first premise, the conclusion that the probability of h_1 is high cannot be drawn.

However, the particular eliminative argument I have constructed is not of form E. The first step in the argument, which leads to (1) above, is not an explanatory step, but one involving causal simplification. The claim is not that the particle and wave theories will both explain the finite rectilinear motion of light, but that in other observed cases when something travels with uniform speed in a straight line this motion is caused by a series of bodies or a series of wave pulses in a medium. Also, the claim in the first step is indeed exhaustive, since it assigns a probability of 1 to the disjunction of hypotheses. But even if it were not exhaustive in this sense, even if (1) were changed to read "$p(T_1$ or $T_2/O\&b)$ is close to but not equal to 1," a fallacy would not emerge (although other changes would need to be made in the argument).

I conclude that reconstructing what Newton does in Queries 28 and 29 in the form of a probabilistic argument that takes us from (1) to (4) above is in conformity with certain important aspects of Newton's methodology. It combines his explanatory reasoning in Query 29 with his criticisms of the wave theory in Query 28 to provide some reason, though not the highest possible in experimental philosophy, to believe the corpuscular hypothesis. Although it is an eliminative argument it is not one of the type Newton rejects. Because the hypothesis in question is inferred with a probability not sufficiently high to be a virtual certainty, Newton could not construe the argument as a "deduction from phenomena." While we should search for phenomena that will sanction such a "deduction," we should acknowledge that, assuming its premises are true, the present argument does provide a legitimate "weak" reason for believing the corpuscular hypothesis.

6. STRONG VERSUS WEAK INFERENCES: AN ASSESSMENT OF ONE TENET OF NEWTONIAN METHODOLOGY

A "strong" inference furnishes the proposition inferred with the highest evidence possible in experimental philosophy; a "weak" inference furnishes some evidence but not the highest possible. I shall suppose that this difference can be interpreted as a difference over probabilities (construed as representing degrees of rational belief). In a strong inference from A to B, the probability of B given A is close to or equal to 1. In a weak inference the probability is high (say greater than 1/2), but is not close to or equal to 1. For Newton, both strong and weak inferences are based on "phenomena."

Now I take it to be a tenet of Newtonian methodology that in experimental philosophy "deductions from phenomena," and only these, are strong inferences. Accordingly, I want to raise two questions of assessment: (a) Are Newton's "deductions from phenomena" *guaranteed* to be strong inferences? (b) Must other kinds of inferences fail to be strong?

To answer the first question we must return to the definition of "deduction from phenomena" offered in section 2. Deductions from phenomena, we recall, include ordinary deductions, inductions, and causal simplification. Inductions are inferences from all observed members of a class to some members of the class that have not been observed, or to all members of the class. Let me simplify the discussion by considering deductive and inductive inferences but omitting causal simplification, which does not lend itself so readily to a general probabilistic treatment. Also, I shall discuss cases involving only deductions (in the ordinary sense) and those involving only inductions.

Deductive cases: Let $O_1, \ldots, O_n$ be descriptions of phenomena the conjunction of which, together with background information b, deductively implies h. Then $p(h/O_1, \ldots, O_n \& b) = 1$. So here we have a "strong" inference from the O's and b to h.

Inductive cases: To discuss these I shall first introduce some probability considerations and afterward apply them to the sorts of cases particularly relevant to Newtonian induction. Let h be a proposition that together with background information b deductively entails some observational statements $O_1, O_2, \ldots$. The following claims are provable.[54]

(a) If $p(h/b) \neq 0$, then $\lim\limits_{n \to \infty} p(O_{n+1}/O_1, \ldots, O_n \& b) = 1$.

(b) If $p(h/b) \neq 0$, then $\lim\limits_{m,n \to \infty} p(O_{n+1} \& \ldots \& O_{n+m}/O_1, \ldots, O_n \& b) = 1$.

(a) tells us that if the prior probability of h is not zero, then as the number n of observed consequences of h and b gets larger and larger, the probability that the $n + 1$ observational consequence of h and b will be true gets higher and higher, approaching 1 as a limit. (b) tells us that if the prior probability of h is not zero, then as the numbers m and n get larger, the probability that the

54. See John Earman, "Concepts of Projectibility and Problems of Induction," *Nous* 19 (1985), pp. 521–535.

next m observational consequences are true, given that n observational consequences obtain, gets higher and higher and approaches 1 as a limit.

To introduce the third probability result some restrictions will need to be made on h and O_i. Let h be some universal generalization of the form $(x)(Fx \supset Gx)$. Let the O's be "instances" of h of the form $Fa_i \supset Ga_i$. The following is provable:

(c) If $p((x)(Fx \supset Gx)/b) \neq 0$, and $\lim_{n \to \infty} p((Fa_1 \supset Ga_1) \ldots$

$(Fa_n \supset Ga_n)/b) = p((x)(Fx \supset Gx)/b)$, then $\lim_{n \to \infty} p((x)(Fx \supset Gx)/(Fa_1 \supset$

$Ga_1) \ldots (Fa_n \supset Ga_n)\&b) = 1.$[55]

(c) gives a set of sufficient conditions for the probability of $(x)(Fx \supset Gx)$, given observed instances of the form $Fa_i \supset Ga_i$, to approach 1 as a limit.

Now let us apply these three probability results to Newtonian inductions. In all three cases let us consider h's of the form $(x)(Fx \supset Gx)$, and O's instances of the form $Fa_i \supset Ga_i$. (a) tells us that if the prior probability of $(x)(Fx \supset Gx)$ is not zero, then as the number of observed instances of $(x)(Fx \supset Gx)$ increases, the probability that the next instance will obtain gets higher and higher, approaching 1 as a limit. A similar claim can be made for (b). (a) and (b) — so construed — correspond to Newton's inductions from some observed members of a class to some other member(s) of that class. (c) corresponds to Newton's inductions from some observed members of a class to all members. In all three cases the probability in question approaches 1 as a limit, under certain very weak assumptions. Intuitively, the probability that the next instance will satisfy $(x)(Fx \supset Gx)$, that the next m instances will, and that all instances will, gets higher and higher as more and more instances are observed. We get more and more certainty in these cases with more and more observed instances of $(x)(Fx \supset Gx)$.

However, it is not the case that *for every number n* of observed instances, the probability that the next instance will satisfy $(x)(Fx \supset Gx)$, that the next m instances will (for any m), and that all instances will, is close to 1. Consider just the latter, and suppose that the prior probability of $(x)(Fx \supset Gx)$ is low, and the O's are such that, with sufficiently small n, the prior probability of the conjunction of O's is high. If $(x)(Fx \supset Gx)$ and b entails the O's, then by Bayes' theorem,

$$p((x)(Fx \supset Gx)/O_1, \ldots ,O_n\&b) = p((x)(Fx \supset Gx)/b)/p(O_1, \ldots ,O_n/b)$$

Now if $p((x)(Fx \supset Gx)/b)$ is low and the O's are such that, with sufficiently

---

55. For proof see Earman, *op. cit.*, p. 529.

small n, $p(O_1, \ldots, O_n/b)$ is high, then the probability on the left will be small, despite the fact that all the observed O's satisfy $(x)(Fx \supset Gx)$. One case of this sort involves Goodmanesque properties such as "grue," where the prior probability of the proposition "All emeralds are grue" is very low but where, given appropriate background information, the probability that observed items are grue if they are emeralds is very high. Strange Goodmanesque properties or classes can prevent the probability on the left from being high for a given n. But as n increases without bound, the probability on the left will approach 1 as a limit, strange properties notwithstanding.

However, Goodmanesque properties are not the only things that can prevent the probability on the left from being high for a given n. Recall the proof of Proposition 1 of the *Opticks*. Here an induction is made from observations of differences in refrangibility of blue and red rays in an experiment with the sorts of prisms used by Newton to differences in refrangibility of any differently colored rays in any sort of refraction, whether or not the latter is produced by a prism. A critic of Newton might argue as follows: (i) The number n of observed instances of Proposition 1 (that lights that differ in color differ in degrees of refrangibility) is quite low. (If we count as instances here the results of *types* of experiments, rather than specific trials, then the critic has some justification, since Newton cites only two experiments.) (ii) The critic might agree that the probability of getting the results Newton obtains *with these types of experiments with prisms* is high, while supposing that obtaining analogous refraction results with other sorts of prisms or without prisms is improbable.[56] (iii) The critic might argue, on the basis of background information b, that the prior probability of Newton's Proposition 1 is very low. At least, the critic might complain, Newton does nothing to dispel doubts expressed in points (i) through (iii). But unless such doubts are removed, the probability of Newton's Proposition 1, given the results of the experiments Newton mentions, cannot be assumed to be high. The most we can say is that this probability will increase toward 1 as the number of observed instances of the proposition increases.

Confining our attention to ordinary deductions and inductions, we can now answer the question "Are Newton's 'deductions from phenomena' guaranteed to be strong inferences?" in the following way. If they are deductions (in the ordinary sense), they are so guaranteed. Any deductive inference from $O_1, \ldots, O_n$ and b to h—no matter what number n is—guarantees that the probability of h given $O_1, \ldots, O_n$ and b is maximal. By contrast, it is not the case that every particular inductive inference is guaranteed to be strong, no matter how many instances are involved and no matter what the character of

---

56. See Simon Schaffer, "Glass Works: Newton's Prisms and the Uses of Experiment," in David Gooding, Trevor Pinch, and Simon Schaffer, eds., *The Uses of Experiment* (Cambridge, England, 1989), pp. 67–104.

the properties or classes in question. If Newton's methodology requires a claim to the contrary, then it is mistaken. However, the previous probability results show that (under certain weak assumptions), as more and more instances are observed, then no matter what the character of properties or classes in question, the strength of the inference is guaranteed to increase and to approach the highest strength in the limit.

Accordingly, there are several ways to interpret Newton's methodology (or to modify that methodology) so as to avoid the problems above. First, instead of saying that every inductive inference from phenomena is a strong one, Newton could say that *some* are, namely, those based on sufficiently many instances (provided that the prior probability of $(x)(Fx \supset Gx)$ is not zero). Second, Newton could restrict those inductions he will allow in the category of "deductions from phenomena" to ones based on sufficiently many instances. On both of these proposals, however, no particular number can be chosen that will count as "sufficiently many." In each case this will depend on the prior probability of $(x)(Fx \supset Gx)$ and on the prior probability of the conjunction of instances. Third, Newton could attempt to impose conditions on the character of the properties or classes that are subject to induction so that inductions involving such properties or classes will guarantee maximal probability no matter how many instances have been observed. Newton does not formulate any such conditions. Whether it would be possible to do so seems very dubious to me, though I shall not pursue this here. Finally, Newton could abandon entirely an "absolute" claim about the strength of inductions in favor of a "comparative" one. He could say simply that, under minimal assumptions, the strength of an induction increases as more and more instances are observed.

Now turning to the other side of the coin we need to ask whether in experimental philosophy there are strong inferences that are not "deductions from phenomena." Is Newton correct in implying that only "deductions from phenomena" can have this feature?

Let us return to result (a) above. (What I say here will be applicable to (b) as well, mutatis mutandis.) Although (a) allows h and O_i to be of forms $(x)(Fx \supset Gx)$ and $Fa \supset Ga$, respectively, it does not require this. All that is necessary is that h and b deductively imply O_i. Accordingly, h might be some proposition that Newton would classify as an hypothesis, for example, that light consists of particles. This hypothesis is not "deduced from phenomena." Let the background information b include Newton's first law of motion that in the absence of forces particles travel with uniform speeds in straight lines. Hypothesis $h + b$ deductively implies (O_1) that in the absence of forces light travels in straight lines, and (O_2) that in the absence of forces light travels with uniform speed. Now result (a) allows us to conclude that the probability that some consequence of an "hypothesis" (in the Newtonian sense) obtains gets higher and higher, approaching 1 as a limit, as more and more consequences of that hypothesis are observed. The only assumption needed is that the prior probability of this hypothesis is not zero. This, of course, does not imply that the probability of the "hypothesis" itself approaches certainty, but only that the probability of its deductive consequences does.

Newton does not appear to be thinking of cases in which we make inferences to deductive consequences of "hypotheses." But such inferences can be strong ones, or at least they can get stronger and stronger as more and more consequences are observed to hold. To be sure, Newton could claim that he is classifying as "inductive" an inference from some observed consequences of h to other not yet observed consequences. But his inductions appear to be simply inductive generalizations from observed F's that are G's to other or all F's being G's.

Let us turn, then, to result (c) involving the probability of h itself. And let us consider the more general case in which h is any proposition that, together with b, deductively implies O_1, O_2, ... Here we cannot obtain the result that $\lim_{n \to \infty} p(h/O_1, \ldots, O_n \& b) = 1$ because we cannot in general assume that $\lim_{n \to \infty} p(O_1, \ldots, O_n/b) = p(h/b)$. Indeed, the following are provable:

(d) Let h (together with b) entail O_1, O_2, ... If h has at least one incompatible competitor h' that together with b also entails O_1, O_2, . . . , and whose probability on b is greater than zero, then $\lim_{n \to \infty}$ $p(h/O_1, \ldots, O_n \& b) \neq 1$.

(e) Let h together with b entail O_1, O_2, ... If h has at least one incompatible competitor h' that together with b also entails O_1, O_2, . . . , and is such that $p(h'/b) \geq p(h/b)$, then for any n, no matter how large, $p(h/O_1, \ldots, O_n \& b) \leq .5$.[57]

So if h has competitors that, like h, deductively imply all the observable phenomena, then h's probability will not approach 1 as a limit; and if the prior probability of one of the competitors is at least as great as h's prior probability, then h's probability will not increase beyond .5, no matter how many deductive consequences of h are observed to be true.

However, the quest for strong inferences to Newtonian "hypotheses" is not necessarily doomed. We need not insist that the limit of the probability of h be 1, but only that the probability of h given the observations be "very high" and remain so with more and more observations. To this end, I shall employ the concept of a *partition* of propositions on b, which is a set of mutually exclusive propositions, the probability of whose disjunction on b is 1, and the probability of each of which on b is not zero. The following is provable (see Essay 4):

---

57. See Earman, *op. cit.*, pp. 528–529.

(f) If $h, h_1, \ldots, h_k$ form a partition on b, then for any O, and for each $h_i (\neq h)$ in the partition, and for any number r greater than or equal to 0 and less than 1, $p(h/O\&b) > r$ if and only if $\sum_{i=1}^{k} p(h_i/O\&b) < 1 - r$.

Now suppose that we have some observed phenomena $O, O_1, \ldots, O_n$ and background information b, and we want to make a strong inference to h by showing that the probability of h given the observed phenomena and background information is greater than some threshold value r for "very high" probability. Using theorem (f), the following strategy is possible:

Strategy for showing that h has a very high probability (greater than some threshold value r for very high probability), given observed phenomena O, $O_1, \ldots, O_n$ and background information b:

1. Find some partition on $b - h, h_1, \ldots, h_k$ — that includes h.
2. Show that phenomenon O is such that for each proposition $h_i \neq h$ in the partition, $\sum_{i=1}^{k} p(h_i/O\&b) < 1 - r$.
3. Show that $O_1, \ldots, O_n$ are derivable from h (together with b).

If we complete steps 1 and 2 in this strategy, then, in accordance with theorem (f), we will have shown that $p(h/O\&b) > r$. By completing step 3, we show that $p(h/O\&O_1, \ldots, O_n\&b) > r$, since $O_1, \ldots, O_n$ are derivable from h together with b.

The question of interest is whether this strategy is applicable to propositions Newton would regard as hypotheses. In fact, it seems applicable to the hypothesis Newton considers in Query 29 of the *Opticks* — that light consists of particles. Indeed, the probabilistic argument I constructed in the last section can be suitably modified and shown to be a legitimate variant of this form. Let me recall the basic steps.

We began with the observation O that light travels in straight lines with uniform speed, which, together with the background information b, yields a probability of 1 that light is corpuscular or undulatory, that is,

(1) $$p(T_1 \text{ or } T_2/O\&b) = 1$$

Accordingly, T_1 and T_2 form a partition on $O\&b$, since T_1 and T_2 are incompatible.

Second, we found some other observed facts O' that cast doubt on the wave theory T_2. We noted this by writing $p(T_2/O\&O'\&b) < 1/2$. But this is too modest, even for Newton, since the actual facts cited, Newton thought, cast much more doubt on T_2 than this. The two mentioned were diffraction and refraction. If light is a wave phenomenon, then, like water waves and sound waves, it ought to be diffracted into the shadow; but Newton observed no such diffraction. Second, Newton (as well as defenders of the wave theory) believed that, *given the wave theory* and the observations of differences in degrees of refraction, the probability that light is modified by the refracting prism is very high, say close to 1. But on the basis of his own refraction experiments, Newton pretty clearly thought he had refuted the modification assumption, that is, the probability of this assumption, given his experimental results, is close to zero. So, where M = the modification assumption, and O' includes the results of Newton's refraction experiments, we have the result that $p(M/T_2\&O'\&O\&b)$ is close to 1, whereas $p(M/O'\&O\&b)$ is close to zero. It follows that $p(T_2/O'\&O\&b)$ is close to zero. Letting O' also contain the observed absence of diffraction into the shadow and b also contain observed diffraction in the case of sound and water, we write

(2) $\qquad p(T_2/O\&O'\&b) \approx 0 \qquad$ ($\approx$ means "is close to")

This completes the second step in the strategy.

From (1), since the probability of T_1 or T_2 is 1, it remains 1 if we add O'. So we have

(3) $\qquad\qquad p(T_1 \text{ or } T_2/O\&O'\&b) = 1$

Since T_1 and T_2 are incompatible, from (2) and (3) we infer

(4) $\qquad\qquad p(T_1/O\&O'\&b) \approx 1$

Since $T_1 + b$ deductively implies other optical phenomena $O_1, \ldots, O_n$, from (4) we derive

(5) $\qquad\qquad p(T_1/O\&O'\&O_1, \ldots, O_n\&b) \approx 1$

which completes the third and final step of the strategy.

Again, I must stress that it is not my claim that this is Newton's actual argument in Queries 28 and 29. Besides the attribution of the probability calculus, the main stumbling block lies in the use of the first step in the strategy, leading to (1) above (even if (1) were weakened by replacing "equals" with "is close to"). Although Newton considers only the wave and particle theories, he does not explicitly claim that the probability of their disjunction on the evidence is maximal (or even very high). Still in the previous section I indicated what type of argument for this claim Newton could have given that would be compatible with his general methodology. If the strategy is launched by this assumption in step (1), then Newton's own arguments against the wave theory can be used to justify the steps leading to the final (5).

Let us suppose that (1) is justified by inference from observed phenomena. And let us assume that the remaining steps are also valid, so that the argument does establish the very high probability of a proposition given certain observations and background information. If so it provides the basis for a "strong" inference to that proposition from those observations and background information. Is the argument a "deduction from phenomena"?

In certain ways it seems quite different from the sorts of arguments Newton has in mind when he uses this expression. First, unlike the "deductions" that Newton gives, it contains an inference to a disjunction of propositions in the first step. Second, the argument is eliminative, whereas the "deductions" Newton offers are not. Indeed, he rejects (certain types of) eliminative arguments. Third, and most important, it makes use of the probability calculus, which Newton never does. The inferences to (3), (4), and (5) are justified by principles of probability. Whether Newton would have been willing to classify such inferences as "deductive" is unclear.

Yet reasons might be offered for classifying the argument as a "deduction from phenomena." First, the previous characterization of causal simplification (as well as that of induction) does not preclude an inference to a disjunction of propositions. Second, although it is eliminative, it is not an eliminative argument of the type that Newton rejects. Indeed, if the previous point is accepted, it is an eliminative argument that uses causal simplification to establish a disjunction of propositions and then to argue against one of the disjuncts. Third, the probability principles generating steps (3), (4), and (5) might be thought of as, or as akin to, mathematical principles, which for Newton can serve as a basis for "deductions."

Accordingly, assuming the argument in question is valid, the following possibilities emerge:

1. In a broad sense the argument is a "deduction from phenomena." If so it does not refute the Newtonian claim that only "deductions from phenomena" guarantee strong inferences. However, if we construe it as a "deduction from phenomena," then with this argument we must deny that the Newtonian corpuscular hypothesis is an hypothesis. With this argument we will have "deduced" the corpuscular hypothesis from the phenomena and thus rendered it no longer hypothetical.

2. In a narrower sense (one that excludes probability arguments) the argument is not a "deduction from phenomena." Yet it provides the basis for a "strong" inference to the corpuscular hypothesis. So if this narrower sense is Newton's, then we need to reject his idea that only "deductions from phenomena" can provide the highest certainty in experimental philosophy.

7. CONCLUSIONS

1. Although neither Newton's professed methodology, nor his actual practice, form consistent sets, my suggestion is that interpretation (3) in section 3 reflects a good deal of both. On that interpretation, the most certainty possible in experimental philosophy is achieved when, and only when, propositions are "deduced from phenomena." The latter involves deduction or induction or causal simplification from generally accepted facts established by observation.

2. However, on this interpretation one is allowed not only to consider propositions not "deduced from phenomena," that is, hypotheses, but to make weak inferences to them in cases in which "deductions" have not been achieved. But we must recognize that such inferences are weak, and we must continue to search for phenomena from which the propositions in question can be "deduced."

3. One sort of non-"deductive" inference to hypotheses is illustrated in Queries 28 and 29 in the *Opticks* in the discussion of the particle and wave theories of light. Here Newton seems to be making a (weak) inference to the particle theory on the grounds that it explains a range of optical phenomena. In section 5 above this argument is reconstructed probabilistically in such a way as to reflect, at least in part, Newton's discussion in Queries 28 and 29, as well as his general methodology.

4. We cannot suppose, as Newton seems to, that "deductions from phenomena" will always yield the maximal certainty possible in experimental philosophy. In the case of induction, for example, such certainty is not guaranteed simply by observing positive instances of an inductive generalization and no negative ones. What we can say is that, granted certain minimal assumptions, an increase in the number of positive instances will increase the strength of such inferences toward maximality. Finally, assuming that probabilistic explanatory reasoning of the type constructed in section 6 can be valid, we may say this: If probabilistic arguments are not construed as "deductive," then we cannot suppose, as Newton seems to, that only "deductions from phenomena" can generate the highest certainty possible in experimental philosophy.*

*For very helpful suggestions I am indebted to Robert Rynasiewicz, Doren Recker, Robert Kargon, and Alan Shapiro.

ESSAY 3

Light Hypotheses

1. INTRODUCTION

At the beginning of the nineteenth century Thomas Young published papers that defended the wave theory of light against the Newtonian particle theory. Following this there occurred a lengthy and sometimes heated dispute between particle theorists and wave theorists which, it is alleged, stemmed from deep divisions over scientific methodology. Particle theorists, it is said, particularly British ones, used the method of induction whereas wave theorists employed the antithetical method of hypothesis. Thus Geoffrey Cantor writes:

> Although in the eighteenth century almost every British natural philosopher accepted without question the corpuscular interpretation of Newton's writings on optics, by the 1830s most British natural philosophers had rejected Newton's corpuscular theory in favor of the wave theory of light. *Intimately bound up with this scientific "revolution" in optical theory was a change in scientific methodology: the replacement of the method of induction by the method of hypothesis.*[1]

According to Cantor, nineteenth-century particle theorists "followed the [eighteenth-century] common-sense philosophers in considering induction to be the proper scientific method" (p. 111), and in rejecting or limiting a reliance on hypotheses; nineteenth-century "supporters of the wave theory, unlike its objectors, championed the method of hypothesis" (p. 114).

Larry Laudan has also emphasized a change in methodology between the late eighteenth and early nineteenth centuries. The wave theory of light re-

---

1. Geoffrey Cantor, "The Reception of the Wave Theory of Light in Britain: A Case Study Illustrating the Role of Methodology in Scientific Debate," *Historical Studies in the Physical Sciences* 6 (1975), p. 109. Emphasis mine. See also his book *Optics after Newton* (Manchester, 1983), pp. 177–186.

quired an imperceptible luminiferous ether, which eighteenth-century inductivists rejected as an untestable hypothesis. Speaking of the reception of ether theories in Scotland, Laudan writes:

> The primary reason for opposition to ether theories was the widespread acceptance among Scottish philosophers and scientists of a trenchant inductivism and empiricism, according to which speculative hypotheses and imperceptible entities were inconsistent with the search for reliable science.[2]

Laudan goes on to argue that nineteenth-century defenders of the wave theory used a form of the method of hypothesis (which I shall consider in this essay).

In 1803 Henry Brougham, a defender of the particle theory of light, wrote a scathing review of Thomas Young's "Bakerian Lecture on the Theory of Light and Colors." Brougham begins by saying:

> As this paper contains nothing which deserves the names either of experiment or discovery, and as it is in fact destitute of every species of merit, we should have allowed it to pass among the multitude of those articles which must always find admittance into the collections of a Society which is pledged to publish two or three volumes every year.[3]

Brougham's principal objection to Young's paper is that it is not based on inductions from experiments but involves simply the formulation of hypotheses to explain various facts. And Brougham writes:

> A discovery in mathematics, or a successful induction of facts, when once completed, cannot be too soon given to the world. But . . . an hypothesis is a work of fancy, useless in science, and fit only for the amusement of a vacant hour. . . . (p. 451). It is scarcely possible to conceive a wider difference than that which subsists between the philosophy of Newton and the philosophy of Dr. Young. While the former utterly rejects hypotheses, and asserts that our stock of facts upon the subject of the ether is insufficient; the latter says that we have enow [sic] of experiments, and that we only require to have a stock of hypotheses. (p. 455)

In this review Brougham defends the Newtonian particle theory on the grounds that it is inductively supported by experiments, while he rejects

---

2. Larry Laudan, "The Medium and its Message," in G. N. Cantor and M. J. Hodge, eds., *Conceptions of the Ether* (Cambridge, England, 1981), p. 170. Unlike Cantor, Laudan's principal aim in this paper is to compare the methodology of those who defended the wave theory in the nineteenth century with eighteenth- (rather than nineteenth-) century inductivist critiques of that theory (and of ether theories generally). Since my main interest in what follows is (like that of Cantor) in the debate between wave and particle theorists in the nineteenth century, Laudan's claim that is of special concern to me is that nineteenth-century wave theorists utilized a method of hypothesis.

3. *Edinburgh Review* 1 (1803), p. 450.

Young's defense of the wave theory on the grounds that it employs an unacceptable method of hypothesis.

In what follows I propose the following:

1. To give an account of the method of hypothesis (or of various such methods).

2. To argue, contrary to Cantor and Laudan, that in their actual practice, as well as in their reflections on this practice, nineteenth-century wave theorists such as Young, Fresnel, Lloyd, and Herschel typically employed a method that is significantly different from the method of hypothesis.

3. To argue that this method contains not only an explanatory component present in the method of hypothesis, but an "independent warrant" component that is not. For wave theorists the strategy for supplying independent warrant is an eliminative one that can be justified by appeal to probabilistic and inductive considerations. Of particular interest in this justification will be probability considerations introduced in section 5 that pertain to the introduction of auxiliary hypotheses.

4. To give an account of what nineteenth-century British particle theorists such as Brougham meant by "induction" and how they utilized this method in developing the particle theory. In doing this some attention will need to be given to Newton's ideas, which exerted considerable influence on later particle theorists.

5. To argue that there are strong similarities, if not identities, between the inductivism of British particle theorists and the methodology of wave theorists, and that the important debate is over particles versus waves, not methodologies. Accordingly, the present case will not support a form of relativism that states that fundamentally different theories employ fundamentally different methodologies.

2. THE METHOD OF HYPOTHESIS

On this method one proposes an hypothesis to explain observed phenomena. If the hypothesis, if true, would correctly explain those phenomena, one can claim support for it, even if the hypothesis postulates unobserved or unobservable entities and processes. Here is a simple use of this method by David Hartley, in defending the hypothesis that an ether exists:

> Let us suppose the existence of the aether, with these its properties, to be destitute of all direct evidence, still, if it serves to explain a great variety of phenomena, it will have an indirect evidence in its favour by this means.[4]

---

4. David Hartley, *Observations on Man, His Frame, His Duty, and His Expectations*, 2nd ed., 2 vols. (London, 1791), vol. 1, p. 15. Quoted by Laudan, *op. cit.*, p. 161.

More generally, the method of hypothesis contains the following idea:

> *Basic method of hypothesis:* The fact that hypothesis h if true would correctly explain observed phenomena $O_1, \ldots, O_n$ constitutes at least some reason to think that h is true.

Frequently, especially in the mathematical physics developed by both wave and particle theorists, the explanations consist of deductive derivations of $O_1, \ldots, O_n$ from h. If so, we get the modern hypothetico-deductive viewpoint. However, the method of hypothesis is also close to the idea of retroduction introduced by Peirce at the end of the nineteenth century and developed in the middle of the present century by N. R. Hanson. According to Hanson, it involves an inference of the following form:

> Some surprising phenomenon P is observed.
> P would be explicable as a matter of course if h were true.
> Hence, there is reason to think that h is true.[5]

Now, according to Laudan, by the 1830s an important change had occurred in the method of hypothesis. Prior to this, hypothesists were willing to conclude that there is some reason to think an hypothesis true if it explains phenomena that have already been observed and for which the explanation was proposed in the first place. (This would make early versions of the method akin to Hanson's form of retroduction.) By the 1830s a requirement was instituted that the hypothesis has to explain states of affairs significantly different from those it was invented to explain. This can be accomplished if the hypothesis can predict (and explain) some new and as yet unobserved phenomenon or some known phenomenon that did not prompt the hypothesis in the first place.[6] Such a view is expounded by William Whewell, who speaks in this connection of a *consilience of inductions*. We might formulate it like this:

> *Method of hypothesis with consilience:* Let h be some hypothesis proposed initially to explain O_1 (and nothing else). The fact that h if true would correctly explain O_1,

---

5. N. R. Hanson, *Patterns of Discovery* (Cambridge, England, 1958), p. 72.

6. See Laudan, *op. cit.*, p. 175. At least one exception to Laudan's thesis is Huygens, who in 1690, in the Preface to his *Treatise on Light*, defends a form of the method of hypothesis that involves deriving or explaining not only known facts but new ones as well. He writes:

> . . . here [in his *Treatise*] the principles are verified by the conclusions to be drawn from them . . . especially when there are a great number of them, and further, principally, when one can imagine and foresee new phenomena which ought to follow from the hypotheses which one employs, and when one finds that therein the fact corresponds to our prevision. (Christian Huygens, *Treatise on Light*, reprinted in Robert Maynard Hutchins, ed., *Newton, Huygens* (Chicago, 1952), p. 551.)

. . . ,O_n (where these are significantly different) provides some reason to think that h is true.

In point of fact, Whewell's version of the method seems even more complex than this. Whewell notes that formulations like those above presuppose that

> the hypothesis with which we compare our fact [is] framed *all at once*, each of its parts being included in the original scheme. In reality, however, it often happens that the various suppositions which our system contains are *added* upon occasion of different researches.[7]

In modifications toward a true theory, Whewell notes:

> all the additional suppositions *tend to simplicity* and harmony; the new suppositions resolve themselves into the old ones, or at least require only some easy modification of the hypothesis first assumed: the system becomes more coherent as it is further extended.[8]

Perhaps, then, Whewell would have espoused the following:

> *"Dynamical" method of hypothesis with consilience:* Let h_1 be some hypothesis proposed initially to explain O_1 but not O_2, . . . ,O_n, where the latter are different in kind from each other and from O_1; let h_2, . . . ,h_k be hypotheses added to h_1 to explain O_2, . . . ,O_n. The fact that h_1, . . . ,h_k if true would correctly explain O_1, . . . ,O_n, and in addition would correctly explain O_{n+1}, . . . ,O_{n+p} (different facts that did not prompt h_1, . . . ,h_k), provides some reason to believe h_1, . . . ,h_k, provided that h_2, . . . ,h_k are "natural" extensions of h_1, so that h_1, . . . ,h_k has "coherence."

These three formulations of the method, although by no means identical, have in common the basic idea that the fact that an hypothesis if true would correctly explain phenomena counts as some reason for believing that hypothesis. There may be restrictions on the kinds of phenomena explained (e.g., they should be different in kind from ones that prompted the hypothesis in the first place). And there may be restrictions on the additions to the hypothesis required for subsequent explanations. But there is no requirement that the hypothesis in question, or any subsequent one, be inductively inferable from any observations. More generally, there is no requirement that there be any independent warrant for the hypotheses introduced, that is, any reason for

---

7. William Whewell, *The Philosophy of the Inductive Sciences* (New York, 1967), vol. 2, p. 68. Emphasis in original.

8. *Ibid.*, p. 68. Emphasis in original.

believing such hypotheses other than the explanatory ones hypothesists mention.

---

3. WHAT METHOD DID NINETEENTH-CENTURY WAVE THEORISTS EMPLOY IN PRACTICE?

In publications setting forth arguments for their theory, a strategy wave theorists typically used is this:

1. *Start with the assumption that light is either a wave phenomenon or a stream of particles.*

According to the wave theory, light consists of a wave motion or pulse transmitted through some medium; the medium itself may be composed of particles that vibrate rather than exhibit translational motion. According to the particle theory, light consists of discrete particles emanating from luminous bodies; these particles are subject to forces obeying Newton's laws of motion; if no such forces are acting the particles move in straight lines with constant finite velocity.

The assumption that light is either a wave or particle phenomenon is made on the grounds that these are the two main theories that have been proposed by the physics community, or on the grounds of some empirical consideration regarding motion, or both. Taking the former line Young writes:

> It is allowed on all sides, that light either consists in the emission of very minute particles from luminous substances, which are actually projected, and continue to move with the velocity commonly attributed to light, or in the excitation of an undulatory motion, analogous to that which constitutes sound, in a highly light and elastic medium pervading the universe; but the judgments of philosophers of all ages have been much divided with respect to the preference of one or the other of these opinions.[9]

Humphrey Lloyd, after a few preliminaries, begins the body of his 1834 report on the present state of physical optics as follows:

> The first property of light which claims our notice is its progressive movement. Light we know, travels from one point of space to another in time, with a velocity

---

9. Thomas Young, *A Course of Lectures on Natural Philosophy and the Mechanical Arts* (London, 1845), p. 359. Also taking the former line, Fresnel, like Young, begins by noting that the particle and wave theories represent "the two systems which have up till now divided scientists with respect to the nature of light." A. Fresnel, "Memoir on the Diffraction of Light" (1816), reprinted (in part) in Henry Crew, ed., *The Wave Theory of Light* (New York, 1900). For parts of this material not in Crew, I have used a translation provided by Laurence Selim.

of about 195,000 miles a second. The inquiry concerning the mode of this propagation involves that respecting the nature of light itself.

There are two distinct and intelligible ways of conceiving such a motion. Either it is the self-same body which is found at different times in distant points of space; or there are a multitude of moving bodies, occupying the entire interval, each of which vibrates continually with certain limits, while the vibratory motion is communicated from one to another, and so advances uniformly. Nature affords numerous examples of each of these modes of propagated movement; and in adopting one or the other to account for the phenomena of light, we fall upon one or other of the two rival systems, — the theories of Newton [particle theory] and of Huygens [wave theory].[10]

Lloyd's assumption that light is either a wave phenomenon or a particle phenomenon is based on the observation that light travels in space from one point to another with a finite velocity, that both particle and wave theories can account for this movement, and that in nature one observes motion from one point to another occurring by the motion of a body and by the motion of vibrations through a set of bodies.

Herschel, another defender of the wave theory, begins his account of physical optics as follows:

Among the theories which philosophers have imagined to account for the phenomena of light, two principally have commanded attention; the one conceived by Newton . . . in which light is conceived to consist of excessively minute molecules of matter projected from luminous bodies. . . . The other hypothesis is that of Huygens . . . , which supposes light to consist, like sound, in undulations or pulses, propagated through an elastic medium.[11]

Although Herschel recognizes that other theories have been proposed, he notes that "these are the only *mechanical* theories which have been advanced." He seems to suppose that these are the most plausible theories.

2. *Show how each theory explains various observed optical phenomena (e.g., rectilinear propagation, reflection, refraction, diffraction, dispersion, etc.).*

Young, for example, begins with diffraction ("when a portion of light is admitted through an aperture and spreads itself in a slight degree in every direction"):

In this case it is maintained by Newton that the margin of the aperture possesses an attractive force, which is capable of inflecting the rays. . . . In the Huygensian

---

10. Humphrey Lloyd, "Report on the Progress and Present State of Physical Optics," *Reports of the British Association for the Advancement of Science* (1834), pp. 297-298.

11. J. F. W. Herschel, "Light," *Encyclopedia Metropolitana* (1845), vol. 4, p. 439.

system of undulation, this divergence or diffraction is illustrated by a comparison with the motions of waves of water and of sound, both of which diverge when they are admitted into a wide space through an aperture. . . . [12]

Young continues by noting other observed optical phenomena and indicating whether or how the two leading theories account for them. Exactly similar strategies are followed by Fresnel, Lloyd, and Herschel.

3. *Show that the particle theory, in explaining one or more of the observed optical phenomena, introduces improbable hypotheses, while the wave theory does not.*

Immediately after introducing the particle explanation of diffraction at an aperture as caused by an attractive force exerted at the margin, Young writes:

> But there is some improbability in supposing that bodies of different forms and of various refractive powers should possess an equal force of inflection, as they appear to do in the production of these effects; and there is reason to conclude from experiments, that such a force, if it existed, must extend to a very considerable distance from the surfaces concerned, at least a quarter of an inch, and perhaps more, which is a condition not easily reconciled with other phenomena.[13]

Fresnel offers a similar argument against the forces introduced by the particle theory to explain diffraction. He presents experiments on the basis of which he concludes that

> The phenomena of diffraction do not at all depend upon the nature, the mass, or the shape of the body which intercepts the light, but only upon the size of the intercepting body or upon the size of the aperture through which it passes. We must, therefore, reject any hypothesis which assigns these phenomena to attractive and repulsive forces whose action extends to a distance from the body as great as that at which rays are inflected.[14]

---

12. Young, *op. cit.*, pp. 359–360. Young's wave explanation of diffraction, which is rather sketchy, is perhaps this: waves (e.g., those of sound and water) diverge when admitted into a wide space through an aperture. Light is a wave motion. That is why it diverges similarly. It remained for Fresnel to give a quantitative wave-theoretic explanation of this and other diffraction phenomena. In one such phenomenon light bends around obstacles into the shadow as well as away from it. Newton (to whom Young refers in the quotation above) observed the external fringes but not the internal ones. This was one of his reasons for rejecting the wave theory (see section 7).

13. *Ibid.* Young proceeds to show how in explaining numbers of other phenomena the particle theory, by contrast to the wave theory, employs dubious hypotheses. This strategy is also evident in one of his earliest papers ("Outlines of Experiments and Inquiries Respecting Sound and Light," *Philosophical Transactions of the Royal Society*, 1800), in which he also argues in favor of the wave theory, though with somewhat less assurance (see pp. 613–616).

14. Fresnel, *op. cit.*, p. 99.

Earlier in this prize essay on diffraction Fresnel presents an argument against Newton's introduction of "fits of easy reflection and transmission" of light particles as an auxiliary hypothesis to explain Newton's rings. He concludes:

> Not only is the hypothesis of fits improbable because of its complexity, and difficult to reconcile with the facts in its consequences, but it does not even suffice in explaining the phenomenon of the colored rings, for which it was imagined.[15]

Fresnel goes on to argue that Newton's rings, as well as diffraction, can be explained as natural consequences of the wave theory, without introducing improbable hypotheses.

Lloyd notes that discoveries of Bradley and Roemer lead to the conclusion that the velocity of light is the same

> whatever be the luminous origin: the light of the sun, the fixed stars, the planets and their satellites, being all propagated with the same swiftness. This conclusion must be allowed to present a formidable difficulty in the theory of emission.[16]

The difficulty is that if light consists of particles (with mass), then a massive object such as a fixed star should exert a force on them that "would be sufficient to destroy the whole momentum of the emitted molecules, and the star would be invisible at great distances" (p. 300). Lloyd asserts that the only way to explain the fact that the velocity we observe is the same for all luminous bodies is to adopt an hypothesis of Arago "that the molecules of light are originally projected with very different velocities: but that among these velocities is but one which is adapted to our organs of vision, and which produces the sensation of light" (pp. 300–301). Lloyd notes that such a supposition has some support from discoveries of invisible rays of the spectrum. But he concludes that the supposition is not "easily reconciled with hypotheses which we are able to frame respecting the nature of vision" (p. 301; for additional discussion of this point, see my "Light Problems: Reply to Chen," *Studies in History and Philosophy of Science* 21 (1990)). By contrast, Lloyd asserts, the fact that the observed velocity of light is the same for all luminous bodies is explained without difficulty by the wave theory:

> This uniformity of velocity, on the other hand, is a necessary consequence of the principles of the wave-theory. The velocity with which vibratory movement is propagated in an elastic medium depends solely on the elasticity of that medium and on its density; and if these be uniform in the vast spaces which intervene between the material bodies of the universe, (and it is not easy to suppose it otherwise) the velocity must be the same, whatever be the originating source. (p. 301)

---

15. *Ibid.*, sec. 7.
16. Lloyd, *op. cit.*, p. 300.

4. *Conclude that the wave theory is (very probably) true, while the particle theory is (very probably) false.*

At the beginning of his paper Lloyd makes explicit the strategy he will follow:

> To take, in the first instance, a rapid survey of the several leading classes of optical phenomena which the labours of experimental philosophers have wrought out in such rich profusion, and afterward to examine how far they are reducible to one or other of the two rival theories which have alone advanced any claim to our consideration. This is, in fact, the only way in which the truth of a physical theory can be established; and the argument in its favor is essentially *cumulative*.[17]

Having seen how the two theories explain (or fail to explain) various optical phenomena, and having argued that the particle theorists introduce hypotheses in these explanations that are improbable, whereas wave theorists do not — or do not to such a great extent — it is concluded that the wave theory is probably true.

4. ANALYSIS OF THIS METHOD

The method described in the previous section is a type of "eliminative" one that consists of four parts. Schematically:

1. Assume that either theory T_1 or theory T_2 is correct, and give grounds for such an assumption.

2. Show how T_1 and T_2 explain various observed phenomena.

3. Show that T_2 in explaining one or more of these phenomena introduces improbable hypotheses, whereas T_1 does not.

4. Conclude that T_1 is probably true.

Let us examine the three steps leading to the conclusion, beginning with the second.

Step 2 introduces the idea of explanation. To conclude that T_1 is probably true, a theorist using this strategy must show that T_1 is capable of explaining certain phenomena (by producing the explanations). Following the method of hypothesis, we might say that such a theorist seeks a theory T that will satisfy a

Basic explanatory condition: T if true would correctly explain observed phenomena $O_1, \ldots, O_n$.

---

17. *Ibid.*, p. 295.

In the light of the discussion in section 2 this explanatory condition, which is associated with the "basic" method of hypothesis, could in principle be broadened to include more sophisticated features of the "dynamical method of hypothesis with consilience." For example, it might be required that theory T explain phenomena different in kind from those that first prompted the theory, and that hypotheses added to T for this purpose be "natural" ones that result in a "coherence" among the theoretical assumptions.[18]

Despite the fact that wave theorists satisfied one or the other explanatory conditions of the method of hypothesis, there is a fundamental difference between the method they employed and the method(s) of hypothesis in section 2. In the latter case, when the explanatory condition is satisfied, it is concluded that there is some reason to think the theory is true. But with the method described in the previous section this is not a sufficient condition, only a necessary one. For each of the rival theories may satisfy the explanatory condition. The particle theory (no less than the wave theory), together with auxiliary assumptions needed, would, if true, correctly explain certain observed phenomena. Indeed, it might be the case that these auxiliary assumptions are "natural" extensions of the particle theory resulting in a "coherent" set of assumptions, and that if the enlarged theory is true it will correctly explain phenomena different from those prompting the theory in the first place. If so, more sophisticated "explanatory conditions" will be satisfied.

For example, in explaining diffraction a particle theorist introduces the auxiliary hypothesis that the margins of the aperture exert an attractive force on the particles of light that is capable of causing the bending of their path. This is a "natural" extension of the particle theory, since the latter seeks to explain optical phenomena in terms of particles subject to forces. The objection to this explanation offered by nineteenth-century wave theorists is not that it introduces ideas foreign to the particle theory, ones that render the set of theoretical assumptions "incoherent," but that it introduces hypotheses that are improbable, given observations made in this case and others. (Fresnel's objection to the Newtonian attractive force at the margins of the aperture in diffraction is based on experiments and observations that show that diffraction does "not at all depend upon the nature, the mass, or the shape of the body which intercepts the light.")

If the satisfaction of an explanatory condition is not sufficient, what else is necessary? Here we must examine steps 1 and 3.

In step 1 wave theorists begin with the assumption that light is either a particle or a wave phenomenon, that is, that one or the other of these two theories is true. This is not simply assumed for the sake of argument to see

---

18. These additional features of an explanation are emphasized by Lloyd, *op. cit.*, pp. 349–350.

what follows. Rather, arguing in the manner of the previous section, wave theorists are committed to the idea that it is likely that one theory or the other is true, and reasons are given for thinking that this is so. What sorts of reasons are these?

Lloyd, we recall, argues "there are two distinct and intelligible ways of conceiving" the observed motion of light, and that "in adopting one or the other [modes of propagated motion] to account for the phenomena of light" we obtain the particle or the wave theory. Accordingly, a part of Lloyd's reasoning is explanatory: both theories will explain the fact that light exhibits motion. But to this claim Lloyd adds importantly that "nature affords numerous examples of each of these modes of propagated movement." Had others been observed, presumably further ways of conceiving the propagation of light would have been noted. Accordingly, if, as seems plausible, Lloyd means that these are the only modes of communication known (or perhaps even just the most prevalent ones), then, in addition to the explanatory reason, there is an inductive one: light is observed to be communicated from one point to another in a finite time; the modes of communication observed in nature consist in the motion of bodies from one point to another and in the vibratory motion of a medium; so it is reasonable to assume that light is either a particle or a wave phenomenon.

Sometimes (as with Young) the claim that light is either a particle or a wave phenomenon is defended by saying that these are the two leading theories proposed by physicists. If, as I am assuming, this is to be understood as providing some reason not simply to examine these theories but to think that one or the other is correct, then, even in this case, the reasoning involves some inductive steps: The fact that these are the leading theories proposed by physicists, together perhaps with an implicit appeal to the reputations of those supporting each theory (e.g., Newton vs. Huygens) and to their other successes, provides some reason to think that one of these theories is true. (Certainly a particle theorist such as Brougham had no qualms about defending his theory, at least in part, by appeal to the success of his authority Newton. And, as noted in Essay 1, Young in an 1802 paper also appealed to the authority of Newton in defense of some of the assumptions of the wave theory.)

Since the claim that light is either a particle or a wave phenomenon is not simply assumed, but grounds are given for it, and since it is recognized that the resulting accounts are not the only possible ones,[19] just the most likely, it

---

19. An alternative theory, which had some defenders until the early years of the nineteenth century, was that light is produced by the rectilinear motion, rather than the vibrations, of a fluid. According to most of these theorists this fluid consists of particles. However, unlike the particle theorists, fluid theorists refused to offer mechanical explanations of the interactions of light and matter, i.e., explanations in terms of attractive and repulsive forces obeying Newtonian

seems appropriate to formulate step 1 in terms of probability. (Wave theorists do use the term "probability" and its cognates in speaking of their theory and that of their opponents.) In what follows I will show how the wave theorist's argument, given in schematic form at the beginning of this section, can plausibly be reconstructed probabilistically. In doing so I will assume that the usual axioms of the probability calculus are satisfied, and that probability is a measure of rational credibility. Beyond that no particular interpretation of probability will be invoked.

We might say, then, that wave theorists using the strategy of the previous section begin with the idea that the probability is very high—say close to 1— that light is either a particle or a wave phenomenon, given certain observed facts O, including ones pertaining to the motion of light. Schematically,

(1) $\qquad p(T_1 \text{ or } T_2/O\&b) \approx 1 \qquad$ ($\approx$ means "is close to")

where T_1 and T_2 are the rival theories, and b is the accepted background information that includes facts about known modes of travel in other cases. To note the required observations and background information and establish (1) is the aim in the first step of the wave theorist's strategy.

Now let us turn to step 3. Here the wave theorist seeks to show that the particle theory in its quest to explain certain observed phenomena introduces improbable hypotheses, whereas the wave theory does not. What role does this step play? Suppose it could be established that the probability of the particle theory, given certain observed facts contained in O and accepted background information b, is very low—say, close to zero. Schematically,

(2) $\qquad\qquad\qquad p(T_2/O\&b) \approx 0$

(In section 5 I will show how wave theorists argue in such a way that (2) follows.) Then, since T_1 and T_2 are rival, incompatible theories, from (1) and (2) we can infer

(3) $\qquad\qquad\qquad p(T_1/O\&b) \approx 1$

Now, let $O_1, \ldots, O_n$ be observed facts about light (e.g., rectilinear propagation, reflection, refraction, etc.) other than those in O and b. What the wave theorist seeks to determine is how probable his theory is in the light of all these facts as well, that is, $p(T_1/O_1, \ldots, O_n\&O\&b)$. Returning to the

---

laws. The theory was frequently given theological associations, and for the most part its defenders were writers outside the mainstream of the scientific community. (See Cantor, *Optics after Newton*, ch. 4.) Accordingly, although such a theory is compatible with the observed transmission of light from one point to another, it was considered very improbable by most nineteenth-century physicists because it postulated particles not subject to Newtonian mechanical principles and hence unlike any observed. (See Cantor, p. 109.)

explanatory step 2 at the beginning of this section, suppose that $O_1, \ldots, O_n$ are explained by the wave theory in such a way that they follow deductively from the theory together possibly with the background information. (When the observed facts are described quantitatively the explanations involve mathematical derivations.) But if the wave theory T_1 (together possibly with b) entails $O_1, \ldots, O_n$, then from the probability calculus it follows that $p(T_1/O_1, \ldots, O_n \& O \& b) \geq p(T_1/O \& b)$. Accordingly, from (3) we get

$$(4) \qquad\qquad p(T_1/O_1, \ldots, O_n \& O \& b) \approx 1$$

And this is the conclusion of the wave theorist's argument. It tells us that the wave theory is highly probable given a range of observed phenomena, including ones explained by that theory.

The explanations of $O_1, \ldots, O_n$ provided by T_1 do not create the high probability for T_1, but they do sustain it. They permit an inference from (3) to (4). The argument leading to (3) shows that $O \& b$ provides independent warrant for T_1, that is, warrant that does not depend on the fact that $O_1, \ldots, O_n$ are explained by T_1. (4) shows that the high probability secured by this independent warrant is retained by T_1 in the light of the additional optical phenomena $O_1, \ldots, O_n$. This is a crucial role played by such explanations in trying to establish the high probability of the wave theory on the basis of a variety of optical phenomena.

More generally, the following probability claim holds:

(5)   For any r such that $0 \leq r < 1$, $p(T/O_1, \ldots, O_n \& O \& b) > r$ if: (i) $p(T/O \& b) > r$, and (ii) $O_1, \ldots, O_n$ are explainable via derivation from T (plus b).

The explanatory condition (ii) by itself will not suffice to yield high probability for T. (See Essay 4 for general arguments showing why derivational explanations, even ones subject to certain "coherence" and "consilience" conditions, cannot guarantee high probability for T.) However, if the independent warrant condition (i) is satisfied, the result will suffice. This suggests one strategy to use when trying to establish the high probability of an hypothesis:

(6)   To show that $p(T/O_1, \ldots, O_n \& O \& b) > k$ (where k represents some threshold value for "high" probability):
  (i)   Show that there is independent warrant for T given some of the observed facts O and background information b, so that $p(T/O \& b) > k$.
  (ii) Show that the remaining observed facts $O_1, \ldots, O_n$ are explainable via derivation from T (together with b).

Independent warrant for T, given O and b, might be shown directly by producing some inductive or analogical argument from O and b to T, or indirectly by producing such an argument against one or more rival theories. Exactly how this works, particularly in the case of the wave theory, will be the subject of the next section. But first it should be noted that wave theorist John Herschel explicitly espouses ideas that commit him to an independent warrant condition. In speaking about the introduction of "hypotheses" in science, Herschel writes:

> Now nothing is more common in physics than to find two, or even many, *theories* maintained as to the origin of a natural phenomenon. For instance . . . with light: one [theory] considers it as consisting in actual particles darted forth from luminous bodies, and acted upon in their progress by forces of extreme intensity residing in the substances on which they strike; another, in the vibratory motion of the particles of luminous bodies, communicated to a peculiar subtle and highly elastic ethereal medium filling all space, and conveyed through it into our eyes. . . .
>
> Now, are we to be deterred from framing hypotheses and constructing theories, because we meet with such dilemmas, and find ourselves frequently beyond our depth. Undoubtedly not . . . it may happen (and it has happened in the case of the undulatory doctrine of light) that such a weight of analogy and probability may become accumulated on the side of an hypothesis, that we are compelled to admit one of two things: either that it is an actual statement of what really passes in nature, or that the reality, whatever it be, must run so close a parallel with it, as to admit of some mode of expression common to both, at least in so far as the phenomena actually known are concerned. . . .
>
> In framing a theory which shall render a rational account of any natural phenomenon, we have *first* to consider the agents on which it depends, or the causes to which we regard it as ultimately referable. These agents are not to be arbitrarily assumed; they must be such as we have good inductive grounds to believe do exist in nature, and do perform a part in phenomena analogous to those we would render an account of; or such whose presence in the actual case can be demonstrated by unequivocal signs. They must be *verae causae*, in short, which we can not only show to exist and to act, but the laws of whose action we can derive independently, by direct induction, from experiments purposely instituted; or at least make such suppositions respecting them as shall not be contrary to our experience, and which will remain to be verified by the coincidence of the conclusions we shall deduce from them, with facts.[20]

What Herschel says here commits him to an independent warrant condition for hypotheses. His insistence on "good inductive grounds" for believing in the existence of the agents introduced by hypotheses, as well as on inductive

---

20. J. F. W. Herschel, *Preliminary Discourse on the Study of Natural Philosophy* (London, 1830), pp. 195–197.

grounds for the laws governing such agents, would seem to require a high probability for such hypotheses on the inductive evidence. To be sure, Herschel does back off a bit at the end by allowing that the suppositions about the agents (though not the suppositions about their existence) must at least "not be contrary to our experience." But even this appears to require at least that the probability of such hypotheses must not be very small given our experience. In either case, the threshold value k in (6) must be "significant."

Also contained in (6) is the idea that a range of observed phenomena is explained by derivation from T. This is certainly part of Herschel's strategy when he develops the wave theory. For example, in his lengthy review article "Light" he begins his discussion of the wave theory by formulating six hypotheses or postulates of his theory (p. 449). He then provides explanatory derivations of various known optical phenomena such as reflection, refraction, interference, and so on. Explaining such optical phenomena seems to be important in showing the believability of the theory. However, this is not sufficient because a rival theory may also, if true, correctly explain the same observed phenomena. Accordingly, Herschel's insistence that an optical theory both provide explanations of observed optical phenomena *and* contain hypotheses with independent warrant reflects the ideas in (6).

Now I suggest that in following the strategy of section 3, wave theorists were adhering to the methodology expressed by (6), rather than to the method of hypothesis in any of the versions in section 2. Wave theorists following the strategy of section 3 wanted to show not only: (a) that their theory if true would correctly explain a range of optical phenomena, but also (b) that their theory had independent empirical warrant. Showing both (a) and (b) would suffice to establish (4), the high probability of their theory given a range of empirical data. They attempted to show (a) by producing the required explanations using the wave theory. They attempted to show (b) by arguing to (3)— that the probability of the wave theory, given a certain subset of all the observations and given accepted background information, is close to 1. Conclusion (3) is inferred by a type of eliminative reasoning from premises (1) and (2). Premise (1), we recall, is that the probability that light is either a particle or a wave phenomenon, given certain observations and background information, is close to 1. Premise (2) is that the probability that light is a particle phenomenon, given those same observations and background information, is close to zero. We get (1) by supposing, among other things, that the observations and background information contain the idea that light travels with a finite velocity and that the only (or perhaps the most common) things known to do this are particles and waves. Accordingly, premise (1) is reached by an argument based, at least in part, on an analogy with observed cases of motion—an argument that Herschel would have classified as inductive. There may in addition be parts of the argument used to establish (1) that are "explanatory" (as with Lloyd), so that both components of (6) are utilized.

And there are other arguments for (1) that can plausibly be construed as inductive.[21]

How (2) is to be established will be the subject of the next section.

5. HOW TO ARGUE FOR THE LOW PROBABILITY OF THE PARTICLE THEORY

The general idea, according to the wave theorists, is this. To explain various optical phenomena the particle theory introduces improbable (auxiliary) hypotheses. For example, to explain diffraction, the particle theory introduces the hypothesis that diffraction is caused by an attractive force at the margin of the aperture—an improbable assumption, given what is known. While this may be the case, how does it show that the particle theory itself is improbable? In what follows I shall present some general probability considerations and show how these can justify the wave theorist's argument.

The particle theory, as I have been construing it, contains the central assumptions that light consists of particles emanating from luminous bodies, that these particles are subject to forces obeying Newton's laws of motion, and that in the absence of such forces the particles move in straight lines with a constant velocity. However, these central assumptions do not include the (auxiliary) assumption that diffraction at a small aperture is caused by a force exerted at the aperture. Call the central assumptions of the particle theory T, call the auxiliary assumption h, and let $O\&b$ be a conjunction of certain observational data together with background information. (O will include information about observed diffraction patterns, in addition to that about the motion of light, and b will include information about other known forces.) Assume that the probability of the auxiliary hypothesis, that is, $p(h/O\&b)$, is low. How, if at all, could this be used to show that the probability of T is low?

It could be so used if the conditional probability of h given T and O is high. Thus, if $p(h/O\&b)$ is close to 0, and $p(h/T\&O\&b)$ is close to 1, then $p(T/O\&b)$ is close to 0. We can establish this in a general way by means of the following theorem:

---

21. Larry Laudan, *op. cit.*, claims that during the 1820s and 1830s proponents of the method of hypothesis such as Herschel and Whewell imposed a "requirement of independent or collateral support," which stated that for an hypothesis to be credible "it must explain (or predict) states of affairs significantly different from those which it was initially invented to explain." This I have labeled "the method of hypothesis with consilience." It is different from what I am here calling "independent empirical warrant," which for the wave theorist is provided by a type of eliminative reasoning involving inductions from observations. The wave theorist is not claiming that the fact that his theory explains (or predicts) states of affairs different from those it was originally invented to explain by itself suffices to render it probable.

$$\text{If } p(h/O\&b) \neq 0, \text{ then } p(T/O\&b) \leq \frac{p(h/O\&b)}{p(h/T\&O\&b)}$$

Proof. According to Bayes' theorem, where

$$p(h/O\&b) \neq 0, \quad p(T/h\&O\&b) = \frac{p(T/O\&b) \times p(h/T\&O\&b)}{p(h/O\&b)}$$

But since $p(T/h\&O\&b) \leq 1$, the theorem follows.

Assume now that $p(h/O\&b) \neq 0$. From the theorem it follows that if the fraction on the right of the inequality is close to 0, then so is the probability on the left. That is,

$$\text{If } \frac{p(h/O\&b)}{p(h/T\&O\&b)} \approx 0, \text{ then } p(T/O\&b) \approx 0$$

Now if $p(h/O\&b) \neq 0$, then $p(h/O\&b)/p(h/T\&O\&b)$ is close to 0 if and only if $p(h/T\&O\&b)$ is much, much larger than $p(h/O\&b)$. Accordingly, we have

(A)   Where $p(h/O\&b) \neq 0$, if $p(h/T\&O\&b) >> p(h/O\&b)$, then $p(T/O\&b) \approx 0$.   ($>>$ means "is much, much larger than").

A more precise expression is this: where a is any constant greater than 0,

$$\lim_{\substack{p(h/O\&b) \to 0 \\ p(h/T\&O\&b) \to a}} p(T/O\&b) = 0$$

One way that $p(h/T\&O\&b)$ can be much, much larger than $p(h/O\&b)$ is if the former probability is close to 1 and the latter probability is close to 0. So from (A),

(B)   If $p(h/O\&b) \approx 0$ (but not equal to 0) and $p(h/T\&O\&b) \approx 1$, then $p(T/O\&b) \approx 0$.[22]

More precisely,

$$\lim_{\substack{p(h/O\&b) \to 0 \\ p(h/T\&O\&b) \to 1}} p(T/O\&b) = 0$$

---

22. The analogue of this for the deductive case is this: If h is false and T entails h, then T is false.

These ideas can be used in analyzing the wave theorist's argument. In explaining some observed optical phenomenon, say diffraction (into the shadow), the particle theorists introduce an auxiliary assumption, for example,

h: diffraction is caused by an attractive force exerted at the edges of the aperture.

Given observed diffraction patterns, the probability of *h, on the assumption of the truth of the particle theory* and on other accepted background information, is extremely high. According to the particle theory, the particles of light obey Newtonian laws. By Newton's first law, when particles are deflected from their motion in a straight line some force must be acting. Since it is observed that only bodies exert forces on other bodies, and since the light bends around each edge of the aperture toward the side of the body with that edge, it is very likely, on inductive grounds, that a force emanates from each edge and that this force is attractive, since that is observed to be the case with other known forces. So, *given that light consists of particles subject to Newtonian laws,* and given what is known about other forces acting on bodies, and given observed diffraction patterns, the probability of *h* we may suppose is close to 1, that is,

(1) $$p(h/T\&O\&b) \approx 1$$

On the other hand, without the assumption of the truth of the particle theory, the probability of *h* looks very different. Thus, according to Young, *h* is improbable because it requires supposing that "bodies of different forms and of various refractive powers should possess an equal force of inflection," which is not observed to be the case with other known forces acting at a distance. With the assumption that light consists of particles, and with the observations of the deflection of light in diffraction, the probability of *h* could be regarded as high, even if *h* requires assuming that bodies of different forms and refractive powers exert the same force. Given that light consists of particles, the inductive weight on the side of *h* from known facts about forces acting to change directions of particles is overwhelming. However, without the assumption that light consists of particles, our other information about the action of forces makes the probability of *h* very low. At least, let us suppose that this is so, that is,

(2) $$p(h/O\&b) \approx 0$$

Then from (B) we may conclude that

(3) $$p(T/O\&b) \approx 0$$

that is, the probability of the (central assumptions of the) particle theory is close to 0.

We get the same result even if we make an assumption weaker than (1), namely, that $p(h/T\&O\&b) >> p(h/O\&b)$, without assuming that the former probability is close to 1. From this assumption, (3) follows using the more general (A).

Let us consider one more example. One standard objection wave theorists raised against particle theorists pertained to the observed constant velocity of light. If light consists of particles emanating from bodies, then a massive body such as a fixed star should exert a force on these particles that would decelerate them more than would a less massive body. Accordingly the velocity of light would not be a constant but would depend on the mass of the body emitting the light. To explain the fact that the observed velocity of light from all bodies is the same, Arago introduced the auxiliary hypothesis that particles of light are emitted with different velocities, but that our eyes are sensitive to light of just one particular velocity. Call this hypothesis h.

Let us assume that, given the particle theory T and background information (which contains Newton's law of universal gravitation), the probability of h is extremely high. (Lloyd, for example, writes that this auxiliary hypothesis "seems to offer the only means of avoiding this difficulty," given the particle theory.)[23] So we have $p(h/T\&O\&b) \approx 1$. However, wave theorists argue that the auxiliary hypothesis without the assumption of the particle theory is very improbable, given what is known about vision. That is, $p(h/O\&b) \approx 0$. With the assumption of the particle theory (let us suppose), the auxiliary hypothesis is very probable, without it, very improbable.[24] Accordingly, wave theorists conclude, the probability of the particle theory, given the observed constant velocity of light and other accepted background information, is very low. This inference is in accord with the earlier probability considerations.

Thomas Young notes that to explain the constancy of the velocity of light some particle theorists introduce the auxiliary hypothesis that a force of emission exists that is about a "million million times as great as the force of gravity" (*Natural Philosophy*, p. 361). Observing that light is produced by such varied sources as decaying wood, pebbles rubbed together, iron burning in oxygen, and the sun, Young points out that "there is no [known] instance in nature . . . of a simple projectile moving with a uniform velocity in all cases, whatever may be its cause. . . . " While one might be willing to concede the

---

23. Lloyd, *op. cit.*, p. 300.

24. The auxiliary hypothesis is probable even though it requires assuming that our eyes can see light of just one velocity. Given the assumption that light consists of particles subject to Newtonian forces, and given the known fact that the force exerted by a body varies with its mass, the weight on the side of the auxiliary hypothesis is strong, despite known facts about vision. Or at least, given the assumptions of the particle theory, the probability of the auxiliary hypothesis is much, much larger than the probability of the auxiliary hypothesis without the assumptions of the particle theory.

probability of such a powerful force residing in luminous bodies, given the assumption that light consists of particles subject to gravity, it is highly improbable without this assumption.

By contrast, wave theorists argue, the explanation of the same observed optical phenomena on the wave theory does not involve the introduction of auxiliary hypotheses whose probability given the wave theory is high, but whose probability without the assumption of that theory is low. For example, in explaining the observed constancy of the velocity of light on the wave theory, Lloyd writes:

> This uniformity of velocity, on the other hand, is a necessary consequence of the principles of the wave theory. The velocity with which vibratory movement is propagated in an elastic medium depends solely on the elasticity of that medium and on its density; and if these be uniform in the vast spaces which intervene between the material bodies of the universe, (and it is not easy to suppose it otherwise), the velocity must be the same, whatever be the originating source.[25]

To the basic assumptions of the wave theory, in explaining the observed constant velocity of light Lloyd adds two auxiliary assumptions: that the velocity of a wave propagated through an elastic medium depends only on the elasticity and density of the medium; and that these are constant in spaces between luminescent bodies in the universe. He regards these assumptions as very probable ("it is not easy to suppose it otherwise"). Accordingly, he believes, the wave theory, in explaining this phenomenon, does not introduce hypotheses that, given the observations and background information, have low probabilities.[26]

Let me now summarize what I take to be a typical strategy of the wave theorists. In accordance with (6) of section 4, the aim of this strategy is to show two things:

1. That the probability of the wave theory is high, given certain observed phenomena and accepted background information.

2. That the wave theory if true would correctly explain a range of observed optical phenomena.

An attempt is made to establish (1) in an indirect way by a type of eliminative reasoning, as follows:

(a) It is argued that it is very probable that light is either a wave or a particle phenomenon. This argument is at least in part an inductive one based on

---

25. Lloyd, *op. cit.*, p. 301. Young, *op. cit.*, p. 361, makes essentially the same point.

26. In the appendix there is a more general discussion of conditions under which the introduction of an auxiliary hypothesis can affect the probability of a theory.

the fact (among others) that light is observed to travel from one point to another with a finite velocity and that the only (or most common) kinds of things that have been observed to do this are waves and particles.

(b) It is argued that in order to explain observed optical phenomena the particle theory introduces auxiliary hypotheses that, although probable given the particle theory, are very improbable without it. (This argument is also an inductive one.) And it is argued that the wave theory does not introduce auxiliary hypotheses with these features.

(c) From (b) it is concluded that the particle theory is improbable.

(d) From (a) and (c) it is concluded that the wave theory is very probable.

An attempt is made to establish (2) by producing wave-theoretic explanations for observed optical phenomena such as rectilinear propagation, reflection, refraction, interference, and so forth. In accordance with probability principle (5) of section 4, the wave theorist can now conclude that the probability of his theory is high in the light of a range of phenomena. The theorist can do so because of the satisfaction of the "independent warrant" condition. On the basis of some of these phenomena and the background information (it is argued) the probability of the wave theory is high. And in light of the wave-theoretic explanations of other phenomena, this probability remains high. Such a strategy, it should be noted, yields high probability for hypotheses about "unobservables." To achieve this, inductions from observables appear in (a) and (b) in order to establish independent warrant. And explanations of other "observables" by means of "unobservables" appear in the explanatory part.

6. OBJECTIONS

In what follows four objections to my account of the wave theorists' strategy will briefly be considered.

Objection 1

It might be suggested that there is a plausible alternative interpretation that places the wave theorists squarely in the hypothesist camp. On this interpretation, the wave theorists do not assume—as I suggest in (a) at the end of the previous section—that it is very probable that light is either a wave or a particle phenomenon. *A fortiori*, they give no arguments for such an assumption. Rather they are only saying that these are the most widely held views. And their strategy is simply to show that the wave theory if true would correctly explain more optical phenomena than the particle theory; they conclude from this (via some form of the method of hypothesis) that the wave theory is probably true, or at least more likely to be true than the particle theory. Such a strategy invokes explanations but no independent warrant, and in particular no inductive reasoning.

This interpretation strikes me as mistaken. Wave theorists do assume that light is either a particle or a wave phenomenon. Recall Young's claim that "it is allowed on *all* sides [presumably including himself] that light either consists in the emission of very minute particles from luminous substances . . . or in the excitation of an undulatory motion. . . . " And, as shown in section 4, wave theorists do have reasons for their assumption that are not simply appeals to its explanatory power. Moreover, it is part of the wave theorist's argument that particle theorists, in explaining various optical phenomena, introduce improbable auxiliary hypotheses. The reason given for this improbability is not that such auxiliary hypotheses fail to explain or do so badly, but that these hypotheses invoke forces (or whatever) unlike any observed. Finally, an argument from the fact that the wave theory, if true, would correctly explain more phenomena than the particle theory to the conclusion that the wave theory is probably true, or at least more probable than the particle theory, would be fallacious. As is shown in the appendix (point 8), it is possible to have two theories T_1 and T_2 that are such that T_1 if true will correctly explain more phenomena than T_2, yet the probability of T_1 is the same as that of T_2 or even less.

Objection 2

It might be claimed that wave theorists do not always proceed by invoking a comparison with the particle theory. Admittedly, for example, Fresnel does use an argument of the previous sort in which support is provided for the wave theory by comparing wave and particle explanations of diffraction and showing how the latter but not the former introduces a very improbable auxiliary hypothesis. Following this discussion Fresnel writes:

> In the first section of this memoir I have shown that the corpuscular theory, and even the principle of interference when applied only to direct rays and to rays reflected at the very edge of the opaque screen, is incompetent to explain the phenomena of diffraction: I now propose to show that we may find a satisfactory explanation and a general theory in terms of waves, without recourse to any auxiliary hypothesis, by basing everything upon the principle of Huygens and upon that of interference, both of which are inferences from the fundamental hypothesis.[27]

Using the wave theory, Fresnel presents mathematical derivations of maximum and minimum intensities of light in diffraction patterns, and he takes the fact that these derivations yield results in conformity with experiment as

---

27. Fresnel, *op. cit.*, p. 99.

helping to establish the theory. Yet he makes no attempt to demonstrate whether or how similar results could be obtained using the particle theory.

Fresnel's strategy is in conformity with that developed in the last section. Having already provided independent warrant for the wave theory by means of a comparison between wave and particle explanations of the existence of diffraction patterns (see section 5), Fresnel now proceeds to show that the wave theory can explain other phenomena, including the mathematically described intensities of the diffraction bands (even if the latter were not previously observed or measured). Because independent warrant is already secured for the theory, these explanations guarantee that the high probability of that theory will be sustained in the light of the new phenomena. This holds true even if the intensities of the diffraction bands could also be derived from the particle theory. If the wave theory entails the observed intensities, then, even if the particle theory does too, p(wave theory/observed diffraction intensities $\&O\&b$) $\geq p$(wave theory/$O\&b$). If the second probability is high, so is the first.

Objection 3

It might be objected that to say that wave theorists argued for their theory in the manner described in the previous section is to imply that they "conclusively refuted" the particle theory and "proved" the truth of the wave theory. It is sometimes held that certain arguments given by wave theorists, in particular one appealing to Young's double-slit experiment producing an interference pattern, did just this. John Worrall has argued against such a claim on the grounds that the particle theorists could and did give various particle explanations of Young's results.[28] For example, there is a physiological explanation according to which destructive interference is produced when the two sets of particles passing through the two slits arrive at the eye and produce vibrations in the retina that destructively interfere. A second possible particle explanation noted by Worrall invokes the idea that the forces emanating from the sides of bodies and acting on light are capable of interfering. Worrall admits that both these explanations are problematic (and indeed that the second one was never actually given by particle theorists). But he argues that the fact that they are possible particle explanations of Young's interference experiments shows that these experiments do not refute the particle theory.

The fact that in response the particle theorists can offer possible particle explanations of interference data does not by itself show very much. Even if Young's experiments did not demonstrate the falsity of the particle theory,

---

28. John Worrall, "Thomas Young and the 'Refutation' of Newtonian Optics: A Case Study in the Interaction of Philosophy of Science and History of Science," in Colin Howson, ed., *Method and Appraisal in the Physical Sciences* (Cambridge, England, 1976), pp. 107–179.

they may well have made that theory very improbable (as wave theorists claimed).[29] This can be shown by appeal to the previous probability results.

Let h_1 be the physiological hypothesis invoked to explain interference, and let h_2 be the "interfering force" hypothesis. Suppose that the disjunction of these two hypotheses is much, much more likely on the assumption of the particle theory than without that assumption, that is,

(1) $$p(h_1 \text{ or } h_2/T\&O\&b) >> p(h_1 \text{ or } h_2/O\&b)$$

where T is the particle theory and O contains the observed interference phenomena. (1) seems reasonable, since (by Worrall's own admission) the disjunction of h_1 and h_2 is problematic given what else is known; but assuming the truth of the particle theory, one of these auxiliary explanations (particularly the one involving interfering forces) would seem much more likely. Now if (1) is the case, then by proposition (A) of the previous section (p. 86),

(2) $$p(T/O\&b) \approx 0$$

While this would not demonstrate that the particle theory T is "conclusively refuted" by the interference data, it would show that it is made very unlikely. I am not claiming to have established (2), but only to show that Worrall's point that the particle theorist can invoke h_1 and h_2 as possible explanations does not suffice to preclude (2).

Objection 4

It might be objected that to claim that wave theorists used the strategy of the previous section in arguing for their theory is to suggest that they were unaware of difficulties in that theory, which is untrue. For example, Herschel, a wave theorist, believed that the wave theory had difficulty explaining the dispersion of light by a prism.[30] On the wave theory, Herschel points out, the refraction of light is a consequence of the difference in velocity of light between the outside medium and the refracting one. When these velocities are given, the amount of the refraction is determined. Hence, light rays of all colors traveling between the same two media should be refracted equally, thus making dispersion impossible.[31] Herschel notes that to explain dispersion Thomas Young introduces the auxiliary hypothesis that the vibrations of the

29. Later in the nineteenth century wave theorists certainly took the interference experiments to show that the wave theory is almost certain to be true and the particle theory almost certain to be false. See J. C. Maxwell, "Ether," in W. D. Niven, ed., *The Scientific Papers of James Clerk Maxwell* (New York, 1965), vol. 2, p. 764.

30. This was also one of Newton's objections to the wave theory.

31. Herschel, "Light," p. 450.

matter of the refracting medium modify the vibrations within it that constitute light, and that they do so differently according to their frequency, producing a difference in the velocity of propagation of different colors. Herschel does not endorse this auxiliary hypothesis. One crucial question is whether he regards the probability of this auxiliary hypothesis, given the wave theory, as very much greater than the probability of this auxiliary hypothesis without the assumption of the wave theory. Young's auxiliary assumption may be the only one that wave theorists had come up with at that time. But that does not mean that its probability on the assumption of the wave theory is very much greater than its probability without this assumption. Herschel may well have been agnostic concerning such a probability. If so he was not in a position to draw an inference from this case that the wave theory has low probability. Still he believed that this theory should be capable of explaining dispersion, and he believed it had not yet adequately done so. Yet he writes:

> We hold it better to state it [the wave theory] at once in its broadest terms, and call on the reader to suspend his condemnation of the doctrine for what it *apparently* will not explain, till he has become acquainted with the immense variety and complication of the phenomena which it will. The fact is, that neither the corpuscular nor the undulatory, nor any other system which has yet been devised, will furnish that complete and satisfactory explanation of *all* the phenomena of light which is desirable.[32]

We have, then, the following situation. As shown by an eliminative inductive argument, certain optical phenomena (e.g., diffraction and the constant velocity of light) together with background information provide independent warrant for the wave theory. In addition there are optical phenomena (rectilinear propagation, reflection, etc.) that are explained via derivation from the wave theory. Accordingly, the probability of the wave theory given all these phenomena is high. However, there are some optical phenomena (dispersion) that wave theorists have not succeeded in deriving from their theory. Yet they want to make sure that the probability of the theory, given such phenomena, remains high. What should their strategy be, assuming that they do not want to modify or discard central assumptions in their theory? Here are several alternatives: (a) Continue trying to derive O (the recalcitrant optical phenomenon) from the wave theory plus the background information. (b) Try to construct some eliminative inductive argument from O to the wave theory (by showing, for example, that the *particle* theorist in explaining O introduces an auxiliary hypothesis whose probability, given the particle theory, is much, much greater than its probability without that theory). (c) Find some auxiliary hypothesis h such that O is derivable from the wave theory plus h.

The strategy wave theorists actually adopted is (c), and it will be successful

---

32. *Ibid.*, p. 450. Italics in original.

if it can be shown that some observed phenomena O_i provide independent warrant for the wave theory & h, so that p(wave theory & h/O_i &b) $> k$. If the recalcitrant phenomenon O is derivable from the wave theory & h, and if $O_1, \ldots, O_n$ are derivable from the wave theory plus b, then it will follow that p(wave theory & h/O_i &O&$O_1, \ldots, O_n$) $> k$.

Accordingly, unexplained optical phenomena do not necessarily show that the wave theory has low probability. But they do present a challenge to wave theorists to demonstrate that their theory retains its high probability in the light of such phenomena. Until they meet such a challenge all wave theorists can say is that their theory is highly probable given the other observed optical phenomena.

7. NEWTON'S STRATEGY

I propose now to contrast the methodological strategy of the nineteenth century wave theorists with that of British particle theorists. To do so it will be useful to begin with Newton's published ideas, since nineteenth-century British particle theorists were largely influenced by them. (A much fuller account has been given in Essay 2.) I will then focus on Henry Brougham, since he was a typical nineteenth-century defender of the particle theory, was a follower of Newton, and both performed experiments in optics and had fairly well-developed methodological views. Following this there will be a much briefer discussion of a case introduced by David Brewster, another nineteenth-century particle theorist.

Newton's published works on the particle theory consist of a few remarks in the *Principia* and several queries in the *Opticks*. In the *Principia*, Book I, Section 14, he proves a theorem to the effect that if a body traveling across a small space separating two media is acted on by a force directed perpendicular to either medium, the body will be refracted in such a way that the sine of the angle of incidence and the sine of the angle of refraction will be "in a given ratio."[33] At this point Newton seems content simply to note an *analogy* between the refraction of light rays when going from one medium to another and the refraction of particles acted on by a force. He explicitly refrains from supposing that light consists of particles. But obviously if it does, and if these particles are subjected to a force of the sort Newton supposes when going from one medium to another, then the refractive property of *light* is explained.

In the *Opticks*, by contrast, Newton does introduce the supposition that light consists of particles:

---

33. Newton, *Principia* (Berkeley, Calif., 1966), vol. 1, p. 226.

Qu. 29: Are not the Rays of Light very small Bodies emitted from shining Substances? For such Bodies will pass through uniform Mediums in right Lines without bending into the Shadow, which is the Nature of the Rays of Light. They will also be capable of several Properties, and be able to conserve their Properties unchanged in passing through several Mediums, which is another Condition of Rays of Light. Pellucid Substances act upon the Rays of Light at a distance in refracting, reflecting, and inflecting them, and the Rays mutually agitate the Parts of those Substances at a distance for heating them; and this Action and Reaction at a distance very much resembles an attractive Force between bodies. If Refraction be performed by Attraction of the Rays the Sines of Incidence must be to the Sines of Refraction in a given Proportion, as we showed in our Principles of Philosophy: And this Rule is true by Experience.[34]

Newton is claiming here that on the supposition that light consists of particles (subject to his laws of mechanics), various known properties of light can be explained, including rectilinear propagation, refraction, and reflection. He goes on to show how the particle theory can explain colors and the fact that light of different colors is refracted differently, "fits of easy reflexion and transmission," and the refraction of Iceland crystal (pp. 372–373).

Accordingly, at least part of Newton's defense of the particle supposition can be put like this:

(1)   The particle theory, if true, would correctly explain a range of optical phenomena.

Another part of Newton's strategy consists in an attack on an alternative type of theory:

Are not all Hypotheses erroneous, in which Light is supposed to consist in Pression or Motion, propagated through a fluid Medium? For in all these Hypotheses the Phenomena of Light have been hitherto explain'd by supposing that they arise from new Modifications of the Rays; which is an erroneous Supposition.

If Light consisted only in Pression propagated without actual Motion, it would not be able to agitate and heat the Bodies which refract and reflect it. If it consisted in Motion propagated to all distances in an instant, it would require an infinite force every moment, in every shining Particle to generate that motion. And if it consisted in Pression or Motion, propagated either in an instant or in time, it would bend into the Shadow. . . . The Waves on the Surface of stagnating Water, passing by the sides of a broad Obstacle which stops part of them, bend afterwards and dilate themselves gradually into the quiet Water behind the Obstacle.[35]

---

34. Newton, *Opticks* (New York, 1979), pp. 370–371.
35. *Ibid.*, p. 362.

Newton offers two types of objections to theories in which light consists of a wave (some pressure or pulse in a medium).

First, such a theory would require extremely improbable auxiliary hypotheses. For example, if light consisted in a motion propagated to all distances in an instant it would require an infinite force, which Newton regards as absurd. The logic of this type of argument can be construed as the same as that described earlier when wave theorists defend their theory: Let T be the theory that light consists of motion propagated through a medium instantaneously to all distances. Let h be the auxiliary hypothesis that an infinite force produces this motion. The probability of h *given* T and the observations and background information (including Newton's mechanics) is close to 1. But the probability of h given just the observations and background information (which includes the fact that no infinite forces have been observed in nature) is close to 0. Accordingly, one can conclude that the probability of T given the observations and background information is low.

Newton employs reasoning of a similar type in connection with the phenomenon of double refraction by Iceland crystal. To explain this phenomenon, Huygens, a wave theorist, introduced the auxiliary hypothesis that there are two vibrating mediums within the crystal. Newton argues against this auxiliary hypothesis by appealing to refraction experiments involving two pieces of Iceland crystal placed together. This argument is part of the query just quoted in which doubt is being cast on the wave theory. The argument will do so if we can suppose that the probability of Huygens' auxiliary hypothesis, given the wave theory, is very much higher than its probability without it.

Second, Newton argues even more directly that a wave theory is refuted or at least made extremely unlikely by observations. His most famous objection is that waves—such as water waves and sound waves—are observed to bend around obstacles into the "shadow," but light rays are not.[36] Accordingly, given these observations, the probability that light is a wave motion is extremely low.

Before attempting to bring together these aspects of Newton's strategy, one important methodological passage in Newton's *Opticks* should be noted:

> As in Mathematicks, so in Natural Philosophy, the Investigation of difficult Things by the Method of Analysis, ought ever to precede the Method of Composition. This Analysis consists in making Experiments and Observations, and in drawing general Conclusions from them by Induction, and admitting of no Objections against the Conclusions, but such as are taken from Experiments, or other certain Truths. . . . By this way of Analysis we may proceed from Compounds to Ingredi-

---

36. Newton performed experiments in which light bent away from the shadow of an obstacle, but not into it. For a discussion of this see Roger H. Stuewer, "A Critical Analysis of Newton's Work on Diffraction," *Isis* 61 (1970), pp. 188–205.

ents, and from Motions to the Forces producing them; and in general, from Effects to their Causes, and from particular Causes to more general ones, till the Argument end in the most general. This is the Method of Analysis: and the Synthesis consists in assuming the Causes discover'd, and establish'd as Principles, and by them explaining the Phenomena proceeding from them, and proving the Explanations.[37]

The "method of analysis," according to Newton's most general description of it, consists in arguing inductively from effects that have been observed to causes of those effects. Such an argument might have this form:

(2)   *X*'s are observed to have property *P*.
      In other cases, when something has *P* this is observed to be caused only (or usually) by a cause of type *C*.
         Therefore (probably)
      The fact that *X*'s have *P* is caused by *C*.[38]

For example, since Newton says we use such reasoning in arguing from motions to the forces producing them, we might construct the following argument:

The planets are observed to accelerate around the sun in a closed orbit.
In other cases (e.g., a stone's being whirled around on a string) when a body accelerates around a central body in a closed orbit this is observed to be caused by a force exerted by the central body.
   Therefore (probably)
The fact that the planets accelerate around the sun in a closed orbit is caused by a force exerted by the sun.

One can use this form of reasoning even when the cause of *X*'s having *P* is unobserved, so long as the causes in the other cases are observed.

Indeed, for Newton this form of reasoning permits inferences to causes that are unobservable. In the *Principia*, Newton's Rule 3 of philosophizing allows an inference from the fact that certain qualities ("which admit neither intensification nor remission of degrees") are found to belong to all bodies within the reach of our experiments to the conclusion that these qualities

---

37. Newton, *Opticks*, pp. 404–405.
38. As noted in Essay 2, in the Rules of Reasoning of the *Principia* Newton seems to distinguish causal from inductive reasoning, his first two rules applying to the former, his third and fourth to the latter. He uses all four rules in arguments leading to his law of gravitation, and he does not claim that his causal rules are reducible to the inductive ones. By contrast, in the present passage from the *Opticks*, when he speaks of the method of analysis he seems to be conflating inductive and causal reasoning in a manner illustrated by Argument (2) above.

belong to all bodies whatever (whether or not these are observable).[39] Newton mentions qualities such as extension, hardness, impenetrability, mobility, inertia, and gravitational attraction. By the latter presumably he has in mind mutual gravitational forces. He writes that "among those in the celestial regions, we have no experiments, nor any manner of observation."[40] Yet by Rule 3, one can infer that such forces exist, even though they are unobservable. Accordingly, if Newton can establish that light consists of bodies, then by using Rule 3 he can attribute to such bodies qualities such as extension, hardness, impenetrability, mobility, inertia, and (presumably) forces, since these are found to be the qualities of all observed bodies.

Newton's method of "composition" or "synthesis" consists in assuming the causes and showing how observed phenomena can be explained by these causes. Although he says that "analysis" should precede "synthesis" in one's investigation, presumably he believes that when these are accomplished both together provide a good reason to believe the theory describing the cause of the phenomena. We might put these ideas as follows:

(3) Where theory T assigns a cause to various effects, T is probable if
  (a) there is independent inductive support for T from observations of other observed causes and effects ("analysis").
  (b) T if true would correctly explain a range of phenomena ("synthesis").

In Book 3 of the *Opticks* Newton provides at least some syntheses for his particle theory of light by arguing that the theory if true would correctly explain observed phenomena such as rectilinear propagation, reflection, and refraction. Does he provide an analysis? Newton himself admits that

> In this third Book I have only begun the Analysis of what remains to be discovered about Light and its Effects upon the Frame of Nature, hinting several things about it, and leaving the Hints to be examin'd and improv'd by the farther Experiments and Observations of such as are inquisitive.[41]

In Newton's discussion of the particle theory there are no explicit inductive arguments of form (2). For example, he does not offer any argument of the following sort:

---

39. See Maurice Mandelbaum, *Philosophy, Science, and Sense Perception* (Baltimore, 1964), who calls such inferences transdictions. He thinks of them as one type of induction. See p. 62.
40. Newton, *Principia*, p. 400.
41. Newton, *Opticks*, p. 405.

(4)   Light is observed to travel in a straight line with uniform speed.

In other cases, when something travels with uniform speed in a straight line this is always or usually observed to be caused by a particle or series of particles.

Therefore (probably)

The fact that light consists of particles is what causes it to travel in straight lines with uniform speed.

How then does Newton proceed?

It is quite possible that Newton thought that he did not have any, or any significant, "analyses" to present for the particle theory; that he simply had "syntheses" (which would not be sufficient to make the theory probable); and that, as he says, further experiments would be needed to provide the independent inductive support required by an analysis. (Perhaps this is why Newton puts the theory as a query rather than a proposition.)

On the other hand, Newton does contrast his particle theory with wave theories. And he raises objections to such theories. It is quite possible he took the fact that such theories have difficulties not shared by his particle theory to be some reason, or at least part of a reason, to believe the particle theory. (Although he puts the particle theory in the form of a query, the question, which is formulated as a negative, seems rhetorical. The mode in which it is expressed, as well as the arguments following the question, strongly suggest that the answer to the question, "Are not the Rays of Light very small Bodies emitted from shining Substances?," is supposed to be Yes!) In view of this, how might Newton be construed, so as to preserve his inductivism and provide support for the particle theory? Here is one possibility (see Essay 2, where this is spelled out probabilistically).

Instead of using an inductive argument of form (2) for the "analysis," Newton is using a slightly more complex version:

(2)′ X's are observed to have property P.

In other cases, when something has P this is observed to be caused by C or C'.

But given the observations and background information, it is unlikely that C' causes X's to have P.

Therefore (probably)

The fact that X's have P is caused by C.

So, for example, instead of (4) we might have

(4)′   (a) Light is observed to travel in a straight line with uniform speed.

(b) In other cases, when something travels with uniform speed in a straight line this motion is observed to be caused by a series of particles or a series of wave pulses produced in a medium (e.g., sound).

(c) But given the observations and background information, it is unlikely that a series of wave pulses in a medium is what is causing light to travel in straight lines.

Therefore (probably)

The fact that light consists of particles is what causes it to travel in straight lines with uniform speed.

Newton believed (a). It might reasonably be said that he was in a position to assert (b) even though he did not explicitly do so. We have already seen how Newton argued for (c): first, by arguing that the wave theory introduces auxiliary hypotheses that are improbable on the basis of the observations (though very probable given the wave theory); second, by arguing more directly that the wave theory is made improbable by the observations.

This would explain why Newton thought it important to criticize the wave theory: doing so, and supposing that observations of other causes suggest that various properties of light are due either to particles or waves, would allow him to conclude, on the basis of observation, that light is a particle phenomenon. On this interpretation, it is possible to satisfy Newton's demand for analysis as well as synthesis. It is possible to satisfy the conditions of schema (3).

8. BROUGHAM'S STRATEGY

In section 1 it was noted that in 1803 Henry Brougham, in a review of Thomas Young's wave theory, defended the particle theory and attacked Young's hypotheses on methodological grounds. According to Brougham, the particle theory receives inductive support from experiments while the wave theory employs an indefensible method of hypothesis. What did Brougham have in mind by an "inductive" inference?

In his *Discourse on Natural Theology* Brougham makes general remarks on the nature of inference in science. He counts it as reasonable to draw conclusions from what we can observe not only to other observable facts but also (following Newton) to unobservable ones. Thus he agrees that "the examination of certain visible objects and appearances enables us to ascertain the laws of light and of vision." But we can also infer from what we can observe to what we cannot:

But that light, which can be perceived directly by none of our senses, exists, as a separate body, we can only infer by a process of reasoning from things which our senses do perceive. So we are acquainted with the effects of heat; we know that it extends the dimensions of whatever matter it penetrates; we feel its effects upon our own nerves when subjected to its operation; and we see its effects in augmenting, liquefying, and decomposing other bodies; but its existence as a separate substance we do not know, except by reasoning and analogy.[42]

Brougham emphasizes that such reasoning is from observed effects to some (unobserved or unobservable) cause:

A certain sensation is excited in the mind through the sense of vision; it is an inference of reason that this must have been excited by something, or must have had a cause. . . . Experience and reasoning, therefore, are required to teach us the existence of external objects; and all that relates to their relations of size, colour, motion, habits, in a word, the whole philosophy of them, must of course be the result of still longer and more complicated processes of reasoning. (pp. 24–25)

Finally, Brougham argues that such reasoning, which he takes to be "common to Natural Philosophy and Natural Theology," (p. 42) is inductive. Speaking of the kind of reasoning used in natural theology and comparing it to that in natural philosophy, he writes:

Is not this last process [reasoning in Natural Theology] as much one of strict induction as the other? It is plainly only a generalization of many particular facts; a reasoning from things known to unknown; an inference of a new or unknown relation from other relations formerly observed and known. (p. 43)

Brougham does not spell out the form or forms of such inferences. But since they proceed from what is observed to what is not (even to what is unobservable, such as heat or light as "bodies"), and since they involve, or can involve, arguing from effects to causes, perhaps Brougham's inductive inferences include ones having argument form (2) of the previous section, or some variant of it such as

(1) X's are observed to have property P.
       X's are observed to have property Q.
       In other cases, when something with Q has P this is observed to be caused only (or usually) by cause C.
          Therefore (probably)
       The fact that X's have P is caused by C.

This form of reasoning would allow Brougham to argue from observed effects to unobserved or unobservable causes.[43]

---

42. Henry Brougham, *Discourse on Natural Theology*, 2nd ed. (London, 1835), pp. 21–22.

43. Later in his book Brougham offers a more general characterization of induction: "The inductive principle is this—that from observing a number of particular facts, we reason to others of the same kind—that from observing a certain thing to happen in certain circumstances, we

In developing his particle theory of light Brougham does employ reasoning that conforms to this pattern, at least in part. He performed an experiment in which rays of light impinge on a curved surface of a small polished pin. The reflected light is decomposed into various colors, and rays of different colors are reflected at different angles. Brougham notes, for example, that when the angle of incidence of the ray is 77°20′ the angle of reflection for red (at one end of the spectrum) is 75°50′, while that for violet (at the other end) is 78°51′. Brougham then proceeds to infer a cause of this phenomenon:

> I shall conclude this part of the subject with a few remarks on the physical cause of reflexibility. As light is reflected by a power extending to some distance from the reflecting surface, the different reflexibility of its parts arises from a constitutional disposition of these to be acted on differently by the power. And as these parts are of different sizes, those which are largest will be acted on most strongly.[44]

Brougham goes on to derive a formula relating the reflecting force to the velocity of the light, the sine of the sum of the angles of incidence and reflection, and the sine of the angle of reflection. From this, together with the assumption that the force exerted on the light of a given color is proportional to the size of the particle of light, he derives the result that "the size of red particles are to the violet as 1275 to 1253" (p. 738). Following this he notes that

> All this follows mathematically, on the supposition that the parts of light are in proportion to their sizes; and to say the truth, I see no other proportion in which we can reasonably suppose them to be influenced; for such an action is not only conformable to the universal laws of attraction and repulsion, and but also to the following arguments.[45]

One important part of Brougham's argument might be reconstructed as follows:

(2) Light of different colors is observed to be reflected from a curved pin at different angles (red is reflected closest to the normal, violet furthest).
Light consists of particles.
In other cases, when particles are reflected from their paths, they are

---

expect the same thing to happen in the like circumstances" (*Discourse*, p. 167). Schema (1) above would conform to this idea, since from an observed causal relationship between *C* and *P* in objects with *Q* we are inferring a causal relationship between *C* and *P* in *X*'s, since *X*'s have *Q*.

44. Henry Brougham, "Experiments and Observations on the Inflection, Reflection, and Colours of Light," *Philosophical Transactions* 1791–1796, p. 738.

45. p. 738. Brougham argues that if the force varied according to some other ratio then we would get unacceptable conclusions regarding intensities of the various colors.

reflected (only) by a force acting on them, and this force acts differently on particles of different sizes (masses); e.g., gravitation.
    Therefore (probably)
Light is reflected from the curved pin by forces acting differently on
different particles according to their size (mass).

This conforms to the inductive pattern (1) above, with the exception of the
second premise. Brougham's argument requires an assumption that light consists of particles which, of course, are not observable. Nor does Brougham
offer an argument for the second premise from observations. He simply
assumes that this is so. In the 1790s, before Thomas Young's revival of the
wave theory, Newton's particle theory was widely believed, and Brougham
probably thought that at this point the assumption that light consists of
particles needed no argument. What was necessary was to work out the
theory in certain areas.
    Assuming, then, that the premise that light consists of particles could itself
be inferred inductively from observations (perhaps in the manner of (4)' of
the previous section), Brougham could offer an argument—namely, (2)—to
the conclusion that the reflected light from the curved pin is caused by forces
on the light particles that vary with the size of the particle. Such an argument
would be inductive in a sense that Brougham could reasonably endorse.
    One additional feature of Brougham's methodology deserves to be noted.
Brougham follows Newton in speaking of analysis and synthesis as parts or
aspects of one's methodology:

> But it may be said that in this classification of the objects of science we omit one
> ordinarily reckoned essential—the explanation of phenomena. The answer is, that
> such a classification is not strictly accurate, as no definite line can be drawn
> between the explanation of phenomena and the analytical process by which the
> truths themselves are established: in a word, between analysis and synthesis in the
> sciences of contingent truth. For the same phenomena which form the materials of
> the analytical investigation—the steps that lead us to the proposition or discov-
> ery—would, in a reversed order, become the subjects of the synthetical operation;
> that is, the things to be explained by means of the proposition or discovery, if we
> had been led to it by another route, in other words, if we had reached it by means of
> other phenomena of the like kind, referable to the same class, and falling within the
> same principle or rule. Thus the experiments upon the prismatic spectrum prove
> the sun's light to be composed of rays of different refrangibility. This being demon-
> strated, we may explain by means of it the phenomena which form the proofs of the
> first propositions of the *"Optics"* that lights which differ in colour differ in re-
> frangibility—as that a parallelogram of two colours refracted through a prism has
> its sides no longer parallel.[46]

---

46. Brougham, *Discourse*, pp. 159–160.

Brougham's point is that if one infers an hypothesis inductively from observed phenomena, one is in a position to use that hypothesis to explain the phenomena themselves as well as other similar ones. This is clearly the case if the inductive arguments Brougham had in mind are arguments from effects to causes, such as (1) above or variants of it. If we infer inductively that the fact that X's have property P is caused by C, then we can appeal to C in explaining why X's have property P. And it may be the case that similar properties of X's can also be explained as due to C. Brougham stresses that the phenomena the inferred hypothesis is used to explain in the process of "synthesis" must be ones that would have provided the basis for an inductive inference to that hypothesis. To use the hypothesis to explain other sorts of phenomena as well would be illegitimate.

Brougham explicitly rejects the method of hypothesis:

> The fundamental rule of inductive science is, that no hypothesis shall be admitted—that nothing shall be assumed merely because, if true, it would explain the facts.[47]

Nevertheless, as we have noted, Brougham admits that explanatory hypotheses about unobservables can be legitimate. Conceivably, he saw the explanatory power of the hypothesis as providing, or helping to provide, some reason to believe it. But if he did, then a necessary condition for this is that the hypothesis have inductive support from the explained phenomena.

9. BREWSTER

The final physicist I shall (very briefly) consider is David Brewster, who defended the particle theory during the first four decades of the nineteenth century. Unlike Brougham, Brewster did not write any general treatise expounding his methodology, although there are methodological claims in some of his papers and reviews. Thus in a short paper criticizing the wave theory, he has this to say in rejection of the method of hypothesis:

> The power of a theory, however, to explain and predict facts, is by no means a test of its truth. . . . Twenty theories, indeed, may all enjoy the merit of accounting for a certain class of facts, provided they have all contrived to interweave some common principle to which these facts are actually related.[48]

---

47. *Ibid.*, p. 164.
48. David Brewster, "Observations on the Absorption of Specific Rays, in Reference to the Undulatory Theory of Light," *Philosophical Magazine* 2 (1833), pp. 360–363.

Although Brewster emphasizes the importance of experiments in physics (which he performed on numerous occasions), and although frequently in his writings he does not adopt physical hypotheses postulating unobserved causes to explain these experiments,[49] he by no means rejects the use of such hypotheses. In a critical review of Comte's *Cours de Philosophie Positive*, Brewster claims that hypotheses can serve three useful roles: as mnemonic devices in organizing observed phenomena, as devices to explain observed phenomena (so long as the explanation makes no assumption incompatible with the observations), and as devices to predict new facts.[50]

Does Brewster ever allow that the explanatory and predictive success of an hypothesis can count as some reason for believing it to be true or probable? He does *under suitable conditions*. To illustrate this, I shall note the results of one of Brewster's investigations of double refraction and the polarization of light.[51]

When polarized light is transmitted along the axis of a uniaxial crystal, circular concentric colored rings are produced that contain all the tints in Newton's table of the colors of thin plates (p. 210). If the crystal is thinner, the rings are larger. Now, notes Brewster, if we combine two crystals and transmit light through them symmetrically, a difference can be noted between two types of crystals. In some (e.g., combining beryl and calcareous spar) the system of rings exhibited will be diminished and will be the same as would be produced by one crystal whose thickness is equal to the sum of the thicknesses of the two combined (p. 215). With other combinations (e.g., zircon and calcareous spar) the system of rings is increased and "is equal to the system which would have been produced by a thin plate of calcareous spar, whose thickness is equal to the difference of the thicknesses of the plate of calcareous spar, that would give rings of the same size as those given by the zircon, etc., alone" (p. 216). Brewster notes that this difference was first observed by Biot, who classified crystals into categories: repulsive (rings diminish) and attractive (rings increase). Biot explained the difference as being due to a single force in a given type of crystal that is either repulsive or attractive. Brewster rejects this as "hypothetical" and suggests that combinations of attractive and repulsive forces could produce the same effect:

> If we consider a material particle in motion as under the influence of forces, the nature and the source of which are unknown, we may ascribe any change of

---

49. For example, "In these enquiries I have made use of no hypothetical assumptions." *Philosophical Transactions of the Royal Society* 105 (1815), pp. 158–159.

50. David Brewster, *Edinburgh Review* 67 (1838), p. 306.

51. David Brewster, "On the Laws of Polarisation and Double Refraction in Regularly Crystallized Bodies," *Philosophical Transactions of the Royal Society* 108 (1818), pp. 199–273. For a brief discussion of this case, and of Brewster's methodological views, see Cantor, *Optics after Newton*, pp. 76–78, 179ff.

direction which it experiences, either to a single attractive, or a single repulsive force, emanating from different sources; or we may regard it as the resultant of a variety of forces of the same, or of opposite characters. . . . The deviation of the extraordinary ray in beryl, may be the result of a repulsive force emanating from the axis of the prism, or of an attractive force emanating from two equal rectangular axes lying in a plane perpendicular to the axis of the prism, or of various other combinations of forces, either of the same or of opposite names.[52]

Despite these various possibilities, Brewster claims that there is some reason to believe in the existence of opposite forces coexisting in crystals:

With regard to the nature of the forces we are not left entirely without some general indications. In magnetism and electricity, the various phenomena are produced by two opposite and co-existent forces which modify each other's action; and since opposite forces are obviously indicated by the phenomena of polarisation, we have the strongest reasons, from analogy, to believe that they are also co-existent in crystals. (pp. 252–253)

Accordingly, Brewster proposes a reason for postulating such unobserved forces that contains an explanatory part. (The hypothesis of opposite forces in a crystal acting on polarized light would, if true, explain certain observed phenomena involving the transmission of polarized light through crystals.) It also contains "independent warrant." (In other known cases such as electricity and magnetism, where we have a modification of actions, there are opposite coexistent forces.) Indeed, Brewster explicitly mentions both the explanatory aspect and the independent warrant (from analogy) in the following passage:

I trust I shall be able to demonstrate, not only that the phenomena of double refraction and polarisation may be explained by forces or combinations of forces different from those which have been given by Laplace and Biot, but that there are certain analogies of nature, and certain physical circumstances in the phenomena, which may lead us to select one combination of forces in preference to others, as the means which nature has employed in the accomplishment for her purposes. (pp. 245–246)

10. ARE THERE IMPORTANT DIFFERENCES BETWEEN METHODOLOGICAL STRATEGIES OF WAVE AND PARTICLE THEORISTS?

By contrast to claims suggested by certain historians and philosophers of science, as well as by Brougham in his attack on Young, wave theorists, in following the strategy of section 3 in their actual practice and in their philosophical reflections about this practice, were not supporters of the method of hypothesis in any of its (simple or sophisticated) versions outlined in sec-

---

52. Brewster, "On the Laws . . . ," p. 246.

tion 2. Rather, they followed a strategy that, in very general terms, can be characterized as consisting of two components: (a) Show that the probability of T is high, given certain observed phenomena and accepted background information. (b) Show that theory T, if true, would correctly explain a range of phenomena beyond those in (a). In the case of the wave theory, at least, (a) is shown by a type of eliminative reasoning. Component (b) requires the satisfaction of an explanatory condition demanded by the method of hypothesis. But component (a) requires the satisfaction of an "independent warrant" condition that is absent from this method.

To compare this with strategies of particle theorists, note to begin with that Brewster, a particle theorist, in defending the hypothesis that opposite forces act on polarized light in crystals, argues that this hypothesis has independent warrant from analogies with electricity and magnetism. And he shows how this hypothesis, if true, would explain certain observed effects of polarization. However, let us focus on inductive strategies of Newton and Brougham, since it is these that are generally picked out when contrasts are drawn between wave and particle theorists.

Newton's inductivism, as well as that of Brougham, permits reasoning from observed effects to unobserved causes. From the fact that X's have observed properties $P_1, \ldots, P_n$ and that, in other cases it is observed that these properties are caused by C, it is concluded that probably C causes X's to have these properties as well. Such an argument can be valid even if cause C in the case of X's is unobservable (e.g., qualities of light particles, forces at the aperture), so long as the fact that C causes these properties in other cases is observable.

Accordingly, one similarity between the methodologies of wave and particle theorists is that both allow inferences to hypotheses about unobservables. It is not true that the inductivism of Newton or Brougham permits inferences only to entities or processes that can be seen. Furthermore, both methodologies, not just that of the particle theorists, stress the need for independent empirical warrant. For the particle theorist in the most general case this will require an inference from observed effects to an unobserved cause via similar causes in other observed cases. But for the wave theorist too, such an inference, or one of a similar type, will typically be involved in showing (a) above, namely, that the probability of T is high given certain observed phenomena and background information. It is possible that, at least in their philosophical doctrines describing their methodologies, particle theorists would have demanded more independent empirical warrant (say higher probabilities or probabilities based on more instances) than wave theorists. But in their *practice* this is not generally so. By his own admission, Newton provides "syntheses" (explanations), but only "hints" of "analyses" (inductions). Even if, as I think reasonable, we count his arguments against the wave theory as inductive, these do not provide stronger independent empirical warrant for his theory than wave theorists, employing a similar strategy, provide for their theory. If anything, it is the reverse.

Is there anything in the inductivist strategy of the particle theorists that corresponds to the wave theorist's explanatory condition that T if true correctly explains a range of phenomena? The answer seems to be yes. As Brougham explicitly notes, an inductive inference of the sort he has in mind — one proceeding from the fact that X's have observed properties $P_1, \ldots, P_n$, and the fact that in other cases these properties are caused by C, to C causes X to have these properties as well — can be used to produce explanations. The cause C that one infers can be used to explain why X's have the properties P_1, $\ldots, P_n$. Brougham does not restrict the explanations that can legitimately be given by postulating C to explanations of the properties $P_1, \ldots, P_n$. One can explain others as well, so long as inductive inferences to C are possible from these properties.

Whether Newton, from whom Brougham took many of his methodological and physical ideas, placed such a restriction on the explanations produced in "synthesis" is not so clear. Newton does add "and proving the Explanation" to his description of synthesis, although he offers no clarification of this. Conceivably this could be construed in a very strong sense as requiring an inductive argument from each type of phenomenon explained to the hypothesis. Alternatively, it might suffice to provide such an argument from only some of the explained phenomena (or other phenomena) to the explanatory hypothesis. And in his actual practice, when he uses the particle theory to explain various phenomena he does not present inductive arguments from each of these phenomena to the postulates of the particle theory. Finally, Brewster in his practice as well as in his methodological remarks on hypotheses does not insist on an inductive argument from each phenomenon explained to the explanatory hypothesis.[53]

Accordingly, with regard to explanation, Brougham may have held the strongest view of the three, which might be formulated as follows. A theory T postulating unobservables may be used to explain various types of observed phenomena $O_1, \ldots, O_n$. But if $p(T/O_1, \ldots, O_n \& b)$ is to be high, then an inductive inference must be possible from each O, together with b, to T. By contrast, the weaker view, which may well have been Brewster's as well as Newton's, allows $p(T/O_1, \ldots, O_n \& b)$ to be high if some though not all of the O's provide an inductive basis for T, so long as T can explain the remaining O's. So when it comes to explanation there is a methodological difference between Brougham and the wave theorists. The latter allow the fact that T explains O to help sustain T's high probability, even where O does not provide

---

53. See, for example, various particle theory explanations, and the comparison with wave theory ones, in his "Optics," *Edinburgh Encyclopedia*, vol. 14 (American ed., Philadelphia, 1832), pp. 589–789.

inductive grounds for T. Brougham disallows this. On the other hand, Newton and Brewster seem more liberal. Indeed the type of reasoning I have supposed Newton might be employing in defending his particle theory is very like that used by wave theorists in defending their theory: given certain observations and background information, it is very likely that light is either a particle or a wave phenomenon. But the wave theory introduces auxiliary hypotheses whose probability on that theory is much, much greater than without it. Therefore, the probability of the particle theory is high, and since that theory explains other phenomena, its probability remains high in the light of these phenomena.

In sum, even if there is a methodological difference between some of the particle theorists and the wave theorists about the use of explanations, there are also close methodological similarities. Both groups reject the method of hypothesis; both allow explanations of observed phenomena that appeal to unobservables; both require independent inductive warrant; and at least Newton and Brewster, like the wave theorists, allow explanations of phenomena to help support an hypothesis even when inductive arguments are not supplied from each of those phenomena to the hypothesis.

By the first third of the nineteenth century, when the wave theorists had obtained the upper hand in the debate, their position was not that they employed a superior methodology, but that using the methodology they did there were good reasons to believe their theory rather than the particle theory. This position was based on two claims, each justifiable in accordance with the methodology I have outlined.

First, wave theorists claimed that experiments and observations such as those involving diffraction and interference supported the wave theory rather than the particle theory. This can be justified on the grounds that although both theories provide explanations for these phenomena, the particle theory in doing so introduces auxiliary hypotheses that are probable given that theory but very improbable without it; by contrast, the wave theory needs to introduce no such hypotheses.

Second, wave theorists claimed support for their theory on the grounds that it explained *numerous* optical phenomena, more than did the particle theory. See, for example, the "success table" (Figure 1 in Essay 1) drawn up in 1833 by Baden Powell. Even though particle theorists could claim that this table was not complete,[54] it was generally thought that the wave theory was more successful in producing explanations than the particle theory. Accordingly, wave theorists could base their (high) probability claim on more observations than could particle theorists.

---

54. See Cantor, *Optics after Newton*, p. 192.

11. CONCLUSIONS

1. Contrary to what some have supposed, in their actual practice as well as in their reflections on this practice, nineteenth-century wave theorists employed a strategy that is importantly different from the method of hypothesis. This strategy requires not only an explanatory part, demanded by hypothesists, but independent empirical warrant as well. For the wave theorist, the latter involved a type of eliminative reasoning from observations that can be analyzed in inductive and probabilistic terms.

2. Particle theorists in their actual practice as well as in their reflections on this followed a strategy that also involves explanatory and independent warrant components. In "analysis" one provides independent empirical warrant for causal hypotheses via inductive arguments from observed causes and effects. In "synthesis" one uses the causal hypotheses to explain observed phenomena. Some particle theorists, unlike wave theorists, may have required an inductive argument from each (rather than only some) of the phenomena explained to the explanatory hypothesis, though this idea is not always reflected in actual practice, which, in this regard, frequently resembles that of the wave theorists.

3. Particle theorists on occasion provided independent warrant by using a type of eliminative argument that is exactly analogous to the one employed by wave theorists. Wave theorists in their eliminative argument introduced inductive steps that are exact counterparts of those employed by particle theorists. And both theorists sanctioned inferences to unobservable entities and processes.

4. I conclude that there are strong similarities, if not identities, between the methodologies of wave and particle theorists, and that the important difference between the two is over questions of physics, not method.

APPENDIX

Suppose that in developing theory T to explain some observed phenomenon O a scientist introduces an auxiliary hypothesis h. Under what conditions can this affect the probability of T, given O and the background information b? Several cases will be considered.

1. We find an auxiliary hypothesis h such that $T + h$ — if true — will correctly explain O. But $p(h/T\&O\&b) >> p(h/O\&b)$. This is the type of case discussed earlier in which (the wave theorist alleges), to explain some optical phenomenon O, the particle theorist introduces an auxiliary assumption h whose probability given the particle theory is much, much greater than its probability without that assumption. In such a case, by proposition (A) of section 5, $p(T/O\&b)$, the probability of the particle theory, given the observations and background information, is close to zero. So in this case, the

introduction of an auxiliary hypothesis h to enable T to explain some observation O shows that T is extremely improbable.

2. We find an auxiliary hypothesis h such that $T + h$ — if true — will correctly explain O and for this h we also find that $p(h/O\&b) > k$ and $p(h/T\&O\&b) > k$. That is, we find that the probability of h with or without the assumption of T is high. Will the explanatory power of T and h, together with these high probabilities for h both with and without T, allow us to conclude that T has a high probability, that is, that $p(T/O\&b) > k$? No, it will not. Under these assumptions T's probability can still be low. Consider the following simple nonscientific case:

T = John has received the news that he has won the lottery.
h = John is happy whenever he wins money.
O = John is happy over the news he has just received.
b = People generally are happy when they receive money; John holds 1 ticket out of 1000 sold in a fair lottery.

$T\&h$ — if true — would correctly explain O. The following probability claims seem reasonable, where, let us say, the threshold value k is 1/2:

$$p(h/T\&O\&b) > k$$

$$p(h/O\&b) > k$$

Yet $p(T/O\&b) < k$. Accordingly, the fact that an auxiliary hypothesis h is such that it, together with a theory T, will — if true — correctly explain O and the fact that this auxiliary hypothesis has high probability both with and without the theory does not suffice to show that the probability of the theory T is high.

3. We find an auxiliary hypothesis h such that $T + h$ — if true — will correctly explain O, and we also find that $p(h/O\&b) < k$, and $p(h/T\&O\&b) < k$. That is, we find that the probability of h with or without the assumption of T is low. Does this suffice to show that $p(T/O\&b) < k$? No, it does not. To show this we can use the case described in point 2, simply switching h and T. Now, $p(h/O\&b) < k$ and $p(h/T\&O\&b) < k$. But $p(T/O\&b) > k$. Accordingly, a theory can have high probability, even when an auxiliary assumption used to explain some phenomenon has low probability with and without the theory.

4. We find an auxiliary hypothesis h such that $T + h$ — if true — will correctly explain O, and we also find that the probability of the auxiliary hypothesis is high, that is, $p(h/O\&b) > k$, but the probability of the auxiliary hypothesis, given the theory T, is low, that is, $p(h/T\&O\&b) < k$. Will this suffice to show that the probability of theory T is low, that is, $p(T/O\&b) <$

k? No, it will not, because under the conditions specified, if $p(T/h\&O\&b) \geq k$, then $p(T/O\&b) > k$. That is,

If (a) $p(h/O\&b) > k$ $(k > 0)$, (b) $p(h/T\&O\&b) < k$, and (c) $p(T/h\&O\&b) \geq k$, then $p(T/O\&b) > k$.

Proof. From (b), using Bayes' theorem

$$p(h/T\&O\&b) = \frac{p(h/O\&b) \times p(T/h\&O\&b)}{p(T/O\&b)} < k$$

So

$$p(T/O\&b) > \frac{p(h/O\&b) \times p(T/h\&O\&b)}{k}$$

Since, from (c), $p(T/h\&O\&b) \geq k$, we get $p(T/O\&b) > n \times p(h/O\&b)$, where $n \geq 1$. But from (a), $p(h/O\&b) > k$; so we can get $p(T/O\&b) > k$. Q.E.D.

This probability theorem shows, for example, that for the wave theorist to argue against the particle theory it is not sufficient to show that some auxiliary hypothesis introduced by a particle theorist to explain some phenomenon has high probability without the assumption of the particle theory but low probability with this assumption. Under these conditions it is still possible for the particle theory to have high probability.

This theorem also suggests one way to provide independent warrant for a theory T: find independent warrant for an auxiliary assumption h used by the theory; however, not just any assumption, but one whose probability given the theory is low, and one on the assumption of which the probability of the theory is high.

5. We find an auxiliary assumption h such that $T + h$—if true—will correctly explain O, and we also find that the probability of h is low, the probability of h on the assumption of T is high, and the probability of T assuming h is low. Under these conditions the probability of T is low. This is established by the following theorem:

If (i) $p(h/O\&b) \leq k$, and (ii) $p(h/T\&O\&b) > k$, and (iii) $p(T/h\&O\&b) \leq k$, then $p(T/O\&b) < k$.

Proof. By Bayes' theorem and assumption (ii),

$$p(h/T\&O\&b) = \frac{p(h/O\&b) \times p(T/h\&O\&b)}{p(T/O\&b)} > k$$

Therefore

$$p(T/O\&b) < \frac{p(h/O\&b) \times p(T/h\&O\&b)}{k}$$

From (i), $p(h/O\&b) \leq k$. So $p(T/O\&b) < n \times p(T/h\&O\&b)$, where $n \leq 1$. But from (iii), $p(T/h\&O\&b) \leq k$. Therefore $n \times p(T/h\&O\&b) \leq nk$. So we get $p(T/O\&b) < n \times p(T/h\&O\&b) \leq nk$. But since $n \leq 1$, we get $p(T/O\&b) < k$.   Q.E.D.

This theorem shows one way to argue against a theory T that introduces an auxiliary hypothesis h to explain some phenomenon O: show that without the assumption of T, h's probability is low, with it is high, while the probability of T given h is low. For example, let

T = John had a ticket marked 3 in a lottery, and the winning ticket was marked 3.

h = John won $1 million.

O = John bought an expensive car.

b = John bought 1 ticket in a fair lottery of 1000 tickets, and the winning ticket received $1 million.

Theory T together with h—if true—correctly explains O. Furthermore, $p(h/O\&b) < k$; $p(h/T\&O\&b) > k$; $p(T/h\&O\&b) \leq k$; and $p(T/O\&b) < k$. Given the truth of the second and third of these probability claims, we can argue against theory T in this case by arguing against hypothesis h, that is, by trying to show that h's probability is low.

6. T by itself, if true, does *not* correctly explain O, and we have as yet found no auxiliary hypothesis h that is such that $T + h$—if true—will correctly explain O. Can we conclude that the probability of T is low? Obviously not, since independently of O, T may have high probability that is not affected by O. For example, let T = this man is mortal, O = this man is 100 years old, b = in the past all men have eventually died. T if true does not correctly explain O, and let us suppose we have found no auxiliary hypothesis h such that $T + h$—if true—will correctly explain O. Yet $p(T/O\&b)$ is high.

This type of case is relevant for theories of light. As noted, Powell in 1833 claimed that although the wave theory could explain many more optical phenomena than the particle theory, there were still certain phenomena that the wave theory (and indeed the particle theory) had not succeeded in explaining. The wave theory by itself did not explain such phenomena, nor had wave theorists found auxiliary hypotheses that would work. This would not be sufficient to show that the wave theory is improbable. Using an eliminative argument of the sort described in section 3, suppose we conclude that the probability of the wave theory, given *other* observed optical phenomena, is high. We incorporate these phenomena into the background information b and write p(wave theory/b) $> k$. Now we take some observed optical phenomenon O (say polarization at metallic surfaces) that neither the wave theory nor the particle theory has yet succeeded in explaining. It may well be the case that p(wave theory/$O\&b$) $= p$(wave theory/b) $> k$. This will occur when $p(O$/wave theory $+ b) = p(O/b)$, that is, when the assumption that the wave theory is true does not alter the probability that the phenomenon O occurs.

7. T by itself, if true, does not correctly explain O, but we find an auxiliary hypothesis h such that $T + h$ — if true — will correctly explain O, and also find some data O' that provide independent warrant for $T + h$, so that $p(T + h/O'\&b) > k$. Then (assuming that $T + h$ entails O), it will follow that $p(T + h/O'\&O\&b) > k$. This type of case is also relevant for theories of light. Certain optical phenomena O (e.g., dispersion) were not explained by the wave theory T. What was sought was some auxiliary assumption h that together with T would yield those phenomena. If independent warrant for $T + h$ could be found, then the probability of $T + h$ could remain high given O.

8. Finally, to consider a type of case that does not involve the introduction of auxiliary hypotheses, we suppose that theory T_1, if true, will explain more phenomena than T_2. Can we conclude that the probability of T_1 is greater than that of T_2? No, we cannot, as is shown by the following type of example. Let O_1 be explainable by derivation from theory T_1 as well as from theory T_2. Let O_2 be explainable by derivation from T_1 but not from T_2 (from which it is not even derivable). And let both O_1 and O_2 be phenomena that are known to be true, so that $p(O_1) = 1 = p(O_2)$. Then, using Bayes' theorem, we can show that $p(T_1/O_1\&O_2) = p(T_1)$ and $p(T_2/O_1\&O_2) = p(T_2)$. So if the prior probability of T_1 is less than or equal to that of T_2, that is, if $p(T_1) \le p(T_2)$, then $p(T_1/O_1\&O_2) \le p(T_2/O_1\&O_2)$, even though T_1 explains more phenomena than T_2.*

*For very helpful suggestions I am indebted to Geoffrey Cantor, John Earman, Gary Hatfield, Robert Kargon, Alan Karr, Larry Laudan, Michael Liston and Robert Rynasiewicz.

John Stuart Mill.

William Whewell.

ESSAY 4

Hypotheses, Probability, and Waves

1. INTRODUCTION

It is well known that Mill and Whewell debated the verification of hypotheses in science. Mill defines an hypothesis as

> any supposition which we make (either without actual evidence, or on evidence avowedly insufficient) in order to endeavor to deduce from it conclusions in accordance with facts which are known to be real; under the idea that if the conclusions to which the hypothesis leads are known truths, the hypothesis itself either must be, or at least is likely to be, true.[1]

The so-called method of hypothesis consists of deriving consequences from an hypothesis, and if the consequences are observed to be true, concluding that the hypothesis is true or at least probable. Mill rejects this as a method for establishing either the truth or the probability of hypotheses, on the grounds that conflicting hypotheses are possible from which the same true consequences can be derived; unless such alternatives can be excluded, nothing can be inferred about the truth or probability of any hypothesis being considered. The fact that the consequences derived from an hypothesis are observed to be true shows only that the hypothesis is *possible*, that it is consistent with the data obtained so far. It will be rendered probable only if the data derived or other data provide the basis for an inductive argument to the hypothesis.

Whewell, of whom Mill was sharply critical, defends a particular version of the method of hypothesis that requires not only that an hypothesis explain known phenomena but that it explain and/or predict new ones as well, partic-

---

1. John Stuart Mill, *A System of Logic* (London, 1959), p. 322.

117

ularly ones different in kind from those it was initially designed to explain
("consilience"). Recognizing that hypotheses being considered are usually additions to larger systems, Whewell also imposes a requirement that such
additions render the system more coherent.[2] If an hypothesis meets these
conditions, Whewell concludes that it is true. Indeed, he is prepared to say
that if it satisfies just consilience then it is "certain" (p. 65). Perhaps because
of this he does not speak in terms of probability. Mill, however, uses the term
probability and its cognates, and he explicitly denies that an hypothesis is
even probable under conditions of the sort Whewell mentions. In what follows only the *probabilistic* thesis will be considered.

Both Whewell and Mill apply their views regarding hypotheses to one of
the most famous controversies in physics of their day: that between wave and
particle theories of light. Whewell defends the wave theory on the grounds
that it meets all of the conditions of the method of hypothesis that he advocates.[3] Mill attacks those who use the method of hypothesis to defend the
wave theory, and in particular the hypothesis of the unobservable luminiferous ether on which that theory depends. Concerning this hypothesis he
writes:

> The existence of the ether still rests on the possibility of deducing from its assumed
> laws a considerable number of actual phenomena. . . . Most thinkers of any degree
> of sobriety allow, that an hypothesis of this kind is not to be received as probably
> true because it accounts for all the known phenomena, since this is a condition
> sometimes fulfilled tolerably well by two conflicting hypotheses; while there are
> probably many others which are equally possible, but which, for want of anything
> analogous in our experience, our minds are unfitted to conceive.[4]

In this passage Mill goes on to deny that the hypothesis "is entitled to a more
favourable reception" if besides accounting for known phenomena it generates
new ones that are later observed.

When Whewell and Mill cite the wave theory as an example of the use of
the method of hypothesis each seems to suppose that it is by the employment
of this method that nineteenth-century physicists such as Young, Fresnel,
Herschel, and others actually developed and defended their theory.[5] Indeed, it
is a thesis of some contemporary writers that nineteenth-century wave theo-

---

2. William Whewell, *The Philosophy of the Inductive Sciences* (New York, 1967), vol. 2, p.
68.

3. *Ibid.*, pp. 71–72.

4. Mill, *op. cit.*, p. 328.

5. Whewell is explicitly committed to this in both his historical and his philosophical writings. (See *History of the Inductive Sciences* (New York, 1873), vol. 2, chs. 11–13; *The Philosophy
of the Inductive Sciences*, vol. 2, pp. 65ff.) And when Mill writes that "the existence of the ether
still rests on the possibility of deducing from its assumed laws a considerable number of actual
phenomena," he seems to be referring to what physicists who defend the theory give in its
defense.

rists used the method of hypothesis, whereas their particle theory opponents in the eighteenth and nineteenth centuries were committed to an antithetical form of inductivism.[6]

There is no doubt that scientists generally, and wave theorists in particular, who introduce hypotheses and from them derive true observational conclusions find some type of support for hypotheses from this fact. Is Mill right in thinking that this shows only that the hypotheses *may* be true, that they are consistent with the data? Is Whewell right in drawing the much stronger conclusion that under appropriate conditions (when there is consilience and coherence), this shows, at least, that the hypotheses are probably true?

2. DEDUCTION, EXPLANATION, AND PROBABILITY

More clarification of the opposing positions is needed. When Mill discusses the method of hypothesis generally he speaks of *deductions* of conclusions from the hypothesis. But on occasion he also speaks of the hypothesis as *explaining* the phenomena. His examples of the relationships between hypotheses and conclusions come from theoretical physics (derivation of Kepler's laws from Newtonian celestial mechanics; wave theory explaining various optical phenomena). Here the explanations tend to be, or at least to involve, derivations of conclusions from hypotheses using mathematics. Accordingly, it is reasonable to suppose that Mill's position on hypotheses is at least this: the fact that we can explain various phenomena by deductively deriving descriptions of them from an hypothesis does not suffice to render that hypothesis probable.

Whewell speaks of both explanatory and predictive relationships between hypothesis and phenomena. Since his examples, even more than Mill's, are from theoretical physics where the explanations (and predictions) are, or involve, deductions of the phenomena, his position is at least this: the fact that we can explain (and/or predict) various phenomena by deductively deriving descriptions of them from an hypothesis will (under certain appropriate conditions) suffice to render that hypothesis probable.

When Mill and Whewell speak of the phenomena as being explained by, or derived from, an hypothesis *h*, the concept of explanation or derivation they employ does not require the truth or probability of *h* itself. In the terminology of the contemporary deductive-nomological model of explanation, what is being supposed is that *h* provides a "potential" explanation—one that would

6. See Geoffrey Cantor, "The Reception of the Wave Theory of Light in Britain: A Case Study Illustrating the Role of Methodology in Scientific Debate," *Historical Studies in the Physical Sciences* 6 (1975), pp. 109–132; Larry Laudan, "The Medium and Its Message," in G. N. Cantor and M. J. Hodge, eds., *Conceptions of the Ether* (Cambridge, England, 1981), pp. 157–185.

be correct if h were true or probable. Otherwise, there would be no debate between Mill and Whewell. If a derivation or explanation of the sort Whewell and Mill had in mind were to require h's truth or probability, then, trivially, the fact that we can explain various phenomena by deriving them from h guarantees that h is true or probable. Nor are Mill and Whewell ruling out, at least as a logical possibility, that conflicting hypotheses may also explain and entail these phenomena. Both, indeed, recognize that various optical phenomena can be accounted for by the wave and particle theories.

Finally, in stating the opposing positions I have spoken of "rendering an hypothesis probable." Two obvious interpretations present themselves: (i) ensuring that the hypothesis has high probability and (ii) increasing the probability of the hypothesis. For the present let us ignore consilience and coherence (which will be taken up in sections 4 and 5) and formulate simplified positions reflecting (i) and (ii). On (i) the position would be that if phenomena $O_1, \ldots, O_n$ (here presumably what Whewell and Mill mean are types rather than tokens) are explainable via a derivation from h, then h's probability, given $O_1, \ldots, O_n$, is greater than some threshold value k for "high" probability. Symbolically, where b is accepted background information, $n \geq 1$,[7] and $p(h/b) \neq 0$ (an assumption made throughout in what follows),

(1a) $p(h/O_1, \ldots, O_n \& b) > k$, if $O_1, \ldots, O_n$ are explainable via derivation from h, or from h together with b.

Alternatively, in a weaker form, the position might be that for each hypothesis h there is some number n such that if n phenomena $O_1, \ldots, O_n$ are explainable via derivation from h, then h's probability is greater than k, that is,

(1b) $p(h/O_1, \ldots, O_n \& b) > k$, for some n, if $O_1, \ldots, O_n$ are explainable via derivation from h and b.

On (ii) the position might encompass one or both of the following ideas. First, h's probability, given observable phenomena $O_1, \ldots, O_n$ ($n \geq 1$), is greater than h's probability in the absence of $O_1, \ldots, O_n$, if the latter are explainable via derivation from h and b:

(2a) $p(h/O_1, \ldots, O_n \& b) > p(h/b)$ if $O_1, \ldots, O_n$ are explainable via derivation from h and b.

---

7. We could take n to be greater than or equal to any number we wish, thus, in effect, requiring a certain number of observed phenomena to be explained by h before we say that h's probability is "high." In what follows what I say for $n \geq 1$ holds for $n \geq a$ where a is any number greater than zero.

Second, h's probability continues to increase toward 1 as a limit as n becomes larger, that is, as the number of observable phenomena explainable via derivation from h increases:

(2b) $\lim_{n \to \infty} p(h/O_1, \ldots, O_n \& b) = 1$, where $O_1, \ldots, O_n$ are explainable via derivation from h and b.

In what follows all four claims will be examined. When Mill writes that "an hypothesis . . . is not to be received as probably true because it accounts for all the known phenomena," I shall construe him to be saying at least this: the fact that an hypothesis accounts for all known phenomena, even where these are numerous, does not ensure either that it is highly probable or that its probability increases toward the maximum possible the more phenomena it explains. That is, Mill is rejecting at least (1a), (1b), and (2b). Whether he is also rejecting the weaker (2a) I shall not speculate. On the other hand, I shall understand Whewell to be saying that, under appropriate conditions, if an hypothesis explains a range of phenomena, then at least its probability has increased (so that (2a) or some variant is correct). But Whewell is committed to more than this, since he claims that we can infer, with considerable assurance, that the hypothesis is true. To achieve such assurance there will need to be concern not only with conditions under which the probability of an hypothesis has increased but also with those under which the probability is "high" and under which it tends to a maximum ("certainty"). The Whewellian position, formulated probabilistically, will be understood as saying that, in some suitable variation, not only is (2a) correct, but so are (1a), (1b), and (2b).

If we wish to assess (1) and (2) we will need to make some assumptions about probability. In what follows it will be supposed simply that the concept of probability satisfies the usual axioms of the probability calculus. Although no particular interpretation of that calculus is assumed, probability will be construed as a measure of rational credibility, since the disputants are disagreeing about the conditions under which there are good reasons to believe an hypothesis.[8]

8. When Mill criticizes probabilistic versions of Whewell's thesis he does not characterize any particular concept of probability for this purpose. In a later chapter on probability (ch. 18) he does urge that probability is a measure of rational credibility. And he speaks of the probability calculus for which he advocates a frequency interpretation and which he believes is applicable to propositions about causes of phenomena. It is not my claim that Mill did apply, or would have applied, the probability calculus to hypotheses about unobservables, or that he and Whewell carried out their debate in the probability terms I shall be discussing. My interest in what follows is in trying to determine whether, and if so to what extent, standard probabilities can be utilized in clarifying issues raised by Mill and Whewell and offering some evaluation of their conclusions.

3. A "COMPETING HYPOTHESES" OBJECTION

Positions (1) and (2), which as yet do not reflect Whewellian consilience or coherence but do express basic ideas of an "hypothesist" viewpoint, can be shown to be objectionable on Millian grounds: (1) and (2) will be false for a given hypothesis h if certain kinds of competitors to h exist. Although Mill does not produce the required probabilistic argument, one way to do so is by introducing the notion of an O_n-partition, defined as follows. A set of hypotheses $h_1, \ldots, h_k$ forms an O_n-partition on b relative to $O_1, \ldots, O_n$ if (i) $h_1, \ldots, h_k$ are mutually exclusive, (ii) $p(h_1$ or $h_2 \ldots$ or $h_k/b) = 1$, and (iii) $O_1, \ldots, O_n$ are derivable from each h_i in the set together with b. Generally in what follows I will speak simply of an O-partition where the subscript n will be omitted and the relativization to $O_1, \ldots, O_n$ and to b will be implicit. Briefly, an O-partition is a set of mutually exclusive hypotheses that is exhaustive on b and that contains members each of which entails the observed phenomena. The following is provable (see the appendix):

(3) If $h_1, \ldots, h_k$ form an O-partition, then for each h_i in the partition
$p(h_i /O_1, \ldots, O_n \& b) = p(h_i /b)$.

This tells us that if we have a set of mutually exclusive hypotheses that is exhaustive on b, and each member of the set plus the background information entails the observed phenomena, then the probability of any hypothesis in the set given those phenomena remains the same as its prior probability, that is, the same as its probability without those phenomena.

Now (3) can be used to show that (1) and (2) will be false for a given h if certain kinds of competitors to h exist. Taking (2) first, suppose that the phenomena $O_1, \ldots, O_n$ are explainable via derivation from h together with b. This does not guarantee that $p(h/O_1, \ldots, O_n \& b) > p(h/b)$, because the fact that $O_1, \ldots, O_n$ are explainable via derivation from h and b is perfectly compatible with the existence of an O-partition containing h. That is, there may be one or more competing hypotheses that, together with h, are exhaustive on b, and that with b also entail $O_1, \ldots, O_n$. If there are, then by (3), h's probability given the phenomena is the same as its prior probability, thus rendering (2a) false for such an h. Extending the argument, suppose that h and b are such that for any n phenomena explainable by derivation from h and b there is an O-partition containing h. If so, then by (3), h's probability will continue to remain the same as its prior probability, thus falsifying (2b) for such an h. Furthermore, if h's probability on b is less than k — an assumption perfectly compatible with h's entailing $O_1, \ldots, O_n$ for any n — then by (3) h's probability on $O_1, \ldots, O_n$ and b will be and will remain less than k, thus falsifying both (1a) and (1b) for this h.

This shows that explaining the observed phenomena by deriving them from your favorite hypothesis will not by itself suffice either to give your hypothesis high probability, or even to increase its probability. A sticking point — as Mill noted — is the possibility that all the phenomena you have are derivable from competitors. (The latter need not have been formulated by you or anyone else, and indeed may include hypotheses that, in Mill's words, "our minds are unfitted to conceive.") If such competitors exist and if they are exhaustive on your background information, then the probability of your favorite hypothesis is not guaranteed to be high no matter how many phenomena it explains, and will not increase as more and more phenomena are explained.[9]

Now let us see what happens when Whewell's additional requirements are added to (1) and (2).

4. CONSILIENCE

Two ideas are usually associated with Whewell's concept. One is that the phenomena derived from h should not all be known to be true by the scientist or community proposing h; at least some should be predictions not yet observed:

> The hypotheses which we accept ought to explain phenomena which we have observed. But they ought to do more than this: our hypotheses ought to *foretel* phenomena which have not yet been observed.[10]

The second idea is that the phenomena derived from h should not all be of the same kind as those that prompted the hypothesis:

> But the evidence in favour of our induction is of a much higher and more forcible character when it enables us to explain and determine cases of a *kind different* from those which were contemplated in the formation of our hypothesis.[11]

To revive (1) and (2) we need to give these ideas probabilistic interpretations. If the phenomena are known by observation, their probability might be

---

9. This is not the only way to show that (1) and (2) can be false for a given hypothesis. Here is another that does not invoke the idea of competing hypotheses. If h and b entail $O_1, \ldots, O_n$, then by Bayes' theorem, $p(h/O_1, \ldots, O_n \& b) = p(h/b)/p(O_1, \ldots, O_n/b)$. Suppose h is such that $p(O_1, \ldots, O_n/b) = 1$ for each O_i explainable via derivation from h. (This is compatible with the assumptions of (1) and (2).) Then $p(h/O_1, \ldots, O_n \& b) = p(h/b)$, which violates (2a) for such an h. If $p(h/b) < k$, then (1a), (1b), and (2b) will also be violated. My aim here is not simply to show that (1) and (2) will be false if certain kinds of hypotheses exist, but to see whether it is possible to give a Millian argument for this, that is, one that appeals to the idea of competing hypotheses that also explain the phenomena. In the next section an even stronger competing hypotheses argument will be presented.

10. Whewell, *The Philosophy of the Inductive Sciences*, vol. 2, p. 62.

11. *Ibid.*, p. 65. Although Whewell clearly espouses both of these ideas, he reserves the phrase "consilience of inductions" for the second. However, Whewell's interpreters frequently include both under "consilience," and I will follow this practice.

construed as maximal; if they are predictions that have not been observed, their probability is not maximal. Accordingly, the first idea might be understood as requiring that in the set $O_1, \ldots, O_n$ derivable from h, not all the O's have a probability of 1 given the current background information. Let me call this weak consilience$_A$. Alternatively, a much stronger requirement would be that in the set $O_1, \ldots, O_n$ derivable from h, *each* of the O's have a probability less than 1 (strong consilience$_A$).[12]

Whewell does not define the notion of "same kind." Presumably he has in mind not simply the concept of a set, but of a "natural" kind—a concept which, as Quine has argued, resists successful definition.[13] However, without defining it, we might note a connection often made between natural kinds and projectibility. (The predicate "green," but not "grue," is projectible because it denotes a natural kind.) This, in turn, suggests a connection with probability. (An arbitrarily chosen emerald's being green increases the probability that another is; the same is not true for grue.) Accordingly, we might say that if two phenomena O_i and O_j are of the same kind from the viewpoint of some body of information b, then the probability that one occurs is increased by the occurrence of the other, that is, $p(O_i / O_j \& b) > p(O_i / b)$. And if two phenomena are of different kinds from the viewpoint of b, then the probability that one occurs is not increased by the occurrence of the other. With this the second consilience idea might be understood as requiring that in the set of phenomena derivable from h, at least two, O_i and O_j, be such that $p(O_i / O_j \& b) \leq p(O_i / b)$.[14] In a much stronger form the requirement might be that this hold for each pair of phenomena derivable from h. Let me call these weak and strong consilience$_B$, respectively. The idea is not that $p(O_i / O_j \& b) \leq p(O_i / b)$ should be construed as sufficient for O_i and O_j to be of "different kinds," only necessary. But this condition might be taken to provide a probabilistic representation of a central thought underlying the second of Whewell's ideas about consilience.[15]

---

12. In both cases we might change the condition and require that (some of) the O's have a probability not just less than 1 but less than some threshold value for "high" probability. This is suggested by one of the several interpretations of consilience offered by Larry Laudan, *Science and Hypothesis* (Dordrecht, 1981), p. 165. In what follows I shall use probability less than 1 since what I shall say about this is applicable as well to the condition suggested by Laudan's interpretation.

13. W. V. Quine, "Natural Kinds," in N. Rescher, ed., *Essays in Honor of Carl G. Hempel* (Dordrecht, 1969), pp. 5–23.

14. Whewell would add that the latter is to hold where O_j but not O_i is among the phenomena that prompted h in the first place. But this is a pragmatic notion not readily captured in probabilistic terms. We can ensure that this further proviso is satisfied with the stronger consilience requirement that follows.

15. This thought might be put in terms of an example of a sort Whewell himself could offer. The wave theory of light explains the refraction of light by a lens, its refraction by a prism, and its reflection by a mirror. The first and second optical phenomena are of the "same kind," but the

Putting these ideas together, a set of phenomena $O_1, \ldots, O_n$ is consilient with respect to h and b (or in more Whewellian terms, an "induction" from $O_1, \ldots, O_n$ and b to h is consilient) if $O_1, \ldots, O_n$ are explainable via derivation from h and b and

(A) $p(O_i / b) \neq 1$ for at least one of the O's (weak consilience$_A$), or for each of the O's (strong consilience$_A$);

(B) $p(O_i / O_j \& b) \leq p(O_i / b)$ for at least two of the O's (weak consilience$_B$), or for each pair of O's (strong consilience$_B$).

Requiring just consilience$_A$ (either strong or weak) will in fact block the particular arguments used against (1) and (2) in the previous section. To see this, let us revise (1) and (2), as follows:

(1a)' $p(h/O_1, \ldots, O_n \& b) > k$, for every n, if the set $O_1, \ldots, O_n$ is consilient$_A$ with respect to h and b, that is, if each member of the set is explainable via derivation from h and b, and $p(O_i / b) \neq 1$ for at least one of the O's (weak consilience$_A$) or for all the O's (strong consilience$_A$).

(1b)' This is like (1a)' except that "for every n" is replaced by "for some n."

(2a)' $p(h/O_1, \ldots, O_n \& b) > p(h/b)$ if the set $O_1, \ldots, O_n$ is consilient$_A$ with respect to h and b.

(2b)' $\lim\limits_{n \to \infty} p(h/O_1, \ldots, O_n \& b) = 1$ if the set $O_1, \ldots, O_n$ is consilient$_A$ with respect to h and b.

The previous arguments against (1) and (2) are now blocked, since if h is a member of an O-partition, then $p(O_i/b) = 1$ for each O_i.[16] (This follows from the fact that if $h_1, \ldots, h_k$ form an O-partition, then $p(h_1$ or $\ldots$ or $h_k/b) = 1$ and the disjunction of the h's entails each O_i.) Accordingly, if we suppose that h is a member of an O-partition—if we suppose that there are conflicting

---

first and third are not. So—and this underlies the consilience$_B$ condition—given that light is refracted by a lens, the probability that it is refracted by a prism is increased; but given that light is refracted by a lens, the probability that it is reflected by a mirror does not increase. Therefore, it is more surprising that the wave theory can explain both refraction by a lens and reflection by a mirror than it is that it can explain both refraction by a lens and refraction by a prism. Accordingly, the wave theory receives more probability from explaining the former pair than from explaining the latter. And this probability becomes "high" as more and more consilient phenomena are explained. If this is Whewell's thinking, or something like it, then the probability condition expressed in consilience$_B$ is central.

16. The argument of note 9 is also blocked since this too makes the assumption that the probability of each O_i is 1.

hypotheses each of which entails the phenomena and the probability of the disjunction is maximal—then the phenomena in question must have maximal probability. If they do, then h's probability given these phenomena cannot be greater than h's prior probability (thus falsifying (2a) outright for such an h, and (1) where h's prior probability is less than k, and (2b) where h's prior probability is less than 1). In short, if h is a member of an O-partition, then we generate the so-called problem of old evidence—evidence that we know to obtain and that cannot increase the probability of h.[17] With the requirement of consilience$_A$ we disallow the possibility that all the evidence that we are considering that is generated by h is old evidence. Does this work?

Partly. It yields (2a)', but not (1a)', (1b)', or (2b)'. If $p(O_i / b) \neq 1$ for some O_i in $O_1, \ldots, O_n$, then $p(O_1, \ldots, O_n / b) < 1$. Using Bayes' theorem, if $h\&b$ entails each O_i, then $p(h/O_1, \ldots, O_n\&b) = p(h/b)/p(O_1, \ldots, O_n/b)$. So if the denominator of the fraction on the right is less than 1, the probability on the left is greater than the numerator of the fraction on the right, thus yielding (2a)'.[18]

However, (1a)' and (1b)'—with $k = 1/2$—and (2b)' will all be false, if certain conditions obtain.[19] To show this we can again appeal to the Millian idea of competing hypotheses. This time, however, we need not suppose that h is a member of an O-partition, but only that h has one competitor of a certain sort. The relevant probability theorems are these:

(4a) Let h together with b entail O_1, O_2, ... If h has at least one incompatible competitor h' that together with b also entails O_1, O_2, ..., and whose probability on b is greater than zero, then $\lim_{n \to \infty} p(h/O_1, \ldots, O_n\&b) \neq 1$.

This result holds even if $p(O_i / b) \neq 1$ for each O_i. So if such a competitor to h exists, then (2b)' is false for h in the case of both strong and weak consilience$_A$.

(4b) Let h together with b entail O_1, O_2, ... If h has at least one incompatible competitor h' that together with b also entails O_1, O_2, ..., and is such that $p(h'/b) \geq p(h/b)$, then for any n no matter how large, $p(h/O_1, \ldots, O_n\&b) \leq .5$.

17. See Clark Glymour, *Theory and Evidence* (Princeton. 1980), pp. 85–92.

18. In fact, something even stronger than (2a)' is readily provable: if $O_1, \ldots, O_n$ are explainable via derivation from h and b, then $p(h/O_1, \ldots, O_n\&b) > p(h/b)$ if and only if $p(O_i/b) \neq 1$ for at least one O_i.

19. They are false even if consilience$_A$ is construed in Laudan's stronger sense as requiring $p(O_i/b) < k$ for some O_i derivable from h. See note 12.

This is so even if $p(O_i /b) \neq 1$ for each O_i, which, for $k = 1/2$, will falsify both (1a)′ and (1b)′ for both strong and weak consilience$_A$ in the case of any hypothesis for which such a competitor exists.[20]

The claim here is not that every hypothesis h that explains some data will in fact have a competitor of the sort described in (4a) and (4b). It is only that if such a competitor does exist — a state of affairs perfectly compatible with h's satisfying strong consilience$_A$ — then h's probability will not increase toward 1 as a limit and will not even be "high." However, it does seem reasonable to suppose that there are at least *some* hypotheses with competitors of the sort in question. If so, then we can conclude that (1a)′, (1b)′, and (2b)′ are false if construed generally as applying to *all* hypotheses satisfying their conditions.[21]

We may conclude, then, that consilience$_A$ will suffice to yield an increase in the probability of the hypothesis. But it will not guarantee that the limit of the probability will be 1 or that the probability will even be "high."

What about consilience$_B$? By itself it will not save either (1) or (2), since it is compatible with $p(O_i /b) = 1$ for each O_i derivable from h. Accordingly, if each of the O's derivable from h has maximal probability, then for any n, $p(h/O_1, \ldots ,O_n \& b) = p(h/b)$, which violates (1a), (1b), and (2a); and if $p(h/b) \neq 1$, it violates (2b) as well.

Suppose, then, we put consilience$_A$ and consilience$_B$ together. Consilience$_A$, we already have seen, is sufficient by itself to yield (2a), but not (1) or (2b). Does adding consilience$_B$ to consilience$_A$ save (1) or (2b)? No, it does not. This is shown by appeal once more to (4a) and (4b), which hold even if $p(O_i /b) \neq 1$ for each O_i and $p(O_i /O_j \& b) \leq p(O_i /b)$ for each O_i and O_j.

Consilience$_B$ is not without value. It can result in higher probabilities for an hypothesis than without it. Suppose O_1 and O_2 are both derivable from h and b, so that

$$p(h/O_1 \& O_2 \& b) = \frac{p(h/b)}{p(O_1 \& O_2 /b)} = \frac{p(h/b)}{p(O_1 /b) \times p(O_2 /O_1 \& b)}$$

---

20. Proofs of (4a) and (4b) can be found in John Earman, "Concepts of Projectibility and the Problems of Induction," *Nous* 19 (1985), pp. 521–535. In note 9 I pointed out that Bayes' theorem, which does not invoke competing hypotheses, can be used to show that (1) and (2) can be false for a given h. Is the same possible here? Not quite. Bayes' theorem will show that (1a)′ can be false for both strong and weak consilience$_A$, and that (1b)′ and (2b)′ can both be false for weak consilience$_A$. But, unlike (4a) and (4b), it will not suffice to show that (1b)′ and (2b)′ can be false for strong consilience$_A$. So (4a) and (4b) have wider applicability. And more important, they allow us to formulate a Millian objection to the Whewellian position.

21. Earman's claim in the reference cited in note 20 is indeed that "once we move beyond direct observational generalizations to theories that outrun the data, it is surely true that there are many rival theories that cover the same data" (p. 529). If at least some of these theories have competitors satisfying the conditions of (4a) and (4b), then (1a)′, (1b)′, and (2b)′ are not true in general.

Now if consilience$_B$ is satisfied, so that $p(O_2/O_1\&b) \leq p(O_2/b)$, the denominator of the fraction on the right will be smaller than it would be if consilience$_B$ is not satisfied and $p(O_2/O_1\&b) > p(O_2/b)$. So if consilience$_B$ is satisfied, the probability on the left, $p(h/O_1\&O_2\&b)$, will be greater than if it is not satisfied.[22] However, even with consilience$_A$, consilience$_B$ will not suffice to ensure that the limit of the probability will be 1 as more and more O's are derived, or even that the probability will be greater than 1/2.

Two replies will be noted. It might be claimed that we should be satisfied if there is a notion of consilience that guarantees increase in probability, that is, (2a)′, even if it does not assure high probability (1a)′ or (1b)′, or an increase toward maximal probability (2b)′. The reason we should be satisfied is that increase in probability is both necessary and sufficient for *evidence*. (O is evidence for h, given b, if and only if $p(h/O\&b) > p(h/b)$.) And the debate between Mill and Whewell can be construed as a debate over what is to count as evidence for hypotheses.

It is extremely dubious that increase in probability is either necessary or sufficient for evidence.[23] But even if we were to accept the idea that there is a concept of evidence for which increase in probability is both necessary and sufficient, it is not the case that evidence *in this sense* is all that Mill and Whewell were arguing about. Whewell claims (and Mill denies) that consilience provides a good reason to believe an hypothesis, something that requires more than merely increasing its probability. (If I buy one ticket in a million-ticket lottery I increase the probability that I will win; but my buying a ticket does not provide a good reason to believe the hypothesis that I will win.) Admittedly it is desirable to seek phenomena that will increase the probability of one's hypothesis. And this aim can be realized by invoking phenomena that

---

22. Assuming that with consilience the prior probability of h will not need to be changed to such an extent that the effect of consilience is canceled. In this argument it is being supposed that O_1 and O_2 stay the same but that the background information b is varied so that we have consilience$_B$ in one case but not the other. Example: Let O_1 = bodies on the earth obey Newton's laws of motion, O_2 = bodies on the moon obey Newton's laws of motion, h = all bodies obey Newton's laws of motion. h entails both O_1 and O_2. Now consider two different, conflicting background assumptions b_1 and b_2. b_1 includes the information that the behavior of things on earth (where motion is not being considered) is generally different from that of things on the moon; b_2 includes the information that it is generally the same. In this case O_1 and O_2 are consilient with respect to h and b_1 but not with respect to h and b_2, since $p(O_2/O_1\&b_1) < p(O_2/b_1)$, but $p(O_2/O_1\&b_2) > p(O_2/b_2)$. Now, consistent with the above, assume the following probabilities: $p(h/b_1) = .1$, $p(O_1/b_1) = .7$, $p(O_2/O_1\&b_1) = .2$, $p(h/b_2) = .3$, $p(O_1/b_2) = .7$, $p(O_2/O_1\&b_2) = .8$, and $p(O_2/b_1) = p(O_2/b_2) = .4$. Then, using the formula in the text above, where the background information is b_1 and there is consilience, $p(h/O_1\&O_2\&b_1) = 20/28$; where the background information is b_2 and there is no consilience, $p(h/O_1\&O_2\&b_2) = 15/28$. So in this case h has higher probability when the O's are consilient with respect to h and b_1 than when they are not with respect to h and b_2. In these two cases the prior probabilities of h are not the same, but the difference is not sufficient to cancel the effect of consilience.

23. For arguments against the necessity and the sufficiency of this condition see Peter Achinstein, *The Nature of Explanation* (New York, 1983), ch. 10.

satisfy consilience$_A$. But if, in addition, one wants to provide a good reason to believe the hypothesis, and for this purpose to determine whether it has "high" probability and whether that probability tends to a maximum as more and more phenomena are explained, then consilience will not suffice. It will save (2a), but not (1a), (1b), or (2b).

A second reply is that the probabilistic concepts of consilience we have introduced, particularly consilience$_B$, are not strong enough to reflect Whewell's ideas completely. Thus, as already noted, even if we construe $p(O_i / O_j) \leq p(O_i)$ as necessary for O_i and O_j to be phenomena of "different kinds," it is not sufficient. And despite the kind of argument offered in note 15, more might be demanded for our representation of Whewell's second consilience idea. If so, can whatever else is required be formulated in probabilistic terms so that (1) and (2b) are generated? This seems dubious for the following reason.

Suppose that some set of phenomena O_1, O_2, . . . is explainable via derivation from h and b where these phenomena are of "different kinds" in some fuller sense intended by Whewell. What theorem (4b) tells us is that if these same phenomena are explainable via derivation from some incompatible h', where the probability of h' on b is at least as great as that of h on b, then h's probability, given these phenomena, cannot be greater than .5. But why should the fact that the O's derived from h and b are of "different kinds" preclude the possibility of such a competitor? I can suggest no logical reason for this. Indeed, even historically it seems false. Various optical phenomena that Whewell himself regarded as being of "different kinds" — for example, rectilinear propagation, reflection, and refraction — are explainable via derivation from the wave theory of light. Yet at the turn of the nineteenth century, before the work of Young and Fresnel on interference and diffraction, the probability of the rival particle theory, which also explained these phenomena, was justifiably regarded as higher than that of the wave theory on the basis of background information then available (which excluded interference and certain diffraction phenomena). If such phenomena are of "different kinds," then even without a probabilistic account of the latter, this is sufficient to reject the general claim that whenever any set of phenomena is explainable via derivation from an hypothesis then that hypothesis receives high probability if the phenomena are of "different kinds."

Let us turn then to another important idea Whewell introduces — coherence. Can it be used to generate (1a), (1b), or (2b)?

---

5. COHERENCE

Coherence is a vague notion, for which Whewell (like most others who invoke this idea) offers no definition. He does say that in a coherent system "different members of the theory run together," and that in a system in which this is lacking "the new suppositions are something altogether additional; — not suggested by the original scheme; perhaps difficult to reconcile with it."[24] Can a probabilistic definition capture something of these ideas and get (1) and (2b) off the ground?

For this purpose we might introduce the idea of coherence in two stages. First, an hypothesis might be said to be *coherent with* a set of hypotheses if that hypothesis has a high probability given all the other hypotheses in the set, higher than without those other hypotheses:

(5) h_1 is coherent with $h_2, \ldots, h_m$, on b, if and only if $p(h_1/h_2, \ldots, h_m \& b) > k$, and $p(h_1/h_2, \ldots, h_m \& b) > p(h_1/b)$.

Then we introduce coherence for a set of hypotheses by saying:

(6)   A set of hypotheses $h_1, \ldots, h_m$ is coherent, on b, if and only if each hypothesis is coherent with the other members of the set on b.

I take this to be a fairly intuitive probabilistic representation of coherence, one intended to provide an interpretation, in terms of probabilities, of Whewell's idea that "different members of the theory run together" (and of Harman's idea that "if one's beliefs are coherent, they are mutually supporting" — see note 24): each hypothesis in a coherent set will be probable given all the other hypotheses in the set, and this probability will be greater than its prior probability.

Now let us apply this concept of coherence to (1) and (2b). Can we show that if $O_1, \ldots, O_n$ (for $n \geq 1$, or at least for some n) are explainable by derivation from the set $h_1, \ldots, h_m$ together with b, *and if the set $h_1, \ldots, h_m$ is coherent*, then (1) $p(h_1, \ldots, h_m/O_1, \ldots, O_n \& b) > k$, and (2b) $\lim_{n \to \infty} p(h_1, \ldots, h_m/O_1, \ldots, O_n \& b) = 1$? No, we cannot. To see this, we note first that from the fact that $h_1, \ldots, h_m$ is coherent on b, it does not follow that $p(h_1, \ldots, h_m/b)$ is high.

Proof: $p(h_1, \ldots, h_m/b) = p(h_1/b) \times p(h_2/h_1 \& b) \times \ldots \times p(h_m/h_1, \ldots, h_{m-1} \& b)$. Now if the set $h_1, \ldots, h_m$ is coherent on b, then by definition the last term on the right $— p(h_m/h_1, \ldots, h_{m-1} \& b) —$ expresses high probability, higher than $p(h_m/b)$. But this is perfectly compatible with the first term on the right $— p(h_1/b) —$ expressing very low probability. Suppose it does. Then because we are multiplying probabilities on the right, and these are less than or equal to 1, the term on the left $— p(h_1, \ldots, h_m/b) —$ will be less than or equal to $p(h_1/b)$. If the latter is low, so will the former be.   Q.E.D.

---

24. Whewell, *The Philosophy of the Inductive Sciences*, vol. 2, p. 68. Compare this with a contemporary account: "According to the coherence theory, the assessment of a challenged belief is always holistic. Whether such a belief is justified depends on how well it fits together with everything else one believes. *If one's beliefs are coherent, they are mutually supporting.*" Gilbert Harman, *Change in View* (Cambridge, Mass., 1986), pp. 32–33. Emphasis mine.

Suppose now that $p(h_1/b)$ is low, so that $p(h_1, \ldots, h_m/b)$ is low too. (Let $p(h_1, \ldots, h_m/b) = r < k$.) And suppose that for any n O's derivable from $h_1, \ldots, h_m$ there is an O-partition containing $h_1, \ldots, h_m$ as one disjunct. Then by (3), $p(h_1, \ldots, h_m/O_1, \ldots, O_n\&b) = p(h_1, \ldots, h_m/b)$. So $p(h_1, \ldots, h_m/O_1, \ldots, O_n\&b) = r < k$. And this violates both (1a) and (1b) despite the fact that $h_1, \ldots, h_m$ is a coherent set of hypotheses on b. Since under these conditions, $p(h_1, \ldots, h_m/O_1, \ldots, O_n\&b) = p(h_1, \ldots, h_m/b)$, we also have a violation of (2b) (as well as (2a)). Accordingly, we do not save (1) or (2b) by adding the requirement that the set of hypotheses from which $O_1, \ldots, O_n$ are explainable by derivation be coherent, as this notion is given by (6).

What about adding (strong) consilience to coherence and explanatory derivations, and requiring that $p(O_i/b) < 1$ for each O_i and $p(O_i/O_j\&b) \leq p(O_i/b)$ for each pair of O's derived? This will block the argument just given, which invokes O-partitions. But it will still not suffice to generate high probability in the sense of (1) or (2b). Suppose that $h_1, \ldots, h_m$ is coherent. Suppose also that there is some competitor to $h_1, \ldots, h_m$, namely, $h_1', \ldots, h_m'$, which, like the former, entails all the O's and is such that $p(h_1', \ldots, h_m'/b) \geq p(h_1, \ldots, h_m/b)$.[25] Then by theorem (4b), $p(h_1, \ldots, h_m/O_1, \ldots, O_n\&b) \leq .5$, no matter how many O's are derivable from $h_1, \ldots, h_m$, even if consilience is satisfied. Thus neither (1) nor (2b) will be satisfied. Coherence together with consilience will not guarantee a high probability or a probability that approaches 1 in the limit.

An advocate of coherence may suggest strengthening that requirement by saying that what should be coherent is not the set of hypotheses by itself but the set containing these *together with the observed phenomena* $O_1, \ldots, O_n$. Using (5) and (6), this will mean that for each h_i (or O_i) in this set $p(h_i (O_i)/$ other h's in set and (other) O's$\&b) > k$, and $p(h_i (O_i)/$other h's in set and (other) O's$\&b) > p(h_i (O_i)/b)$. Although this gives us much more coherence

---

25. Is this possible? Here is an example. Background information tells us that a coin being tossed is perfectly symmetrical. Let h_i = God intervenes to make the ith toss result in heads. Let h_i' = the Devil, not God, intervenes to make the ith toss result in heads. Each h_i is incompatible with each h_i'. Let O_i = the ith toss results in heads. For any m, the phenomena $O_1, \ldots, O_m$ can be explained by derivation from $h_1, \ldots, h_m$, as well as from $h_1', \ldots, h_m'$. Also for some m and for any h_i not in $h_1, \ldots, h_m$, $p(h_i/h_1, \ldots, h_m\&b) > k$, $p(h_i/h_1, \ldots, h_m\&b) > p(h_i/b)$. Equally, $p(h_i'/h_1', \ldots, h_m'\&b) > k$ and $p(h_i'/h_1', \ldots, h_m'\&b) > p(h_i'/b)$. So $h_1, \ldots, h_m$ and the competing $h_1', \ldots, h_m'$ are both coherent on b in the sense of (6). Assuming our background information is such as to provide no more reason to think that God exists and intervenes in coin-tossing events than that the Devil does, we may also suppose that the prior probability of the Devil-intervening set of hypotheses is no less than that of the God-intervening set. Finally, strong consilience$_A$ is satisfied if we assume that the tosses have not yet been observed, so that $p(O_j/b) < 1$ for each O_j. And strong consilience$_B$ is satisfied since the background information tells us that the coin is perfectly symmetrical; accordingly, in the absence of intervention assumptions involving God or the Devil, we may assume probabilistic independence, so that for each pair of O's, $p(O_j/O_i\&b) = p(O_j/b)$. The conditions in the text are now satisfied.

than before, it still will not yield (1) or (2b). Even if $h_1, \ldots, h_m, O_1, \ldots, O_n$ is coherent on b, it can be the case that for some h_i in this set, $p(h_i / O_1, \ldots, O_n \& b)$ is low for any n.[26] If it is, then since $p(h_1, \ldots, h_m / O_1, \ldots, O_n \& b)$ can never be greater than $p(h_i / O_1, \ldots, O_n \& b)$, we have a violation of both (1) and (2b) with or without consilience.

Despite all this, it is possible to propose a coherence condition that will yield high probability in the sense of (1). Instead of requiring that some set of hypotheses $h_1, \ldots, h_m$ (and phenomena) be coherent — as we have been doing so far — we may simply require *that $h_1, \ldots, h_m$ be coherent with the observed phenomena $O_1, \ldots, O_n$* in the sense given by (5).[27] This will mean that $p(h / O_1, \ldots, O_n \& b) > k$. Accordingly, (1) will be satisfied immediately.

The problem is that this does not at all do justice to the Whewellian idea of coherence. Suppose that a set of hypotheses $h_1, \ldots, h_m$ is coherent with phenomena $O_1, \ldots, O_n$ and b in the sense given by (5). This will mean that $p(h_1, \ldots, h_m / O_1, \ldots, O_n \& b) > k$, and $p(h_1, \ldots, h_m / O_1, \ldots, O_n \& b) > p(h_1, \ldots, h_m / b)$. But this is perfectly compatible with the following situation: the original theory contains h_1 and h_2, proposed on the basis of phenomena O_1 and O_2 in such a way that $p(h_1 \& h_2 / O_1 \& O_2 \& b) > k$ and $p(h_1 \& h_2 / O_1 \& O_2 \& b) > p(h_1 \& h_2 / b)$. Now a completely unrelated hypothesis h_3 is added in light of a completely unrelated phenomenon O_3. It is possible that $p(h_1 \& h_2 \& h_3 / O_1 \& O_2 \& O_3 \& b) > k$ and $p(h_1 \& h_2 \& h_3 / O_1 \& O_2 \& O_3 \& b) > p(h_1 \& h_2 \& h_3 / b)$, even though the new hypothesis h_3 is (in Whewell's words) "something altogether additional — not suggested by the original scheme; perhaps difficult to reconcile with it." We may continue adding new unrelated hypotheses to the system, each of which has high probability on the basis of some new unrelated phenomenon. The resulting system of hypotheses $h_1, \ldots, h_m$ may be coherent with the set of phenomena $O_1, \ldots, O_n \& b$ in the sense of (5). Yet the system of hypotheses created is an incoherent monster containing hypotheses that in no reasonable sense "run together." (Note that $h_1, \ldots, h_m$ can be coherent with the phenomena $O_1, \ldots, O_n$ in the sense of (5) without being a coherent set in the sense of (6).)

Is it possible to find a coherence requirement of the sort desired? We seek one that captures the idea of a set of hypotheses "running together" in a more or less natural way. Suppose some set of hypotheses $h_1, \ldots, h_m$ satisfies this (admittedly vague) description, and that phenomena $O_1, O_2, \ldots$ are explainable by derivation from this set. What we must ask is this: Are there some incompatible hypotheses $h_1', \ldots, h_m'$ that also "run together" in a more or less natural way and from which $O_1, O_2, \ldots$ can be explained by derivation? If so, and if the prior probability of this alternative set is at least as great as the prior probability of $h_1, \ldots, h_m$, then by theorem (4b), the probability of $h_1, \ldots, h_m$ will never rise above .5 no matter how many phenomena that set

26. For a case of this sort see the example in note 25.

27. Keith Lehrer, *Knowledge* (Oxford, 1974), ch. 8, offers a somewhat similar account of "coherent with."

entails. This violates (1) for $k = 1/2$, and (2b) (even if there is consilience). So the question is whether the idea of coherence necessarily precludes the possibility of two competing systems of hypotheses that are coherent, both of which explain by derivation the observed phenomena, and that satisfy the prior probability condition mentioned. Those such as Whewell who introduce the idea of coherence, but characterize it simply as "running together" in a natural way or "mutually supporting," give no reason to suppose such competing coherent systems to be impossible. Nor can I supply any. If they are possible, then the coherence of a set of hypotheses from which the phenomena can be explained by derivation will not suffice to guarantee "high" probability for that set.[28]

Whewell claims that in practice in the history of science you cannot find two conflicting scientific theories or sets of hypotheses of this sort. If you look at competing theories or systems which were in fact defended (his examples include Copernican vs. Ptolemaic astronomy, the Cartesian system of vortices vs. Newton's theory of gravitation, and the wave vs. particle theories of light), you will find that one system in each pair is not coherent. Even if we grant Whewell's historical claim, the logical point remains. If coherence allows conflicting systems of the type mentioned in the previous paragraph, even ones that were never in fact defended or proposed, then "high" probability is not guaranteed.

A coherence requirement that does preclude such conflicting systems is that $h_1, \ldots, h_m$ be coherent with the observed phenomena in the sense given by (5). But this fails to reflect adequately what Whewell (and others) mean by the coherence of a set of hypotheses. By contrast, the sense of coherence defined in (6) does more justice to that concept (especially the sense of "mutual support"). But the requirement that the set of hypotheses $h_1, \ldots, h_m$ be coherent on b in this sense (or even that it be coherent on $O_1, \ldots, O_n \& b$) will not exclude a competing set of the sort in question. So (1) and (2b) are not generated.

6. INDEPENDENT WARRANT AND AN ELIMINATIVE STRATEGY

Where do we stand? We began by asking whether the explanatory derivation of phenomena from an hypothesis will suffice to make the hypothesis probable. The answer is that it will not, either in the sense of "high" probability,

---

28. The competing sets of "God-intervening" and "Devil-intervening" hypotheses in note 25 both satisfy coherence in the sense of (6); phenomena $O_1, O_2 \ldots$ are explainable via derivation from each set; and both satisfy the prior probability condition. Are these sets "coherent" in the intended sense? If they are, then in the intended sense the coherence of a set of hypotheses from which the phenomena can be explained by derivation does not guarantee the high probability of the set.

(1a) or (1b), or of "increase in probability," (2a) or (2b). Next the question was whether consilience or coherence will suffice (if taken together with explanation). Consilience, understood in the proposed manner, will guarantee an increase in probability in the sense of (2a) but not (2b), and it will not guarantee high probability. Coherence, if understood in one fairly intuitive way, will not yield either high probability or increase in probability. If understood in another way it will yield high probability. But this interpretation seems foreign to Whewell's idea that coherent hypotheses must "run together" naturally. So the question remains whether we can find some plausible condition that, together with explanation, will guarantee high probability. In the present section such a condition will be noted, and a strategy for satisfying it will be explored. At the end of the section increase in probability in the sense of (2b) will briefly be discussed.

By contrast to Whewell, Mill and a number of other nineteenth-century theorists, including John Herschel, do not invoke consilience or coherence but a very different condition. Their basic idea is that in addition to requiring that an hypothesis postulating unobservables explain observed phenomena, there should be data providing some independent warrant for the hypothesis. This is warrant independent of the explanatory power of the hypothesis, whether the latter includes the number of phenomena explained, their consilience, or the coherence of the system.

In place of the method of hypothesis (which he also calls the "hypothetical method") Mill speaks of the "deductive method." It consists of three parts: an induction to the hypothesis, "ratiocination" (which includes explanation by derivation), and verification.[29] The "hypothetical method," Mill writes, "suppresses the first of these three steps, the induction to ascertain the law, and contents itself with the other two operations, ratiocination and verification."

John Herschel, one of the more philosophical physicists defending the wave theory in the nineteenth century, advocates a doctrine that combines explanations with the idea that the explanatory hypothesis should receive independent inductive support from data. He writes:

In framing a theory which shall render a rational account of any natural phenomenon, we have *first* to consider the agents on which it depends, or the causes to which we regard it as ultimately referable. These agents are not to be arbitrarily assumed; they must be such as we have good inductive grounds to believe do exist in nature, and do perform a part in phenomena analogous to those we would render an account of; or such whose presence in the actual case can be demonstrated by unequivocal signs.[30]

---

29. Mill, *op. cit.*, p. 323.
30. J. F. W. Herschel, *Preliminary Discourse on the Study of Natural Philosophy* (London, 1830), pp. 196–197. See Essay 3 for a more extensive excerpt from this passage and further discussion.

On both accounts we might say that for the fact that an hypothesis that explains a range of phenomena to count as (part of) a good reason to believe the hypothesis, the latter should be probable in the light of other data that provide inductive grounds for believing it. I shall not at this point be concerned with the character of these grounds but simply with the requirement that h be probable in the light of other data. (In section 7 when the idea of independent warrant is illustrated by means of the wave theory, the kinds of inductive grounds Herschel and other wave theorists had in mind will be noted.) Let the data providing independent warrant for h be included in the background information b. Then (1) could be given this new formulation:

(1)″ $p(h/O_1, \ldots ,O_n\&b) > k$ (for any $n \geq 1$) if $O_1, \ldots ,O_n$ are explainable via derivation from h and b, and if $p(h/b) > k$.

The second clause reflects the warrant for h supplied by the data in b. The condition that $p(h/b) > k$, if added to (2a) and (2b), would not suffice to make these true. *However, (1)″ is true.* If $O_1, \ldots ,O_n$ are derivable from h and b, then $p(h/O_1, \ldots ,O_n\&b) \geq p(h/b)$. So if $p(h/b) > k$, then $p(h/O_1, \ldots ,O_n\&b) > k$.

This result suggests an important, nonsuperfluous role for explanation. Suppose there are some initial data b in the light of which the probability of h is high. Now some seemingly relevant phenomena $O_1, \ldots ,O_n$ are observed, and we would like to determine the probability of h on these phenomena plus the initial data, that is, $p(h/O_1, \ldots ,O_n\&b)$. Without any further assumptions, this probability is not necessarily the same as $p(h/b)$. However, if we can show that the phenomena $O_1, \ldots ,O_n$ are explainable by derivation from h together with b, then it follows necessarily that $p(h/O_1, \ldots ,O_n\&b) \geq p(h/b)$. So if our initial data b give h high probability, then the explanatory power of h with regard to the other phenomena guarantees that h retains this high probability.

Accordingly, while explanations (no matter how numerous or varied) do not suffice to give an hypothesis high probability, they will ensure that the hypothesis retains whatever probability it has on other data. If the latter is high then the probability of h on all the evidence will be high. This sustaining role of explanations will be illustrated later when I turn to the form of argument used by nineteenth-century wave theorists.

Let us assume now that we have an hypothesis h together with some phenomena $O_1, \ldots ,O_n$ and some background information b. We want to determine whether $p(h/O_1, \ldots ,O_n\&b) > k$. (1)″ provides a

Basic Strategy:

1. Determine whether $p(h/b) > k$;
2. Determine whether $O_1, \ldots ,O_n$ are explainable via derivation from h.

In step 1 we determine the independent warrant for h, in step 2 the explanatory warrant. If both are found, then, by (1)$''$, $p(h/O_1, \ldots, O_n \& b) > k$. One way to determine whether $p(h/b) > k$ is directly by showing that b provides some type of inductive support for h. Another way—one that nineteenth-century wave theorists adopted—is indirectly by elimination: on the basis of inductive reasoning from b we establish that some set of h's competitors has low probability. Various eliminative strategies are possible for determining whether $p(h/O_1, \ldots, O_n \& b) > k$, of which I shall note one here, since it is, I believe, reflected in the wave theorist's procedures.

To introduce it we will speak simply of a *partition* of hypotheses on b as a set of mutually exclusive hypotheses, the probability of whose disjunction on b is 1. The strategy requires finding some observed phenomenon O that renders improbable each of the other hypotheses in some partition that includes h. The following is provable (see appendix):

(7) If $h, h_1, \ldots, h_k$ form a partition on b, then for some O and for each h_i ($\neq h$) in the partition, $\sum_i p(h_i/O \& b) < 1 - r$ if and only if $p(h/O \& b) > r$.

This tells us that if we have a set of mutually exclusive hypotheses that are exhaustive on b, then the probability of any hypothesis in the set, given some phenomenon, will be greater than r if and only if the sum of the probabilities of all the other hypotheses in the set, given that phenomenon, is less than $1 - r$. In view of this, the following strategy is possible for determining whether $p(h/O_1, \ldots, O_n \& O \& b) > k$:

Eliminative Strategy:

1. Find some partition on b that includes h;
2. Find some observable phenomenon O such that for each of the other hypotheses h_i in the partition $\sum_i p(h_i/O \& b) < 1 - k$;
3. Determine whether $O_1, \ldots, O_n$ are derivable from h.

In step 2, if we find such an O, then from (7) it follows that $p(h/O \& b) > k$. From this, assuming (via step 3) that $O_1, \ldots, O_n$ are derivable from h, it follows that $p(h/O_1, \ldots, O_n \& O \& b) > k$. This is an eliminative strategy, since we determine that h has a probability on all the phenomena that is greater than k by showing that there is some phenomenon on the basis of which the sum of the probabilities of each competing hypothesis in a partition that includes h is less than $1 - k$.

This strategy can be viewed as one form of the basic strategy, in which we determine h's probability on b and whether the observed phenomena are explainable via derivation from h. The eliminative strategy makes the first determination by considering competitors to h and determining whether the sum of their probabilities is $< 1 - k$. If it is, then independent warrant for h is secured. Moreover, if the observed phenomena are explainable by derivation from h, then this explanatory fact will ensure that h retains the high probability supplied by independent warrant.

I am not claiming that an eliminative strategy such as the one above is necessary for establishing high probability for an hypothesis, only that it is sufficient. But in addition I am saying this: *If our strategy for trying to establish high probability for h depends on an appeal to the fact that certain phenomena are explainable via derivations from h, then this is not sufficient.* An explanatory strategy of the sort advocated by Whewell and other supporters of the method of hypothesis will not be enough to guarantee high probability for h, no matter how many phenomena h explains, even if consilience and coherence, as understood earlier, are satisfied. In this regard Mill was correct, Whewell mistaken.

Indeed, taking this further, to establish the high probability of h on the phenomena $O_1, \ldots, O_n$ it will not be sufficient to show that these phenomena are all derivable from h and that none is derivable from any of h's competitors in some partition containing h. To see this, suppose that h is a member of some O-partition. Then h entails $O_1, \ldots, O_n$, and by (3), $p(h/O_1, \ldots, O_n\&b) = p(h/b)$. We may take $p(h/b)$, and therefore $p(h/O_1, \ldots, O_n\&b)$, to be as low as we like. Now h is always a member of the partition containing h and not-h. And, assuming that the O's are not logical truths, if h entails $O_1, \ldots, O_n$, it will not be the case that not-h entails $O_1, \ldots, O_n$. Accordingly, we have a partition containing an hypothesis h that entails the phenomena $O_1, \ldots, O_n$, and no competing hypothesis in that partition entails these phenomena. Yet the probability of h, given those phenomena, is not high.

In this section I have been discussing a role that explanation by derivation can play in establishing the high probability of an hypothesis on all the observed phenomena. High probability has been construed as probability greater than some threshold value, that is, in accordance with (1). And an eliminative strategy that involves explanation has been shown sufficient to yield high probability in this sense. However, this strategy does not guarantee that this probability approaches 1 as a limit as more and more phenomena are explained. Let us return to (2b) and ask whether we can supply general conditions that are both necessary and sufficient for the limit of the probability of h to be 1 as the phenomena increase. The following is provable (see appendix):

(8) $\lim\limits_{n \to \infty} p(h /O_1, \ldots, O_n\&b) = 1$ if and only if there is at least one partition on b containing h such that for each h_i $(\neq h)$ in the partition, $\lim\limits_{n \to \infty} p(h_i/O_1, \ldots, O_n\&b) = 0$.

In accordance with this theorem, one strategy to show that h's probability increases toward 1 is eliminative: show that the probability of each of h's competitors in at least one partition decreases toward 0. However, in pursuing this strategy, explanation by itself will not suffice. Nor will it suffice if conjoined with consilience and independent warrant from b. This is shown as follows.

Suppose we have a partition containing h in which each of the O's is explainable by derivation from h but from no other hypothesis h_i in the partition. We cannot conclude from this that, for each $h_i \neq h$, $\lim\limits_{n \to \infty} p(h_i / O_1, \ldots, O_n \& b) = 0$. (We cannot even conclude from this that $p(h / O_1, \ldots, O_n \& b) > p(h_i / O_1, \ldots, O_n \& b)$, i.e., that h's probability is greater than that of each competitor in the partition.) If the O's are explainable by derivation from h, and if $p(O_i / b) < 1$ for $each$ O_i derivable (strong consilience$_A$), we can conclude that $p(h/O_1, \ldots, O_n \& O_{n+1} \& b) > p(h/O_1, \ldots, O_n \& b)$ for each n (i.e., that as more and more phenomena are explained by h, h's probability rises where these phenomena are not certain). But we cannot conclude from this that h's probability approaches 1 as a limit under such conditions even if h has strong independent inductive warrant from b so that its probability on b is high. By theorem (4a), if h has some competitor that also explains all the O's and whose probability on b is greater than zero, then h's probability cannot approach 1 as a limit no matter how many O's it explains, even if h's probability on b is high.

The conclusion to be drawn is this. If we can find independent warrant for h from b, then h's explaining phenomena $O_1, \ldots, O_n$ will (a) at least sustain the probability supplied by that warrant, and (b) increase that probability if the O's exhibit consilience. But it will not suffice to increase that probability to 1.

7. WAVES[31]

The methodological points in the previous section pertaining to the achievement of high probability will now be illustrated by means of the nineteenth-century wave theorists' defense of their theory of light. Their strategy depends in part on invoking the fact that the wave theory explains a variety of optical phenomena. To this extent both Whewell and Mill, who cite the wave theory as an example of the use of the method of hypothesis, are correct. But in conformity with the remarks in the last section, the wave theorists' strategy contains an important eliminative part as well, which Whewell and Mill fail to mention. The explanatory part of the strategy will not suffice to give the theory high probability. For this purpose the eliminative part is essential.

31. Much of the material in this section is covered in Essay 3. Readers familiar with the latter might wish to turn straightway to the last two paragraphs of the present section.

A typical strategy actually used by wave theorists in defending their theory is this:

1. *Start with the assumption that light is either a wave or a particle phenomenon.* On the wave theory, light consists of a wave motion transmitted through a medium, the luminiferous ether. On the particle theory, light consists of a stream of particles emanating from luminous bodies; these particles are subject to forces obeying Newton's laws, so that if no forces are acting they move in straight lines with constant speed. Thomas Young (who first resuscitated the wave theory at the beginning of the nineteenth century), Fresnel (who developed it mathematically and applied it to diffraction), and Herschel and Lloyd (each of whom gave detailed presentations and defenses of the theory), all begin with this assumption in their actual presentations of the wave theory.[32]

Wave theorists who make the first assumption do not do so simply for the sake of argument to see what follows, but offer reasons. These involve either an appeal to what the best authorities believe ("leading physicists support one or the other assumption"), or an appeal to certain observed facts about light. In the latter category, for example, Lloyd notes that it is an observed fact about light that it travels in space from one point to another with a finite velocity, and that in nature generally one observes that finite motion is communicated from one point to another by the motion of a body and by the motion of a wave disturbance through a medium.[33]

2. *Show how each theory explains various optical phenomena.* A host of optical phenomena had been observed, including rectilinear propagation, reflection, refraction, dispersion, and diffraction. The wave theorist typically proceeds in his argument by showing not only how his theory proposes to explain a given phenomenon, but how the rival particle theory does so as well. Both wave and particle theorists had worked out explanations of many (though by no means all) of the known optical phenomena.

3. *Argue that in explaining one or more of the observed optical phenomena the particle theory introduces improbable hypotheses but the wave theory does not.* Light is observed to bend around (be diffracted by) small obstacles and to form diffraction bands both inside and outside the shadow. As wave theorists note, particle theorists explained this phenomenon by postulating the existence of both attractive and repulsive forces emanating from the obstacle and acting at a distance on the particles of light so as to bend some of

32. Thomas Young, *A Course of Lectures on Natural Philosophy and the Mechanical Arts* (London, 1845), pp. 359ff.; A. Fresnel, "Memoir on the Diffraction of Light" (1816), reprinted (in part) in Henry Crew, ed., *The Wave Theory of Light* (New York, 1900); J. F. W. Herschel, "Light," *Encyclopedia Metropolitana* (1845), vol. 4, pp. 341–586; Humphrey Lloyd, "Report on the Progress and Present State of Physical Optics," *Reports of British Association for Advancement of Science* (1834), pp. 295–413.

33. Lloyd, *op. cit.*, pp. 297–298.

them away from the shadow and others into it. Wave theorists such as Fresnel point out that observed data show that diffraction patterns do not vary with the mass or shape of the obstacle. Since known attractive and repulsive forces do depend on such factors, they conclude that the existence of such forces in the case of diffraction is very improbable.[34] By contrast, wave theorists argue that diffraction is explainable from the wave theory (on the basis of Huygens' principle that each point in a wave front can be considered a source of waves), without the introduction of any new assumptions (at least without any new ones that are improbable given the data). Wave theorists try to show how in the explanations of numbers of other optical phenomena (particularly interference and the observed constant velocity of light), the particle theorists introduce improbable auxiliary assumptions which are avoided with their own theory.

4. *Conclude from steps 1 through 3 that the probability of the wave theory is high.*

Now let us try to reconstruct this argument probabilistically. In step 1 the wave theorist begins by assuming that the probability is very high—close to 1—that light is either a particle or a wave phenomenon. (We may simplify the argument a bit if we suppose this probability to be equal to 1; for an argument based on the less idealized assumption see note 35.) Schematically,

(i) $$p(W \text{ or } P/b) = 1$$

where W asserts that light consists of a wave motion in some medium; P asserts that light consists of discrete particles emanating from luminous bodies and subject to forces obeying Newton's laws of motion; the background information includes facts about the known modes of travel in other cases (the only known ones being waves and bodies), and about the reputation and previous success of the advocates of each theory. (i) is defended inductively on the basis of such facts.

Let us avoid step 2 for the moment, turning our attention to step 3. Here wave theorists argue that to explain some observed optical phenomenon particle theorists introduce some new ("auxiliary") hypothesis h that is very improbable, given all the background information available. For example, h might be that attractive and repulsive forces emanate from an obstacle in the path of light and act at a distance to produce the observed diffraction patterns. O_d describes these patterns and includes the observed fact that they do not vary with the mass or shape of the obstacle. Hypothesis h is very improbable, given O_d and given the character of other known forces. So we may write:

---

34. Fresnel, *op. cit.*, p. 99.

(ii) $p(h/O_d \& b) \approx 0$ ($\approx$ means "is close to")

Somehow the wave theorist gets from (i) and (ii) (and the claim in step 2 that the wave theory explains a range of observed phenomena) to the conclusion that the wave theory is very probable given all the data. How can this inference be justified? It can if the conditional probability of the auxiliary assumption h is close to 1, given the particle theory P and the diffraction phenomena O_d, that is, if

(iii) $p(h/P \& O_d \& b) \approx 1$

Even more weakly, the inference can be justified if the probability in (iii) is much, much greater than that in (ii), even if the probability in (iii) is not close to 1, that is, if

(iv) $p(h/P \& O_d \& b) >> p(h/O_d \& b)$
                    ($>>$ means "is much, much greater than").

From (ii) and (iii), or from (iv) by itself, it follows that

(v) $p(P/O_d \& b) \approx 0$

That is, the probability of the particle theory, given observed diffraction phenomena and the background information, is close to zero. So we need to defend assumption (iii), or at least the weaker (iv), and to prove that (v) follows from (ii) and (iii), and from (iv) by itself. For proofs of these entailments see Essay 3, section 5. Here I shall show how (iii) — or at least (iv) — is defensible.

If by P light consists of particles subject to Newton's laws, and if by O_d light is diffracted from its rectilinear path into as well as away from the shadow, then by Newton's first law some force or set of forces must be acting on the light. Since it is observed that only bodies exert forces on other bodies, and since the only body observed to be present is the obstacle, it is very likely on inductive grounds that the obstacle exerts a force (or set of forces) on the light particles. Moreover, since some particles are deflected away from the obstacle and others toward it, it is likely, by analogy with other known forces, that both attractive and repulsive forces emanate from the obstacle, and that these act at a distance, that is, h. Now, to be sure, in the case of other known forces that act at a distance, varying the mass and shape of the body from which the force emanates will alter the observed path. However, given the assumption P that light consists of particles subject to Newton's three laws of motion, the inductive weight on the side of h from known facts about the action of forces in producing changes of directions in particles would overwhelm contrary evidence against h, making the probability of h, given P and

O_d, much, much greater than the probability of h without P (thus yielding (iv)) and perhaps even close to 1 (which would generate (iii)). In short, very extensive information about forces acting to produce changes in direction is considered to swamp less extensive information about forces emanating from bodies and varying with the mass and shape of those bodies. In this manner (iv) (if not the stronger (iii)) can be justified.

Now let us return to (i). In general, for any propositions h, e_1, and e_2, if $p(h/e_1) = 1$, then $p(h/e_1 \& e_2) = 1$ (where e_2 is assumed to be compatible with e_1 and h). So from (i) we get

(vi) $$p(W \text{ or } P/O_d \& b) = 1$$

where we have simply added the diffraction phenomena to the background information. In virtue of the fact that the classical wave and particle theories are mutually exclusive, from (v) and (vi) we get

(vii) $$p(W/O_d \& b) \approx 1$$

that is, the probability of the wave theory, given the diffraction phenomena and background information, is close to 1.

Finally, we can turn to step 2—the explanatory one. The wave theorist is confronted with the existence of numerous observed optical phenomena in addition to diffraction O_d and the observed motion of light (in b). Let us call these other observed optical phenomena $O_1, \ldots, O_n$. The wave theorist wants to know something about the probability of his theory, given all these phenomena as well. That is, he wants to know something about $p(W/O_1, \ldots, O_n \& O_d \& b)$. It does not follow that this probability ≈ 1 just because $p(W/O_d \& b) \approx 1$. (This would follow only if the former probability = 1.) Enter explanation. If the wave theorist can explain each of the phenomena $O_1, \ldots, O_n$ by deriving it from the wave theory, then he can show that $p(W/O_1, \ldots, O_n \& O_d \& b) \geq p(W/O_d \& b)$. That is, explanation will at least sustain whatever probability the wave theory has on other data. Accordingly, where $O_1, \ldots, O_n$ are the optical phenomena derivable from the wave theory, it follows from (vii) that

(viii) $$p(W/O_1, \ldots, O_n \& O_d \& b) \approx 1$$

which is the conclusion of the wave theorist's argument.

Explanation is an important part of the wave theorist's strategy, since it is used in getting from (vii) to (viii). But the present argument also conforms with my earlier claim that explanation is not sufficient to establish the high probability of an hypothesis. In fact it is readily seen that the preceding argument follows the eliminative strategy outlined in the previous section. In step (i) there is a partition on b that consists of the wave theory and the particle theory.[35] This reflects the first part of the eliminative strategy, which requires some partition on b that includes the hypothesis in question. Steps (ii) through (v) argue to the conclusion that the probability of the particle theory, given the observed diffraction phenomena, is very low, and thus that of the wave theory is very high. This conforms to the second part of the eliminative strategy, which requires that some phenomenon O be found that makes the sum of the probabilities of the other hypotheses in the partition $< 1 - k$. (Assume that k, the threshold value for high probability, is greater than or equal to 1/2.) Finally, from the fact that the observed optical phenomena $O_1, \ldots, O_n$ are explainable by derivation from the wave theory, it is concluded in step (viii) that the probability of the wave theory, given these phenomena, is very high. This reflects the third part of the eliminative strategy, which requires determining whether $O_1, \ldots, O_n$ are derivable from h.

From this example we may draw several conclusions. Contrary to the claims of Whewell and Mill (and some contemporary historians of science), wave theorists were not employing a method of hypothesis. Their strategy is not reflected in principles (1) and (2), or in these modified by consilience and coherence. These principles will not suffice to generate either a probability greater than some threshold value, or, in the limit, a probability of 1 as more and more phenomena are explained. And although explanatory derivations of phenomena will suffice to increase the probability of the hypothesis if the phenomena derived are consilient, this does not yet adequately reflect the wave theorists' strategy. Their aim was not simply to increase the probability of their theory but to show that it was highly probable. Moreover, they were attempting to provide not only explanations of phenomena (whether or not these phenomena were consilient), but also independent warrant for their theory. This they did by using an eliminative strategy that contains inductive steps. If such warrant could be secured, then explanations of other phenomena would play the important role of sustaining whatever high probability the theory achieved from the independent warrant.

---

35. This assumption can be relaxed by supposing there are other theories with very low, but nonzero, probabilities. Let us define a "virtual" partition on b to be a set of mutually exclusive hypotheses each of which has a nonzero probability, and the disjunction of which has a probability, given b, that is close to but not equal to 1. A strategy based on the use of a virtual partition is this: (a) Find a virtual partition on $O\&b$ that includes h. (b) Determine whether O is derivable from $h\&b$ but is such that for each other hypothesis h_i in the partition, $p(h_i/O\&b) \approx 0$. (c) Determine whether $O_1, \ldots, O_n$ are derivable from h. If the results are positive, it will follow that $p(h/O_1, \ldots, O_n\&O\&b) \approx 1$. It is possible to interpret the wave theorist as following this strategy, which is a variant of the eliminative strategy of section 6, where $O =$ observed diffraction phenomena.

8. CONCLUSIONS

If the Mill–Whewell debate is viewed in the present terms, who won? Although both are correct in certain judgments and mistaken about others, Mill, I think, should be given the edge.

Mill claims that an hypothesis is not probable simply because it explains observed phenomena, even if those phenomena are consilient. If we construe "probable" in the sense either of probability greater than some threshold value, say .5, or of probability that approaches 1 as the number of phenomena increases, then what Mill says is correct, and the reason he gives is valid. Conflicting hypotheses can also explain the observed data. Even if there is just one competing hypothesis that like h entails the O's and whose probability on b is at least as great as that of h on b, the probability of h cannot rise above .5 no matter how many phenomena it explains even if they are consilient. Mill does claim that the fact that h explains some range of phenomena shows only that h is possible. If this means that such an explanatory fact can show nothing at all about h's probability, then Mill is mistaken. When h explains the phenomena and the latter are consilient, h's probability increases. On the other hand, Mill correctly sees the value of independent warrant. His "deductive method" requires such warrant in addition to ratiocination and verification. This comports with the basic strategy of section 6, although Mill does not formulate this strategy, or its eliminative variation, in the way that I have done.

Whewell's position, expressed in probabilistic terms, is that an hypothesis is probable if it explains observed phenomena where those phenomena are consilient and where h introduces greater coherence into a system. If we construe "probable" in the sense of "increase in probability," and "consilience" in the sense of section 4, then what Whewell says is correct. (Coherence understood in the sense of (6) of section 5 becomes irrelevant.) Explanation of the phenomena by derivation from h does suffice to increase h's probability, if the phenomena are consilient. However, if we construe "probable" either as probability greater than some threshold value for high probability, say .5, or as probability that approaches 1 as the number of phenomena increases (which seems quite appropriate for a probabilistic formulation of Whewell's position), then what Whewell says is mistaken. The fact that the observed phenomena are explainable by derivation from h does not suffice to make h probable in either of these senses, even with consilience and coherence.

Moreover, Whewell is mistaken in supposing, as he seems to do, that where h explains the phenomena h's probability is high *only if* consilience and coherence are satisfied. If h has independent inductive warrant from b so that h's probability on b is high, then if $O_1, \ldots, O_n$ are explainable by derivation from h and b, h's high probability on the O's and b is sustained, whether or not there is consilience or coherence. This last consideration is important in understanding the strategy of nineteenth-century wave theorists who, contrary to what both Whewell and Mill say about it, were not defending their theory simply by employing some variant of the method of hypothesis.

APPENDIX

Proof of Theorem (3)

We need the following:

> *Lemma:* If $h_1, \ldots, h_k$ comprise a set of mutually exclusive hypotheses and if $p(h_1 v h_2 v \ldots v h_k / b) = 1$, then $\sum_{i=1}^{k} p(h_i / O_1, \ldots,$
>
> $O_n \& b) = 1$, for any n.

Proof: Since $p(h_1 v \ldots v h_k / b) = 1$, it follows that $p(h_1 v \ldots v h_k / O_1, \ldots, O_n \& b) = 1$. But since the h's are mutually exclusive the lemma follows.

Proof of (3): Suppose $h_1, \ldots, h_k$ form an O-partition. Then for each h_i in this O-partition, $h_i + b$ entails $O_1, \ldots, O_n$. If so, then using Bayes' theorem, $p(h_i / O_1, \ldots, O_n \& b) = p(h_i / b)/p(O_1, \ldots, O_n / b)$. Now $p(O_1, \ldots, O_n / b) \leq 1$, so

$$(1) \qquad p(h_i / O_1, \ldots, O_n \& b) \geq p(h_i / b) \qquad \text{for each } h_i$$

Since $h_1, \ldots, h_k$ form an O-partition,

$$(2) \qquad \sum_{i=1}^{k} p(h_i / b) = 1$$

Now suppose that there is some h_j such that

$$(3) \qquad p(h_j / O_1, \ldots, O_n \& b) > p(h_j / b)$$

Then from (1) and (2),

$$(4) \qquad \sum_{i=1}^{k} p(h_i / O_1, \ldots, O_n \& b) > 1$$

But from the lemma, since $h_1, \ldots, h_k$ is a set of mutually exclusive hypotheses, and since $p(h_1 v \ldots v h_k / b) = 1$,

$$(5) \qquad \sum_{i=1}^{k} p(h_i / O_1, \ldots, O_n \& b) = 1$$

Since (4) and (5) conflict, assumption (3) is false. That is, there is no h_j such that $p(h_j /O_1, \ldots, O_n \& b) > p(h_j /b)$. Therefore, from (1), each h_i is such that $p(h_i /O_1, \ldots, O_n \& b) = p(h_i /b)$.   Q.E.D.

Proof of Theorem (7)

A:

1. Suppose $h, h_1, \ldots, h_k$ form a partition on b, and $\Sigma p(h_i /O \& b) = \Sigma a_i < 1 - r$, for each $h_i \neq h$. We want to show that $p(h/O \& b) > r$.
2. Since we have a partition on b, $p(hvh_1 v \ldots vh_k/b) = 1$, and therefore $p(hvh_1 v \ldots vh_k/O \& b) = 1$, so $p(h/O \& b) + \Sigma p(h_i/O \& b) = 1$; that is, $p(h/O \& b) + \Sigma a_i = 1$, or $\Sigma a_i = 1 - p(h/O \& b)$.
3. From 1 and 2, $1 - p(h/O \& b) < 1 - r$, so that $p(h/O \& b) > r$.   Q.E.D.

B:

1. Suppose that $h, h_1, \ldots, h_k$ form a partition on b and $p(h/O \& b) > r$. We want to show that for each $h_i (\neq h)$, $\Sigma p(h_i /O \& b) < 1 - r$.
2. Since we have a partition, $p(hvh_1 v \ldots vh_k/b) = 1$. Therefore, $p(hvh_1 v \ldots vh_k/O \& b) = 1$, so $p(h/O \& b) + \Sigma p(h_i /O \& b) = 1$.
3. Let $p(h_i /O \& b) = a_i$. From 2, $p(h/O \& b) + \Sigma a_i = 1$, so $p(h/O \& b) = 1 - \Sigma a_i$.
4. From 1 and 3, $1 - \Sigma a_i > r$; so $1 - r > \Sigma a_i$, that is, $\Sigma a_i < 1 - r$. Q.E.D.

Proof of Theorem (8)

Only if:

1. Suppose $\lim_{n \to \infty} p(h/O_1, \ldots, O_n \& b) = 1$.
2. There is a partition on b, namely, h, $-h$, such that $p(h/O_1, \ldots, O_n \& b) = 1 - p(-h/O_1, \ldots, O_n \& b)$.
3. So $\lim_{n \to \infty} p(h/O_1, \ldots, O_n \& b) = 1$ iff $\lim_{n \to \infty} p(-h/O_1, \ldots, O_n \& b) = 0$.
   Q.E.D.

If:

1. Suppose there is some partition on b containing h such that for each h_i ($\neq h$) in the partition $\lim_{n \to \infty} p(h_i /O_1, \ldots, O_n \& b) = 0$. Call this partition $h, h_1, \ldots, h_k$.
2. Since we have a partition, we have $p(hvh_1 v \ldots vh_k/b) = 1$.

3. So $p(h/O_1, \ldots, O_n\&b) + \Sigma p(h_i/O_1, \ldots, O_n\&b) = 1$. So $p(h/O_1, \ldots, O_n\&b) = 1 - \Sigma p(h_i/O_1, \ldots, O_n\&b)$.

4. From 1, $\lim_{n\to\infty} p(h_i/O_1, \ldots, O_n\&b) = 0$ for each h_i. So $\sum_i \lim_{n\to\infty} p(h_i/O_1, \ldots, O_n\&b) = 0$.

5. From 4, $\lim_{n\to\infty} \Sigma p(h_i/O_1, \ldots, O_n\&b) = 0$.

6. From 3, $\lim_{n\to\infty} [p(h/O_1, \ldots, O_n\&b) + \Sigma p(h_i/O_1, \ldots, O_n\&b)] = 1$. So $\lim_{n\to\infty} p(h/O_1, \ldots, O_n\&b) + \lim_{n\to\infty} \Sigma p(h_i/O_1, \ldots, O_n\&b) = 1$.

7. From 5 and 6, $\lim_{n\to\infty} p(h/O_1, \ldots, O_n\&b) = 1$. Q.E.D.*

---

*For this essay Robert Rynasiewicz offered important criticisms and suggestions.

PART II

Maxwell and the Kinetic Theory of Gases

James Clerk Maxwell.
(Courtesy National Portrait Gallery, London.)

ESSAY 5

Introduction

1. HISTORICAL BACKGROUND[1]

James Clerk Maxwell, the first Cavendish Professor of Physics at Cambridge and probably the greatest theoretical physicist of the nineteenth century, made substantial contributions to the kinetic theory of gases. His first paper on the subject, "Illustrations of the Dynamical Theory of Gases,"[2] published in 1860, begins as follows:

> So many of the properties of matter, especially when in the gaseous form, can be deduced from the hypothesis that their minute parts are in rapid motion, the velocity increasing with the temperature, that the precise nature of this motion becomes a subject of rational curiosity. Daniel Bernouilli, Herapath, Joule, Krönig, Clausius, etc. have shewn that the relations between pressure, temperature, and density in a perfect gas can be explained by supposing the particles to move with uniform velocity in straight lines, striking against the sides of the containing vessel and thus producing pressure. (vol. I, p. 377)

The basic assumption of the kinetic theory was that observable properties of gases, including pressure, volume, and temperature, are to be explained by the motions of the unobservable particles, the molecules, of which gases are

---

1. For detailed historical accounts, various works of Stephen G. Brush are recommended, particularly *The Kind of Motion We Call Heat* (Amsterdam, 1976), *Kinetic Theory* (Oxford, 1965), and *Statistical Physics and the Atomic Theory of Matter* (Princeton, 1983). Maxwell's published and unpublished writings on kinetic theory are collected in Elizabeth Garber, Stephen G. Brush, and C. W. F. Everitt, eds., *Maxwell on Molecules and Gases* (Cambridge, Mass., 1986). The latter contains a very informative 47-page historical introduction by the editors. I reviewed this volume in *Foundations of Physics* 17 (1987), pp. 425–433, and in what follows I have used some material from this review.

2. W. D. Niven, ed., *The Scientific Papers of James Clerk Maxwell* (New York, 1965), vol. I, pp. 377–409. Unless otherwise specified, page references to Maxwell will be from this collection.

composed. This was contrary to a number of other accounts. There was a static theory, derived from Newton, according to which gas particles are stationary, not kinetic, and retain their positions because of the mutually repulsive forces they exert. This idea was incorporated into the caloric theory, the account of heat widely accepted during the eighteenth and early nineteenth centuries, according to which heat is a fluid that penetrates all matter. It consists of particles that repel each other but at the same time are attracted to the particles of ordinary matter. A second, contrasting theory was the wave theory of heat, developed particularly by Ampere in articles in 1832 and 1835. By that time, as noted in Part I of this volume, the wave theory of *light* had become much more widely accepted, as a result of the work of Young and Fresnel. This, together with experiments on radiant heat which, like light, exhibits reflection, refraction, and interference, made it quite easy for some to accept the idea that heat is associated with the vibrations of the ether, in particular with the kinetic energy of those vibrations.

The kinetic theory rejects the assumption of the caloric theory that heat is a substance; and it rejects the assumption of the wave theory that heat is a property of the all-pervading ether. Instead it takes it to be a property of the particles of ordinary matter comprising bodies, namely, molecular motion. It remains for kinetic theorists to say what sort of motion this is, and how molecules of a gas interact with each other and with the walls of the gas' container.

In the passage just quoted Maxwell mentions Bernouilli, Herapath, Joule, Krönig, and Clausius. Daniel Bernouilli, a Swiss mathematician, is generally regarded as the first to develop the kinetic theory in the eighteenth century. In Chapter 10 of his book *Hydrodynamica*, published in 1738, Bernouilli proposed to explain various properties of gases, including their weight and their capacity to expand and to be compressed, by assuming that they consist of "very small particles in rapid motion."[3] These particles he assumed to be spherical, each with the same diameter. He supposed that all the particles of the gas have the same velocity, and that the temperature of the gas is a function of this velocity. Using these assumptions he derived Boyle's law — that at a given temperature, the pressure of the gas is inversely proportional to its volume — for the case in which the diameter of a particle is much smaller than the distance between the centers of particles. Despite this result, Bernouilli's speculations did not convince anyone, since at that time heat was widely thought to be a substance rather than a property of matter.

In 1820, the Englishman John Herapath submitted a manuscript to the Royal Society which was rejected but subsequently published in the *Annals of Philosophy* in 1821. In it he developed a kinetic theory of gases based on various postulates, including that matter is composed of perfectly hard, indestructible atoms; that in gases atoms move with "perfect freedom"; that heat

---

3. Reprinted in Brush, *Kinetic Theory*, vol. 1, p. 58.

arises from the "intestine" motion of the atoms and is proportional to their momentum.[4] From the latter proportionality Herapath derived the result that the pressure of a gas times its volume is proportional to the square of the temperature (rather than to the first power, as in the ideal gas law). Another British scientist, John James Waterston, although not mentioned by Maxwell, developed a more sophisticated version of the kinetic theory in 1845. Unlike Herapath, he assumed that molecules are perfectly elastic, so that he could introduce the principle of conservation of mechanical energy. Moreover, unlike Herapath who assumed that temperature is proportional to momentum, Waterston took it to be proportional to mean square translational velocity of the molecules, as in contemporary formulations. He derived various results including that the pressure of a gas with a constant mean molecular velocity is proportional to the number of molecules per unit volume, from which Boyle's law follows. He also deduced that the pressure of a gas is proportional to its density times mean square molecular velocity, from which the ideal gas law (PV α T) follows. Like Herapath's paper, Waterston's was rejected by the Royal Society. However, in this case the Royal Society retained the paper and published it posthumously in 1892 when Lord Rayleigh discovered it. Because of this delay Waterston's work had no impact on other scientists during the mid-nineteenth century when kinetic theory was most extensively developed.

James Prescott Joule's major contribution was to establish a quantitative relationship between mechanical work and heat. During the 1840s he conducted a series of experiments from which he concluded

> . . . 1st that the quantity of heat produced by the friction of bodies, whether solid or liquid, is always proportional to the quantity of force expended; 2nd that the quantity of heat capable of increasing the temperature of a pound of water . . . by 1 degree F. requires for its evolution the expenditure of a mechanical force represented by the fall of 772 lbs through the space of one foot.[5]

Joule took the idea of the mechanical equivalent of heat to suggest that heat is not a substance but some form of molecular motion. However, unlike other kinetic theorists, he associated temperature with the rotation of molecules about their axes, rather than with translational motion.

In 1856, the German chemist August Karl Krönig published a short paper on kinetic theory in which he derived various results, including the ideal gas law, from assumptions involving perfectly elastic spherical molecules moving with the same velocity. The paper did not make new advances, but because of Krönig's professional status it was influential in generating study and responses by others. For example, Rudolf Clausius begins his important 1857

---

4. Reprinted in Henry A. Boorse and Lloyd Motz, eds., *The World of the Atom* (New York, 1966), vol. 1, pp. 198–205.

5. Reprinted in Boorse and Motz, *op. cit.*, p. 255.

paper, "The Nature of the Motion Which We Call Heat,"[6] with reference to Krönig's views, with which he is in substantial agreement, although he proceeds to show how the theory needs to be much further developed. It was this paper of Clausius', together with one published in 1859, that sparked Maxwell's interest in kinetic theory.

Clausius begins his 1857 paper by assuming that in addition to the translatory motion postulated by Krönig, molecules exhibit rotational motion and vibrations due to the atoms they contain. He gives qualitative kinetic theory explanations of various phenomena, including the pressure of a gas, Boyle's law, the claim that temperature is proportional to the translatory *vis viva* (kinetic energy) of the molecules, and the specific heat of a gas. Then introducing certain idealizations he derives three quantitative relationships. The first relates the product of pressure and volume to the mean square velocity of a molecule. Using this he derives values of mean molecular velocities for oxygen, nitrogen, and hydrogen at the temperature of melting ice (461 m/s, 492 m/s, 1844 m/s). Finally, he derives a formula relating the ratio of translatory kinetic energy of the molecules in a gas and total internal energy of the gas to specific heats.

In 1858 the Dutch meteorologist C. H. D. Buys-Ballot, responding to the mean molecular velocities Clausius computed, observed that if the molecules of a gas move as fast as Clausius claimed, then mixing of gases by diffusion should occur much more rapidly than it does. For example, malodorous hydrogen sulfide emitted in one corner of the room should be detected much more quickly than it is. Clausius replies in a paper in 1858 by modifying the theory in an important way. He attributes the phenomenon Buys-Ballot notes to the forces between molecules, which prevent molecules from covering large distances quickly. Accordingly, he abandons the idealizing assumption used for his quantitative derivations that intermolecular forces act only at infinitesimally small distances. Instead he introduces the idea of two intermolecular forces: one, a force of attraction between molecules that is exerted at some significant distance and increases as the distance diminishes; the other, a force of repulsion exerted when molecules are in the immediate neighborhood of one another. He speaks of a "sphere of action" as a sphere of radius r surrounding a molecule in which the force of repulsion acts. He then proposes what turned out to be an important new concept, that of *mean free path*, "how far on an average can the molecule move, before its center of gravity comes into the sphere of action of another molecule."[7]

Following this Clausius introduces the first probabilistic considerations in kinetic theory. He supposes that the gas in which a molecule is moving is divided into parallel layers perpendicular to the motion of the molecule. And

---

6. Reprinted in Brush, *Kinetic Theory*, pp. 111–134.

7. Rudolf Clausius, "On the Mean Lengths of the Paths Described by the Separate Molecules of Gaseous Bodies," reprinted in Brush, *Kinetic Theory*, p. 139.

he asks for the probability that a molecule will pass through a layer of a certain thickness without encountering the sphere of action of another molecule. He derives the formula $W = e^{-(\pi\rho^2/\lambda^3)x}$, where W = the probability of the molecule traveling a distance x, λ = the mean distance between the centers of neighboring molecules for a gas at a given density, and ρ = the radius of the sphere of action of the molecule. Using this formula Clausius then derives the formula $\ell = 3/4\lambda^2/\pi\rho^2$, which, for the case in which all molecules move with equal velocity, relates the mean free path of a molecule to the quantities above. However, Clausius did not know how to compute an actual magnitude for ℓ, since he had no way to determine the radius of the sphere of action or the mean distance between molecules for a gas at a given density.

Maxwell's 1860 kinetic theory paper, which begins with the quotation given earlier, makes very considerable advances on Clausius' work. On the first page, Maxwell notes that Clausius derived the formula relating mean free path to λ and ρ without being able to determine either of the latter. However, he claims that (what are now called) transport phenomena—internal friction of gases (viscosity), heat conduction, and diffusion—may lead to a numerical determination of the mean free path. And, he continues:

> In order to lay the foundation of such investigations on strict mechanical principles, I shall demonstrate the laws of motion of an indefinite number of small, hard, and perfectly elastic spheres acting on one another only during impact. (vol. I, p. 377)

Maxwell uses the term *sphere*, and more frequently *particle*, rather than *molecule*. And in this paper, as indicated by the quotation, he assumes that the only forces between the particles are contact forces. Maxwell proceeds to furnish a unified, comprehensive, mathematical treatment of various known gaseous phenomena, particularly heat conduction, viscosity, and diffusion, which prior to this had been investigated only rarely and had not been integrated. He introduces the idea that these processes involve a transfer of energy, momentum, and mass, respectively.

In his theoretical treatment of viscosity Maxwell derives a formula relating the coefficient of viscosity to the mean molecular velocity. From this, together with experimentally determined values of viscosity and density, he computes the mean free path for molecules of air at 60 degrees to be 1/447,000th of an inch. Even more important, the theoretical viscosity equation implies that the coefficient of viscosity is independent of the density of the gas and, therefore, of its pressure, a result Maxwell found intuitively very surprising. Not content with his role as armchair theoretician, in 1865 Maxwell together with his wife performed experiments on viscosity at various pressures and temperatures. In a Bakerian lecture of 1866 Maxwell describes these experiments and notes that at constant temperature the value of the coefficient of viscosity does indeed remain the same for different densities. This experimental verification of a surprising theoretical consequence of his 1860 theory increased Maxwell's confidence that he was not simply building castles in the air.

While Clausius had recognized that molecular velocities exhibit a wide range, he used only averages in his calculations. Maxwell in his 1860 paper concentrated on the range of velocities and derived the first velocity distribution law for molecules. It gives a mathematical expression for the number of molecules whose speed is between v and $v + dv$ as an exponential function of v. This is the most important contribution of the paper and the law has come to bear his name. (A precise formulation of the law and Maxwell's derivation of it are presented in Essay 6.) With this law Maxwell followed Clausius in continuing to introduce statistical methods into physics.[8] In 1871, commenting on this important methodological innovation, he writes:

> The method of dealing with groups of atoms, which I may call the statistical method, and which in the present state of our knowledge is the only available method of studying the properties of real bodies, involves an abandonment of strict dynamical principles, and an adoption of the mathematical methods belonging to the theory of probability. (vol. II, p. 253)

For someone steeped as Maxwell was in the Newtonian mechanical tradition, in which problems of motion are solved by analyzing a system into component parts and determining the forces acting on each, this is a bold departure.

Maxwell's 1860 paper is based on a billiard-ball model involving perfectly elastic spheres interacting only at impact. From this, together with other assumptions, he derives the theoretical result that the ratio of total molecular kinetic energy to translational kinetic energy is 2. But he notes that the experimentally obtained value is 1.634, a result that he thinks is "decisive against the unqualified acceptation of the hypothesis that gases are such systems of hard elastic particles" (p. 318). There is another result Maxwell obtains in his 1860 paper which, he realized later, is incompatible with experiments. He derives the theorem that the coefficient of viscosity μ is proportional to the mean molecular velocity v. But since absolute temperature T is proportional to v^2, μ must be proportional to the square root of T. Yet experiments he performed a few years later showed that μ is proportional to T, not to the square root of T. In the Bakerian lecture of 1866 he takes this experimental result to require a change in kinetic theory from contact forces between molecules to action at a distance.

This work led directly to Maxwell's second major paper on kinetic theory, published in 1867, in which he proposes "to consider the molecules of a gas,

8. See Elizabeth Garber, "Aspects of the Introduction of Probability into Physics," *Centaurus* 17 (1972), pp. 11–39; Theodore M. Porter, "A Statistical Survey of Gases: Maxwell's Social Physics," *Historical Studies in the Physical Sciences* 12 (1981), pp. 77–116.

not as elastic spheres of definite radius, but as small bodies or groups of smaller molecules repelling one another with a force whose direction always passes very nearly through the centres of gravity of the molecules, and whose magnitude is represented very nearly by some function of the distance of the centres of gravity" (vol. II, p. 29). From his experiments on viscosity Maxwell "deduces" that the repulsive force varies inversely as the *fifth* power of the distance, "any other law of force being at variance with the observed fact that the viscosity is proportional to the absolute temperature."[9] In this second paper Maxwell develops a new generalized transport theory based on molecules as centers of repulsive force. However, later experiments on viscosity by Meyer and others, which Maxwell acknowledged in an 1879 paper, showed that the viscosity of air does not vary with the first power of the temperature but with a lower one, "probably the 0.77 power." These experiments seemed to vitiate the model based on an inverse fifth-power repulsive force. Moreover, other phenomena noted by Maxwell suggested that attractive forces between molecules also exist.

The final atomic model to which Maxwell gave some support was that of the atom as a vortex ring. The proposal was made by Kelvin following some ideas of Helmholtz regarding rotational motion of a homogeneous incompressible fluid devoid of viscosity. Vortex rings, Maxwell wrote in an 1870 address to the British Association, "may be seen when an experienced smoker sends out a dexterous puff of smoke into the still air" (vol. II, p. 223). Once generated in the absence of viscosity, vortex rings "would go on whirling forever, would always consist of the very same portion of the fluid which was first set whirling, and could never be cut in two by any natural cause." Accordingly, they have the properties of individuality and permanence required of atoms. Moreover, unlike the elastic sphere and action-at-a-distance models

> In the vortex theory we have nothing arbitrary, no central forces or occult properties of any kind. We have nothing but matter and motion, and when the vortex is once started its properties are all determined from the original impetus, and no further assumptions are possible. (vol. II, p. 223)

Maxwell recognized that these ideas provided only the qualitative beginnings of a theory and that "the difficulties of this method are enormous, but the glory of surmounting them would be unique" (vol. II, p. 472).

Although Maxwell used each of the atom models noted here on different occasions—billiard ball, center of force, and vortex—he was never altogether satisfied with any of them. Each had significant problems and could be used only to apply to a restricted set of experimental facts. Indeed, even after Maxwell realized that the billiard-ball model was incompatible with experi-

---

9. Garber, Brush, and Everitt, *op. cit.*, p. 416.

mental data giving the relationship between viscosity and temperature, in an 1873 paper on Loschmidt's experiments on diffusion he relied on that very model to "proceed for a few steps on more hazardous ground, and inquire into the actual size of molecules" (vol. II, p. 348). For this purpose he assumed that molecules are spherical and that they collide only at impact, so that a mean-free-path formula could be used to derive values for diameters of various molecules. Estimates of the size of molecules were important to physicists such as Maxwell who came to believe in their real existence and wanted to develop a precise and comprehensive, quantitative theory about them. It also led Maxwell to an estimate of another very important quantity, Avogadro's number, the number of molecules in the gram equivalent of the molecular weight of a substance.

2. METHODOLOGICAL ISSUES

Maxwell's work in kinetic theory is a gold mine for the philosopher of science, especially since Maxwell himself held methodological views that he expressed in numerous writings and that influenced his own work in physics. A basic methodological problem—one that Maxwell explicitly addresses—is how one should understand and justify a theory that postulates entities such as molecules which one has no idea how to observe and for which there is scanty evidence at best.

In his two major kinetic theory papers of 1860 and 1867 Maxwell notes the results of only a few experiments conducted by himself and others, and he does not describe how they were done. The papers are highly theoretical, mathematical, and abstract. They consist almost entirely of *theoretical derivations*, which proceed by using the basic assumptions of the theory, together with others, and applying mathematical and logical operations to generate a conclusion in a series of steps. What role do these play? Do they serve to justify Maxwell's molecular hypotheses?

According to standard methodologies, such as hypothetico-deductivism and Millian inductivism, the only, or at least the principal, role of any theoretical derivation is to provide an empirical test for a theory or to explain some known empirical fact. Once theoretical postulates have been proposed these methodologies focus on generating observational conclusions: either new predictions to test the theory or old observations that the theory can explain. Yet this does not seem to be true in the case of Maxwell's most famous and important derivation in kinetic theory, that in which he derives his distribution law for molecular velocities. That law was not a "known empirical fact" or even "observational." Indeed, its truth was first established experimentally only in the 1920s with molecular beam experiments. Nor did Maxwell or anyone else at the time regard its derivation as providing an empirical test for kinetic theory. Why did Maxwell and others consider it so important? If the derivation failed to yield an empirical test for the theory or explain some known fact, did it serve some other function that helped to secure Maxwell's theoretical hypotheses? This question is considered in Essay 6, and the various roles of theoretical derivations in general are examined. By reference to Maxwell's case it is shown how a derivation may enable a scientist to discover some new theoretical proposition and provide a foundation for it that is theoretical rather than observational.

Throughout his career as a physicist Maxwell showed a concern for the proper scientific method to use in dealing with theories postulating entities that cannot be observed or measured. Should such theories be construed in a "realist" manner as making commitments to the existence of such hypothetical entities and attributing properties to them? Or should they be understood without such commitments, perhaps as providing useful *analogies* with observed items? Even before turning to kinetic theory, Maxwell confronted this issue in 1855 in his first paper on electromagnetic theory, "On Faraday's Lines of Force" (vol. II, pp. 155–229).

Maxwell notes that "electrical science" at that time contained various laws of electricity and magnetism that had been empirically established but not related or systematized. His aim is to produce a "simplification and reduction of the results of previous investigation to a form in which the mind can grasp them." But he rejects two scientific methods for doing so: the use of purely mathematical formulas, and the use of physical hypotheses that postulate the existence of unobservable entities and causes. Using the first method, we "entirely lose sight of the phenomena to be explained" and we lack a "clear physical conception." The second method, although employing a physical conception, leads to a "blindness to facts and rashness in assumption," since hypotheses are generated on the basis of little or no evidence. Instead, Maxwell advocates the *method of physical analogies*, which, unlike pure mathematical formulas, yields a physical conception but, unlike the use of physical hypotheses, avoids unwarranted speculations about unobservables. In this paper Maxwell constructs an analogy between the electromagnetic field and a purely imaginary, incompressible fluid flowing through tubes of varying section. An electrical property (e.g., the electrical force at a point in the field) is represented by some appropriate fluid property (e.g., velocity of the fluid at a point), and it is demonstrated that the electrical property satisfies a law mathematically similar to one satisfied by the corresponding fluid property (e.g., an inverse square law). In constructing the analogy Maxwell makes no assumptions about unobserved features of the electromagnetic field that cause it to have the properties and to satisfy the laws mentioned in the analogy. Indeed, he emphasizes that the incompressible fluid is purely imaginary and is not being assumed to exist. A physical analogy serves to organize ideas in one domain by providing such an organization in an analogous one. It also affords a way of working out unsolved problems in one system by considering solutions achieved in the analogue system.

Does Maxwell rely on this method in the development of kinetic theory? In his 1860 paper he does speak in terms of an analogy. After introducing his kinetic theory assumptions about the system of particles, he writes:

> If the properties of such a system of bodies are found to correspond to those of gases, an important physical analogy will be established which may lead to more accurate knowledge of the properties of matter. (vol. I, p. 378)

And just before writing this paper, in a letter to Stokes in 1859, Maxwell says that he intends to arrange his "propositions about the motions of elastic spheres in a manner independent of the speculations about gases" (Garber et al., p. 282). Accordingly, it may seem that in this paper Maxwell is simply constructing a physical analogy between a gas and a dynamical system of particles by showing that the latter has a set of properties and satisfies laws that are analogues of ones associated with gases. As with the earlier electromagnetic analogy, this would be possible to do without assuming the hypothesis that the "original" system, a gas, is composed of the particles comprising the analogue system, or indeed that the latter even exists. Yet in actual practice in this 1860 paper, despite what he writes to Stokes, Maxwell seems to go beyond the analogy by introducing the speculative physical hypothesis that gases are composed of the system of unobservable particles he postulates. For example, after he derives the pressure law for gases he writes:

> We have seen that, on the hypothesis of elastic particles moving in straight lines, the pressure of a gas can be explained by the assumption that the square of the velocity [of the particles] is proportional directly to the absolute temperature [of the gas], and inversely to the specific gravity of the gas at constant temperature. . . . (vol. I, p. 389)

Whether it is possible to construct a Maxwellian physical analogy between a gas and a dynamical system of particles, whether Maxwell's paper should be viewed solely in this analogical manner, and if Maxwell needs to go beyond the analogy, why he does, are questions explored in Essay 7. It is a conclusion of this essay that Maxwell does in fact transcend analogy and assume that gases are composed of the particles he describes. Indeed, he has to do so. Only in this way can he generate *dynamical explanations* of gaseous phenomena. Analogies that preclude hypotheses about the unobserved constituents of gases would not give Maxwell explanations of the properties and laws of gases of the sort he wants.

An important question remains for Maxwell, which is discussed in Essay 8. When can we say that one's hypotheses — particularly those postulating unobservables — have been shown to be verified or at least probable? Maxwell explicitly rejects the method of hypothesis, or hypothetico-deductivism, which in a paper of 1875 he characterizes as follows:

Forming an hypothesis and calculating what would happen if the hypothesis were true. If these results agree with the actual phenomena, the hypothesis is said to be verified, so long, at least, as someone else does not invent another hypothesis which agrees still better with the phenomena. (vol. II, p. 419)

Maxwell claims that those who employ this method are "compelled either to leave their ideas vague and therefore useless, or to present them in a form the details of which could be supplied only by the illegitimate use of the imagination" (*ibid.*).

If one wants to go beyond analogies and introduce explanatory hypotheses about unobservables, for example, molecules, but if one rejects the flights of fancy of hypothetico-deductivism, what method should one choose? Maxwell's answer is what he calls the "method of physical speculation" (p. 420). On this idea, the fact that an hypothesis entails or explains known phenomena will be considered a reason for believing it to be true provided that there is independent empirical warrant for the hypothesis from other observed phenomena. Maxwell offers no general definition of independent empirical warrant, only a few examples. But it is this idea that distinguishes his viewpoint from the method of hypothesis, which requires no such warrant.

As far as kinetic theory is concerned, Maxwell believed he had independent warrant for *some* of the hypotheses of this theory. For example, in his article "Atom" in the *Encyclopedia Britannica* (1875), he writes:

We begin by assuming that bodies are made up of parts, each of which is capable of motion, and that these parts act on each other in a manner consistent with the principle of the conservation of energy. In making these assumptions, we are justified by the facts that bodies may be divided into smaller parts, and that all bodies with which we are acquainted are conservative systems, which would not be the case unless their parts were also conservative systems. We may also assume that these small parts are in motion. This is the most general assumption we can make, for it includes, as a particular case, the theory that the small parts are at rest. The phenomena of the diffusion of gases and liquids through each other show that there may be a motion of the small parts of a body which is not perceptible to us. (vol. II, p. 451)

However, there are important assumptions that Maxwell introduces in one version or another of kinetic theory for which he has no independent empirical warrant. For example, in his 1860 paper he assumes that the force between molecules is zero except at impact. This allows a calculation of momentum transfer, and thus a derivation of Boyle's law relating the pressure and density of a gas. But because Maxwell provides no independent empirical warrant for the molecular force law, the fact that Boyle's law is derivable using it does not constitute a reason for believing that theoretical force law. And indeed in his 1860 paper Maxwell makes no claim that his derivation supports the assumption that molecules interact only when colliding. Despite this it may be very reasonable on pragmatic grounds to introduce such an assumption. Maxwell seeks to develop kinetic theory in a quantitative way "on strict mechanical principles"—an aim facilitated by some assumption about the forces governing molecules. In the absence of any empirical reason for choosing this rather than another force law, the fact that the one in question is simple and mathematically tractable may suffice to make it worth trying out to see what consequences will follow from its use.

In short, in kinetic theory from the very beginning Maxwell permits "speculations." He allows hypotheses about unobservables to be used to see what conclusions, if any, they yield about observed gaseous phenomena. In a second letter to Stokes in 1859 when speaking about his first kinetic theory paper he makes this explicit:

> I do not know how far such speculations may be found to agree with facts, . . . and at any rate as I found myself able and willing to deduce the laws of motion of systems of particles acting on each other only by impact, I have done so as an exercise in mechanics. Now do you think that there is any so complete a refutation of this theory of gases as would make it absurd to investigate it further so as to found arguments upon measurements of strictly "molecular" quantities before we know whether there be any molecules?[10]

Maxwell here expresses the thought that it can be worthwhile to consider and mathematically work out theoretical principles even if one hasn't any idea whether they are likely to be correct. This idea is reflected again in Maxwell's treatment of the vortex atom. He allows speculations about a vortex atom and shows how, if they are true, various observable properties of matter are explained. But he refrains from concluding, with the method of hypothesis, that this shows the vortex theory to be true or probable. To return to an earlier point, it is possible for Maxwell to be an opportunist about molecular models—to introduce various models and mathematically derive consequences pertaining to diffusion, viscosity, and so forth—without definitely committing himself to any particular model. This raises a general methodological question: Under what conditions is it reasonable to consider, "play with," or take seriously an hypothesis in the absence of independent empirical warrant? Is a speculative hypothesis worth considering when, or only when, it explains known phenomena? Are other conditions required? These issues, in addition to the ones mentioned in the last few paragraphs, are discussed in Essay 8.

Part II concludes with a general philosophical essay that examines one particularly interesting defense of the method of hypothesis against a standard attack. As we saw in Part I, a typical criticism of this method is one raised by Mill in the mid-nineteenth century: There may be competing hypotheses that entail the same observed phenomena as the favored hypothesis.

---

10. Garber et al., p. 279.

In response to Mill, William Whewell (as well as some philosophers in the twentieth century) offers an "only-game-in-town" argument. Suppose that hypothesis h entails a range of observed phenomena — some observed before the hypothesis was formulated and some afterward. And suppose that the experts in the scientific community cannot find a plausible competitor that will also generate these phenomena. Under these conditions we can say that the hypothesis h is "the only game in town." The fact that it is, is taken by some to count strongly in its favor.

In Essay 9 I consider various probabilistic and nonprobabilistic ways an only-game defense might be construed, and I argue that none of these is legitimate. Among the examples I invoke is Maxwell's 1860 kinetic theory, since in 1860 it was the only game in town with respect to a considerable range of observed gaseous phenomena. Yet, I argue, this fact did not render the probability of that theory high, or even increase it. Nor did it make the theory worth pursuing. I conclude that Mill's attack on the method of hypothesis is not vitiated by an only-game argument.

ESSAY 6

Theoretical Derivations

Scientific papers, especially the more theoretical ones, often contain derivations that may be the most important and novel parts of the material presented. These derivations proceed by using assumptions of one or more theories and applying mathematical and logical operations to generate some conclusion in a series of steps. I call them *theoretical derivations*. They are intended to show that something follows from something else. But why is it important do to that? What role do such derivations play? Why would a theoretical paper without them often be regarded as inferior to one in which they are present?

There is, I think, a serious lacuna on this topic in standard accounts of scientific method. I will begin by sketching four widely discussed methods in sufficient detail to bring out the role each accords theoretical derivations. This will be important later in defending my claim that these views offer a very incomplete account.

1. FOUR METHODOLOGIES

The Method of Hypothesis

The physicist Richard Feynman is a staunch supporter of this method, which today is usually called the hypothetico-deductive (h-d) method. He writes:

In general we look for a new law by the following process. First, we guess it. Then we compute the consequences of the guess to see what would be implied if this law that we guessed is right. Then we compare the result of the computation to nature, with experiment or experience, compare it directly with observation, to see if it

165

works. If it disagrees with experiment it is wrong. In that simple statement is the key to science.[1]

Feynman thus notes three stages in the development of a new scientific law (or hypothesis generally). First, a "guess" is made. Second, consequences are "computed." Third, these consequences are tested by experiment and observation. Presumably the second stage is the one in which derivations appear. We have a derivation — using mathematics and (at least implicitly) logic — because we need to test the law or hypothesis we have guessed. If the latter is highly theoretical, as it often is, then it cannot be tested directly. What must be done is to derive observable consequences from it together with auxiliary assumptions. The derivation is the intermediate step between the guess and the experiment or observation.[2]

This is not to say that every derivation from a new law or theory will necessarily result in a directly testable proposition. There may be intermediate stages, as Braithwaite, another h-d theorist, notes.[3] A derivation from a "high-level" law (Braithwaite's example is Galileo's law that unsupported bodies fall with an acceleration of 32 ft/s^2) may lead, via mathematical operations, to a lower level hypothesis ("unsupported bodies fall $16t^2$ feet in t seconds"); and this in turn, through the application of logic, will generate "singular" propositions that are directly testable ("this unsupported body falls 16 feet in 1 second"). Such a series of derivations, says Braithwaite, is meant to yield propositions of "diminishing generality" in order that the highest level propositions in the theory — those that are underived — can be empirically tested.

Many who defend a version of the method of hypothesis also emphasize the role of derivations in *explaining* and *predicting* observed phenomena. Whewell, 100 years before contemporary hypothetico-deductivists, asserted that new hypotheses, which are discovered by guessing,

> ought to explain phenomena which we have observed. But they ought to do more than this: our hypotheses ought to *foretel* phenomena which have not yet been observed.[4]

To do so, according to Whewell, deductive reasoning is required:

> . . . in Deduction we infer particular from general truths; while in Induction we infer general from particular. . . . Deduction is a necessary part of Induction. Deduction justifies by calculation what Induction had happily guessed.[5]

---

1. Richard Feynman, *The Character of Physical Law* (Cambridge, Mass., 1965), p. 156.

2. Similar accounts are to be found in Karl Popper, *The Logic of Scientific Discovery* (New York, 1968), and Carl G. Hempel, *Philosophy of Natural Science* (Englewood Cliffs, N.J., 1966).

3. R. B. Braithwaite, *Scientific Explanation* (Cambridge, England, 1953), pp. 12–21.

4. William Whewell, *The Philosophy of the Inductive Sciences* (New York, 1967), vol. 2, p. 62.

5. *Ibid.*, pp. 92–93.

For Whewell, the role of deduction is to derive — and therefore explain or predict — particular observable facts from general hypotheses that have been selected by sagacious guesswork.

Mill's "Deductive Method"

When the phenomena to be investigated are too indirect and complex for observation and experiment alone we use what Mill calls the "deductive method":

> The mode of investigation which, from the proved inapplicability of direct methods of observation and experiment, remains to us as the main source of the knowledge we possess or can acquire respecting the conditions and laws of recurrence of the more complex phenomena, is called, in its most general expression, the Deductive Method, and consists of three operations — the first, one of direct induction; the second, of ratiocination; the third, of verification.[6]

According to Mill, we use the "deductive method" when we want to discover some effect, or some law of effect, when a given phenomenon is governed by a multitude of causes. He cites as an example determining the velocity and range of a cannon ball (p. 302). We need to determine the various "causes," for example, the force on the cannonball by the gunpowder, the angle of elevation of the cannon, the density of the air, and the strength and direction of the wind. These causes and the laws governing them are inferred by induction from previous observations and experiments. This is Mill's "first operation."

Second, there is "ratiocination," which is an operation of

> . . . determining from the laws of the causes what effect any given combination of those causes will produce. This is a process of calculation. . . . when our knowledge of the causes is so perfect as to extend to the exact numerical laws which they observe in producing their effects, the ratiocination may reckon among its premises the theorems of the science of number, in the whole immense extent of that science.[7]

From the "causes" (or determining factors) of the motion of a projectile we use mathematics to compute the effect (e.g., the velocity and range) — which as Mill notes, can be a very difficult task indeed.[8]

---

6. John Stuart Mill, *A System of Logic* (London, 1959), p. 299.

7. *Ibid.*, p. 302.

8. Mill admits that mathematical reasoning is not always a part of ratiocination, especially in those sciences that are not quantitative. In ratiocination, "all that is essential," he writes, "is reasoning from a general law to a particular case, that is, determining by means of the particular circumstances of that case what result is required in that instance to fulfill the law" (p. 303).

The third process is verification:

> To warrant reliance on the general conclusions arrived at by deduction, these conclusions must be found, on careful comparison, to accord with the results of direct observation wherever it can be had.[9]

For Mill, then, derivations occur in "ratiocination," the second process in the deductive method. Such derivations yield the effect of a set of causes governed by various laws. And this effect must accord with the results of direct observations. Mill makes it clear that ratiocination is a process directed toward the "calculation" of propositions capable of direct empirical testing. On this issue Mill is in agreement with hypothetico-deductivists. Their principal difference lies in the fact that Mill requires an induction in the first stage of theorizing, h-d theorists do not.

Retroduction

Champions of retroduction such as Peirce and Hanson reject the h-d idea that a new hypothesis is simply guessed: it is inferred. However, they do not regard the reasoning as inductive generalization (à la Mill), but as retroductive or explanatory. The scientist begins with some observed phenomenon and then reasons that an hypothesis is plausible, or worth considering, on the grounds that if true it would correctly explain that phenomenon. Peirce believes that retroduction has "a perfectly definite logical form," which he puts as follows:

The surprising fact C is observed.
But if A were true, C would be a matter of course.
   Hence
There is reason to suspect that A is true.[10]

What role, if any, do derivations play in this account? They may enter at two points. First, they may be part of the retroductive reasoning itself, employed in showing that the observed fact does follow from, or is explained by, the hypothesis which is retroduced. Despite the fact that both Peirce and Hanson use the expression "(as) a matter of course" in describing the manner in which the observed fact would follow from, or be explained by, the hypothesis, I do not think this commits them to the view that the observed fact is

---

9. *Ibid.*, p. 303.

10. Charles Peirce, *Collected Papers*, Charles Hartshorne and Paul Weiss, eds. (Cambridge, Mass., 1960), vol. 5, 5.189. Hanson offers various schemas. One of his simplest, which makes explicit the explanatory character of the reasoning, is this: "Some surprising phenomenon P is observed; P would be explicable as a matter of course if H were true; hence, there is reason to think that H is true." N. R. Hanson, *Patterns of Discovery* (Cambridge, England, 1958), p. 86.

necessarily an obvious or immediate corollary of the hypothesis, requiring no demonstration. Thus, Hanson offers the following as an example of retroductive reasoning to Newton's law of universal gravitation:

1. The surprising, astonishing discovery that all planetary orbits are elliptical was made by Kepler (1605 to 1619).
2. But such an orbit would not be surprising or astonishing if, in addition to other familiar laws, an inversely varying law of gravitation obtained. Kepler's first law would follow as a matter of course; indeed the hypothesis could even explain why (since the sun is in but one of the foci) the orbits are ellipses on which the planets travel with non-uniform velocity.
3. Therefore, there is good reason for elaborating this hypothesis further, for proposing it as that from the assumption of which Kepler's first law might be explained.[11]

Now Kepler's first law is no obvious, immediate consequence of Newton's law of gravitation together with the three laws of motion. A derivation is required. More generally, derivations may need to be constructed in showing that the observed phenomenon would indeed follow "as a matter of course" from the retroduced hypothesis.

There is a second use of derivations that retroductivists recognize. This comes after the hypothesis has been retroduced, after the scientist discovers that if H were true the observed phenomenon P would follow. It comes in the "context of justification" when the hypothesis is being tested. Here, by contrast to the "context of discovery," Hanson is willing to follow the h-d theorist. Consequences (in addition to those observed phenomena from which the hypothesis H is originally retroduced) are derived from H, and these are subject to empirical test. However, Hanson urges that although such reasoning exists, it is not reasoning of the most original kind:

By the time a law has been fixed into an H-D system, really original physical thinking is over. The pedestrian process of deducing observational statements from hypotheses comes only after the physicist sees that the hypothesis will at least explain the initial data requiring explanation. This H-D account is helpful only when discussing the argument of a finished research report, or for understanding how the experimentalist or the engineer develops the theoretical physicist's hypotheses; the analysis leaves undiscussed the [retroductive] reasoning which often points to the first tentative proposals of laws.[12]

---

11. N. R. Hanson, "The Logic of Discovery," in *The Concept of Evidence*, Peter Achinstein, ed. (Oxford, 1983), pp. 60–61.

12. Hanson, *Patterns of Discovery*, pp. 70–71.

Bootstrapping

Clark Glymour, who introduces this idea as an alternative to the method of hypothesis, is particularly concerned with the testing of theories.[13] On this view an hypothesis in a theory is tested by using the theory to make computations from observed experimental values to instances of the hypothesis to be tested. Let e be observed values of certain quantities, h the hypothesis we are testing, and T a theory. Then according to the bootstrapping idea, e confirms hypothesis h with respect to theory T if and only if from e it is possible, using the theory T itself, to derive an instance of h, where the derivation is such as not to guarantee an instance of h no matter what e had been chosen.

Glymour offers a simple schematic example of a theory T consisting of the following linear equations:

(1) $A_1 = E_1$

(2) $B_1 = G_1 + G_2 + E_2$

(3) $A_2 = E_1 + E_2$

(4) $B_2 = G_1 + G_2$

(5) $A_3 = G_1 + E_1$

(6) $B_3 = G_2 + E_2$

The A's and B's are directly measurable quantities; the E's and G's are "theoretical" quantities whose values can be determined only indirectly through the theory by determining the values of the A's and B's. Here is how we obtain evidence for hypothesis (1). We determine a value for A_1 directly from experiment. We obtain a value for the "theoretical" quantity E_1 by obtaining values for the "observables" B_1, B_3, A_3 and then, by using hypotheses (2), (5), and (6) from the theory, we mathematically compute a value for E_1. If the value for A_1 determined by experiment is the same as the computed value for E_1, then the observed values of A_1, B_1, B_3, and A_3 constitute confirming evidence for hypothesis (1) in the theory.

On this view, derivations will occur in the testing of a theory. They will begin with observed values of certain quantities, and by using the principles of the theory together with mathematics and logic they will proceed to compute values for theoretical quantities. Glymour notes an important difference between this view and the method of hypothesis. According to the latter, derivations go from theories to observations. According to bootstrapping, derivations go from observations via a theory to an instance of a theoretical hypothesis.

---

13. Clark Glymour, *Theory and Evidence* (Princeton, 1980).

Conclusions

On all four methodologies theoretical derivations are used in the testing of a theory. Hypothetico-deductivists, Mill, and retroductivists may disagree on the conditions necessary for the initial proposing of a hypothesis. But once it has been proposed it is tested by constructing a derivation, or perhaps a series of derivations, that will lead from that hypothesis, together with the theory in which it appears, to observational conclusions, which are then tested directly. On the bootstrap idea, derivations occur in the testing of hypotheses, but the direction is reversed. In addition, hypothetico-deductivists and retroductivists, at least, emphasize the role of derivations in the explanation of observed phenomena.

In sum, then, on all four methodologies derivations are constructed

> to test theories empirically, or to explain some known fact that has already been tested empirically, or both.

If those who defend these methodologies hold that there are other major roles for theoretical derivations they do not say. It is possible they think these are the only ones, or perhaps the only important ones.

---

2. MAXWELL'S DISTRIBUTION LAW

To examine these ideas I shall begin with a famous derivation. In 1860 James Clerk Maxwell published the first of his two great papers on kinetic theory. It was entitled "Illustrations of the Dynamical Theory of Gases."[14] In it he derives a law—the distribution for molecular velocities—that may well be the most important contribution of the paper. The derivation is fairly brief (unlike that given in some contemporary texts), and I will reconstruct it, frequently using Maxwell's own words.

Let N be the total number of molecules in a sample of gas. Let x, y, z be the components of velocity for a molecule using rectangular coordinates. Let $Nf(x)dx$ be the number of molecules whose x-component of velocity lies between x and $x + dx$, where $f(x)$ is some function of x to be determined. ($f(x)dx$ can be thought of as the fraction of molecules with x velocities between x and $x + dx$, or as the probability that a molecule in the sample has an x coordinate of velocity in that range.) Similar definitions are given for $Nf(y)dy$ and $Nf(z)dz$.

Now Maxwell assumes that the velocities x, y, and z are independent, so

---

14. W. D. Niven, ed., *The Scientific Papers of James Clerk Maxwell* (New York, 1965), vol. I, pp. 377–409.

that the number of molecules with x-components of velocity between x and $x + dx$, *and* with y-components between y and $y + dy$, *and* with z-components between z and $z + dz$, is

(1) $$Nf(x)f(y)f(z) \; dx \, dy \, dz$$

If we think of $f(x)dx$ as the probability that a molecule will have an x-component of velocity between x and $x + dx$, then what Maxwell is assuming here is that this probability is independent of the probability that the same molecule has a y-component between y and $y + dy$, and also of the probability that it has a z-component between z and $z + dz$. Since these probabilities are independent, they can be multiplied to yield the probability that the molecule has an x-component between x and $x + dx$, a y-component between y and $y + dy$, and a z-component between z and $z + dz$.

Now we suppose that the N molecules in the sample of gas start from some common origin at the same time. Then from (1), the number of molecules in an element of volume $dx \, dy \, dz$ will be

(2) $$Nf(x)f(y)f(z)$$

And the fraction of the total N in that volume element will be

(3) $$f(x)f(y)f(z)$$

Another way to look at this is to think of a three-dimensional "velocity" space, each coordinate of which represents one of three velocity coordinates. A point in this space will represent the velocity of some molecule. The number of points in some small volume $dx \, dy \, dz$ in this space represents the number of molecules with components of velocity between x and $x + dx$, y and $y + dy$, and z and $z + dz$. The number of molecules in this unit volume is given by (2), the fraction of the total by (3).

Maxwell next assumes that since the directions of the coordinates are arbitrary, the number of molecules in the unit volume $dx \, dy \, dz$ depends only on the distance of this volume element from the origin. This is to assume that the fraction of molecules in a unit volume of velocity space is a function of the distance of that volume from the origin (i.e., the fraction does not depend on the direction of molecules in that volume but only on their speeds). But the square of the distance of a point in a space given by coordinates x, y, z is $x^2 + y^2 + z^2$. So Maxwell is assuming that the fraction of molecules with velocities between x and $x + dx$ and y and $y + dy$ and z and $z + dz$ is some function ϕ of $x^2 + y^2 + z^2$, that is,

(4) $$f(x)f(y)f(z) = \phi(x^2 + y^2 + z^2)$$

The only mathematical solution possible is an exponential one

$$f(x) = Ce^{Ax^2}$$

and similarly for y and z, where C and A are to be determined. If A is positive, then the number of molecules given by (2) will increase with velocity toward infinity. Therefore, we make A negative and equal to $-1/\alpha^2$ so that the number of molecules with x-components of velocity between x and $x + dx$ is

(5) $$NCe^{-x^2/\alpha^2}dx$$

Now if we integrate this from $x = -\infty$ to $x = +\infty$ the result is equal to N, the total number of molecules, since we are integrating over all possible x-components of velocity. The result of this integration is $NC\sqrt{\pi}\alpha$. Equating this to N and solving for C we get $C = 1/\alpha\sqrt{\pi}$. Therefore, from (5) we derive that the number of molecules whose x-components of velocity lie between x and $x + dx$ is

(6) $$N\frac{1}{\alpha\sqrt{\pi}} e^{-x^2/\alpha^2}dx$$

We get similar expressions for y- and z-components of velocity.

The number of molecules whose speed (independent of direction) is between v and $v + dv$ can be determined to be

(7) $$N\frac{4}{\alpha^3\sqrt{\pi}} v^2e^{-v^2/\alpha^2}dv$$

(6) and (7) express Maxwell's formulation of the distribution law for molecular velocities and speeds.

The "independence" assumption leading to (1) Maxwell later regarded as questionable,[15] and in his second major paper on kinetic theory, "The Dynamical Theory of Gases," written in 1866, he gave a different derivation of the distribution law based on assumptions about molecular encounters. But in what follows I will focus on the original derivation.

3. METHODOLOGIES REVISITED

According to the method of hypothesis, the scientist begins by guessing a new law, rather than by inferring it deductively or inductively. Now Maxwell's

---

15. For a defense of this assumption and a critique of another part of the derivation, see John Maynard Keynes, *A Treatise on Probability* (London, 1921), pp. 173–174.

distribution law for molecular velocities was certainly a new law in physics. Earlier formulations of kinetic theory by Bernoulli, Herapath, and Clausius, for example, contained no such law. Yet there is no strong reason to suppose that Maxwell began simply by guessing the law after which he sought to derive formally what he had conjectured informally. Some nine years before the publication of his paper Maxwell may have read a review of a work of Adolphe Quetelet written by John Herschel in the *Edinburgh Review* in 1850.[16] In this review Herschel gives an argument for the law of errors that is similar in certain respects to Maxwell's derivation of the velocity distribution law.

Herschel cites as an example a ball dropped from a given height with the intention that it fall on a given mark. The "error" is the deviation from the mark. Herschel makes two assumptions that are analogous to ones Maxwell makes for velocities. He assumes that the error along one coordinate is independent of errors along the others (so that the probabilities can be multiplied). And he assumes that the probability of any deviation depends solely on its magnitude and not on its direction. This will yield an equation with the same form as Maxwell's (4), whose solution is an exponential function involving the square of the error. If Maxwell did read Herschel's review, which is by no means certain, and if he used Herschel's derivation as a basis for his own, then Maxwell could not properly be said to have begun by guessing the distribution law. If these were the conditions that obtained, then he began by making assumptions about the distribution of molecular velocities that were analogues of those made by Herschel about the distribution of errors; from which he derived a law about the distribution of molecular velocities that is analogous to a law about the distribution of errors. But even if Herschel's review had little if any influence on Maxwell, there is no evidence to show that Maxwell began by simply *guessing* that the law is exponential in character or that the function will involve a term for the square of the velocity. The exponential function he introduces is not the simplest or most intuitive one he might have tried; nor is there any record of Maxwell systematically trying out a number of functions, as might be the case if he first guessed the result and afterward tried to derive it. Rather what seems most plausible is that Maxwell arrived at the law not first by guessing it but by deriving it in the manner he indicates in his paper.

If this is right then Maxwell did not arrive at his law by making an inductive inference in Mill's sense. According to Mill,

---

16. John Herschel, *Edinburgh Review* 92 (1850), pp. 1–57. For discussions of the possible effect of Herschel's review on Maxwell, see Stephen G. Brush, *The Kind of Motion We Call Heat* (Amsterdam, 1976), book I, pp. 183–186; Elizabeth Garber, "Aspects of the Introduction of Probability into Physics," *Centaurus* 17 (1972), pp. 11–39; Theodore M. Porter, "A Statistical Survey of Gases," *Historical Studies in the Physical Sciences* 12 (1981), pp. 77–116.

Induction is the process by which we conclude that what is true of certain individuals of a class is true of the whole class, or that what is true at certain times will be true in similar circumstances at all times. . . . it proceeds from the known to the unknown. . . . [17]

But Maxwell did not arrive at his distribution law by inferring from the fact that it is known to hold of such and such gases that it holds of all gases. Although Maxwell asserts the applicability of the law to all gases (i.e., to all molecular systems of which gases are supposed to be composed), he does not infer this from the fact that he has established this for particular ones.

Nor is there evidence to suggest that Maxwell began with some set of observations and proceeded to infer the law retroductively on the grounds that it explains those observations. He mentions no observations leading to the proposing of his law that would be explained by the law if it were true. Gas molecules are unobservable, and Maxwell had no empirical data regarding molecular velocities that could be organized and explained using his law.

Well, what is so surprising about that? Don't h-d theorists, Mill, retroductivists, and bootstrappers all recognize the deductive character of science? Don't they admit that the scientist spends a good deal of time *deriving* conclusions? So here is how Maxwell operated, they will say. First, he set down his basic assumptions of kinetic theory. Never mind how he got these—whether by guessing, inductive inference, or retroduction. Then from the assumptions he proceeded to derive conclusions, including the distribution law, which can be subjected to empirical test (perhaps even by bootstrapping). As I will try to show in the next two sections, this gives an inaccurate picture of Maxwell's problem situation when he attempted to derive the distribution law, as well as a questionable account of the role of this derivation and others in the testing of theories.

4. PROBLEM SITUATIONS

Maxwell does, indeed, begin his paper with basic assumptions of the kinetic theory. He assumes that gases are composed of minute molecules in rapid motion; that the velocity of the molecules increases with the temperature of the gas; that the molecules move with uniform velocity in straight lines striking against the sides of the container, thus producing pressure; that the molecules are perfectly elastic spheres acting on each other only during impact; and that the motion of the molecules is subject to mechanical principles of Newtonian mechanics.[18] These are fairly standard assumptions of kinetic

17. Mill, *op. cit.*, p. 188.
18. Maxwell, *op. cit.*, p. 377.

theory which, as Maxwell notes, were made by numbers of previous physicists.

However, the most important assumptions he needs for the proof are not ones in this set, but rather (a) the assumption of the independence of the x-, y-, and z-components of velocity of a molecule and (b) the assumption that the fraction of molecules in a unit volume in velocity space is a function of the distance of that volume from the origin. Both of these are special assumptions Maxwell introduces just for the purposes of this derivation.

What is strange about that? Philosophers of science frequently recognize that you cannot derive very much from the basic assumptions of the theory alone. You need a set of "auxiliary assumptions" that pertain to the special systems to which you are applying the more general theory. Hilary Putnam, who has discussed various "schemas for scientific problems," calls this "schema I," which he thinks is emphasized by standard philosophy of science[19]:

Schema I

Theory
Auxiliary statements (A.S.)
_____
Prediction — true or false?

"In the first type of problem," writes Putnam, "we have a theory, we have some A.S., we have derived a prediction, and the problem is to see if the prediction is true or false. . . . "

H-D theorists, Mill, and retroductivists do indeed recognize situations of the schema I variety, in which one has already derived a prediction from the theory + A.S. and the problem is to test that prediction. But another sort of problem situation occurs in what Feynman calls the "computational" stage and Mill calls "ratiocination." It is a situation in which one has a theory + A.S., one has some observed facts that the theory may be able to explain, and the problem is to see whether the theory can do so. The problem is to be solved by constructing a derivation of those facts from the theory. Let me call this

Schema IA

Theory
Auxiliary statements
_____   ???
Observed facts

The question marks to the right of the line indicate that what is sought is a derivation of the observed facts from the theory + A.S.

---

19. Hilary Putnam, *Mathematics, Matter and Method* (Cambridge, England, 1975), p. 261.

Now Maxwell's situation is not that of schemas I or IA. Maxwell does not begin with a theory and a set of auxiliary statements. He begins with a theory and his problem is to find a set of auxiliary statements from which he can derive a distribution law. Indeed, Maxwell's Proposition 4 sets the following problem:

> To find the average number of particles [molecules] whose velocities lie between given limits, after a great number of collisions among a great number of equal particles.

To solve this problem he has to discover auxiliary statements to add to this theory.

Putnam would agree with this. He thinks that "standard philosophy of science" has concentrated only on schema I and has failed to recognize other schemas. Putnam's second schema, which seems closer to Maxwell's situation, is this:

Schema II

Theory
???
_____

Fact to be explained

"In this type of problem," writes Putnam, "we have a theory, we have a fact to be explained, but the A.S. are missing: the problem is to find A.S. if we can, which are true, or approximately true (i.e., useful oversimplifications of the truth), and which have to be conjoined to the theory to get an explanation of the fact."[20] Putnam believes that schema II, rather than schema I, is exhibited in the Kuhnian "puzzle solving" of "normal science."[21] And he thinks that schema II will "enable us better to appreciate both the relative unfalsifiability of theories which have attained paradigm status, and the fact that the 'predictions' of physical theory are frequently facts which were known beforehand, and not things which are surprising relative to background knowledge."[22]

If Putnam's question marks represent what is sought in a problem situation, then schema II does not completely reflect what Putnam has in mind. We begin with a theory and a fact to be explained. What we seek is not only a set of auxiliary statements which when added to the theory will yield the fact, but also a *derivation* showing how to get the fact to be explained from the theory + A. S. (Maxwell was searching not simply for a set of additional assumptions that, when added to the theory, would entail the distribution

---

20. *Ibid.*, p. 261.
21. *Ibid.*, p. 264.
22. *Ibid.*, p. 265.

law; he sought to construct a derivation showing this entailment.) Accordingly, as with schema IA, we can introduce question marks to the right of the line separating premises and conclusion in schema II to indicate that what is also sought is a derivation of the conclusion from the premises:

Schema IIA

Theory
???
——————— ???
Fact to be explained

In one respect Maxwell's situation is represented by schemas II and IIA. Maxwell does begin with certain standard assumptions of kinetic theory, and his problem is to find auxiliary assumptions and to generate a distribution law. But there are two features of Maxwell's situation that schemas II and IIA do not reflect very accurately. First, the auxiliary assumptions Maxwell seeks are not of the sort that Putnam seems to have in mind. They are not initial or boundary conditions of some particular system (such as earth and sun), or of some particular type of system (such as two bodies) to which the more general theory is applicable. Rather they are assumptions about molecular velocities that are as general as those with which Maxwell begins his paper. More important, at least on one reasonable historical interpretation, Maxwell did not start with kinetic theory plus his distribution law (given by (6) and (7)) and then seek additional assumptions from which to derive that law. The reason is that he did not begin with the distribution law at all. His task, as he says himself in Proposition 4, is "to find" such a law. It is not to explain a law that he has already found.

Before he begins his derivation of the law Maxwell explains why he thinks there is such a law:

> If a great many equal spherical particles were in motion in a perfectly elastic vessel, collisions would take place among the particles, and their velocities would be altered at every collision; so that after a certain time the *vis viva* [kinetic energy] will be divided among the particles according to some regular law, the average number of particles whose velocity lies between certain limits being ascertainable, though the velocity of each particle changes at every collision.[23]

If the molecules were simply point particles colliding elastically there would be no changes in speeds (only in directions). But Maxwell is assuming that molecules are spherical, and spheres can collide in different ways, with different speeds resulting. Since Maxwell is assuming that the collisions are elastic, the total kinetic energy of all molecules remains constant. So the different

---

23. Maxwell, *op. cit.*, p. 380.

speeds of molecules must be consistent with conservation of kinetic energy, which leads him to think that there may be a general law governing the number of molecules with velocities within given limits, even if individual molecules are constantly changing their velocities.

Maxwell, in short, does not begin with the distribution law, but with a general description of the *type* of law he seeks (one that will give the number of molecules with velocities within given limits), and with some reason why he thinks there may be such a law. Putnam's schema II (or IIA) is therefore not quite applicable to Maxwell's situation, since the law was not a "fact known beforehand" by Maxwell.

Putnam does give a third schema, his final one, which like schema II he thinks is "neglected by standard philosophy of science":

Schema III

Theory
Auxiliary statements
_____

???

Here one begins with a theory and auxiliary statements, and the problem is to discover what consequences we can derive (and presumably to derive them, so that we might add question marks to the right of the line). "Knowing whether a set of statements has testable consequences at all depends upon the solution to this type of problem, and the problem is frequently of great difficulty. . . . "[24]

I think Putnam is mistaken when he claims that standard philosophy of science neglects schema III. For hypothetico-deductivists, as well as for Mill, this schema represents one possible problem situation in the "computational" stage of theorizing (the other possible situation in this stage for these methodologists is that of IA). After the theory and auxiliary statements have been proposed the problem is to determine what new observational conclusions follow that can be tested directly. Schema III — or rather a variation of it in which there are question marks to the right of the line indicating the need to construct a derivation — reflects this quite nicely.

Schema III partly captures Maxwell's situation, since his problem is to discover a velocity distribution law that will be a consequence of kinetic theory plus additional assumptions. But in several respects it is not applicable to Maxwell. As noted in the discussion of schema II, Maxwell does not begin with a set of auxiliary statements. He needs to find such statements. Second, unlike the situation suggested by schema III, Maxwell's problem is not to discover what (interesting, testable) consequences, if any, follow from his theory + A.S., but to discover a *law of a particular type*, one that gives

---

24. Putnam, *op. cit.*, p. 262.

molecular velocities. Third — and this is something I will discuss in section 5 — contrary to what I believe Putnam would claim about schema III, Maxwell, at least at the point at which he is attempting to find a distribution law, is not seeking consequences of his theory *that he can test.*

Included among Putnam's schemas and variations of them I have suggested are ones represented in standard methodologies of section 1 as applied to problem situations in which derivations are constructed from theories. But the schemas given above fail to do justice to Maxwell's problem situation.[25] To give a schema that would fare better here we might write:

Schema IV

Theory
???
——————————   ???
???   (fact of a certain specified kind to be derived)

Here one begins with a theory, say standard assumptions Maxwell gives for kinetic theory. One seeks to discover a fact or law *of a certain kind* (e.g., one that gives the number of molecules with velocities between given limits), although the particular fact or law is not known beforehand. One seeks to discover new assumptions to be added to the theory presented at the outset, which, together with that theory, will yield a specific fact or law of the kind desired. And one seeks to construct a derivation that will demonstrate this (hence the question marks to the right of the line). The specific fact to be derived may or may not be directly testable. And the new assumptions to be added to the theory may or may not involve initial or boundary conditions for a particular type of system to which the more general theory applies.

As noted earlier, Putnam thinks that schema II rather than schema I represents the "puzzle solving" of "normal science." And he holds that this observation will enable us to appreciate the "relative unfalsifiability of theories which have attained paradigm status." In the problem situation of schema II the theory is not a candidate for confirmation or falsification, since "it is not functioning in a hypothetical role."[26] Putnam also claims that schema II will enable us to understand why what is derived from a theory are frequently

———————————

25. Nor would the bootstrapping schema, which would look like this:

Observations
Theory + A.S.
——————————————   ???(Computation)
Instance of hypothesis tested

Maxwell does not begin with observations and then compute values for quantities in the distribution law. See section 5.

26. Putnam, *op. cit.*, p. 264.

facts already known. Now, with schema IV, as with Putnam's II, we are dealing with a problem situation in which the theory is "unfalsifiable in the context."[27] In attempting to derive a velocity distribution law Maxwell is assuming basic tenets of kinetic theory. In this context the point is not to find confirmation or disconfirmation for those tenets. However, with schema IV, unlike Putnam's II, we have a problem situation in which the fact to be derived is not known beforehand, although the type of fact is. This situation may well be as common as the one Putnam emphasizes. Admittedly, some of the propositions that Maxwell derives in his paper were known beforehand by Maxwell and other kinetic theorists. Prime examples are the law relating the pressure of a gas to the mean square molecular velocity,[28] and Avogadro's law that equal volumes of gases under the same pressure and temperature have the same number of molecules.[29] But there are many other derivations yielding propositions (laws, formulas, etc.) not known beforehand. For example, given two systems of particles moving in accordance with his distribution law, Maxwell derives a formula for the number of pairs of particles, one from each system, whose relative velocity lies between given limits (Proposition 5); and he derives a formula relating the coefficient of internal friction to the mean velocity of molecules, their mean free path, and the density of the gas (Proposition 13).

I am not, of course, saying that all derivations are constructed in problem situations represented by schema IV. But many are. And when they are, as with Maxwell's distribution law, we have examples of one sort of scientific *discovery* (a theme that will be developed in section 6). The previous methodologies, which emphasize schemas I, IA, and III, as well as Putnam's II, fail to represent problem situations of this sort adequately.

It is this failure, I think, that accounts for the thought on the part of some that the "computational" stage of theorizing—when derivations are constructed—is of no physical interest (though it may present mathematical challenges). Thus, recall Hanson's view that when a law or hypothesis is fixed into an h-d system "original physical thinking is over."[30] The rest is just the "pedestrian process of deducing observational statements." But this is to ignore the fact that a law or an hypothesis fixed into an h-d system may generate questions calling for the discovery of new laws of certain types. And the deduction of such laws may require the introduction of new hypotheses and thus very original physical thinking. It is also to ignore the fact that what is to be derived may be just as "theoretical" as the hypotheses employed as premises. The derivation of Maxwell's distribution law is no "pedestrian process of

---

27. *Ibid.*
28. Maxwell, *op. cit.*, p. 389.
29. *Ibid.*, p. 390.
30. Hanson, *Patterns of Discovery*, p. 70.

deducing observational statements." Moreover, the derivation introduces important new physical assumptions that are statistical in nature.

5. TESTING AND EXPLAINING

The methodologies of section 1 stress the idea that derivations are constructed

> (a) To test theories empirically, or to explain some known fact that has already been tested empirically, or both.[31]

This thesis can be given different interpretations. But only on the weakest of these ((a_4) and (a_5) below) — ones that I think say considerably less than standard methodologies intend — does the thesis become plausible. According to the first interpretation, the claim that (a) is the reason for constructing a derivation is to be understood as implying that

> (a_1) A theoretical derivation is constructed by a scientist solely or principally to enable him or scientific contemporaries to test a theory empirically or to explain something that has been or can be tested by him or contemporaries.

If a scientist derives a proposition that neither he nor his peers know how to test, then his principal aim in producing the derivation has been defeated, since neither he nor his peers are in a position to use the result to test the theory.

Now the distribution law that Maxwell derived was not a tested fact known beforehand by him or other physicists. Nor was it tested empirically by Maxwell following its derivation. Indeed, he offers no clues about how it could be tested. Gas molecules are not directly observable, and Maxwell had no experimental way to determine or compare molecular velocities. Nor was Maxwell in a position to test the law by bootstrapping, a procedure that would require a computation of specific values for each quantity in the law from observed values of quantities. Expressing the distribution law for velocities as

$$N_{v,dv} = \frac{4}{\alpha^3 \sqrt{\pi}} \, v^2 e^{-v^2/\alpha^2} dv$$

the left-hand side gives the number of molecules whose velocity lies between v

---

31. This is represented in Putnam's schema I, in which what is derived are predictions, and the problem is to see whether the predictions are true. It is also represented in Putnam's schema III, in which we begin with a theory + A.S. and the aim is to discover testable consequences. And it is represented in schemas IA, II, and IIA, in which what is derived is a fact already known, presumably having been tested.

and $v + dv$. Although Maxwell was able to compute a value for α (see below), and a value for v is chosen arbitrarily, he did not know how to compute N—the number of molecules in the gas.[32] But even if Maxwell had been able to determine all the quantities on the right side of the equation, he had no procedure for computing a value for $N_{v,dv}$ for a given v, other than by computing values for quantities on the right side, which is precluded in bootstrapping. There are no other hypotheses in his theory that will permit an independent computation of a value for $N_{v,dv}$. In fact, direct experimental tests of Maxwell's distribution law became possible only in the twentieth century with molecular beam experiments.[33]

A defender of (a_1) can remain undaunted. It is not required that every derivation yield a prediction or fact that has been, or can be, tested by the scientist or the community. Following Braithwaite we can stress the idea of intermediate stages. The scientist constructs a series of derivations to propositions of diminishing generality. The point of a derivation is to generate some proposition that is itself testable by the scientist or community, or to generate something that, by means of other derivations, will ultimately yield such a proposition. So if Maxwell's derivation does not generate a testable distribution law, that is not sufficient to show that (a_1) fails to express the central role this derivation is intended to serve. We must look to see what, if anything, Maxwell derives from his distribution law.

Maxwell does indeed use this law as a premise in other derivations. But none of the propositions derived is empirically testable by Maxwell or his contemporaries. For example, from the distribution law Maxwell derives the following formulas for the mean velocity of molecules and for the mean square velocity:

(1) $$\text{Mean velocity} = \frac{2\alpha}{\sqrt{\pi}}$$

(2) $$\text{Mean value of } v^2 = \frac{3}{2}\alpha^2$$

---

32. Maxwell did not know how to determine Avogadro's number; if he had he could have determined N by choosing a quantity of gas equal in mass to the molecular weight of the gas.

33. For a description of some initial experiments in the 1920s see Jas. P. Andrews, "The Direct Verification of Maxwell's Law of Molecular Velocities," *Science Progress* 23 (1928-1929), pp. 118-123. Andrews does not regard even these experiments as conclusive but only as a beginning. Indeed he remarks at the outset of his paper: "It is a curious fact that a law of such fundamental importance as Maxwell's Law of Distribution of Molecular Velocities should have so little direct experimental verification, and should have had to wait so long for such verification as does exist. So far as I am aware, no frontal attack was made upon such a problem until well into this [twentieth] century, in spite of the fact that Maxwell's first paper on the subject appeared in 1860" (p. 118).

where α is the undetermined constant in Maxwell's distribution law. (The first derivation, for example, proceeds by solving the integral

$$\int_0^\infty N \frac{4}{\alpha^3 \sqrt{\pi}} v^2 e^{-v^2/\alpha^2} dv$$

whose function is Maxwell's velocity distribution function, and dividing the result by N, the total number of molecules in the sample.) Since α is undetermined, the consequences are obviously not testable. Later in his paper Maxwell does relate α to the pressure and the density of the gas. (He derives the law $p = (1/3)MNv^2$, relating the pressure p of a gas to the mean square velocity v^2. Taking Boyle's law as $p = k\rho$, where ρ = density, from the pressure law and (2) above he derives $\alpha^2 = 2k$. So if we know the pressure and the density of the gas at constant temperature we can compute α.) Therefore, at a given temperature, from measurements of pressure and density we can compute values for mean velocity and mean square velocity. But this is not by itself enough to test (1) and (2). For this purpose, as emphasized in the bootstrap approach, we need either another, independent way to compute α, or a way to compute mean molecular velocity independently of (1), neither of which Maxwell supplies.

In an earlier (1857) paper on kinetic theory that Maxwell read, Rudolf Clausius also computes mean velocities of various molecules at a temperature of $0°C$.[34] He computes specific speeds for molecules of oxygen, nitrogen, and hydrogen. And although Maxwell makes no such specific computations in his paper, we might suggest using the ideas he does present to compute these values. If they conform to the values computed by Clausius, this might be thought to be some empirical test, albeit indirect, for Maxwell's distribution law.[35]

Unfortunately, this is not the case. Clausius' computation, like Maxwell's derivation of $\alpha = 2k$, is based on the use of the formula relating pressure to mean square molecular velocity. Clausius' calculation of mean molecular velocity at a given temperature depends on determining pressure, volume, and total mass of the gas. This is essentially the same in Maxwell, whose calculations (if he gave them) of mean molecular velocity, at a given temperature, would depend on determining pressure and density (total mass divided by volume). And Clausius, like Maxwell, offers no other method for determining molecular velocities.

Once more, however, defenders of (a_1) need not abandon course. If the law derived is not testable by the scientist or community, and if it is not used as a

34. Rudolf Clausius, "The Nature of the Motion Which we call Heat," in S. G. Brush, ed., *Kinetic Theory* (Oxford, 1965), vol. 1, pp. 111–134; see pp. 130–131.

35. This would not satisfy Glymour's bootstrapping, which would require in this case that $N_{v,dv}$ be computable.

premise in a derivation of something testable, then at least some proposition that is derived at some point from that law or from some consequence of the law is used as a premise in the derivation of something testable. In other words, the law generated in a derivation ultimately plays some role, however minimal and indirect, in the derivation of something that can be, or has been, tested by the scientist or his contemporaries. This, I think, is true of Maxwell's distribution law.

Maxwell does use a proposition derived from his distribution law, namely, (1) above (mean velocity = $2\alpha/\sqrt{\pi}$) as one assumption, among many, in a derivation of a formula for the mean free path of a molecule. (He gives the derivation in the course of discussing the internal friction of a gas.) The derived formula for mean free path (ℓ) is this:

$$\ell = 3/2 \frac{\mu}{\rho} \sqrt{\frac{\pi}{2k}}$$

where μ is the coefficient of internal friction of a gas. He takes a value for μ/ρ supplied by Stokes in experiments on air, and from this and the value $\sqrt{k} = 930$ feet per second for air at 60° (for which he provides no calculation) he derives $\ell = 1/447{,}000$th of an inch for the mean distance traveled by a molecule between collisions. Later in the paper (when he is discussing the diffusion of two gases through each other) he also uses the same consequence of the distribution law, namely (1), as one assumption, among many, in deriving a different formula for mean free path. Using this second formula,[36] and using the results of an experiment by Graham, which is quoted by Herapath, he derives a value of $\ell = 1/389{,}000$th of an inch for mean free path. Maxwell at the end of the paper[37] notes that these two values for ℓ are "not very different." Although he does not say so explicitly, he may well have taken this fact to provide some support for the hypotheses of kinetic theory. (On the bootstrapping approach the results of the experiments would provide support for the hypothesis

$$\ell = 3/2 \frac{\mu}{\rho} \sqrt{\frac{\pi}{2k}}$$

but not necessarily for other hypotheses in the theory.)

Maxwell also uses a consequence of the distribution law in a complex derivation of a proposition according to which the final state "of any number of systems of moving particles of any form is that in which the average *vis*

---

36. Maxwell, *op. cit.*, p. 403 (formula [57]).
37. *Ibid.*, p. 409.

viva of translation along each of three axes is the same in all systems, and equal to the average *vis viva* of rotation about each of the three principal axes of each particle."[38] This result can be tested by comparison with experiments on the ratio of specific heat at constant pressure to specific heat at constant volume. The experimental value of the specific heat ratio is 1.408, which requires that the ratio of total *vis viva* to translational *vis viva* be 1.634, whereas Maxwell's theoretical value for the latter ratio is 2. Accordingly, by contrast with the mean-free-path results, he takes the present results to be "decisive against the unqualified acceptation of the hypothesis that gases are such systems of hard elastic particles" (p. 409). (I take Maxwell at his word here. He does not regard this as a complete refutation of the ideas of kinetic theory, but only as decisive against the particular version he is considering, which depends on molecules exerting only contact forces; in his later 1866 paper he modifies this idea by assuming that molecules exert forces on each other that vary as the inverse fifth power of the distance.)

In any case, it seems clear — in the two instances I have mentioned — that there are some propositions derived from his distribution law that Maxwell uses as premises in the derivation of something testable. Accordingly, he does satisfy the aim expressed in a weak version of (a_1). But if a derivation is to generate consequences that can be tested by the scientist or community, or to lead to other derivations that do, then, although Maxwell's derivation of his distribution law satisfies this condition, it does not do so in a particularly robust way. So far as I can determine, these are the only testable consequences Maxwell generates in which at least some use is made of a consequence of the distribution law. (In general, although Maxwell constructs numerous derivations in his paper, not very many yield testable or tested conclusions.)

Do we want to say that at least the weak condition on derivations must be satisfied? If a derivation constructed by a scientist leads to a conclusion he cannot test, must he use this conclusion to construct another derivation, or a series, that eventually yields a testable proposition? Even if this were required, it would not follow that the only or even the principal role of any derivation is ultimately to generate such consequences. There may be other equally important roles (which will be discussed in subsequent sections). With this in mind, we might weaken (a_1) still further:

(a_2) Among the reasons a theoretical derivation is constructed by a scientist (though not necessarily the only or even the principal one) is to obtain some proposition — either from the derivation itself or from other derivations that use the conclusion of this one — that he or his peers can test and use to support or disconfirm the theory.

---

38. *Ibid.*, pp. 408–409.

However, even the aim expressed here is not always satisfied by papers in theoretical physics.

In an important paper that preceded Maxwell's, Clausius gives three derivations from kinetic theory.[39] In none of the three does he generate a proposition that he or his peers could test; nor does he use the proposition derived, or any consequence of it, to generate testable propositions. Clausius first derives the pressure law in the form

$$3/2pv = \frac{nmu^2}{2}$$

in which p = pressure of a gas, v = volume, n = total number of molecules, m = mass of a molecule, and u = mean velocity of a molecule. This is not a testable proposition, since Clausius has no independent way to determine u. He then uses this law, as a premise in a second derivation, to derive values of mean velocities of various molecules, also not testable. In his third and final derivation he derives a numerical value for the ratio of translatory kinetic energy of the molecules in a gas to the total internal energy of the gas (again not testable). And, of course, Clausius offers no experimental evidence in favor of any of the three propositions derived.

It is interesting to note that, unlike some kinetic theorists, Clausius does not derive the ideal gas law PV = constant $\times T$, which might be taken to be a known empirical fact. Instead he uses this law as a separate assumption, and from it, together with the pressure law, derives

$$\frac{nmu^2}{2} = \text{constant} \times T$$

Thus he deduces that the absolute temperature of a gas is proportional to u^2, the mean square velocity of the molecules.

To reject (a_1) and (a_2) is not to imply that testing a theory or using it to explain what has been tested is unimportant to the physicist or that it is done without benefit of derivations. Indeed many theoretical derivations do perform one or both of these functions. Maxwell gives a derivation of Boyle's law from kinetic theory that can be said to explain that law — one previously tested. (Unlike Clausius, Maxwell does not use Boyle's law, or rather the ideal gas law, as an additional assumption, from which to deduce that the temperature of a gas is proportional to the mean square molecular velocity.) Moreover, Maxwell does derive a new observational prediction from kinetic theory, namely, that the coefficient of internal friction of a gas (the coefficient of viscosity) is independent of the density of the gas. (Indeed, he remarks that

---

39. Clausius, *op. cit.*, pp. 125–134.

the only experiment he has met with on this subject does not seem to confirm this prediction, but he does not indicate what this experiment is.)[40] What I am questioning is the idea that a derivation is always constructed by a scientist to enable him or peers to test a theory empirically or to explain something that has been or can be tested. If this idea were true, then we could not accord a very high value to Maxwell's derivation of his velocity distribution law in his first paper on kinetic theory or any value to Clausius' three derivations in his paper.

As I construe the four methodologies of section 1 they imply: (i) that at least one of the purposes in constructing any derivation (if not the only or the principal one) is to test a theory empirically, or to explain some tested fact, or both, and (ii) that a derivation should generate some proposition (either from the derivation itself or from subsequent ones) that can be tested by the scientist constructing the derivation or by peers. Therefore, I regard these methodologies as being committed at least to (a_2), if (a_1) seems too strong. However, it is possible that some defenders of one of these methodologies might propose a view weaker than either of these:

(a_3) Among the reasons a theoretical derivation is constructed by a scientist is to obtain some proposition (either from the derivation itself or a subsequent one) that may someday be capable of being used to test the theory, even if neither those who construct the derivation nor their peers have or will have any idea how to test the proposition derived from this derivation or the subsequent ones.

This introduces "testability at some later date"; such testability need not be the only or even the principal aim in producing a derivation; and it does not require each conclusion of the derivation to be testable even at a later date.

The idea that a theory should be testable, at least at some point in time, would seem to be a basic, if minimal, commitment of empiricist methodology. And if the theory is highly "theoretical," then constructing derivations may be necessary, even if not sufficient, for generating propositions that can be used to test the theory. Even so, (a_3) is too strong.

To see why, we need to distinguish the (or a) purpose or reason for which something is constructed or created from conditions that (one hopes or intends) the construction will satisfy. A bridge may be constructed over a channel to enable cars to cross the channel. A condition may be imposed that the bridge is to be aesthetically attractive. But the bridge is not (or need not be) constructed for the purpose of making something that is aesthetically attractive. Similarly, a theoretical derivation may be constructed subject to the condition (or with the hope or intention) that it is mathematically valid, or that it generate something testable that can be used to test the theory. But it does not necessarily follow that the derivation is constructed for the purpose

---

40. Maxwell, *op. cit.*, p. 391.

of producing something that is mathematically valid or for the purpose of generating something testable that can be used to test the theory. Accordingly, we might put the acceptable ideas of (a_3) as follows:

> (a_4) Although this is not necessarily a reason or purpose for which a scientist constructs a given theoretical derivation, a scientist wants the derivation to satisfy the condition that what is derived should at some point in time be capable of being tested and being used to test the theory.

I am prepared to accept (a_4). But it is substantially different from the position of standard methodologies, which I take to be a thesis about at least one (principal) reason or purpose for which theoretical derivations are constructed, and not simply about a condition that scientists impose on such derivations or hope they will satisfy. Moreover, when standard methodologies speak of testing theories and of the role of derivation in this regard, I construe this to require something stronger than "testability at some later date." A scientist can hardly be testing a theory if he derives consequences from it that neither he nor anyone else in the scientific community knows how to test.

All of this is not to deny

> (a_5) *Some* theoretical derivations are constructed by a scientist principally to enable him or his peers to test a theory empirically or to explain something that has been or can be tested by him or his peers.

This is the only plausible thesis I can suggest that speaks of a role of derivations and contains a reasonably strong notion of testability. What I reject is a generalization of this to all derivations. Because standard methodologies mention only the "testing" and "explanatory" roles of theoretical derivations, someone reading such methodologies may be left with two false impressions: that derivations are always constructed to serve these roles and that there are no others.

---

6. THE ROLE OF THEORETICAL DERIVATIONS IN DISCOVERY

There is, I suggest, a different role a theoretical derivation may have, namely, that of enabling a scientist

> (b) To discover a new theoretical proposition (law, etc.)

I do not mean that a derivation necessarily yields a discovery that some proposition is true. (The derivation may contain false assumptions or incorrect mathematical steps.) I mean only that such a derivation enables the scientist to discover some new proposition (putative law). What's so important about that?

Let us look again at Maxwell's kinetic theory. The basic assumptions of his theory—those he gives at the outset, which are the well-known ones shared by most other kinetic theorists—do not provide a wealth of information about gases. They tell us that gases are composed of minute particles moving rapidly in straight lines, that collide elastically with each other and with the container, and that act on each other only during impact. Maxwell also assumes that these particles are spherical rather than simple point masses, and that they obey Newtonian mechanics.

But without further effort on Maxwell's part by way of drawing conclusions from these assumptions and adding new ones, those in the basic set are silent on many issues. What exactly is the motion of molecules after collision? Are all directions of rebound equally likely? What is the distribution of molecular velocities? What is the mean distance traveled by a molecule before striking another (mean free path)? What is the precise relationship between the pressure of a gas and the velocity of the molecules? What is the friction between layers of molecules in a gas? And so on. Maxwell's main concern at this point is to articulate the theory further, to develop it so that it can answer these theoretical questions. The method he adopts for this purpose is that of deriving answers from the basic assumptions together with new ones that must be added. In short, his situation is that of schema IV, which can now be developed further.

In schema IV, how does the scientist decide what type of fact needs to be discovered? Maxwell's kinetic theory entails that in a gas containing N molecules there is some number of molecules (ranging from zero to N) with velocities within some small range between v and $v + dv$ for each v. Maxwell raises the question: What is that number for each different velocity? The answer he seeks is to be subject to certain constraints, or as I prefer to say, it is to satisfy certain instructions.[41] The instructions Maxwell is following include at least these: find a mathematical formula; one that gives the number of molecules with velocities between v and $v + dv$ as a function of v and dv; one containing a fairly simple function. Such instructions, of course, do not determine a unique answer, but they do aid in the search. They tell us something about the kind of answer wanted (e.g., one involving a function of v and dv) as well as about kinds not wanted (e.g., a qualitative answer like "molecular velocities are distributed in the same manner as bullet holes around the bull's eye"—an answer Maxwell gives in his later paper "On the Dynamical Evidence of the Molecular Constitution of Bodies.")[42]

41. For a discussion of the concept of "instructions" and its role in explanations, see Peter Achinstein, *The Nature of Explanation* (New York, 1983).

42. Maxwell, *op. cit.*, vol. II, p. 428.

More generally, I shall say that a theory T *generates* a question Q_x of the form

Q_x: What is the quantity or relationship x?

if T entails that there is a quantity or relationship x. (If Q_x is generated by T, then we may refer to the question as $Q_{x,T}$.) Maxwell's kinetic theory generates the question: What is the number of molecules with velocities between v and $v + dv$ for each v?, because it entails that there is such a number. His theory also generates the question: What is the relationship between the pressure of a gas and the motion of its molecules?, since it entails the existence of such a relationship.

Let me speak of I as a set of *instructions* for answering a question Q if I is a rule or set of rules imposing conditions on answers to Q. The instructions may be brief or detailed; they may reflect very general methodological values ("give an answer that is quantitative") or specific empirical constraints ("give an answer that satisfies the principle of conservation of kinetic energy"). Among the constraints a scientist imposes on his answer to Q will be some pertaining specifically to theory T (e.g., that the answer be compatible with T or that it satisfy some particular principle in T). But there may be conditions imposed in I (e.g., give a numerical formula) that do not presuppose any particular claims of T.

Now let us construct the following schema to replace IV:

Schema V

$T, Q_{x,T}, I$
???
——————— ???
??? (proposition that answers Q_x in a way that satisfies I)

Schema V represents a problem situation in which the scientist begins not just with a theory T, but with a question $Q_{x,T}$ generated by the theory, and a set of instructions I for answering that question; and in which some new proposition is to be discovered rather than tested or explained. That proposition is to answer the question generated by the theory in a way that satisfies the instructions, and it is to be discovered by constructing a derivation from the theory together with additional assumptions. These conditions are obviously not sufficient to generate a new proposition. But they set a direction for research. We know what kind of proposition we are seeking (one that answers $Q_{x,T}$ in a way that satisfies I); we know a theory whose assumptions, among others, we must use; and we know we must derive the law from these assumptions plus others. These conditions provide at least as much guidance for the discovery of a new proposition as the h-d maxim "first guess the new law," or as Mill's condition that the law be inductively inferred from instances, or as the retroductivist condition that the new law, if true, be capable of explaining observed phenomena.

Still, it might be asked, what advantage is there in articulating a theory further by discovering new propositions in this manner if not to provide a means of testing that theory empirically or of using it to explain what has been tested empirically? Isn't doing (b) simply a means along the way of doing (a)? Here we face the fundamental question of the aims of scientific theorizing. Without attempting to deal exhaustively with this issue, let me simply note that the latter question would be answered in the negative by each of two opposing viewpoints — realism and antirealism — as these have been formulated by Bas van Fraassen. According to van Fraassen's realist, "Science aims to give us, in its theories, a literally true story of what the world is like; and acceptance of a theory involves the belief that it is true."[43] By contrast, van Fraassen's particular form of antirealism — "constructive empiricism" — is the view that "Science aims to give us theories which are empirically adequate; and acceptance of a theory involves a belief only that it is empirically adequate."[44]

If you are a realist, then, you view (b) — the discovery of new theoretical propositions — as a means of giving "a literally true story of what the world is like" (though, of course, not a means that is guaranteed to produce literal truth). Accordingly, you will find Maxwell's derivation of scientific value to the extent that it enables the construction of such a story by adding new parts to that story, and not simply to the extent that it enables kinetic theory to be tested empirically or to be used in explanations of observable phenomena.

By contrast, if you are an antirealist of van Fraassen's sort, you view (b) — the discovery of new theoretical propositions — as a means of furnishing "theories that are empirically adequate." A theory is empirically adequate "if what it says about observable things and events in the world is true — exactly if it 'saves the phenomena'. . . . Such a theory has at least one model that all the actual phenomena fit inside."[45] But you may supply a theory that is empirically adequate in van Fraassen's sense — a theory that has a model for all observable (not just observed) phenomena — without showing that it does have such a model, without testing that theory. In other words, the discovery of a new theoretical proposition via derivation can be of value to van Fraassen's antirealist, it can serve the aim of scientific theorizing, independently of whether it enables the scientist to test the theory empirically.

On both of these views, then, we can value a derivation for yielding new theoretical propositions, and thus for articulating a theory further, whether or not that derivation furnishes a test for the theory or an explanation of what has been tested.

---

43. Bas van Fraassen, *The Scientific Image* (Oxford, 1980), p. 8.
44. *Ibid.*, p. 12.
45. *Ibid.*

Maxwell's own views on the aims of theorizing are not easy to determine. And he may have changed them from one paper to another. But I think it is clear that although some of the theoretical derivations in his first kinetic theory paper are constructed to enable the physicist to test the theory empirically or to explain known phenomena, many others, such as the velocity distribution derivation, are given (among other reasons at least) to discover new theoretical propositions, particularly quantitative ones. At the outset of his paper he indicates that his aim is to investigate the "precise nature" of molecular motion, and to do so he seeks to "demonstrate the laws of motion of an indefinite number of small, hard and perfectly elastic spheres acting on one another only during impact."[46] Some of the laws giving this precise nature — such as the velocity distribution law — are not yet known. His aim is to discover them "by demonstration" — by deriving them from mechanical principles applied to a large number of elastic particles. Accordingly, at least part of what Maxwell is trying to do in such derivations is given by (b) above. His situation in these cases is depicted in schema V.

Maxwell does add the following famous paragraph:

> If the properties of such a system of bodies are found to correspond to those of gases, an important physical analogy will be established, which may lead to more accurate knowledge of the properties of matter. If experiments on gases are inconsistent with the hypothesis of these propositions, then our theory, though consistent with itself, is proved to be incapable of explaining the phenomena of gases. In either case it is necessary to follow out the consequences of the hypothesis.[47]

I take Maxwell to be saying the following. If the mechanical hypotheses he makes about the elastic spheres lead (via derivations) to observed properties of gases or to properties of gases that later become observed via experiments, we can conclude that there is a physical analogy between gases and such systems of elastic spheres. Even if we don't *identify* gases and systems of particles, the derivations will allow us to discover dynamical theorems about systems of elastic spheres, some of which may have analogues in the theory of gases; such derivations will also enable us to test the claim that gases and such mechanical systems are analogous. In point of fact, Maxwell in this paper does not stick consistently to his analogy talk, but frequently assumes that gases are, or are composed of, such systems of elastic spheres.[48] Several theorems he obtains pertaining to viscosity and specific heats are expressed in terms of gases, and these are taken to provide some test for the theory.

So it seems clear that Maxwell did want to produce derivations that would test kinetic theory, or minimally that would test whether there is a "physical

---

46. Maxwell, *op. cit.*, p. 377.
47. *Ibid.*, p. 378.
48. There is a discussion of this issue in Essay 7.

analogy" between gases and systems of elastic spheres. Such derivations would yield propositions about observed or at least observable properties of gases, so that they would satisfy (a). But it is equally clear that Maxwell wanted to produce derivations that would enable the discovery of new theoretical propositions about the "precise nature" of molecular motion, and hence satisfy (b). In the paper there are some derivations of the former sort. However, there are others that lead to the discovery of new theoretical propositions but only minimally and indirectly to the testing of the theory.

7. THE FOUNDATIONAL ROLE OF THEORETICAL DERIVATIONS

So far I have noted the role of theoretical derivations in enabling a scientist

> (a) To test theories empirically, or to explain what has been tested empirically, or both.

> (b) To discover a new theoretical proposition.

There is a third major role a derivation may have, namely, that of enabling a scientist

> (c) To provide a theoretical foundation for some proposition (law, etc.).

In using the term "foundation" I deliberately follow Maxwell who says that his aim is "to lay the foundation of such investigations on strict mechanical principles. . . . "[49] Here and elsewhere Maxwell advocates a program of "strict mechanical reasoning" in which the motions of particles and the forces producing such motions are considered. Maxwell recognizes that there are sciences (he mentions astronomy and "molecular mechanics") that need assumptions beyond those of ordinary mechanics. Admittedly, he writes,

> this science of molecular mechanics rests upon a much less certain basis than that of Astronomy. The superstructure however is an example of strict mechanical reasoning and may be found of use even when the fundamental assumptions have proved to be erroneous.[50]

The theoretical foundation supplied by mechanical reasoning will provide *explanations* of various things, and in doing so it will (under conditions I will note in a moment) provide theoretical *support* and *systematization* for certain

---

49. Maxwell, *op. cit.*, p. 377.
50. Maxwell, "Inaugural Lecture at Aberdeen," *Notes and Records of the Royal Society*, 1973, pp. 69–81.

propositions. To be sure, in discussing (a), the role of derivations in producing explanations has already been noted. But these are explanations of empirically tested or at least testable laws, such as Boyle's law. What I have in mind in (c) is something broader. It includes explanations (as well as justifications and systematizations) of theoretical facts that are not directly testable.

For example, Maxwell produces a derivation of Avogadro's law—that equal volumes of gases at the same pressure and temperature contain the same number of molecules. This law is not directly testable. Yet Maxwell seems to regard his derivation as providing a proof of the law, something indicated at the end of his paper when he summarizes his results:

> We have also proved that when two different gases act freely on each other (that is, when at the same temperature), the mass of the single particles of each is inversely proportional to the square of the molecular velocity; and therefore, at equal temperature and pressure, *the number of particles in unit of volume is the same.* [Maxwell's italics; they give Avogadro's law][51]

Even if Maxwell is using "proof" here only in the sense of "derived from the assumptions"—a sense that does not entail that what is proved is true—I think he regards the derivation as providing some theoretical support for the law. Avogadro's law when first proposed in 1811 had no such support. Avogadro did not derive it from mechanical assumptions about gases, but postulated it to help explain Gay-Lussac's law that gases combine in simple ratios by volume. In a later paper entitled "On the Dynamical Evidence of the Molecular Constitution of Bodies," Maxwell gives a more qualitative derivation of Avogadro's law (which he mistakenly identifies as being due to Gay-Lussac), and he writes:

> This law, however, has hitherto rested on purely chemical evidence, the relative masses of the molecules of different substances having been deduced from the proportions in which the substances enter into chemical combination. *It is now demonstrated on dynamical principles.*[52]

At the beginning of this paper Maxwell emphasizes the importance of "dynamical" explanations:

> When a physical phenomenon can be completely described as a change in the configuration and motion of a material system, the dynamical explanation of that phenomenon is said to be complete. We cannot conceive any further explanation to be either necessary, desirable, or possible, for as soon as we know what is meant by the words configuration, motion, mass, and force, we see that the ideas which they

---

51. Maxwell, *Scientific Papers* I, p. 409.
52. Maxwell, *Scientific Papers* II, p. 430; emphasis mine.

represent are so elementary that they cannot be explained by means of anything else.[53]

I take Maxwell to be claiming something like this. The derivation of Avogadro's law from kinetic theory (a theory built on dynamical principles pertaining to the configuration, motion, mass, and forces of molecules in gases) shows that kinetic theory provides theoretical support for that law. It does so because (i) the dynamical principles of the kinetic theory, if true, would in all probability correctly explain that law via the derivation, and because (ii) those principles themselves have some evidential support.

More generally, we might say that, given background information b, a theory T provides (at least some) theoretical support for a proposition L by means of a derivation d if and only if

1. $p(T$ correctly explains L via $d/T\&L\&b$ & $\text{Der}(L,T,d)) > k$
   ($\text{Der}(L,T,d)$ means that L is derivable from T via d).

2. b is or contains some evidence for T.[54]

---

53. *Ibid.*, p. 418. Peter Heimann (now Harman), "Molecular Forces, Statistical Representation, and Maxwell's Demon," *Studies in History and Philosophy of Science* 1 (1970), pp. 189–211, claims that after 1870 Maxwell used the expression "dynamical method" to refer to one involving equations of motion that permit tracing the course of each particle in a system; and that he contrasted this with the "statistical method." Consequently (according to Harman) Maxwell came to regard the statistical method, but not the dynamical one, as applicable to gases. In a review of a book on kinetic theory by H. W. Watson [*Nature* 16 (1877), pp. 242–246], Maxwell does use "strict dynamical method" in the manner Harman indicates. But in "The Dynamical Evidence of the Molecular Constitution of Bodies" (1875)—from which the quotation in the text is taken—Maxwell is clearly using a broader concept of dynamical. Maxwell's characterization of "dynamical" in this paper does not require the possibility of tracing each particle in the system; nor does it preclude statistical concepts. All that Maxwell requires for a dynamical approach is that the system contain bodies in motion subject to forces obeying Newtonian laws and that it be describable using concepts such as configuration, motion, mass, and force (and others definable by reference to these). Statistical concepts such as mean square velocity can be readily introduced by definition in terms of these. And there are numerous occasions in the paper on which Maxwell claims to be applying a "dynamical method" to gases, even when he is employing statistical concepts.

54. Definitions of "correct explanation" and "evidence" that can be used to supplement this are to be found in Peter Achinstein, *The Nature of Explanation*, ch. 10. For a general account of when and how derivations are explanatory, see *ibid.*, pp. 237–243, and "A Type of Non-Causal Explanation," *Midwest Studies in Philosophy* IX (1984), pp. 221–243. It should not be assumed that any derivation of L from T is explanatory (and therefore that the probability value in the definition is necessarily 1). Also, it should be noted that the definition of theoretical support given above is relativized to the background information. If a part b' of b is evidence for T, then it must be so relative to b. On the definition of evidence I advocate in *The Nature of Explanation*, this entails that $p(T/b'\&b)$ must be greater than some threshold value k. If this condition for evidence is satisfied, and if $k \geq 1/2$, then, given b, if b' is evidence for T, there can be no part of b that is evidence that T is false. Finally, if L is derivable from T, then the occurrence of L on the right side of the probability in condition 1 is redundant. However, it will be retained for ease of comparison with other concepts in the appendix.

The first condition is that the probability that T correctly explains L via d, given that T and L and b are true and that L is derivable from T via d, is greater than some threshold value k. The second condition will be construed as requiring some evidence for each of the theory's assumptions, or at least for those utilized in d. (See the appendix for a discussion of a weaker version of this second condition and for other matters pertaining to theoretical support.)

Is this a reasonable interpretation of Maxwell's claim for Avogadro's law with respect to kinetic theory? Since Maxwell derives Avogadro's law from dynamical assumptions about molecules—assumptions he explicitly regards as providing the very best sort of explanation—I believe that condition 1 is satisfied (at least as far as he is concerned). To determine whether condition 2 is satisfied we need to know whether Maxwell had background information that provided at least some evidence for kinetic theory.

There were, I suggest, two sorts of considerations that Maxwell regarded as relevant here. First, there were observations concerning heat. In his book *Theory of Heat*, published in 1871, Maxwell invokes in support of kinetic theory certain facts known to him well before the publication of his first kinetic theory paper. He points out that heat is transferable from a hotter to a colder body by radiation, which must involve some motion of matter in the intervening space between the bodies. Such motion could only be caused by motion in the body radiating the heat. But, Maxwell continues, this is not a motion of the body as a whole, nor of any of its visible parts (which during heat transfer are observed to be stationary). So, he concludes,

> The motion which we call heat must therefore be a motion of parts too small to be observed separately. . . . We have now arrived at the conception of a body as consisting of a great many small parts, each of which is in motion. We shall call any one of these parts a molecule of the substance. . . . [55]

Thus, Maxwell believed that known facts about heat radiation constituted at least some evidence for the assumption that invisible particles exist as constituents of bodies, that these particles are in motion, and that their motion is responsible for heat radiation. In fact Joule (who discovered the mechanical equivalent of heat) had offered a somewhat similar argument in 1847, and Maxwell was aware of Joule's work.

Second, Maxwell explicitly cites the success of dynamical theories in other domains as providing at least some evidential support for kinetic theory. In his paper "On the Dynamical Evidence of the Molecular Constitution of Bodies," Maxwell claims that astronomy has been successful in analyzing observed motions of the heavenly bodies in accordance with dynamical prin-

---

55. Maxwell, *Theory of Heat* (London, 1875), pp. 304–305.

ciples applied to systems of bodies. He notes that "electrical science" has had similar success in analyzing the observed motions of electrified bodies. His reasoning seems to be this. If bodies are composed of particles in motion, then the success of Newtonian dynamical theory in other domains provides at least some evidence that this theory is applicable to the moving parts of bodies such as gases, even though these moving parts are unobservable. (Reference to the success of dynamical theories elsewhere is also made in Maxwell's Inaugural Lecture at Aberdeen in 1856, four years before his first kinetic theory paper was published, as well as in his Inaugural Lecture at King's College, London, in 1860.)

Of course, this is not to say that the background information establishes the kinetic theory or makes it extremely probable—a point Maxwell would have strongly urged, since he emphasizes the tentative and speculative character of the assumptions of kinetic theory. But he may well have been committed to the plausibility of that theory, based on what he regarded as some evidential support provided by observations of heat radiation and the success of other dynamical theories.

Unfortunately, this is something of an idealization. At best, Maxwell's background information provides evidence for only part of kinetic theory. He had no evidence for a number of crucial assumptions he makes in his theory. For example, he had no evidence to support his assumption that the only forces between molecules are contact forces (and hence that molecules travel in straight lines between collisions), or that molecules are spherical in shape (assumptions he in fact abandons in his second kinetic theory paper). Although these assumptions are fairly simple ones on the basis of which to make calculations, and perhaps for that reason alone are worth trying out, he had no empirical reason to support them. Both of these assumptions play central roles in Maxwell's derivation of Avogadro's law. On the definition of "theoretical support" given above—as I have been construing it—for Maxwell's kinetic theory to provide theoretical support for Avogadro's law by means of Maxwell's derivation, it is required that each of the assumptions of the theory—or at least those used to derive and explain the law—have some evidential support.

Perhaps this requirement is unnecessary. Why isn't the first condition— that $p(T$ correctly explains L via $d/T\&L\&b$ & $Der(L,T,d)) > k$—by itself sufficient for theoretical support? As I am construing theoretical support if, given background information b, a theory provides such support for a proposition L by means of a derivation, then, given b, there is at least some reason to think that L is true. But given b, the fact that the probability is greater than some threshold value that T correctly explains L via d, given $T\&L\&b$ & $Der(L,T,d)$, by itself yields no reason at all to think that L is true. There are numerous theories—some perfectly wild—which, *if true*, would probably correctly explain L via some derivation. But these provide no support for L.

To take a simple nonscientific example, let L = my car won't start. Let theory T = last night five monkeys escaped from the zoo, siphoned all the gas from my tank and substituted crushed bananas; let T also contain the principle that a car without gas won't start. An obvious derivation d may be constructed from T to L. Let b be "normal" background information which includes the fact that monkeys have never been known to do such things. Still T *if true* would in all probability correctly explain L via d.[56] But, given b, no support is accorded L by means of the derivation in theory T. The problem in such a case is that b provides no evidence whatever in support of T; if anything, it provides evidence that T is false.

The fact that a proposition can be derived from a theory in a way that would count as a correct explanation if the theory were true does not necessarily mean that the proposition receives support from that theory. However, when a theory that satisfies the explanation condition 1 does have some evidence in its favor, it can provide support for theoretical propositions that it explains. Even if, given Maxwell's background information, his kinetic theory did not furnish theoretical support for Avogadro's law by means of his derivation, this does not preclude theoretical support for this law based on other versions of kinetic theory or on additional background information. Under appropriate conditions there may be theoretical support for the law derived.

In discussing a "theoretical foundation" for a proposition I have spoken of explanation and support. There is one further aspect that deserves mention, the idea of *systematization*. The scientist may seek an explanation not just for a single law but for many. And if he thinks that these laws govern the same or similar systems, then he seeks one set of theoretical principles to explain them all. Let me say that

> Theory T can be used to systematize $L_1, \ldots, L_n$ if and only if, for each L_i, T if true correctly explains L_i.

A systematization will be construed as a set of explanations:

> A set of explanations $E_1, \ldots, E_n$ is a systematization of $L_1, \ldots, L_n$ relative to theory T if and only if T can be used to systematize $L_1, \ldots, L_n$, and for each pair (E_i, L_i) in which E_i is an explanation of L_i, E_i uses principles of T.

Even if Maxwell's kinetic theory does not provide theoretical support for laws he derives from it, the theory can be used to systematize a set containing,

---

56. The probability here is not necessarily 1, since even assuming the truth of T it is possible that my car won't start for a different reason. For example, although the monkeys did siphon all the gas from my tank, they later replaced it; but my car won't start because the battery is dead.

among other things, the velocity distribution law, Boyle's law, and Avogadro's law. Maxwell constructs a set of derivations of these laws which explain why they hold. These explanatory derivations systematize this set of laws relative to the principles of kinetic theory. In general, derivations can play central roles in systematizing sets of laws that might otherwise be regarded as independent.

Suppose that, given the background information b, theory T provides theoretical support for each of the laws $L_1, \ldots, L_n$ by means of a set of derivations. Suppose further that for each L_i, T if true correctly explains L_i. Then by the foregoing definition, theory T can be used to systematize $L_1, \ldots, L_n$. But the converse is not true, since for each L_i, T if true can correctly explain L_i even though b contains no evidence for T. Capability of systematization is one reason for valuing a theory. It is not by itself a reason to think that what the theory says is true.

8. CONCLUSIONS

The derivation of Maxwell's distribution law has been used to challenge the idea that the only or at least a principal role of any theoretical derivation is (a) to provide an empirical test for a theory or to explain some known empirical fact. Such an idea is based on several schemas for problem situations. In one (schema IA) the scientist has a theory + auxiliary statements, together with some observed facts that the theory may be able to explain. The problem consists in constructing a derivation of those facts from the theory. In another (schema III) the scientist has a theory + auxiliary statements, and the problem is to construct a derivation or a series of derivations yielding new observational conclusions. Admittedly, theoretical derivations are constructed in such problem situations. But there are other problem situations—including the one faced by Maxwell in arriving at his distribution law—that are substantially different and that usual methodologies ignore. In these (represented by schema V) the scientist begins with a theory, a question generated by the theory, and instructions for answering that question. The problem is to find a proposition that will answer the question in a way satisfying the instructions, and to do so by adding new assumptions to the theory and constructing a derivation from them plus the theory to such a proposition. In this situation a derivation may enable the scientist (b) to discover some new theoretical proposition and (c) to provide a foundation for it that is theoretical rather than observational.

These are major roles of theoretical derivations which standard methodologies fail to explore. Such methodologies, I suggest, tend to be overly empirical in their orientation. Once a set of theoretical postulates has been proposed, these methodologies tend to stress only generating observational conclusions, either new predictions to test the theory or old observations that the theory can explain. And derivations are looked upon as the means of generating these observational conclusions. But if we think more broadly about the aims of theorizing—whether these include the answering of questions, or the telling of a "literally true story of what the world is like" (van Fraassen's realist) or even the search for "empirical adequacy" (van Fraassen's antirealist)—then the discovery of new theoretical propositions, and the furnishing of a theoretical foundation for them, become important desiderata. Theoretical derivations can play crucial roles in satisfying these ends.

APPENDIX. THEORETICAL SUPPORT

Several questions raised by the definition of theoretical support in section 7 are discussed in the following.

1. The proposed definition requires evidence for each assumption in the theory. Can we supply a plausible evidence condition for theoretical support that is weaker than this? Here is one possibility:

> (2)′ There are assumptions T^* in theory T such that b contains evidence for T^*; there are no assumptions T' in T such that b contains evidence that T' is false.

This requires that the background information contain evidence for *some* assumptions in the theory, while not containing evidence that other parts of the theory are false. If we combine (2)′ with the first condition—namely, that $p(T$ correctly explains L via $d/T\&L\&b$ & $\text{Der}(L,T,d)) > k$—then we can show that, given Maxwell's background information b, his kinetic theory does provide theoretical support for Avogadro's law. (His background information, we agreed, does contain evidence for some, though not all, assumptions in his theory.) Moreover, (2)′ is still strong enough to prevent the "monkey theory" of section 7 from providing theoretical support for the claim that my car won't start. (In this case there is an assumption in the theory, namely, the monkey hypothesis, for which the background information provides disconfirming evidence.)

Unfortunately, (2)′ permits too much. Again consider a simple nonscientific example. Let L = Jones is dead. Let theory T contain three assumptions: (i) Smith disliked Jones; (ii) Smith decapitated Jones in a duel; (iii) a person who is decapitated in a duel dies. (There is an obvious derivation from T to L.) Let the background information b contain the fact that Jones insulted Smith, which, I shall assume, is evidence that (i) is true but is not strong enough to be evidence that (ii) is true. Furthermore, I shall assume that b contains no evidence that (ii) is false, or that L is true. (The background information simply gives us a reason to think that Smith disliked Jones, but gives us no reason to think that Smith did—or did not—dislike Jones enough to decapitate him in a duel, or indeed to think that Jones is dead.) Therefore, condition (2)′ is satisfied. So is the first condition for theoretical support, which requires that $p(T$ correctly explains L via $d/T\&L\&b$ & $Der(L,T,d)) > k$. If we combine (2)′ with the latter we shall have to say that, given our background information, by means of the derivation from T to L, theory T above provides theoretical support for the claim that Jones is dead. But this conclusion seems unwarranted since, despite the theory and the derivation, there is no reason to think that Jones is dead. Our background information does furnish evidence for part of the theory (for the claim that Smith disliked Jones). But it does not supply evidence for a central part of the theory needed to explain Jones' putative death (*viz.*, that Smith decapitated Jones in a duel)—which seems to be required in order to obtain theoretical support for the claim of death. Accordingly, I suggest retaining the stronger evidence condition in section 7.

2. If we adopt the definition of theoretical support in section 7, could there be theoretical support for a law in the absence of observational evidence in its favor? If, given observational background information b, theory T provides theoretical support for a law L by means of derivation d, must b itself be or contain evidence for L?

To try to answer this, let me invoke a definition of evidence that I defend elsewhere,[57] according to which

> (1) b is evidence that L if and only if (i) b is true; (ii) b does not entail L; (iii) $p(L/b) > k$; (iv) p(there is an explanatory connection between L and $b/L\&b) > k$.

There is an "explanatory connection" between L and b if L correctly explains b, or b correctly explains L, or some hypothesis correctly explains why both b and L are true.

Now recall our definition of theoretical support, according to which:

> (2) Given b, theory T provides theoretical support for L by means of d if and only if (a) $p(T$ correctly explains L via $d/T\&L\&b$ & $Der(L,T,d)) > k$; (b) b is or contains some evidence for T.

Suppose that, given b, theory T does provide theoretical support for L by means of d. To simplify, suppose that b (rather than some proper part) is evidence for T. Then from (1) and (2) we have

> (3) (i) b is true; (ii) b does not entail T; (iii) $p(T/b) > k$; (iv) p(there is an explanatory connection between T and $b/T\&b) > k$.

---

57. *The Nature of Explanation*, ch. 10.

From (3) (iii) we have $p(T/b) > k$. But if L is derivable from T, then

(4) $p(L/b) > k$

And (4) is one condition that must be satisfied if [by definition (1)] b is to be evidence that L. So far so good.

Now, if given b, T provides theoretical support for L by means of d, then from (2)

(5) $p(T$ correctly explains L via $d/T\&L\&b$ & $\mathrm{Der}(L,T,d)) > k$

I am not assuming that (5) is true for every T, L, b, and d. Whether the probability is high that T correctly explains L via d depends on the particular theory and derivation. I am simply supposing that if, given b, T provides theoretical support for L by means of d, then (5) will hold.

Let us assume further that

(6) $p(T$ correctly explains b via $d'/T\&L\&b$ & $\mathrm{Der}(b,T,d')) > k$

This is to make an assumption about the relationship between theory T and the background information b that is analogous to that made about the relationship between T and L in (5). Finally, to construct the most favorable case for the claim we are considering, let us assume that

(7) $p(T$ correctly explains L via d, and T correctly explains b via $d'/$ $T\&L\&b$ & $\mathrm{Der}(L,T,d)$ & $\mathrm{Der}(b,T,d')) > k$

Now "T correctly explains L via d" entails "T correctly explains L." Therefore, from (7) we get

(8) $p(T$ correctly explains L, and T correctly explains $b/T\&L\&b$ & $\mathrm{Der}(L,T,d)$ and $\mathrm{Der}(b,T,d')) > k$

In virtue of the definition of "explanatory connection" given above, "T correctly explains L, and T correctly explains b" in (8) entails "there is an explanatory connection between L and b." Therefore, from (8) we infer

(9) $p($there is an explanatory connection between L and $b/T\&L\&b$ & $\mathrm{Der}(L,T,d)$ and $\mathrm{Der}(b,T,d')) > k$

If it were not for the appearance of T, $\mathrm{Der}(L,T,d)$, and $\mathrm{Der}(b,T,d')$ on the right side of the conditional probability in (9), then (4) and (9)—together with the assumption that b is true and does not entail L—would yield the conclusion that b is evidence that L.

The problem is just that for the probability of an explanatory connection between L and b to reach the k-threshold we need to relativize to theory T and to the fact that L and b are derivable from T. For b to be evidence that L— where, given b, T provides theoretical support for L by means of d—we want to derive

(10) p(there is an explanatory connection between L and $b/L\&b$) $> k$

But we have only been able to derive (9), which is not strong enough. *Given the theory T and the facts that Der(L, T, d) and Der(b, T, d'), and given L and b*, the probability of an explanatory connection between L and b is greater than k (in virtue of the fact that T explains L via d and b via d'). But without the assumption of T and of $\text{Der}(L, T, d)$ and $\text{Der}(b, T, d')$—given just L and b—we are not able to guarantee that the probability of an explanatory connection between L and b is greater than k. We are unable to guarantee that (10) is true. Nor can we do so even if we drop the relativization to the derivations and make the following assumption, which is even stronger than (8):

(11) p(T correctly explains L, and T correctly explains $b/T\&L\&b$) $> k$

From (11) we infer p(there is an explanatory connection between L and $b/T\&L\&b$) $> k$, which is still not strong enough, since it relativizes the probability to T. I suggest, therefore, that it is possible for a theory to provide theoretical support for a law L by means of some derivation, where b is evidence for T, without b's being evidence for L. This can occur when, given just b and L, the probability of an explanatory connection between b and L is less than k.

Suppose (counterfactually) that Maxwell did have evidence that the only forces between molecules are contact forces, and that molecules are perfectly elastic spheres. (Ignore gravity and electromagnetic forces and suppose that all the other forces in nature known to Maxwell were contact forces, and that all small particles he had observed were elastic spheres.) Combine this with the evidence he did have pertaining to heat radiation and the success of dynamical theories in other domains, and assume that he had evidence for each of the assumptions in kinetic theory he needs to produce a derivation of Avogadro's law. Would all this evidence also be evidence for Avogadro's law? Not necessarily. Given just this evidence and Avogadro's law—and not assuming the postulates of kinetic theory or any derivations from those postulates— the probability of an explanatory connection between just this evidence and Avogadro's law might not be high. In the absence of kinetic theory and derivations, facts of the sort we have described concerning heat radiation, the success of dynamical theories elsewhere, and observations of contact forces between spherical particles, do not by themselves constitute evidence for

Avogadro's law, even if they do constitute evidence for the postulates of kinetic theory, from which Avogadro's law can be derived.

We might be reminded here of the controversy surrounding the "special consequence" condition of evidence, according to which if e is evidence for h, and h entails h', then e is evidence for h'. On the definition of evidence given in (1), and on the concept of explanation which I advocate, this condition is not always satisfied.[58]

3. Can we broaden the account of theoretical support in section 7 to include the possibility of an "explanatory connection" between T and L, so that (2a) above is changed to

(2a)' p(there is an explanatory connection between T and L via d/ T&L&b & via d either L is derivable from T, or T from L, or both from some other hypothesis) $> k$

This is too broad for theoretical support. For example, let L = Boyle's law, and let T = kinetic theory. Then, where b is background information that includes results of tests on Boyle's law, and d is a derivation of Boyle's law from kinetic theory,

(i) p(there is an explanatory connection between L and T via d/T&L&b & Der(L,T,d)) $> k$

(ii) b contains evidence for L.

We would then have to conclude that Boyle's law provides theoretical support for kinetic theory by means of derivation d, which is false.

4. It might be noted that on the definitions of "evidence" and "theoretical support," some L could be evidence that T, while T provides theoretical support for L. For example, let L give the regularities observed in molecular beam experiments; let T be Maxwell's distribution law; let d be a derivation of the results of the experiments from the law; and let the background information b include L among other things. Then, given b, L is evidence that T. But given b, T provides theoretical support for L by means of d. Since this theoretical support for L is relativized to b, which includes L, there may appear to be something untoward here. But all we are saying is that given the observed results of molecular beam experiments, we have a theoretical reason—in addition to an observational one—for believing that those results obtain.

---

58. See *The Nature of Explanation*, pp. 362ff.

5. Is a more general definition of theoretical support possible that does not require a derivation (but includes the latter case as a possibility)? An obvious candidate is

(12) Given b, theory T provides theoretical support for L if and only if (a) $p(T$ correctly explains $L/T\&L\&b) > k$; (b) b is or contains some evidence for T.

This permits T to provide theoretical support for L by means other than a derivation. (We need not assume that all theoretical explanations require derivations.)

6. Finally, it will be noted that on the definitions of theoretical support given by (2) and (12) it is possible for a theory T to provide theoretical support for L even though T does not in fact correctly explain L. (Indeed T might not correctly explain L even though both T and L are true and L is derivable from T.) Following a procedure I advocate in the case of evidence,[59] we might want to distinguish two concepts of theoretical support. First, and most basically, there is a concept given by (2) and (12). (We might call this "potential" theoretical support.) Second, and derivatively, there is a concept of "veridical" theoretical support. Given b, theory T provides veridical theoretical support for L if and only if, given b, it provides potential theoretical support for L and T correctly explains L.*

---

59. *Ibid.*, ch. 10.

*For helpful comments I am indebted to Robert Kargon, William Taschek, Michael Liston, Abner Shimony, and John Earman.

ESSAY 7

Maxwell's Analogies
and Kinetic Theory

"In studying the constitution of bodies we are forced at the very beginning to deal with particles which we cannot observe."

J. C. MAXWELL

In the middle of the nineteenth century James Clerk Maxwell promulgated the use of analogies as a legitimate method of science. In his paper, "On Faraday's Lines of Force,"[1] Maxwell focused on what he called "electrical science," which, at the time, contained various laws of electricity and magnetism that had been empirically established but had not been related or systematized. His aim was to produce a "simplification and reduction of the results of previous investigation to a form in which the mind can grasp them" (vol. I, p. 155). There were two scientific methods for doing so that Maxwell rejected. First, the simplification might "take the form of a purely mathematical formula." But to use such formulas is to "entirely lose sight of the phenomena to be explained; and though we may trace out the consequences of given laws, we can never obtain more extended views of the connexions of the subject" (*ibid.*). The second method involves the use of physical hypotheses, which Maxwell treated as postulating the existence of unobservable, or at least unobserved, parts, structures, or causes. This he rejected on the grounds that it leads to a "blindness to facts and rashness in assumption which a partial explanation encourages." Hypotheses are generated on the basis of little or no evidence. By contrast, Maxwell sought a method of investigation that, unlike the use of pure mathematical formulas, would yield a "clear physical conception," but that, unlike the use of physical hypotheses, would not involve empirically unwarranted speculations about unobservable causes

---

1. W. D. Niven, ed., *The Scientific Papers of James Clerk Maxwell* (New York, 1965), vol. I, pp. 155–229. Unless otherwise noted, page references for Maxwell will be to this collection.

of electromagnetic phenomena. The method he advocated is the use of physical analogies.

Four years after the appearance of his first major paper on electromagnetism Maxwell published his first important work on kinetic theory ("Illustrations of the Dynamical Theory of Gases," vol. I, pp. 377–409). Here, as in the case of electromagnetism, Maxwell was aware of numerous empirically established generalizations about properties of gases, including pressure, temperature, volume, density, and specific heats, which he sought to relate and systematize. And, as might be expected, he says that he will do so by constructing a physical analogy. Yet his use of the concept of analogy in the latter case seems very different from that in electromagnetism — something that historians of methodology who have discussed Maxwell's analogy program have not, I think, sufficiently appreciated.[2]

In this essay I propose to describe Maxwell's method of physical analogy in his early work on electromagnetism, to ask whether he is employing an analogy when he first develops his kinetic theory, and to consider to what extent he goes beyond the idea of analogy in that theory and introduces hypotheses. This will help to illuminate both the advantages and limitations of the method. It will also have implications for the use of hypotheses about unobserved causes. Are such hypotheses methodologically important for a theory such as the one Maxwell develops about gases, and if so, why? Can they serve useful purposes even if the scientist who employs them is not committed to their truth or probability?

1. MAXWELL'S CONCEPT OF ANALOGY IN EARLY ELECTROMAGNETIC THEORY

Maxwell characterizes a physical analogy as follows:

> By a physical analogy I mean that partial similarity between the laws of one science and those of another which makes each of them illustrate the other. (vol. I, p. 156)

The best way to see what Maxwell means is to study his examples, particularly the one to which his paper is devoted. Let me characterize a part of this analogy briefly; this will suffice to enable us to draw a contrast between the present case and kinetic theory.

---

2. For papers on Maxwell's use of analogies that focus on electromagnetism, see Joseph Turner, "Maxwell on the Method of Physical Analogy," *British Journal for the Philosophy of Science* 6 (1955), pp. 226–238; Robert Kargon, "Maxwell and Analogy in Victorian Science," *Journal of the History of Ideas* XXX (1969), pp. 423–436; A. F. Chalmers, "Maxwell's Methodology and His Application of It to Electromagnetism," *Studies in History and Philosophy of Science* 4 (1973), pp. 107–164; Mary Hesse, *The Structure of Scientific Inference* (Berkeley, Calif., 1974), ch. 11.

Maxwell constructs an analogy between the electromagnetic field and a purely imaginary, incompressible fluid flowing through tubes of varying section. The velocity of the fluid at a given point represents the electrical force at that point, and the direction of the tube represents the direction of the electrical force. Particles of electricity are represented in the analogue as sources and sinks of fluid. And the electrical potential is represented by the pressure of the fluid. Maxwell shows that the velocity of the imaginary fluid at a distance r from a source will vary as $1/r^2$. Since velocity in the fluid represents the electrical force, we have a law for the fluid that is analogous in form to the law in the electrical case that the electrical force at a distance r from a source of electricity varies as $1/r^2$. We can tabulate these analogues as follows:

Electromagnetic field	*Incompressible fluid*
Electrical force at a point in the field	Velocity of fluid at a point in the fluid
Particle of positive electricity	Source of fluid
Electrical potential at a point	Pressure of fluid at a point
Satisfies law that the force due to a charged particle at a distance r from the particle varies as $1/r^2$	Satisfies law that the velocity of fluid at a distance r from the source of fluid varies as $1/r^2$

The general idea is to represent an electrical property P_i by some appropriate fluid property Q_i, and then demonstrate that Q_i satisfies a law similar to one satisfied by P_i. Maxwell makes it clear that in utilizing the analogy he is not supposing that the electromagnetic field is identical with, or is composed of, an incompressible fluid. Nor is he supposing that the fact that the electromagnetic field has a certain property is caused by an incompressible fluid's having some property. He is not assuming, for example, that what causes a charged body to exert an electrical force at a distance r is the fact that some fluid has a certain velocity at a distance r from its source (or that it is some fact that causes the fluid to have that velocity). As Maxwell writes,

> The substance here treated . . . is not even a hypothetical fluid which is introduced to explain actual phenomena. It is merely a collection of imaginary properties which may be employed for establishing certain theorems in pure mathematics in a way more intelligible to many minds than that in which algebraic symbols alone are used. (vol. I, p. 160)

Finally, in constructing the analogy Maxwell is making no assumptions about unobserved features of the electromagnetic field which cause it to have the properties and to satisfy the laws mentioned in the analogy. Although he may describe such causes for the analogue system, he does not assume that corresponding causes exist in the original system.

More generally, then, in a Maxwellian physical analogy we start with an original system that is known by observation to have properties $P_1, \ldots, P_n$ and to satisfy laws $L_1, \ldots, L_k$. We make assumptions about a second system (which may or may not exist) by ascribing properties to that system that represent properties of the original system, and we demonstrate that (and how) such properties satisfy laws similar to known laws governing corresponding properties in the original system. In the description of the second system we may invoke causes of properties ascribed to that system. But we do not assume that analogous causes exist in the original system if doing so would commit us to the existence of unobserved features of that system.

In what does the similarity between laws of the two systems consist? Maxwell uses the expression "resemblance *in form*" between the laws of the two systems. For example, the law of the velocity of the imaginary fluid has the same mathematical form $(1/r^2)$ as the law of electrical force. However, I do not think he means to deny the fact that certain *physical* resemblances in properties involved in these laws are part of the analogy.[3] In both cases, for example, we have a point that is at a distance r from the source of something (in the one case a source of fluid, in the other, of electricity). The important point for present purposes is only that in constructing an analogy between two systems involving two sets of properties, Maxwell does not suppose that the systems are identical, or that one system is contained in the other, or that the fact that one system has a certain property is caused by the other system's having some property. Nor does he assume that whatever causes the second system to have one of the mentioned properties has some (unobserved) analogue in the original system that causes it to have the corresponding property.

---

3. Mary Hesse, *op. cit.*, pp. 265–266, emphasizes this point. However, I take issue with her over a number of claims she goes on to make. First, she says that a Maxwellian physical analogy "begins with two or more *existing* physical systems" (p. 268, emphasis mine). Sometimes this is so, sometimes not. In "On Faraday's Lines of Force," where the idea of physical analogy is first introduced, the analogy is between the electromagnetic field and a nonexisting, imaginary, incompressible fluid. Second, she claims that "the general laws constituting the formal analogy between systems are themselves derived by direct inductive generalization from experiments." Again, this is not necessarily the case. In "On Faraday's Lines of Force," Maxwell does not derive laws governing the imaginary fluid by direct inductive generalization from experiments. He makes certain arbitrary assumptions about the fluid in order to generate laws that will be formally similar to those governing the electromagnetic field. Third, Hesse agrees that a Maxwellian physical analogy does not *postulate* unobservable entities or causes. Nevertheless, she seems to think (although I do not find this completely clear in her account) that such analogies permit some analogical *inferences* to unobservable entities or causes—perhaps to the laws that govern them—even if they do not permit a detailed specification of these entities or causes. However, in "On Faraday's Lines of Force," Maxwell seems to be denying this. He does not assume, or permit an inference to the assumption, that whatever causes the incompressible fluid to have a certain property has some unobserved analogue (however indefinitely described) in the electromagnetic field that causes it to have the corresponding property. Nor (*a fortiori*) does he permit an inference to laws that govern such an unobserved cause.

In general, to make these suppositions would be to introduce "physical hypotheses" about the unobserved parts and structure of the original system, which is something Maxwell's method of physical analogy is designed to avoid. Moreover, although he does use mathematical formulas in his construction, they are not "pure" ones. They describe a physical situation that the "mind can grasp," namely, the relationship between properties of the imaginary fluid.

Although a physical analogy does not introduce hypotheses about unobserved causes in the original system, it might be asked whether it provides the basis for analogical *inferences* to such causes. That is, given such an analogy, from the fact that C is the cause of some property in the analogue system can one legitimately infer that some unobserved analogous cause C' is responsible for the corresponding property in the original system? Maxwell does not discuss this, but I suggest that his answer ought to be: not necessarily. There are several types of physical analogies, including the following, in which such inferences would be precluded: (a) A physical analogy (such as the present electromagnetic one) in which the analogue system is purely imaginary and in which causes of properties $P_1, \ldots, P_n$ in the analogue are stipulated but these are "arbitrary" in the following sense: no reason is known or given to preclude the description of other analogue systems with properties $P_1, \ldots, P_n$, or with other analogues of properties in the original, that are produced by quite different causes. (b) A physical analogy that is based on purely formal similarities between laws governing the systems, not on physical similarities between the systems or between the properties invoked in the laws. (c) A physical analogy in which no causes for properties of the analogue system are postulated or known. (d) A physical analogy between some of the properties of the two systems that, because of the disanalogies that also exist, is too limited or weak to permit inferences from causes in one system to causes in the other.

However, even if some physical analogies provide a basis for analogical inferences to unobserved causes of properties in the original system, this would not alter what Maxwell says about the use of physical analogies. His aim in using an analogy is to "obtain physical ideas without adopting a physical theory" (vol. I, p. 156). By "adopting" a physical theory (concerning unobserved causes or parts) I take Maxwell to include one or both of the following: assuming, for the sake of argument, that such a theory is true and using it to explain and predict phenomena; believing such a theory to be true or probable. Should some physical analogy provide the basis for an analogical inference to a physical theory concerning unobserved causes, one can still utilize the analogy—one can use certain properties in the analogue system to represent properties in the original and show that laws relating these properties are similar in form to laws relating corresponding properties in the original—without adopting that physical theory. In constructing and employing the analogy one need not assume or believe that such a theory is true and use it to explain and predict phenomena. One need not draw the inference for which the analogy may provide some basis.

Nevertheless, I take Maxwell's viewpoint to be stronger than this. If a physical analogy provides the basis for a legitimate inference to an hypothesis regarding unobservable features of the original system, then, even if the scientist does not "adopt" that hypothesis, he is in a position to do so. If there is a physical analogy that sanctions such an inference, why should such an hypothesis be avoided? Yet in "On Faraday's Lines of Force" Maxwell explicitly seeks to avoid such hypotheses. Accordingly, at least in this paper I take Maxwell's position to be this: Granted it is possible to construct a physical analogy that makes use of hypotheses about unobservables, or that provides the basis for an analogical inference to such hypotheses, the method of physical analogy is to be used when there is no legitimate basis for such hypotheses (from the analogy or elsewhere). Therefore, when Maxwell speaks of this method I take him to have in mind the use of those analogies that avoid such hypotheses and that do not sanction valid inferences to them.

2. KINETIC THEORY

In 1860, four years after "On Faraday's Lines of Force," Maxwell published "Illustrations of the Dynamical Theory of Gases," his first major contribution to kinetic theory. He begins the paper thus:

> So many of the properties of matter, especially when in the gaseous form, can be deduced from the hypothesis that their minute parts are in rapid motion, the velocity increasing with the temperature, that the precise nature of this motion becomes a subject of rational curiosity. (vol. I, p. 377)

He proceeds to indicate assumptions that have been made about such particles by Bernoulli, Herapath, Joule, Krönig, and Clausius, among others, and that (as it turns out) he also makes in his paper. For example, it is assumed that gases are composed of unobservable particles, that these particles are in motion, that their velocity increases with the temperature of the gas, that they move with uniform velocity in straight lines striking against the sides of the container, producing pressure, that the particles are perfectly elastic spheres acting on each other only during impact, and that their motion is subject to mechanical principles of Newtonian mechanics (p. 378).

At this point Maxwell introduces the idea of physical analogy:

> If the properties of such a system of bodies are found to correspond to those of gases, an important physical analogy will be established, which may lead to more accurate knowledge of the properties of matter. (p. 378)

At the end of the paper just before summarizing his results Maxwell speaks once more in terms of analogy:

> We have now followed the mathematical theory of the collisions of hard elastic particles through various cases, in which there seems to be an analogy with the phenomena of gases. (p. 409)

Although Maxwell uses the analogy idiom in his paper, there seems to be an important difference between the use of the method of analogy here and that in "On Faraday's Lines of Force." In the latter Maxwell uses the method of analogy to avoid physical hypotheses. That is one of its chief merits, since it can be used in such a way that unestablished speculations are excluded. Yet in his kinetic theory paper Maxwell seems not to be avoiding physical hypotheses about gases but to be reveling in them! He introduces the very speculative idea that gases are composed of an enormous number of unobservable spherical bodies of the sort he describes. Using these physical hypotheses about gases he proceeds to derive various theoretical and observational results about gases, including his distribution law for molecular velocities, Avogadro's law, Boyle's law, and a host of others.

Indeed, his procedure here might be thought to involve a fairly typical use of the method of hypothesis, or hypothetico-deductive method, which Maxwell characterized in later writings and rejected:

> In attempting the extension of dynamical methods to the explanation of chemical phenomena, we have to form an idea of the configuration and motion of a number of material systems, each of which is so small that it cannot be directly observed. We have, in fact, to determine, from the observed external actions of an unseen piece of machinery, its internal construction.
>
> The method which has been for the most part employed in conducting such inquiries is that of forming an hypothesis, and calculating what would happen if the hypothesis were true. If these results agree with the actual phenomena, the hypothesis is said to be verified, so long, at least, as some one else does not invent another hypothesis which agrees still better with the phenomena. (vol. II, p. 419)

In this later paper, Maxwell rejects the method of hypothesis on the grounds that those who use it either "leave their ideas vague or . . . present them in a form the details of which could be supplied only by the illegitimate use of the imagination" (p. 419). In its place he advocates, not the method of physical analogy, but what he calls the "method of physical speculation," which I shall not pursue here but will comment on in section 5.

The important point for present purposes is that in his first kinetic theory paper Maxwell introduces a set of very speculative hypotheses about the unobserved physical composition of gases and uses these to derive conclusions, some of which at least he hopes will enable the theory to be tested. Yet he refers to what he is doing as attempting to establish a physical analogy between gases and the system of particles he describes. How can this be if the method of physical analogy is supposed to be used to avoid speculative hypotheses? Is Maxwell simply misleading us and himself by speaking of analogies here? Does he perhaps have some concept of analogy in his kinetic theory paper that differs from that in the earlier electromagnetic paper? Or is there a way of rendering Maxwell's earlier views about analogies consistent with what he does in the kinetic theory?

3. A CONCEPT OF ANALOGY IN KINETIC THEORY

Let me suggest a way of understanding Maxwell's use of physical analogy in kinetic theory that will render this use compatible with that in his earlier paper. (Whether Maxwell actually viewed the situation in this way I shall take up in section 4).

Our "original" system is a gas that exists within the walls of a container. The analogue system consists of particles of the sort Maxwell describes at the beginning of his paper. It is a dynamical system that contains "an indefinite number of small, hard, and perfectly elastic spheres acting on one another only during impact," and that satisfies Newtonian mechanics. Suppose we want to establish a physical analogy between a gas in its container and such a system within the walls of a second container. One way to proceed is to focus on various properties and laws of gases and ask how a dynamical system of particles could exhibit those properties and laws.

For example, a gas exerts pressure on the walls of the container. How could a dynamical system of particles of the sort Maxwell describes exert pressure on the walls of its container? Maxwell's answer: " . . . the particles . . . move with uniform velocity in straight lines, striking against the sides of the containing vessel and thus producing pressure" (vol. I, p. 377).

A gas has a certain density. How could a dynamical system of particles have density? The answer: Each particle has mass, and the density of the system of particles is the sum of the masses of the particles divided by the total volume which the particles occupy.

A gas exhibits viscosity (internal friction). How could a dynamical system of particles do so? Maxwell's answer: The particles exist in various layers with those in different layers having different mean velocities. But particles in one layer may pass out of that layer into another, striking the particles in another layer and exerting a tangential force, which constitutes the viscosity of the system.

A gas has a certain temperature. How could a dynamical system of particles have temperature? The answer: The system has this property in virtue of the fact that it contains particles that have motion, and thus kinetic energy, the mean value of this kinetic energy for the system being proportional to the temperature of the system.[4]

A gas satisfies Boyle's law, which Maxwell writes as $p = k\rho$, where p is pressure, k is a constant at constant temperature, and ρ is the density. How could the dynamical system of particles satisfy Boyle's law? The answer: From the assumptions he makes about the dynamical system Maxwell derives

(1) $$p = 1/3 \; MNv^2$$

where p = pressure of the system of particles on the walls of its container, M = mass of each particle, N = number of particles in a unit volume, and v = mean velocity of a particle. Now Maxwell notes that the product MN gives the density of the system of particles (the total mass divided by volume). If we then assume that $v^2 = 3k$, we can transform (1) into

(2) $$p = k\rho$$

which is Boyle's law, understood now as being applied not to a gas but to a dynamical system of particles. In such an application the law is to be understood as saying that the pressure exerted by the dynamical system is equal to k times the density of that system.

In general, then, we might construe Maxwell's analogy program in kinetic theory as follows. We have a system—a gas that has known properties P_1, . . . ,P_n and satisfies known laws L_1, . . . ,L_k. We describe a second system— a dynamical system of particles—in terms of a set of assumptions (including Newtonian mechanics). Our problem is to determine whether (and how) the second system also has the properties P_1, . . . ,P_n and satisfies the laws L_1, . . . ,L_k (understood now as applying to the second system). To the extent that it does, we have established a physical analogy between the two systems.

The result of our investigation can be tabulated as follows:

---

4. Temperature, unlike pressure, density, and viscosity, is not a mechanical property that can be understood solely in terms of concepts such as force, mass, distance, and time. And Maxwell in this paper, although he notes that the velocity of ʌhe particles increases with the temperature of the system, says little else about it. To produce the present analogy with respect to temperature it is assumed that the dynamical system of particles exhibits temperature and that this is explained by the fact that the system exhibits kinetic energy. What is left open is why the system exhibits temperature in virtue of its having kinetic energy. For example, does one cause the other? Are the properties identical? The above explanation of temperature in terms of mean kinetic energy of particles seems less complete than explanations of those properties of the dynamical system that can be understood entirely in mechanical terms.

Gas	*Dynamical System of Particles*
Exerts pressure on sides of its container	Exerts pressure on sides of its container (in virtue of particles striking sides)
Has temperature	Has temperature (in virtue of its having mean kinetic energy)
Satisfies Boyle's law	Satisfies Boyle's law (in virtue of satisfying $p = 1/3MNv^2$)

.

.

.

Has a physical analogy been produced of the sort Maxwell has in mind in his earlier electromagnetic paper? There are, I think, three features of physical analogies that Maxwell stresses in the earlier paper.

1. Such an analogy gives a *physical* conception for the mind to grasp. It is not a pure mathematical formula.

Maxwell would certainly regard this feature as satisfied by kinetic theory, which introduces physical assumptions about spherical particles.

2. A physical analogy between system 1 (a gas) and system 2 (a dynamical system of particles) avoids speculative physical hypotheses about system 1 that attribute to that system unobserved parts or an unobserved structure or an unobserved causal relationship to other systems. To achieve this end it does not assume that the two systems are identical, or that system 2 is contained within system 1, or that the fact that system 1 has a certain property is caused by system 2's having some property. And even when it postulates a cause of system 2's having one of the mentioned properties, it does not assume, or provide a basis for inferring, that there is some (unobserved) analogue in system 1 causing that system to have the corresponding property.

Are the features in (2) present in the kinetic theory analogy? The answer is: *Yes, as we have set up the analogy in the present section.* We have avoided any speculative hypotheses about gases. In particular, we have not assumed that gases are identical with, or are composed of, a dynamical system of particles of the sort Maxwell describes. Nor have we assumed that the fact that gases have a certain property (e.g., that they exert a force on the walls of their container) is caused by the fact that some dynamical system of particles exerts a force on its container. We have made no assumptions about what gases are composed of, or about what causes gases to exhibit the properties they do. Indeed, we have not even assumed as an hypothesis that the analogue system of particles exists. We can treat the analogue system as a purely "imaginary" one, just as Maxwell treats the incompressible fluid in the earlier electromagnetic analogy. And we may as yet have no reason to preclude the description of other imaginary analogue systems in which properties such as pressure and temperature are not caused by the motions of particles. (Presumably if no assumptions are made about the existence of the analogue system we cannot be said to be introducing hypotheses about that system either.) The only system whose existence the analogy commits us to is that of gases, and the only properties and laws we are assuming gases to have are the known observational ones. No assumptions are made or sanctioned about what causes gases to have such properties and exhibit these laws.

3. We construct a physical analogy between system 1 and system 2 by indicating properties of system 2 that "represent" (are the analogues of) those in system 1 and by showing that these properties satisfy similar laws.

This too has been accomplished. For example, *pressure* in the case of a gas is represented by (is analogous to) *pressure* in the case of the dynamical system of particles (just as the color red in Napoleon's uniform can be represented by the color red in a portrait). And both pressure, as exerted by a system of particles, and pressure, as exerted by a gas, satisfy a form of Boyle's law.

If these are the important features of physical analogies, then, at least in the present section, we have constructed (the beginnings of) a physical analogy between a gas and a system of dynamical particles.

Still there is a difference between the present case and Maxwell's electromagnetic analogy. In the latter the properties in system 2 (the imaginary fluid) are not identical with the properties they represent in system 1 (the electromagnetic field). For example, the electrical force at a point a distance r units from a source is represented by the velocity of a fluid at a distance r units from a source. But the property denoted by "electrical force at a point" is not identical with that denoted by "velocity of fluid at a point." Nevertheless, the properties are analogous because they both satisfy an inverse square law. By contrast, in the kinetic theory analogy we do have identical properties, for example, pressure (due to a gas) and pressure (due to the system of particles). In both cases the term *pressure* has the same meaning (force per unit area) and the property denoted is subject to the same laws. Does this difference with the electromagnetic situation make a difference, as far as classifying both as physical analogies in the sense Maxwell intended?

The three features of Maxwellian physical analogies that I have mentioned do not preclude the possibility that analogous systems have certain properties that are identical—so long as it is not being supposed that the systems themselves are identical. Do the roles Maxwell construed physical analogies as playing allow identical properties of the sort found in the kinetic theory analogy?

Maxwell saw two important roles for physical analogies. First, they aid the mind in organizing, simplifying, and understanding laws, generalizations, and concepts. We have a set of ideas about system 1, involving electromagnetism, that are incompletely related, organized, or understood. Let us construct an analogous system, involving an imaginary fluid, and see whether we can produce analogues of these ideas in a way that will aid us in better relating, organizing, and understanding our ideas in electrical science.

Second, physical analogies may afford a way of working out certain unsolved problems (particularly mathematical ones) in one system by considering solutions already achieved, or more readily produced, in the analogue system; and they may suggest new problems for the first system that can be solved using the analogue system. Thus, Maxwell observes that there is a physical analogy (noted first by Kelvin) between the laws of heat conduction in uniform media and laws of electrostatic attraction. And he writes:

> We have only to substitute *source of heat* for *centre of attraction*, *flow of heat* for *accelerating effect of attraction* at any point, and *temperature* for *potential*, and the solution of a problem in attraction is transformed into that of a problem in heat. (vol. I, p. 157)

Both of these roles seem to be served by the kinetic theory analogy. The results of gas theory consisted of a not well-related or organized set of laws and generalizations pertaining to the pressure, volume, temperature, viscosity, diffusion, and specific heats of gases. Maxwell no doubt thought that the mind would be aided in organizing and relating these ideas if corresponding laws and generalizations about the pressure, volume, temperature, and so on of an analogue system of dynamical particles could be derived from assumptions about that system. Even more important, the analogy permitted the formulation and solution of new problems about gases by considering corresponding ones for the particles. For example, by "representing" the viscosity, or internal friction, of a gas in terms of internal friction between layers of particles, Maxwell is able to obtain a possible solution for the problem of the mathematical relationship between the viscosity of a gas and its density. By working out the corresponding problem for the system of particles, he arrives at the surprising result that the coefficient of viscosity of a gas is independent of its density. Moreover, both of these functions can be satisfied even though (a) certain properties in both systems are identical and (b) no speculative hypotheses are being stated or inferred about the unobserved structure of gases or about what causes gases to exhibit viscosity or any other observable property.

No wonder Maxwell thought so highly of physical analogies. They seem able to produce so much with so little commitment!

4. AN IMPORTANT DIFFERENCE BETWEEN ANALOGIES IN KINETIC THEORY AND ELECTROMAGNETISM

In actual fact Maxwell does not present his kinetic theory quite in the way I have done in the previous section. As noted, he does speak of what he is doing as constructing an analogy. Moreover, his paper contains twenty-three numbered propositions, each of which sets a task. (For example, Proposition 13 is "To find the internal friction in a system of moving particles.") And these propositions refer only to the system of particles and not to gases.[5] So it may seem as if Maxwell in working out the problems he sets for himself is making assumptions only about particles and not about gases (in accordance with the procedure of the previous section). But in practice he does not always follow this strategy. For example, after explaining how a system of particles can exhibit viscosity and deriving the equation $\mu = 1/3\rho\ell v$, which relates the coefficient of viscosity μ to the density ρ of the system of particles, the mean free path ℓ of those particles, and their mean velocity v, Maxwell writes:

> A remarkable result here presented to us in equation 24 [$\mu = 1/3\rho\ell v$] is that if this explanation of gaseous friction be true, the coefficient of friction is independent of the density. (vol. I, p. 391)

Maxwell here is clearly treating assumptions about moving particles as a possible explanation of *gaseous* friction, not just of the internal friction of the system of particles. In doing so he is supposing that gases might be composed of unobserved moving particles of the sort he describes.

Again, after deriving Boyle's law $p = k\rho$, Maxwell writes:

> We have seen that, on the hypothesis of elastic particles moving in straight lines, the pressure *of a gas* can be explained by the assumption that the square of the velocity is proportional directly to the absolute temperature and inversely to the specific gravity of the gas at constant temperature. . . . (p. 389; my emphasis)

Once more Maxwell supposes that a property of a *gas*, in this case its pressure, can be explained by hypotheses about unobserved moving particles, which (presumably) comprise the gas.

In sum, although Maxwell could in principle have avoided speculative hypotheses about unobserved parts of gases by following the method of analogy of section 3, in practice he does not always do so. There is a good reason for this.

---

5. In a letter to Stokes of October 8, 1859, Maxwell emphasizes this point: "I intend to arrange my propositions about the motions of elastic spheres in a manner independent of the speculations about gases, . . . " *Memoir and Scientific Correspondence of the Late Sir George Gabriel Stokes, Bart.*, J. Larmor, ed. (Cambridge, England, 1907), vol. 2, p. 11.

Suppose we construct a physical analogy between systems 1 and 2 of the following kind (which I shall call an *identical property* analogy):

(a) System 2 is described as exhibiting properties $P_1, \ldots, P_n$ and laws $L_1, \ldots, L_k$, that are the same as (not just formally similar to) some set that system 1 is known to exhibit.

(b) For system 2 principles are invoked that explain why system 2 has properties $P_1, \ldots, P_n$ and satisfies laws $L_1, \ldots, L_k$.

Then (going beyond the analogy) if we assume as an hypothesis about system 1 that system 1 is identical with, or is composed of, system 2,[6] we could use the principles invoked in system 2 to explain why system 1 has $P_1, \ldots, P_n$ and satisfies $L_1, \ldots, L_k$.

Suppose, for example, that we construct a physical analogy of the sort described in section 3. Both gases and the dynamical system of particles exert pressure on the walls of the container; both have density, temperature, viscosity, and so on. And both obey Boyle's law. Furthermore, in the case of the dynamical system of particles, Maxwell uses a set of principles about the motion of the particles to explain why the system of particles exerts pressure on the walls of its container, why it has density, temperature, viscosity, and so on, and why it obeys Boyle's law. If we now assume as a speculative hypothesis about gases that gases are, or are composed of, such dynamical systems of particles, then we can explain why a gas exhibits $P_1, \ldots, P_n$ by simply taking over the explanation of why dynamical systems of particles exhibit those properties. For example, a gas exerts pressure on the walls of its container for the reason that the particles comprising it strike the walls of the container, exerting pressure on it.

By contrast, this procedure is not possible if we use as a basis a physical analogy in which the analogous properties and laws are not identical or in which properties of the analogue do not cause those of the original system. Recall Maxwell's analogy between the electromagnetic field and the incompressible fluid. One of the important features of this analogy is that the electric force at a distance r from a charged particle varies as $1/r^2$, while the velocity of a fluid at a distance r from a source of fluid varies as $1/r^2$. Suppose (contrary to what Maxwell intends) we were to assume that an electromagnetic field is composed of the incompressible fluid flowing through tubes of varying section. Under this assumption could we explain why the electromagnetic field satisfies the law $F \propto 1/r^2$ by explaining why the fluid that comprises it satisfies the law $v \propto 1/r^2$? Only if we assume either that electric force is the same (property) as fluid velocity or that the velocity of the fluid of which the

---

6. This assumption, of course, commits us to assuming that system 2 exists, since we are assuming that system 1 does.

electromagnetic field is composed causes the electrical force. Otherwise all we have explained is why the fluid of which the electromagnetic field is composed satisfies $v \propto 1/r^2$. We still have to explain what this has to do with electrical force. But in this analogy Maxwell is unwilling to make the assumption that analogous properties are identical or causally related.

Accordingly, there is an important difference between those physical analogies involving identical properties and those involving properties that are not identical or causally related. In the former case, but not the latter, it is possible to go beyond the analogy and use principles explaining the properties and laws of the second system to construct speculative hypotheses about the first system — by supposing that the two systems are identical or that system 1 is composed of system 2. This is precisely what Maxwell does on a number of occasions when he develops the kinetic theory where analogous properties of gases and systems of particles are identical. By contrast, he does not proceed in this manner when he develops the electromagnetic analogy where analogous properties (he is supposing) are not identical or causally related.

5. HYPOTHESES

Now we must squarely face the issue of hypotheses. Let us suppose that Maxwell does use an identical property analogy — such as the one in kinetic theory — as a basis for constructing speculative hypotheses about gases. Even if such hypotheses are not part of the analogy itself, isn't he violating his own cherished idea that physical analogies are used when we want to avoid hypotheses? And if he is, why does he go beyond the analogy to introduce such hypotheses? Does he need to do so? In what follows I will argue (a) that the introduction of speculative hypotheses about gases does not commit Maxwell to the truth or even the probability of such hypotheses and (b) that he needs to introduce such hypotheses in order to give dynamical explanations of why gases have the properties and satisfy the laws they do — something that he wants to do but that cannot be done using only a Maxwellian physical analogy.

As shown in section 3, it is possible to construct a physical analogy in kinetic theory without introducing, or providing the basis for a legitimate inference to, any speculative physical hypotheses about the unobserved structure of gases. We show that (and how) it is possible for dynamical systems of particles to have properties of gases such as pressure, temperature, density, and to obey laws such as Boyle's law — without assuming that gases are or are composed of such systems of particles (indeed, without even assuming that such a system of particles exists), and without assuming any other hypotheses about the unobserved structure of gases.

In actual practice, however, Maxwell goes beyond this and does identify gases as such systems of unobserved particles. This procedure is possible since various analogues in the analogy are identical. However, introducing such speculative hypotheses about gases is not the same thing as using the "method of hypothesis," which Maxwell explicitly rejects. This, I suggest, is quite important in understanding exactly what commitments Maxwell is making in his kinetic theory paper, so I will pursue this further.

Recall that according to the method of hypothesis, as Maxwell formulates it (and as it is ordinarily understood), the physicist proceeds by

> forming an hypothesis, and calculating what would happen if the hypothesis were true. If these results agree with actual phenomena the hypothesis is said to be verified, so long at least as some one else does not invent another hypothesis which agrees still better with the phenomena. (vol. II, p. 419)

The crucial point for our purposes is the second sentence. According to the method of hypothesis, if the results of the hypothesis agree with actual phenomena—if the hypothesis explains known phenomena or correctly predicts some new ones, or both—then (in the absence of more successful hypotheses) it is verified, or at least strongly supported.

I suggest that when Maxwell introduces hypotheses about gases on the basis of the kinetic theory analogy he is not employing the method of hypothesis. The hypothesis that gases are dynamical systems of particles of the sort he describes would, if true, correctly explain why gases obey Boyle's law and Avogadro's law (as Maxwell notes). However, it does not follow that such an hypothesis is verified, strongly supported, or even probable. For there are conflicting hypotheses that, if true, would also explain the same laws.[7] Maxwell is aware of this methodological point and explicitly notes it in commenting on a model of the electromagnetic field he constructs in a later paper entitled "On Physical Lines of Force" (1861–1862; vol. I, pp. 451–513). (Maxwell shows how a purely mechanical fluid containing rotating vortices and particles between the vortices to act as idle wheels could produce electromagnetic properties. As in the kinetic theory paper he proceeds to invoke speculative hypotheses by explicitly identifying the electromagnetic field with the mechanical system he describes.) In his *Treatise on Electricity and Magnetism* (1873), Maxwell makes the following comment about this:

> The attempt which I then made [in "Physical Lines of Force"] to imagine a working model must be taken for no more than it really is, a demonstration that mechanism may be imagined capable of producing a connexion mechanically equivalent to the actual connexion of parts of the electromagnetic field. The problem of determining the mechanism required to establish a given species of connexion between the motions of the parts of a system always admits of an infinite number of solutions.[8]

---

7. See earlier essays, especially Essay 4.

8. James Clerk Maxwell, *A Treatise on Electricity and Magnetism* (New York, 1954), vol. 2, p. 470.

For Maxwell, in order for an hypothesis about the unobserved structure of a system to be considered verified, supported, or even probable it is not enough that the hypothesis be capable of explaining observed facts about that system, since a multitude of different structures might do that. What more does Maxwell require?

In section 2, I mentioned that in his paper "On the Dynamical Evidence of the Molecular Constitution of Bodies" Maxwell rejects the method of hypothesis in favor of what he calls the "method of physical speculation." This requires that an hypothesis have independent warrant for it to be believable. Although he never formulates this method in a general or precise way, when applying it to molecular hypotheses he begins by saying:

> Of all hypotheses as to the constitution of bodies, that is surely the most warrantable which assumes no more than that they are material systems, and proposes to deduce from the observed phenomena just as much information about the conditions and connections of the material system as these phenomena can legitimately furnish.
>
> When examples of this method of physical speculation have been properly set forth and explained, we shall hear fewer complaints of the looseness of the reasoning of men of science, and the method of inductive philosophy will no longer be derided as mere guess-work. (vol. II, p. 420)

Following this, Maxwell assumes that bodies are composed of unobservable particles, an hypothesis he regards as warranted by "experimental proof" (which he does not give). He then shows how a form of Clausius' virial equation relating the pressure and volume of a gas to the kinetic energy of the system of particles it contains and to the distance between particles and the forces between them can be used to explain observed deviations from Boyle's law at high densities (vol. II, pp. 421–423). And he takes this as providing some support for the virial equation. He does so because he believes there is independent warrant for this equation.

Maxwell offers only a few general remarks about how independent warrant is to be demonstrated. As noted above, he speaks of the need to "deduce from the observed phenomena just as much information about the conditions and connections of the material system as these phenomena can legitimately furnish." And he claims that those speculators employing the flawed method of hypothesis are not provided with a means "to express the results of their induction in its early stages" (vol. II, p. 419). It is reasonable to suppose that he thought that independent warrant accrued to the general form of the virial equation in virtue of its derivability from Newton's second law, which is inductively supported.

More generally, we might represent Maxwell's idea of independent warrant by the condition that the hypothesis have some significant probability in the light of observed phenomena.[9] I take this condition to be satisfied for Maxwell if there is an inductive (or causal-inductive) connection between these phenomena and the hypothesis in question (or between the phenomena and principles from which the hypothesis follows). Whether Maxwell allows other types of independent warrant is not clear. He explicitly rejects the idea that the phenomena support the hypothesis simply in virtue of the fact that they are explained by it (if they are). The phenomena providing the independent warrant will be part of the background information and will typically include ones different from those explained by the hypothesis.

To draw a contrast with the method of hypothesis, let us consider Maxwell's method of physical speculation in so far as it is applicable to explanations, and formulate the two views as follows:

Method of hypothesis: Given the background information b, the fact that h, if true, would correctly explain observed phenomena $O_1, \ldots, O_n$ constitutes at least some reason for believing h.

Maxwell's method of physical speculation: Given b, the fact that h, if true, would correctly explain observed phenomena $O_1, \ldots, O_n$ constitutes some reason for believing h only if $p(h/b) > k$.

The latter proviso in the second method, which requires that the probability of h given the background information be greater than some threshold value k, represents the idea that independent warrant is required.[10] If explanations involve deductions, as they so frequently do for Maxwell, then, as we saw in Part I of this book, the independent warrant condition together with explanation will guarantee significant probability in light of *all* the data: If $p(h/b) > k$, and if $O_1, \ldots, O_n$ are explainable via derivation from h and b, then $p(h/O_1, \ldots, O_n \& b) > k$.

Now we can return to hypotheses that are formulated by considering identical property analogies such as the kinetic theory analogy. Suppose that on the basis of an analogy between a gas and a system of dynamical particles of the sort outlined in section 3 we construct the hypothesis that gases are, or are composed of, such systems of dynamical particles. We then explain various properties and laws of gases by means of the principles we have used to explain those properties and laws in the case of the particles. Let h represent these principles as applied to gases, and let $O_1, \ldots, O_n$ be the statements describing various known properties and laws of gases. We are supposing that

9. Richard Olson, *Scottish Philosophy and British Physics* (Princeton, 1975), ch. 12, ties Maxwell's requirement for independent warrant to basic tenets of Scottish Common-Sense philosophy. See particularly pages 308–309.

10. For a somewhat different interpretation of Maxwell's method of physical speculation see Jon Dorling, "Maxwell's Attempts to Arrive at Non-Speculative Foundations for the Kinetic Theory," *Studies in History and Philosophy of Science* 1 (1970), pp. 229–248.

h if true would correctly explain $O_1, \ldots ,O_n$. On the method of hypothesis, which Maxwell rejects, this would constitute at least some reason to believe the hypothesis h about the unobserved structure of gases. On Maxwell's method of physical speculation this would constitute such a reason only if $p(h/b) > k$, that is, only if the hypothesis h has some independent warrant. But the fact that h if true would correctly explain $O_1, \ldots ,O_n$ does not by itself guarantee that h has any independent warrant — a point Maxwell makes by noting that, in general, innumerably many conflicting hypotheses, if true, could also correctly explain $O_1, \ldots ,O_n$. So unless such independent warrant is forthcoming, the fact that an identical property analogy can be used to generate an hypothesis that, if true, will correctly explain a range of facts, does not lead to any commitment whatever to that hypothesis.

In short, the use of identical property analogies to generate hypotheses about unobservables carries no epistemic risk. And this absence of epistemic risk is one of the important things that Maxwell sees in physical analogies:

> We must therefore discover some method of investigation which allows the mind at every step to lay hold of a clear physical conception, *without being committed to any theory founded on the physical science from which that conception is borrowed.* . . . (vol. I, p. 156; emphasis mine)

The fact that the kinetic theory hypotheses would if true correctly explain a range of facts about gases carries no commitment to such hypotheses. This is crucial to Maxwell, especially in his first kinetic theory paper, in which he is extremely guarded about kinetic theory.

If there is, or at least needs to be, no epistemic commitment to the kinetic theory hypotheses, why invoke them at all? Why should Maxwell have gone beyond constructing an analogy between a gas and a system of dynamical particles? A Maxwellian analogy avoids an epistemic commitment to hypotheses about unobservable constituents of a gas, but it also avoids the use of such hypotheses for any purposes. What advantage is gained if one now introduces the hypothesis that gases are systems of dynamical particles?

Maxwell wants to be able to *explain* a range of phenomena about gases (and not just about the analogue system). This is clear from the numerous occasions in his paper in which he explicitly claims to be explaining viscosity, pressure, diffusion, and other properties of gases. Moreover, the explanations he seeks are *dynamical* ones. They are to invoke a system containing parts in motion between which forces are acting. Recall the statement at the beginning of his paper:

> So many of the properties of matter, especially when in the gaseous form, can be deduced from the hypothesis that their minute parts are in rapid motion . . . that the precise nature of this motion becomes a subject of rational curiosity. (vol. I, p. 377)

As he stresses in a later paper, dynamical explanations appealing to the motions of a system of material parts are the most desirable and the most fundamental explanations to be found:

> . . . when a physical phenomenon can be completely described as a change in the configuration and motion of a material system, the dynamical explanation of that phenomenon is said to be complete. We cannot conceive any further explanation to be either necessary, desirable, or possible, for as soon as we know what is meant by the words configuration, motion, mass, and force, we see that the ideas which they represent are so elementary that they cannot be explained by means of anything else.[11] (vol. II, p. 418)

Now to produce a dynamical explanation of gaseous phenomena will require assumptions about some dynamical system — a system whose parts are in motion and are subject to forces. If these parts are ones of which gases are composed then the explanation will require *hypotheses* about gases — since no moving parts of gases are observable.[12] If these parts are not ones of which gases are composed, but are ones of some second, analogue system, then no hypotheses about gases will be invoked. But then no explanations of gaseous phenomena will be forthcoming either. A dynamical *analogy* of the sort Maxwell wants (one neither containing nor supporting hypotheses about gases) will not explain properties and laws of gases. One cannot explain why a gas exerts pressure on the walls of its container by saying only that the reason the analogue system of dynamical particles exerts pressure on the walls of its container is that the particles being in motion continually strike the walls, producing pressure. The only way the analogy will generate a dynamical explanation of gaseous phenomena is by generating the hypothesis that gases are, or are composed of, such systems of (unobserved) particles, or that there is some (unobserved) causal relationship between the two systems. The formulation of some such hypothesis about the nature of gases is a necessary condition for the program of dynamical explanation that Maxwell wants to pursue.

It is a necessary condition but not a sufficient one. Maxwell's program is not simply to formulate dynamical hypotheses that, if true, would correctly explain gaseous phenomena, but to produce dynamical hypotheses that do

---

11. This emphasis on dynamical explanation also appears in Maxwell's earlier writings, for example, in his Inaugural Lecture at Aberdeen in 1856. But see Essay 6, note 53.

12. Comparing dynamical explanations in molecular theory with those in astronomy and electrical theory, Maxwell writes: "The investigation of the mode in which the minute particles of bodies act on each other is rendered more difficult from the fact that both the bodies we consider and their distances are so small that we cannot perceive or measure them, and we are therefore unable to observe their motions as we do those of planets, or of electrified and magnetized bodies." James Clerk Maxwell, *Matter and Motion* (New York, n.d.); pp. 121–122.

correctly explain these phenomena. As he says in commenting on the hypotheses generated by his analogy:

> If experiments on gases are inconsistent with the hypothesis of these propositions, then our theory, though consistent with itself, is proved to be incapable of [correctly] explaining the phenomena of gases. (vol. I, p. 378)

Hypotheses about gases are necessary (but not sufficient) for correct dynamical explanations of gaseous phenomena, which is something Maxwell seeks. A physical analogy, such as the one expressed in section 3, neither contains nor provides a legitimate inference to hypotheses about the unobserved dynamical structure of gases (only about the analogue system of particles, and even then it does not assume such particles actually exist). This is why Maxwell goes beyond such an analogy and constructs dynamical hypotheses about the unobserved structure of gases.

This is not to assert that analogies can never be explanatory. An analogy may contain some explanatory hypothesis, even a dynamical one, about the original system. We might draw an analogy between the way in which (real) molecules that comprise a gas cause the gas to exert pressure on the walls of its container and the way imagined (idealized) particles in a second dynamical system cause that system to exert pressure on the walls of its container. But this is not a Maxwellian physical analogy, in which the original system is described so as to avoid hypotheses about its unobserved structure.

In this early kinetic theory paper Maxwell wants to have his cake and eat it too. He wants to be able to offer dynamical explanations of the properties and laws of gases, which he can do only by introducing physical hypotheses about gases. Yet he wants to avoid physical hypotheses about gases, since he has insufficient evidence to establish them. That is the advantage of using the method of physical analogy, and that is why he speaks in terms of such an analogy. *The outcome is a compromise.* Hypotheses are introduced for explanatory purposes, so they are not avoided. What Maxwell does avoid is an epistemic commitment to the ones he uses based on their explanatory success. He is not saying (with the method of hypothesis) that because kinetic theory hypotheses, if true, would correctly explain various facts about gases, such hypotheses are confirmed or probable. The compromise allows him to use hypotheses to explain phenomena, while remaining a skeptic about their validity once the explanations have been produced. (In his second paper on kinetic theory, and in later articles "Molecules" and "Atom," where Maxwell is more confident about his hypotheses, the analogy talk is dropped.)

Why, then, doesn't Maxwell do the same in his early paper on electromagnetic theory? Why doesn't he go beyond the analogy he constructs between the electromagnetic field and the imaginary fluid and assume as an hypothesis that the electromagnetic field is composed of such an unobserved fluid? Wouldn't this allow Maxwell to explain properties and laws of the electromagnetic field? It would, I have suggested, only if he is prepared to say that analogous properties are identical or causally related. Only if Maxwell assumes that the electric force is the same property as the fluid velocity, or that the velocity of the fluid causes the electric force to be what it is, can he explain why the electric force varies as the inverse square of the distance from its source by explaining why the velocity of the fluid varies as the inverse square of the distance from its source. But Maxwell is not prepared to make such assumptions. The analogy here is not an identical property analogy nor one involving causally related properties. This is why in describing the imaginary fluid Maxwell writes: "It is not even a hypothetical fluid which is introduced to explain actual phenomena" (vol. I, p. 160).

6. MAXWELL'S COMMITMENT TO KINETIC THEORY

In his kinetic theory, I have argued, Maxwell sought to introduce hypotheses about the unobserved parts and structure of gases; otherwise dynamical explanations of gaseous phenomena would not be forthcoming. But he wanted to avoid an epistemic commitment to those hypotheses that is based solely on their explanatory success. This was certainly possible for him to do. He could show that such hypotheses if true could explain gaseous phenomena without concluding from this fact that the hypotheses are true or even probable. But this does not necessarily mean that Maxwell remained epistemically neutral with respect to those hypotheses. There may have been facts other than the explanatory success of the theory that Maxwell took to provide some support (or disconfirmation) for the theory. To what extent did Maxwell actually remain uncommitted?

During the period in which he wrote his first kinetic theory paper he certainly had no empirical evidence that he thought would establish the theory. Nor did he have evidence that would altogether refute it. Nevertheless, his position was not complete epistemic neutrality. Let me mention four facts that are relevant here.[13]

1. In the paper he obtains the theoretical result that the ratio of the total *vis viva* (kinetic energy) to translational *vis viva* is 2, whereas, he notes, the experimental value is 1.634. And he takes this result to be "decisive against the unqualified acceptation of the hypothesis that gases are such systems of hard elastic particles" (vol. I, p. 409). I take Maxwell's word "unqualified" seriously here. This result does not, I think, lead him to reject the total theory, only that part of it that assumes particles act on one another only during impact. In his second kinetic theory paper he replaces this with the idea that intermolecular forces vary as the inverse fifth power of the distance between mole-

---

13. These have been noted in a different context in Essay 6, sections 5 and 7.

cules. Still this result led him to believe that theory *in the exact form presented in his first kinetic theory paper* was false and would require modification.

2. Maxwell derives the theoretical result that the coefficient of viscosity is independent of the density of the gas. He writes that this is "very startling, and the only experiment I have met on the subject does not seem to confirm it," (vol. I, p. 391), although there is no mention of the experiment or how it is disconfirming. In addition, it follows from his theoretical result concerning viscosity that the coefficient of viscosity μ is proportional to the mean molecular velocity v. But since absolute temperature T is proportional to v^2, it follows that μ is proportional to $\sqrt{T}$. Maxwell does not mention this in the present paper. But in a later (1865–1866) paper "On the Viscosity or Internal Friction of Air and Other Gases," (vol. II, pp. 1–25), he indicates how elaborate experiments he performed show that μ is proportional to T. However, in this later paper Maxwell does not take this experimental result as refuting kinetic theory but as requiring a change in that theory from contact forces between molecules to forces varying inversely as the fifth power of the distance (vol. II, p. 11).

3. Maxwell obtains results pertaining to mean free paths that, given certain experimentally determined values, he takes to provide some positive support for the theory. He derives the following theoretical formula for mean free path:

$$\ell = \frac{3}{2} \frac{\mu}{\rho} \sqrt{\frac{\pi}{2k}}$$

where μ is the coefficient of internal friction of a gas and ρ is density. From a value for μ/ρ supplied by Stokes in experiments on air, and from the value $k = 930$ ft/s for air at 60°, he derives $\ell = 1/447,000$th of an inch for the mean distance traveled by a molecule between collisions. Later in the paper when discussing the diffusion of two gases through each other, he derives a different formula for mean free path (formula (57), vol. I, p. 403). On the basis of this formula, using the result of an experiment by Graham, he calculates a value of $\ell = 1/389,000$ for mean free path. At the end of his paper he notes approvingly that these two values for ℓ are "not very different."

4. It is reasonable to suppose that Maxwell thought that at least the basic ideas of kinetic theory—that gases are composed of unobservable particles, that these particles are in motion, that this motion is responsible for heat, and that the motion satisfies Newtonian dynamics—have some independent warrant. There are two reasons, the first of which derives from observations of heat. In his book *Theory of Heat*, first published in 1871, Maxwell invokes certain facts about heat known to him before the publication of his first kinetic theory paper. He notes that heat is transferable from a hotter to a colder body by radiation, which must involve some motion of matter in the

intervening space between the bodies. This motion can only be produced by motion in the body radiating the heat. But this is not a motion of the body as a whole, nor of any of its observable parts (which during the heat transfer are stationary). So Maxwell concludes:

> The motion which we call heat must therefore be a motion of parts too small to be observed separately. . . . We have now arrived at the conception of a body as consisting of a great many small parts, each of which is in motion. We shall call any one of these parts a molecule of the substance. . . . [14]

Thus facts about heat transfer (together with certain assumptions about motion) provided Maxwell with some reason to suppose that invisible particles exist as constituents of bodies, that these particles are in motion, and that their motion is responsible for the radiation of heat. In fact Joule, the discoverer of the mechanical equivalent of heat, had proposed a somewhat similar argument in 1847, and Maxwell was aware of Joule's work.

The second reason Maxwell regarded basic ideas of kinetic theory as having some independent warrant is that they involve *dynamical* hypotheses. This is explicit in his later paper "On the Dynamical Evidence of the Molecular Constitution of Bodies," in which he mentions that both astronomy and electrical science have been successful in analyzing the observed motions of bodies in accordance with dynamical principles applied to systems of bodies. He seems to count this success as some reason, albeit by no means conclusive, to suppose that the same dynamical principles can be applied to the parts of which gases are composed, even though these parts are not observable. This reference to the success of dynamical theories is also made in Maxwell's Inaugural Lecture at Aberdeen in 1856, four years before the publication of his first kinetic theory paper, and in his Inaugural Lecture at Kings College, London, in 1860. I suggest that Maxwell was committed at least to the plausibility of (some form of) kinetic theory, based on the success of other dynamical theories dealing with systems of moving parts.

Accordingly, at the time of his first kinetic theory paper Maxwell had some commitment to basic ideas of kinetic theory, though he recognized that certain assumptions (particularly those pertaining to intermolecular forces) would need altering. Experimental results concerning specific heats and viscosity contradicted kinetic theory, precluding an "unqualified" acceptance of the theory. But there was an experimental result pertaining to mean free paths that obviously impressed Maxwell. And there was some independent warrant for (central parts of) the theory from observations of heat transfer and the success of dynamical theories in other domains—perhaps even enough to reach the k-threshold of the method of physical speculation discussed in

---

14. James Clerk Maxwell, *Theory of Heat* (London, 1875), pp. 304–305.

section 5. If so, he had at least some reason for believing the theory, even though his commitment was guarded and tentative. Many more experimental results would be needed to establish (or refute) the theory. In any case his commitment was not generated by using the method of hypothesis. He did not suppose that the success of kinetic theory in explaining gaseous phenomena by itself provided support for that theory.

7. CONCLUSIONS

It is possible to construct a physical analogy between a gas and a dynamical system of particles by showing that (and how) the dynamical system has a set of properties $P_1, \ldots, P_n$ and satisfies laws $L_1, \ldots, L_k$, which gases also do. Such an analogy can have the features Maxwell requires of physical analogies. It gives a physical rather than a purely mathematical conception for the mind to grasp; it avoids speculative hypotheses about the unobservable structure of gases; it represents properties of the gas by analogous (in this case, identical) properties of the dynamical system and by showing that these properties satisfy similar (in this case, identical) laws; and it serves the two important roles that Maxwell imputes to analogies: organization and simplification of ideas, and working out of problems in one system by solving them in the other.

In his first kinetic theory paper Maxwell speaks of the kinetic theory as providing a physical analogy for gases. Yet he goes beyond this analogy by introducing the speculative physical hypothesis that gases are composed of systems of unobservable particles. Only in this way can he generate *dynamical explanations* of gaseous phenomena. Analogies that preclude hypotheses about gases will not give Maxwell dynamical explanations of properties and laws of gases. But the introduction of hypotheses about unobservable parts of gases violates one of the principal aims of the method of physical analogy. So a compromise is effected. Maxwell uses explanatory hypotheses about gases but avoids becoming epistemically committed to them just because they are explanatorily successful. He does not employ the "method of hypothesis," since he does not conclude from the fact that the hypothesis if true would explain known facts that the hypothesis is true or probable. The reason it is possible for Maxwell to use the analogy between a gas and a dynamical system of particles to generate explanatory hypotheses about gases is that this analogy involves properties in both systems that are identical. By contrast, Maxwell's analogy between the electromagnetic field and the imaginary fluid does not involve properties Maxwell regarded as identical (or causally related). Consequently, he could not use it to produce hypotheses about the electromagnetic field.

Although Maxwell avoided becoming committed to kinetic theory on the grounds of its explanatory success, he did not adopt a stance of complete epistemic neutrality. Some experimental results, as well as consideration of heat transfer and the success of dynamical theories in other areas, tended to support the theory. And although other experimental results were negative, he may well have thought that these did not completely refute the theory but showed only that it requires modification.*

---

*I have benefited considerably from discussions with Robert Kargon, Gary Hatfield, Michael Liston, and Mary Hesse.

ESSAY 8

Scientific Discovery and Maxwell's Kinetic Theory

"Physics is play."

R. FEYNMAN

"We must bear in mind that the scientific or science-producing value of the efforts made to answer these old standing questions is not to be measured by the prospect of ultimately obtaining a solution, but by their effect in stimulating men to a thorough investigation of nature."

J. C. MAXWELL

For the hypothetico-deductivist the initial proposing of a new hypothesis or theory in the "context of discovery," by contrast to its testing in the "context of justification," is a nonrational event. It involves a guess or conjecture, that may have a variety of causes, but not an inference subject to logical analysis. Since N. R. Hanson's revival in the 1950s of Peirce's account of retroduction, this h-d view has become much less popular than it once was. Using as an example James Clerk Maxwell's early kinetic theory, I want to argue that there is an important element of truth in what h-d theorists say about the context of discovery.

1. MAXWELL'S EARLY KINETIC THEORY

In 1860 Maxwell published "Illustrations of the Dynamical Theory of Gases," the first of his two great papers on kinetic theory.[1] In it he proposes to work out a theory of gases "on strict mechanical principles" by demonstrating "the

---

1. W. D. Niven, ed., *The Scientific Papers of James Clerk Maxwell* (New York, 1965), vol. I, pp. 377–409.

laws of motion of an indefinite number of small, hard, and perfectly elastic spheres acting on one another only during contact" (p. 377). At the beginning of the paper he sets down basic assumptions of the theory: that gases are composed of minute particles in rapid motion; that the velocity of the particles increases with the temperature of the gas; that the particles move with uniform velocity in straight lines striking against the sides of the container, producing pressure; that the particles are perfectly elastic spheres; that they act on each other only during impact; and that their motion is subject to mechanical principles of Newtonian mechanics.

These assumptions suggest to Maxwell a set of questions: What exactly is the motion of the particles after they collide? Are all directions of rebound equally likely? What is the distribution of velocities among the particles? What is the mean distance traveled by a particle before striking another? And so forth. Maxwell's project in this paper is to develop the kinetic theory so that it can answer these and other theoretical questions. The method he employs to carry out this task is to construct mathematical derivations from the basic assumptions to theorems that will contain answers to these questions. In the course of doing so Maxwell introduces further underived assumptions. (For example, in deriving his important distribution law he assumes that the x-, y-, and z-components of velocity are independent; see Essay 6.)

With the exception of the first page, the paper is devoted entirely to the derivation of the theorems. Very little attention is given to the origin of the basic assumptions of the theory. How did Maxwell arrive at them? They are highly speculative, involving as they do the postulation of unobserved particles exhibiting unobserved motion. Maxwell does provide two clues concerning their origin. One is that other physicists—Bernoulli, Herapath, Krönig, and Clausius—also supposed that gases contain particles moving with uniform velocity in straight lines. (Hypothetico-deductivists, as we shall see, will make something of this.) The other is the claim that various observable properties of gases can be deduced and explained from the assumptions of kinetic theory postulating motions of particles. (Retroductivists, as we shall see, will make something of this.)

Let me begin with hypothetico-deductivism. On this view, Maxwell did not *infer* his basic assumptions from anything; he guessed them. The physicist Richard Feynman offers a succinct version of the h-d position:

In general we look for a new law by the following process. First, we guess it. Then we compute the consequences of the guess to see what would be implied if this law that we guessed is right. Then we compare the result of the computation to nature, with experiment or experience, compare it directly with observation, to see if it works. If it disagrees with experiment it is wrong. In that simple statement is the key to science.[2]

---

2. Richard Feynman, *The Character of Physical Law* (Cambridge, Mass., 1965), p. 156.

The initial stage in the process—the guess—may occur as a result of various causal influences. As with Maxwell, these may include the fact that certain other physicists had proposed similar ideas. Maxwell was particularly influenced by reading a paper of Clausius entitled "The Nature of Motion Which We Call Heat," which was published in 1857, some three years before his own publication. But Maxwell does not draw an inference from the fact that Clausius and some others have proposed the basic assumptions to the assumptions themselves. He simply appropriates some of the assumptions as part of his own theory. He makes the same, or some of the same, guesses as Clausius does. And he proceeds to use these guesses, as well as new ones of his own, to develop the theory mathematically.

To be sure, guessing is not incompatible with inferring. "Educated" guesses are inferences from somewhat meager data to conclusions deemed plausible. However, when h-d theorists speak of guessing they mean guessing that is not based on an inference from any data or facts. On this view Maxwell did not draw an inference, did not engage in any reasoning, to the fundamental assumptions of kinetic theory. In the context of discovery, when Maxwell first arrived at the hypotheses he wished to consider further he had no data or facts that provided reasons for believing them.

By contrast, the retroductivist would say that Maxwell did not blindly guess the basic assumptions of his theory, or simply plagiarize them from others. He inferred them. He did have reasons for believing them before he constructed the derivations that constitute the bulk of his paper. More generally, according to the retroductivist, in the context of discovery a scientist does and should have some reasons to believe an hypothesis before considering it further. He or she does and should engage in a type of reasoning that does not *establish* an hypothesis but provides (at least some) basis for thinking it is true. Hanson proposes that it takes this form:

Some surprising phenomenon P is observed.
P would be explicable as a matter of course if H were true.
Hence there is reason to think that H is true.[3]

Peirce suggests

The surprising fact C is observed.
But if A were true, C would be a matter of course.
Hence there is reason to suspect that A is true.[4]

And Peirce makes it clear that he has in mind an explanatory relation between A and C.

3. N. R. Hanson, *Patterns of Discovery* (Cambridge, England, 1958), p. 86.
4. Charles Peirce, *Collected Papers*. C. Hartshorne and P. Weiss, eds. (Cambridge, Mass., 1960), vol. 5, 5.189.

In general, I take retroductivists to be claiming that in the context of discovery, when an hypothesis is first proposed (and before conclusions from it — other than those that prompted it in the first place — are drawn and tested), there is an inference, the conclusion of which is that there is some reason to believe the hypothesis. The inference is based on the idea that the hypothesis if true would explain certain observed data.

Maxwell indeed notes at the beginning of his paper that various properties of gases can be explained by supposing that gases are composed of minute parts in rapid motion. Thus, in the paper that preceded his, Clausius, by means of this assumption, offered qualitative explanations of the pressure exerted by gases, the work performed by gases when heated, and Gay-Lussac's law of combining volumes. And Maxwell, before he begins to derive consequences from the theory, explicitly notes that if gases are composed of minute particles in motion, then the pressure of the gas on the container is thereby (qualitatively) explained as being due to the impact of the particles on the sides of the container. However, whether (as retroductivists would claim) Maxwell concluded from this and similar explanatory facts that there is a reason to think his kinetic theory hypotheses are true — whether he made a retroductive inference — is another matter, to which I will now turn.

2. MAXWELL'S DEMAND FOR "INDEPENDENT WARRANT"[5]

To begin with, Maxwell does not explicitly draw an inference of the retroductive sort described above. He does not say that the previous explanatory success of kinetic theory provides some reason to think that kinetic theory is true. His conclusion is much more guarded. It is that the previous explanatory success of a theory that assumes that gases have their minute parts in rapid motion makes "the precise nature of this motion . . . a subject of rational curiosity" (vol. I, p. 377). The most that Maxwell concludes from the (preliminary) explanatory success of the theory is that it is reasonable to consider it further. (As I will argue below, it may be reasonable to consider a theory further without there being reasons to think that it is true.)

Second, in later writings (particularly in a paper published in 1875) Maxwell explicitly rejects reasoning similar in important respects to that described above. He notes that a method frequently used in getting from the observed to the unobserved

> is that of forming an hypothesis, and calculating what would happen if the hypothesis were true. If these results agree with the actual phenomena, the hypothesis is said to be verified, so long, at least, as some one else does not invent another hypothesis which agrees still better with the phenomena. (vol. II, p. 419)

---

5. Much, although not all, of the material in this section is covered in Essay 7, sections 5 and 6.

In accordance with this method, if the hypothesis entails and (thereby) explains known phenomena, then (in the absence of more successful hypotheses) it is verified or at least strongly supported. Maxwell objects to this method on the ground that if the hypotheses are not left vague and useless but their details are filled in, there will be an "illegitimate use of the imagination." There will be insufficient empirical grounds to favor one hypothesis over a multitude of others that also entail and explain the known phenomena.

Moreover, although Maxwell does not explicitly mention this, there will be "crazy" hypotheses—ones that, given all of our background information, have a probability as close to zero as you like—that nevertheless (together with background information) entail observed data, and *if true*, would explain those data.[6] Yet this would constitute no reason for thinking them true. To take a nonscientific example, let the observed fact be that I am happy about the news I have just received. Let the hypothesis h be that I have just received the news that I have won the Nobel prize in literature. Let the background information include the fact that anyone who is awarded a Nobel prize is happy when he or she receives the news. Hypothesis h together with this background information entails that I am happy about the news I have just received, and if h were true it would correctly explain my happiness. But this fact provides no reason for thinking I have just received news I have won the Nobel prize.[7]

To avoid these illegitimate flights of fancy, but still allow certain hypotheses to be introduced, Maxwell in this paper of 1875 proposes what he calls a "method of physical speculation" (vol. II, p. 420), which requires that an hypothesis have independent warrant for it to be believable. It is not sufficient that some observed phenomena be derived or explained via an hypothesis. However, Maxwell does derive and explain known phenomena from hypotheses, and there are occasions on which he takes such derivations

---

6. Peirce was aware that retroductive reasoning can yield such hypotheses, but he seems not to take this as a mark against retroduction. To the question: Why then do scientists make retroductions to the hypotheses they do—retroductions to the "reasonable" rather than the "unreasonable" ones?, his answer is that we possess a certain faculty of insight: "This Faculty is at the same time of the general nature of Instinct, resembling the instincts of the animals in its so far surpassing the general powers of our reason and for its directing us as if we were in possession of facts that are entirely beyond the reach of our senses" (Peirce, *op. cit.*, 5.173).

7. In this example there is only one observed fact being explained. But the same problem arises even if the hypothesis inferred is required to explain or to entail numerous, varied observations. Let $O_1, \ldots, O_n$ be a conjunction containing as many and varied observed facts as you like, including, for example, "the sky is blue," "grass is green," and "the sea is salty." Our hypothesis h is a conjunction of two propositions, the first of which postulates the existence of X, where X is anything you like, however implausible. The second conjunct in h is of the form "If X exists, then X causes it to be the case that $O_1, \ldots, O_n$," where the latter are the many and varied observation reports above. Hypothesis h entails these observation reports, and if true correctly explains them. Yet this fact provides no reason for thinking that h is true.

or explanations as providing some positive support for the hypotheses. For example, he cites a version of Clausius' virial equation that relates the pressure and volume of a gas to the kinetic energy of the particles it contains and to the distances between particles and the forces between them. He shows how this equation can be used in deriving and explaining Boyle's law as well as observed deviations from Boyle's law at low temperatures and high densities. And he takes this as providing support for ideas contained in the virial equation. From the fact that the virial equation entails and explains deviations from Boyle's law at high densities and the fact that such deviations are observed, Maxwell concludes that at high densities there are significant forces between molecules and that these are mainly attractive—in accordance with the ideas of the virial equation. But if the h-d and retroductive accounts are to be rejected, how can these facts provide such support? What Maxwell is assuming, I suggest, is that they can provided there is independent warrant for the virial equation, which Maxwell thought there was, since this equation in its general form is derivable from Newton's second law, which enjoys inductive observational support.

Although Maxwell does not use this terminology, the requirement of independent warrant might be understood as demanding that the hypothesis have some significant probability in the light of observed phenomena that are part of the background information. I take this to be satisfied for Maxwell if there is an inductive, or causal-inductive, connection between such phenomena and the hypothesis, or between the phenomena and principles from which the hypothesis follows—connections of the kinds illustrated in Part I of this volume in the case of wave and particle theories of light. Maxwell himself insists that the independent warrant is to be supplied by the "observed phenomena"; and he uses the term *induction*, to be sure without defining it, although the example he employs in the present context, and others I shall note below, are plausibly understood as involving inductive and causal-inductive generalizations. (See also the quote from his article "Atom" in Essay 5, p. 161.) Since he explicitly rejects the method of hypothesis, Maxwell's requirement of independent warrant will not be satisfied simply if the hypothesis explains the observed phenomena. (Perhaps Maxwell would recognize other sources of independent warrant, but if so this is not clear.)

To draw a contrast with retroduction, I shall consider Maxwell's method of physical speculation insofar as it is applicable to explanations. Both methodologies can be understood as committed to views about when the fact that an hypothesis explains something can be taken as some reason to believe it true. Let me formulate these two views initially as follows:

Basic retroduction. Given the background information *b*, the fact that hypothesis *h*, if true, would correctly explain observed facts $O_1, \ldots, O_n$ constitutes at least some reason for thinking that *h* is true.

Maxwell's method of physical speculation. Given the background information *b*, the fact that *h*, if true, would correctly explain observed facts $O_1, \ldots, O_n$ constitutes at least some reason for thinking that *h* is true provided that $p(h/b) > k$.

Basic retroduction has as its only condition that *h* if true correctly explains *O*. Further conditions can be added (for example, conditions on the explanation) to obtain more complex versions. But as I will understand retroduction, it will not require that there be independent warrant for *h*.[8] The second condition in Maxwell's method represents this requirement. My Nobel prize hypothesis, if true, would correctly explain why I am happy over the news I have received. But this fact constitutes no reason for thinking this hypothesis is true, since, given the relevant background information, its probability is as close to zero as you like. It has no independent warrant. I suggest that Maxwell was right in rejecting basic retroduction, and that his independent warrant condition, or something like it, is required in addition. (If it is satisfied, then *h* at least retains its significant probability in the light of

---

8. Do retroductivists such as Hanson and Peirce have in mind additional conditions for retroduction? If so do these include independent warrant? Hanson, after introducing the retroductive inference form cited earlier, indicates two conditions he attaches to the idea of "explicable as a matter of course" (pp. 87–88). One involves the idea of providing what he calls a "pattern" in terms of which to understand the observed phenomena. The other stipulates that "if *h* is meant to explain *P*, then *h* cannot itself rest upon the features in *P* which require explanation" (p. 88). (His example is that you can't explain the green color of chlorine by appeal to green atoms.) Whatever these conditions amount to, they do not seem to require any significant probability for *h*. Just before Peirce introduces his retroductive schema he writes:

Long before I first classed abduction [retroduction] as an inference it was recognized by logicians that the operation of adopting an explanatory hypothesis — which is just what abduction is — was subject to certain conditions. Namely, the hypothesis cannot be admitted, even as a hypothesis, unless it be supposed that it would account for the facts or some of them. (5.189)

In the present passage the only condition on retroductive inference that Peirce suggests is the explanatory one. In other writings, however, Peirce mentions two additional conditions (7.220). One is that the hypothesis be empirically testable. The other is that it be "economical." Among the several considerations that Peirce includes under economy is the "expectation that a given hypothesis may be true," which may be based on "positive facts which render a given hypothesis objectively probable." However, Peirce does not demand such probability as a necessary condition for a retroductive inference. He writes:

Nothing has caused so much waste of time and means, in all sorts of researches, as inquirers becoming so wedded to certain likelihoods as to forget all the other factors of the economy of research; so that, unless it be very solidly grounded, likelihood is far better disregarded, or nearly so; and even when it seems solidly grounded, it should be proceeded upon with a cautious tread, with an eye to other considerations, and a recollection of the disasters it has caused. (7.220)

Accordingly, while Peirce's position in the present passage is more complex than that expressed in his own retroductive schema given above, it would be incorrect to equate it to Maxwell's method of physical speculation.

$O_1, \ldots, O_n$ if the latter are explainable via derivation from h and b; if some of the O's are predictions with a probability less than one, then h's probability increases. See Essays 3 and 4.)

To return now to his first kinetic theory paper, for Maxwell to have reasonably concluded that the success of kinetic theory in explaining the pressure and other observed properties of gases constitutes some reason for believing true the assumptions of kinetic theory, there would need to be background information that gave some significant probability to these assumptions. Did Maxwell have such independent warrant?

There are, I think, two plausible candidates for such warrant: observations of heat and the success of dynamical theories.

Argument from Observations of Heat

In his book *Theory of Heat*, first published in 1871, Maxwell offers independent support for certain basic ideas in kinetic theory from facts about heat (facts known to him and the physics community before the publication of his first kinetic theory paper), together with widely shared assumptions about motion. Heat is known to be transferable from a hotter to a colder body by radiation. Now, says Maxwell,

> Whatever theory we adopt about the kind of motion which constitutes radiation, it is manifest that radiation consists of motion of some kind, either the projection of the particles of a substance called caloric across the intervening space, or a wave-like motion propagated through a medium filling that space. In either case, during the interval between the time when the heat leaves the hot body and the time when it reaches the cold body, its energy exists in the intervening space in the form of motion of matter.[9]

Now this motion of matter in the intervening space can only be caused by motion in the body radiating the heat.

> Every hot body, therefore, is in motion. We have next to enquire into the nature of this motion. It is evidently not a motion of the whole body in one direction, for however small we make the body by mechanical processes, each visible particle remains apparently in the same place, however hot it is. The motion which we call heat must therefore be a motion of parts too small to be observed separately. . . .
>   We have now arrived at the conception of a body as consisting of a great many small parts, each of which is in motion. We shall call any one of these parts a molecule of the substance. . . . (pp. 303–305)

Maxwell's argument from considerations of heat transfer depends on various assumptions about motion that he seems to regard as plausible, for example, that motion can only be caused by other motion, that if something is moved

---

9. James Clerk Maxwell, *Theory of Heat* (London, 1875), p. 303.

from A to B there is motion at A, and that if there is motion at A but this is unobservable, then there is unobserved matter in motion. Presumably, such assumptions are based on inductions from observable cases of motion. The argument is written with a degree of certainty about the existence of molecules that was lacking years earlier when he published his first kinetic theory paper. But it is conceivable that the known facts about heat transfer, together with assumptions about motion, would have provided Maxwell with at least some independent warrant for (a) the existence of invisible particles as constituents of bodies, (b) the claim that these particles are in motion, and (c) the claim that the motion of these particles is responsible for the radiation of heat. In fact a somewhat similar argument had been given in 1847 by Joule (who discovered the mechanical equivalent of heat).[10] And Maxwell was aware of Joule's work.

I will not here try to assess the claim that these observations of heat radiation (in the light of assumptions about motion) provide at least some independent warrant for (a) through (c). It is plausible to suppose that Maxwell took them to do so. More generally, kinetic theorists of this period cited such facts, together with Joule's discovery of the mechanical equivalent of heat and the problems besetting the caloric theory, as providing some support for the idea that heat is molecular motion.

Argument from the Previous Success of Dynamical Theories

In 1856 in his Inaugural Lecture at Aberdeen, as well as in 1860 in his Inaugural Lecture at King's College, London, Maxwell stressed the success of *dynamical* theories—those that describe systems containing parts in motion between which forces that obey Newtonian laws are acting. He notes the success of dynamical theories in astronomy and he takes this success as providing at least some inductive reason, though by no means a conclusive one, to think that dynamical principles are applicable to any physical system composed of moving parts, whether or not these parts and their motion are observable. In 1875 in his paper "On the Dynamical Evidence of the Molecular Constitution of Bodies" Maxwell reiterates the success of dynamical theories in other domains—this time adding "electrical science" to astronomy—and he again takes this as some reason to suppose that Newtonian principles are applicable to unobservable parts of bodies.

In sum, then, we have the following two ideas:

(i) Considerations of heat transfer (together with widely held assumptions about motion, and also, let us say, with Joule's determination of the mechanical equivalent of heat and the difficulties of caloric theory) lend some support to

---

10. See James Joule, "On Matter, Living Force, and Heat," in S. G. Brush, ed., *Kinetic Theory*, vol. 1 (Oxford, 1965), pp. 78–88.

the claim that bodies contain unobservable parts, that these parts are in motion, and that this motion is responsible for heat.

(ii) Considerations of the success of Newtonian dynamical principles in other domains suggest that if bodies are composed of unobservable parts in motion, then this motion too is subject to Newtonian dynamical principles.

Combining (i) and (ii) we get some independent warrant for basic ideas of kinetic theory. I shall assume that Maxwell did have both (i) and (ii) on his mind when he proposed his fundamental assumptions of kinetic theory. If so, it looks as if retroductivists are right on at least one important point. Maxwell did not simply guess these assumptions. He *inferred* them from certain facts. Where those who support the basic retroductive position go awry — at least from the Maxwellian point of view — is in supposing that the fact that kinetic theory, if true, would correctly explain certain observed properties of gases suffices to justify an inference to that theory. As required by Maxwell's own method of physical speculation, such an inference is reasonable only if there is at least some independent warrant for the assumptions of kinetic theory. On the present considerations such an inference is reasonable, since there was independent warrant.

3. IS HYPOTHETICO-DEDUCTIVISM REFUTED?

If Maxwell inferred the basic assumptions of kinetic theory, and if his inference was reasonable, is hypothetico-deductivism refuted? I want to challenge this conclusion by challenging the premises. Although Maxwell was in a position to reasonably infer some of his assumptions in kinetic theory — and for the sake of the argument let us suppose he did so — he was not in a position to reasonably infer the entire set. From the fact that $h_1, \ldots, h_k$ if true would correctly explain $O_1, \ldots, O_n$ we are permitted to infer that (there is some reason to think that) $h_1, \ldots, h_k$ are true only if there is independent warrant for $h_1, \ldots, h_k$. But from the fact that there is independent warrant for some members of this conjunction, it does not follow that there is independent warrant for the entire conjunction.

Let us look again at the two independent warrant considerations. What they make plausible are certain assumptions about matter generally, not just about gases. Considerations of heat radiation — whether from gases, liquids, or solids — suggest that there is motion of unobservable parts in the matter that is heated. And considerations from the success of dynamical theories suggest that the motion of these parts obeys Newtonian dynamics. But these considerations have nothing to say about:

1. *The paths of the molecules in a gas.* Maxwell assumes that the particles travel in straight lines only. But considerations from heat transfer and

from the success of dynamical theories in astronomy and electrical science do not preclude stationary molecules that exhibit rotational motion. (A rotational theory had been suggested in 1847 by Joule.[11]) And if we do not assume that the forces acting between the particles are contact forces, the independent warrant considerations permit nonlinear translatory motion. (Indeed, in his second paper on kinetic theory Maxwell abandons contact forces in favor of a law according to which the force between two molecules varies as the inverse fifth power of the distance between them.)

2. *The particular force law governing molecules in a gas.* Maxwell assumes in this paper that the only forces are contact forces. Newtonian principles require that the force, whatever it is, satisfy $F = ma$. But these principles do not require contact forces. As in astronomy and electrical theory, molecules may exert forces at a distance. That is, what is known about other forces in nature does not provide more support for contact than for noncontact forces.

3. *The shape of molecules.* Although Maxwell assumes molecules are spherical, this is not required by Newtonian dynamics or by considerations from heat transfer. In his second kinetic theory paper Maxwell abandons this assumption.[12]

4. *The relationship between components of molecular velocity.* Although it is not one of the assumptions given at the outset of his paper, to derive a velocity distribution law Maxwell assumes (without any argument) that the different spatial components of velocity are independent. This allows him to suppose that the probability that a molecule has an x-component of velocity between x and $x + dx$ is independent of the probability that it has a y-component between y and $y + dy$, and of the probability that it has a z-component between z and $z + dz$. (See Essay 6.) This assumption is not required by Newtonian dynamics or by heat transfer considerations. In his second kinetic theory paper he abandons this assumption and offers an alternative derivation of his distribution law.

At most, the two independent warrant considerations provided the basis for an inference to assumptions that Maxwell made that gases are composed of unobservable particles, that these particles are in motion that is also unobservable, that this motion is responsible for heat (so that the temperature of

---

11. *Ibid.*, p. 86.

12. "In the present paper I propose to consider the molecules of a gas, not as elastic spheres of definite radius, but as small bodies or groups of smaller molecules repelling one another with a force whose direction always passes very nearly through the centres of gravity of the molecules, and whose magnitude is represented very nearly by some function of the distance of the centres of gravity" (Maxwell, *Scientific Papers*, vol. II, p. 29).

the gas increases with the velocity of the particles), and that the motion of the particles satisfies Newtonian dynamics. But the independent warrant considerations do not provide a basis for an inference to a number of very central assumptions that Maxwell made pertaining to the paths of molecules, the forces between them, their shapes, and the relationships between components of their velocity. At best, the retroductivist is right in claiming that there were fundamental assumptions in kinetic theory to which Maxwell made, or was in a position to make, a reasonable inference at the outset when he proposed them. But unless we can find more independent warrant than we have so far, there were other fundamental hypotheses to which Maxwell was not in a position to make a reasonable inference at the outset. Indeed, Maxwell most likely introduced the method of physical speculation with just this situation in mind. Certain quite general assumptions concerning the existence and motion of gas particles have independent warrant. But these are not enough to yield a specific model, which requires further hypotheses concerning the forces between particles, their shapes, and so on. Can we conclude with the hypothetico-deductivist that Maxwell made no inferences to such hypotheses but simply guessed them?

4. SIMPLICITY AND ANALOGY

Before we draw this conclusion, two additional factors might be noted. The first is *simplicity*. Doesn't the fact that Maxwell's basic explanatory assumptions were simple ones provide some reason to believe them? That depends on the source of their simplicity.

Consider Maxwell's assumption about the paths of molecules. Straight-line motion is simpler than rotational motion or than translation along, say, an elliptical path. The source of this simplicity is mathematical. Linear equations of the form $Ax + By + C = 0$ are mathematically simpler than those for conic sections (which include ellipses) of the form $Ax^2 + By^2 + Cxy + Dx + Ey + F = 0$. But does the fact that the equation for a straight line is simpler than that for an ellipse make the hypothesis that molecules travel in straight lines more probable than that they travel in elliptical orbits? (Keep in mind that we are assuming nothing about the motion of particles except that it obeys Newton's laws; in particular we are making no assumption about the type of force between molecules.) Suppose you take the same walk each night, but I know nothing about the path you take. Does the fact that the equation for a straight line is simpler than that for an ellipse make it more likely that your path is linear than elliptical? Such a conclusion seems very dubious.

Or take Maxwell's assumption about the forces between molecules. A force law of the form $F = 0$ (except when the distance between the centers of two molecules equals the sum of their radii) is mathematically simpler than one of the form $F \propto 1/r^n$. But does this fact make the hypothesis that molecules exert no forces on each other except at contact more probable than that they exert a noncontact force that varies inversely as some power of the distance between them? Again the reasoning is not persuasive.

I am not here making the more general claim that simplicity is always irrelevant for probability. I assume only that where one physical hypothesis is simpler than another solely because an equation in one is mathematically simpler than an equation in the other we cannot on this basis alone conclude that one is more probable than the other. Since the source of simplicity in the hypotheses about the paths of molecules and the forces between them derives (as I see it) entirely from such mathematical simplicity, we do not yet have a reason to believe such hypotheses. This does not mean that the mathematical simplicity of the equations is irrelevant in determining whether to *consider* a certain hypothesis (more of this later). What I am disputing is only that it necessarily enhances the probability of the hypothesis or renders it high.

It has been argued that *analogies* can provide support for basic assumptions of a theory.[13] Maxwell himself emphasizes the use of analogies in developing theories, particularly in his early work in electromagnetism. In the present paper on kinetic theory he also mentions at two points that he is seeking to draw a "physical analogy" between a gas and a system of unobservable particles of the sort he describes in his basic assumptions. Unfortunately, Maxwell does not spell out his analogy idea in kinetic theory the way he does in electromagnetism. But he may have had in mind something like this (see also Essay 7).

We have an "original" system—in this case a gas—that has certain known properties and satisfies known laws. For example, a gas exerts pressure on the walls of its container; it has a certain density and temperature; it exhibits viscosity; and it satisfies Boyle's law. We now describe a second system, the "analogue" system, in terms of a set of assumptions. For example, we describe a dynamical system containing an enormous number of unobservable particles satisfying all of the assumptions that Maxwell makes at the beginning of his paper, including the assumption that molecules are spherical, that they travel in straight lines, that they are subject only to contact forces, and so forth. We then show that (and how) this analogue system has (some or all of) the same properties and satisfies (some or all of) the same laws as the original system. Thus we show that (and how) the dynamical system of particles exerts pressure on the walls of its container; that it has density, temperature, and viscosity; and that it satisfies Boyle's law.

Could this analogy provide some support for those assumptions of kinetic theory for which we found no independent warrant in section 3? If so, presumably there would be a reasonable argument with a form such as this:

13. See Mary Hesse, *The Structure of Scientific Inference* (Berkeley, Calif., 1974); Robert McLaughlin, "Invention and Appraisal," in R. McLaughlin, ed., *What? Where? When? Why?* (Dordrecht, 1982), pp. 69–100.

Gases have properties $P_1, \ldots, P_n$.
The analogue system of particles also has properties $P_1, \ldots, P_n$, and it does so because it satisfies molecular assumptions $h_1, \ldots, h_n$.
Hence there is reason to suppose that gases also satisfy molecular assumptions $h_1, \ldots, h_n$ (or assumptions similar to these).

But such an argument is legitimate only if there is some reason to preclude the description of analogue systems in which properties $P_1, \ldots, P_n$ are produced by quite different causes. If no reason is given to think that a system satisfying molecular assumptions $h_1, \ldots, h_n$ is the only one capable of manifesting properties $P_1, \ldots, P_n$, or, if not the only one capable, is more likely to exist than the others, then the argument above carries no force.

Now from our earlier discussion let us grant that there is some reason to believe that there exists a set of unobservable particles that satisfy Newtonian laws and are responsible for heat transfer. But (so far at least) we have no support for the assumption that in addition those particles are spherical, move in straight lines, exert contact forces, and have independent components of velocity. We have no support for the claim that there exists a set of particles of just the kind postulated by Maxwell in his kinetic theory. Nor do we have support for the claim that only such a system of particles can satisfy the properties and laws of gases, or that if various systems can, this one is the most likely to exist. The fact that we can imagine such particles and show that as a consequence of all of Maxwell's assumptions a set of such particles has certain properties (for example, pressure and viscosity) and satisfies certain laws (for example, Boyle's law) identical to those of gases does not by itself provide a reason for thinking that gases are such systems.

The situation here is similar to the earlier one involving basic retroduction. The fact that we can describe a hypothetical system that, if it existed (as described), would explain some phenomenon cannot by itself, according to Maxwell, be taken as a reason to suppose that system exists. Similarly, the fact that a certain system, if it existed (as described), would have many of the same properties as gases cannot by itself be taken as a reason to suppose that such a system exists, or to conclude by analogy that gases have many properties identical or similar to the ones attributed to the hypothetical system. Indeed, in his early work on electromagnetism Maxwell makes it clear that his use of analogies avoids any commitment to hypotheses about unobservables. In his paper "On Faraday's Lines of Force" Maxwell constructs a physical analogy between the electromagnetic field and an incompressible fluid flowing through tubes of varying section. But from the fact that the fluid he describes has certain properties and satisfies certain laws analogous to those of the electromagnetic field, he does not conclude that there is any reason to suppose that such a fluid exists or that the electromagnetic field has analogous microproperties.

5. WHAT MAKES AN HYPOTHESIS WORTH CONSIDERING?

Let us grant that Maxwell inferred some of his basic assumptions, and that he did so on the basis of considerations from heat transfer and the success of dynamical theories in other domains. This still leaves important assumptions for which these considerations provide no independent warrant. To be sure, these assumptions (plus the others) if true would correctly explain a range of gaseous properties. But unless there was some independent warrant for them, Maxwell was not in a position to infer from this that there is a reason to think that these assumptions are true. He (rightly) rejected the basic retroductive account.

Here I propose to agree with the hypothetico-deductivists. Maxwell did not make any inference to a number of his central postulates when he first proposed them for consideration. *He had no reason at all to think they were true.* Although Maxwell had some reason to think that gases are composed of unobservable particles in motion satisfying Newtonian laws, he had no reason at all to think that such particles are spherical in shape, or that they exert only contact forces, or that their motion is linear rather than nonlinear, or that their velocity components are independent.

Does this mean that h-d theorists would be correct in saying that Maxwell simply guessed these hypotheses? Suppose that a detective has ruled out all but ten suspects as perpetrators of the crime. The rest have airtight alibis. He then chooses one at a time to investigate. In choosing a particular one of these to investigate first the detective is not, or need not be, guessing that this person is guilty. That would be too strong an epistemic commitment for him to have. Rather, the detective is investigating the possibility that the person in question is guilty. Similarly, although Maxwell did not infer that molecules are spherical from any considerations, neither did he guess that this is so. In proposing this as a basic assumption he was simply considering that possibility. In doing so he was exhibiting no epistemic commitment to the truth or probability of this assumption.

But if Maxwell had no reason at all to think that molecules are spherical how could he have rationally proposed to consider that possibility? Such an hypothesis was *worth considering* even if it had no independent warrant, even if there was no reason to think it was true. How can this be so?

For the retroductivist, as we have described his position so far, it cannot be so. An hypothesis is worth considering only if there is some reason to think it is true. However, we might alter retroductivism by dropping this requirement and substituting

(1) Given observations O, hypothesis h is worth considering if and only if h if true would correctly explain O.

We would then be construing retroductivism as a position about when an hypothesis is worth considering, and not about when there is reason to think it true. Indeed, although Hanson does formulate retroductive reasoning in such a way that it has "therefore there is reason to think that h is true" as the conclusion, on occasion he also formulates it so that the conclusion is "therefore h is worth considering" or "therefore there is good reason for elaborating h."[14] If we do not construe this as implying that there is reason to think that h is true, we allow for the possibility that h may be worth considering even if there is no reason to think it is true.

Unfortunately, the alternative retroductive thesis (1) provides a condition that is neither necessary nor sufficient. That it is not necessary will be shown by an example below used to criticize an even stronger version (2). That it is not sufficient is demonstrated by means of examples that invalidate the previous version as well. There are numerous hypotheses that if true would correctly explain some observations but are not worth considering on the basis of those observations. To use an earlier example, let O be that I am happy about the news I have just received. Let h be that I have just received the news that I have won the Nobel prize in literature. Hypothesis h if true would correctly explain O. But h is not worth consideration given O and background information.[15]

Maxwell and others who reject retroduction as well as the h-d method might suggest that the reason the Nobel hypothesis is not worth considering is that it is absolutely crazy. That is, given my background information b, the probability of h on b is approximately zero. Accordingly, we might write

(2) Given background information b and observations O,
   hypothesis h is worth considering if and only if
   (a) h if true would correctly explain O.
   (b) $p(h/b)$ is not (approximately) 0.

This can be construed as weaker than the Maxwellian independent warrant condition, since the second clause requires only that the probability of h given b not be very close to 0. It does not require that there be some independent reason to think h true, only no overwhelming reason to think h false.

I suggest that (2) is too strong. Neither (a) nor (b) is a necessary condition. Given the background information and a set of observations O, h may be worth considering even if h is incompatible with O—so that h if true would not correctly explain O. For example, given Maxwell's background information, and given observations about the viscosity of gases—including the ob-

---

14. See N. R. Hanson, "The Logic of Discovery," in P. Achinstein, ed., *The Concept of Evidence* (Oxford, 1983), pp. 60–61.

15. The same problem arises even if we strengthen (1) by requiring that h explain a variety of observations. See note 7.

servation that the coefficient of viscosity varies with the absolute temperature of the gas — Maxwell's molecular hypothesis about viscosity may well have been worth considering. (Maxwell's hypothesis was that molecules exist in various layers in the gas, those in different layers having different mean velocities; those in one layer may pass into another layer, striking the particles in it and exerting a tangential force that produces the viscosity of the gas.) Yet Maxwell's molecular hypothesis about viscosity (together with the rest of his kinetic theory) entailed that the coefficient of viscosity is proportional not to the temperature of the gas but to the square root of the temperature. Accordingly, his hypothesis, if true, would not correctly explain an important observed fact about viscosity, thus violating (2a).

Moreover, suppose we consider some different observation entailed by his theory, for example, that the coefficient of viscosity of a gas is independent of the density of the gas. This observational conclusion would be correctly explained by Maxwell's "layer" hypothesis if the latter were true. Suppose now we include in the background information b the observed fact that the coefficient of viscosity varies with the absolute temperature of the gas. Since Maxwell's "layer" hypothesis h is incompatible with the latter, $p(h/b) = 0$. Despite this fact, given the observed independence of viscosity and density, Maxwell's "layer" hypothesis might have been worth considering, thus violating (2b).

One might be tempted to weaken (2) by requiring not that (a) and (b) be true but that they be reasonable to believe (thus obviating the last objection). But this is still too strong a requirement. Maxwell may have had no reason whatever to believe that his molecular hypothesis about viscosity, if true, would correctly explain various known facts about gaseous viscosity. He did have a good reason to suppose that if true it would correctly explain (in a qualitative way) the *existence* of viscosity. But whether, if true, it would offer a quantitative explanation of the observed relationship between viscosity and other known quantities such as temperature was another matter. His hope was that it would. But he may have had no reason to suppose that it would. Moreover, he may have had no reason to believe anything about the probability of his molecular hypothesis about viscosity, given his background information and given the observation that viscosity varies with temperature. It may have been reasonable to suspend belief on this probability. Still on the basis of the background information and observed facts about viscosity his particular hypothesis about viscosity may well have been worth considering.

Indeed, an hypothesis may be worth considering even when the scientist as yet has no observational data that that hypothesis could in principle explain. Maxwell had no observational data regarding the distribution of molecular velocities. (See Essay 6. Such data became available only in the 1920s with the introduction of molecular beam experiments.) Yet in order to determine a theoretical law giving the distribution of molecular velocities, Maxwell introduced the hypothesis that velocity components are independent. This hypothesis was worth considering even though it did not explain observational data that Maxwell had concerning molecular velocity components or the distribution of velocities.

How can these things be so? How can an hypothesis be worth considering even though, if true, it would not explain the data one has, or if one as yet has no data for it to explain?

6. A BROADER PROPOSAL

Let me propose a new way of looking at the situation. On the basis of certain considerations, Maxwell makes these assumptions:

1. Gases are composed of unobservable particles.
2. These particles are in motion, which is also unobservable.
3. The motion of the particles is responsible for heat transfer.
4. The motion of the particles satisfies Newtonian dynamics.

Call this set T_i (initial assumptions). In Maxwell's case T_i consists of those assumptions for which he had some independent warrant. But we need not suppose that this is necessary. Perhaps T_i contains assumptions made by others, or just formulated de novo by the scientist — assumptions for which the scientist has no independent warrant and with respect to which he or she is, for the moment, epistemically neutral.

The assumptions in T_i generate a set of questions, for example,

a. What is the motion of the particles? What paths do they take?
b. What are the forces between particles?
c. What is the shape of the particles?
d. How are velocities distributed among particles?

More generally, T (together possibly with other background assumptions being made) will be said to generate a question Q if T (together with these additional assumptions) entails a *complete presupposition* of Q. A question such as (a) presupposes a number of propositions, for example,

(i) There are particles.
(ii) There is motion.
(iii) The particles have some motion.

Any proposition entailed by a proposition presupposed by a question will also be said to be presupposed by that question. A complete presupposition of a question is a proposition that entails all and only the presuppositions of that question.[16] Of the three propositions in the foregoing set only (iii) is a complete presupposition of question (a). Since this proposition is entailed by T_i the question (a) is generated by T_i. Similarly, questions (b), (c), and (d) are generated by T_i (together with certain other assumptions Maxwell was making). For example, assumptions (1), (2), and (4), together with the additional assumption (which Maxwell would have taken as plausible) that particles are three-dimensional bodies, entail "the particles have some shape." Since this is a complete presupposition of question (c), the latter is generated by T_i. By contrast, question

e. Why did God create unobservable moving particles?

also presupposes (i) through (iii). But its complete presupposition:

God created unobservable moving particles for some reason

is not entailed by T_i. Accordingly, T_i does not generate (e).

Sometimes an answer to a generated question is mathematically or logically derivable from the set T_i. But very often it is not. Such an answer, when forthcoming, will be a new underived assumption in the theory. Many such answers to a given question may be possible. For example, to question (b) one might respond with the law $F = 0$ (except at impact), or with any law of the form $F \propto 1/r^n$. Such answers to (b) would entail different answers to (a). When is it reasonable to consider one of the assumptions? Let me offer the following sufficient condition:

Given T_i, a new assumption A is worth considering if it answers a question Q generated by T_i in such a way as to satisfy a set of appropriate instructions for Q.

Instructions are rules for answering a question. They provide constraints on the answer, and include typical methodological considerations, for example,

1. Very general methodological criteria valued in science. Instructions may require that the answer to Q satisfy some standard of generality (for example, that it employ laws), that it be mathematically formulated, that there be some empirical evidence supporting it, that it be simple, unifying, and so on.
2. More specific empirical constraints. Instructions may require that the answer to Q satisfy Boyle's law, or the principle of conservation of energy, or the principle that there are no preferred directions in space.

16. See Peter Achinstein, *The Nature of Explanation* (New York, 1983) pp. 29ff.

3. Pragmatic constraints. The instructions may require that the answer be one that is mathematically tractable, or one the empirical testing of which is relatively simple.

Obviously given considerations of types (2) and (3), the question of whether some set of instructions is *appropriate* is highly contextual. What specific empirical constraints it is appropriate to impose will depend upon what is known or knowable by the scientist and his community. It would not be appropriate to require Maxwell to propose answers that satisfy special relativity. Similarly, whether a given answer is mathematically tractable or testable depends on the mathematical and empirical procedures usable by those in the scientific community. Indeed, even the applicability of criteria in (1) is context dependent. These criteria (I have argued in *The Nature of Explanation*, ch. 4) provide neither necessary nor sufficient conditions. Whether generality, precision, empirical support, simplicity, or other conditions are needed for an hypothesis to be worth considering will depend in part on the specific knowledge of the community and on the kinds of answers it is interested in achieving. Yet they are relevant criteria. They set a direction for what kind of hypotheses scientists should try to consider at some point. To determine whether some particular set of instructions is appropriate, these criteria must be used in conjunction with contextual facts.

Moreover, whether a particular answer to Q satisfies appropriate instructions will depend on whether the question itself is worth pursuing. Questions generated by a theory that pertain to some quantity such as motion or to some quantitative relationship such as mutual forces — questions such as (a) and (b) — are usually of intrinsic interest to those articulating the theory, and will also be of value because of their tendency to aid in further developing the theory, especially mathematically. But this can vary depending on knowledge and interests. (In certain contexts there may be no appropriate instructions for Q even though it is generated by T.)

Let us see how this works in the case of Maxwell. Maxwell has the set T_i given at the beginning of this section. He proposes to add assumption

> p: The force between molecules is zero except at impact.

p answers the question

> Q: What is the force between molecules?

which, in virtue of Newtonian dynamics, is generated by T_i. Does p satisfy some set of appropriate instructions for Q? It satisfies *some* of the broad methodological criteria valued in science: it is very general, it is mathematically formulated, and it is quite simple. Moreover, it satisfies the pragmatic constraint of being mathematically tractable. It readily allows a calculation of momentum transfer, and thus a derivation of the pressure law. To be sure, there is no empirical evidence supporting it (or any other force law). But where there is no empirical evidence for this or any other force law, it may still be worth considering if the hypothesis satisfies instructions incorporating other desirable ends. This is precisely the case with Maxwell's force law. It was worth considering because it answered a question generated by a theory he was developing, and did so by providing a general, mathematically formulatable, simple answer, that could readily be used by Maxwell to generate answers to further questions. Moreover, this question was one Maxwell was interested in answering. His avowed aim at the beginning of his paper was to develop kinetic theory in a quantitative way "on strict mechanical principles"—an aim that requires, or at least is facilitated by, some assumption about the forces governing molecules. In the absence of any empirical reason for choosing this rather than another force law, these facts suffice to make his answer worth considering. In the context in which Maxwell was operating—given his knowledge and that of his community—it would not have been appropriate to invoke instructions requiring that the answer considered have empirical support.

If this is so how do we preclude considering "crazy" hypotheses such as the Nobel hypothesis? We begin in this case not with a theory, but with the observed fact that I am happy over the news I have just received, and with the assumption that there is some reason for my happiness. These generate the question: Why am I happy?, which, let us assume, members of the audience want to answer. If empirical support for an hypothesis is not always required, what makes the Nobel hypothesis unworthy of consideration? In this situation we have much more information than in Maxwell's case. Maxwell had no empirical reasons to prefer one force law over another. But we know that philosophers have rarely won the Nobel prize and we know something about my literary talents. Moreover, we know from past experience that there are other much more likely explanations. In short, we do have strong empirical reasons for not considering the Nobel hypothesis. Maxwell, at the outset at least, had no such reasons for not considering contact forces between molecules.

The physicist Feynman in the quote at the beginning of this essay asserts that physics is play. I interpret this to mean that it can be worthwhile to consider and work out theoretical principles even if one hasn't any idea whether they are likely to be correct, even if they have no independent warrant. One can play with an idea and see where it leads, even if there is no reason to think it is true. However, it is crucial to distinguish between (a) having a reason to think an hypothesis is true (having a reason to believe it), and (b) having a reason to consider it. Maxwell had a perfectly good reason to consider (to "play with") the hypothesis that forces between molecules are contact forces, even if he had no reason to think it true or likely. His reason was that it answered a question generated by his theory—one that he was interested in answering so that his theory could be further developed — and did so in a way that satisfied appropriate instructions calling for a general, quantitative, simple answer that is mathematically tractable. He was not in a position to satisfy instructions calling for an answer for which there was independent warrant. Such instructions would have been inappropriate for his situation. They would have prevented further development of the theory.

Having argued that an hypothesis can be worth considering even if one has no reason to think it is true, let me take this further. An hypothesis can be worth considering even if one has some reason — indeed a conclusive one — for thinking it is false. What matters is the aim of the consideration. Here are several situations in which this is possible.

1. Criticizing a theory. There is a theory accepted by most in the community that I want to criticize. I consider a certain hypothesis from that theory — which on independent grounds I know or believe to be false — and show that it leads to false predictions. The hypothesis is worth considering because of its widespread acceptance. Yet I have strong reason for thinking it false.

2. Showing that a certain type of theory is possible. In his paper "On Physical Lines of Force," Maxwell's aim is to show that a mechanical theory of the electromagnetic field is possible by imagining a purely mechanical system that will reproduce known electromagnetic properties. He is not supposing that the particular mechanism he introduces for this purpose is true or even probable. At certain points he introduces hypotheses that he believes are probably false (for example, the idea of vortices within the electromagnetic field connected by particles that are in rolling contact with the vortices).[17] In this situation Maxwell is trying to determine whether there could in principle be a mechanical conception of the electromagnetic field. There is also a premium on hypotheses that can be easily investigated mathematically. Accordingly, it can be reasonable to consider specific mechanisms even if one has independent reasons for believing them false or improbable.

3. Producing idealizations. I introduce an hypothesis that I have some independent reason for believing to be false; yet it may be approximately true. If the hypothesis has other virtues (mathematical tractability, etc.), it may be worth considering.

_____

17. Maxwell (*Scientific Papers*, vol. I, p. 487) writes: "The conception of a particle having its motion connected with that of a vortex by perfect rolling contact may appear somewhat awkward. I do not bring it forward as a mode of connexion existing in nature, or even as that which I would willingly assent to as an electrical hypothesis. It is, however, a mode of connexion which is mechanically conceivable, and easily investigated. . . . "

No doubt those who defend the idea that an hypothesis is worth considering only if it has some independent warrant will reply that they are not
speaking of situations of types (1) through (3). They are speaking of:

4. Proposing a theory in order to correctly explain a range of phenomena.

While doing (1) through (3) may serve as a useful prolegomenon to (4), it is
not sufficient. What I have been arguing is that in the case of (4), no less than
in (1), (2), and (3), hypotheses which there is no reason to believe true or
probable may be worth considering.

There is a moral here for agencies that provide financial support for scientific research projects. Suppose that in 1858 Maxwell had submitted a proposal to a government agency to support his theoretical research in kinetic theory.
He proposes to "lay the foundation of such investigations on strict mechanical principles" by deriving consequences from a set of assumptions he makes
about molecules. For some of these he has some independent warrant. But for
a number of the central ones he has no such warrant; he has no reason at all to
think they are true. Nor does his proposal contain a description of any
experiments he will conduct to test these or any other assumptions in the
theory. Whether his proposal should be funded will depend on several factors
in addition to its scientific value (for example, the amount of money available, the quality of other proposals, his scientific credentials, etc.). But most
important, it will depend on whether the theory he proposes to develop is
worth considering. Accordingly, in his proposal to the funding agency he
should provide good reasons for considering the theory. If he has reasons for
thinking that the theory, or some part of it, is true, he should say what they
are. But he may not yet be in a position to do so. Depending on the circumstances, it may be legitimately decided to fund his proposal to work out the
idea that molecules are perfectly elastic spheres subject to contact forces, even
though there are no reasons to think that this idea is true. Funding agencies
should not require such reasons as a necessary condition for support.

As noted, Maxwell had independent warrant for some of the assumptions
of kinetic theory. But suppose he didn't have. Suppose that he had simply
appropriated the four kinetic theory assumptions comprising T_i from
Clausius and others, and could offer no independent warrant for any of
them. He then proposes to consider the hypothesis p that the force between
molecules is zero except at impact. On the proposal of the present section, this
hypothesis could still be worth considering. There is no requirement that the
assumptions in the initial set have independent warrant. We must keep in
mind, however, that the condition for "worth considering" is relativized to the
assumptions in the initial set: p is (or is not) worth considering, given T_i.
Relative to some other set the verdict may be quite different. But this just
prompts the question: What about the initial set itself? Are these hypotheses

worth considering? On the present account they could be even in the absence of independent warrant for any of them. How could this be so? Here is one possible scenario.

Maxwell begins with certain background information about known regularities exhibited by gases — regularities concerning pressure, viscosity, heat transfer, and so forth. On the basis of these he makes the supposition

> S: There is some set of (relatively simple, unified) hypotheses about gases that can explain, or can be further developed to explain, the variety of observed regularities associated with gases.

S generates the question

> Q: What set of (simple, unified) hypotheses about gases can explain, or can be further developed to explain, the variety of observed regularities associated with gases?

Now, in accordance with the present proposal, given the supposition S, the set T_i containing kinetic theory assumptions can be worth considering. T_i answers question Q generated by S. And, in the extreme case, even in the absence of any independent warrant for T_i, it may do so in a way satisfying appropriate instructions for Q. For example, the context may be one in which no other simple, unifying theory has as yet been proposed, or in which any others proposed (for example, caloric theory) have devastating objections, although T_i does not. To be sure, there may be independent warrant for the supposition S. But since S makes no assumptions about the content of the set of simple, unifying hypotheses, there need be no independent warrant for theory T_i. In the absence of independent warrant for any of the assumptions of kinetic theory, those assumptions can still be worth considering.

7. IMPLICATIONS FOR HYPOTHETICO-DEDUCTIVISM AND RETRODUCTION

Hypothetico-deductivism is correct in one important respect. To consider an hypothesis, to take it seriously, one does not need a reason to think it is true or probable. In the context of discovery there need be no inference from any data to the truth or probability of an hypothesis before one attempts to construct derivations from that hypothesis to testable conclusions. However, to say this much one need not adopt some of the other tenets of the h-d position. Hypothetico-deductivists seem eager to avoid making restrictions on which hypothesis it is worth considering (with the possible exception that it provide an answer to a question being raised). Their restrictions are saved for the context of justification in which the hypothesis is being tested. Here I part company with them. Even if one does not demand a reason to believe each hypothesis being considered, there are constraints to be imposed on which hypotheses to consider. The "context of discovery" is not irrational or arational or one in which "anything goes." There may be good reasons for considering a given hypothesis, or for considering hypothesis 1 before hypothesis 2. Maxwell had very good reasons for considering the hypothesis that gas molecules exert contact forces, even if he had no reason for supposing this true or probable.

Similarly, I reject that version of retroduction that requires at least some reason to think each of the assumptions of one's theory to be true before one draws new conclusions from the theory and begins empirical testing. Instead I would support that version that requires only reasons for considering h (which need not be reasons for thinking h true). However, I reject the retroductive position that makes the requirement that h if true would correctly explain some observed data either a necessary or a sufficient condition for h's being worth considering. An hypothesis h may not be worth considering even when h, if true, would correctly explain O (for example, the Nobel prize hypothesis). And an hypothesis may be worth considering even when, if true, it would not correctly explain any observed data we have. The hypothesis may be incompatible with our data—as in the case of Maxwell's viscosity hypothesis. Or we may as yet have no observational data that that hypothesis could explain—as in the case of Maxwell's independence assumption about components of molecular velocity. In the latter case the hypothesis was worth considering even though it did not explain observational data Maxwell had, but because it enabled him to derive, in a fairly simple way, a quantitative answer to the question: How are velocities distributed among particles in a gas? This question was generated by the initial assumptions of his theory. It was one that Maxwell was particularly interested in pursuing, both for its own sake and for enabling the kinetic theory to be given further mathematical development.*

---

*I am indebted to Gary Hatfield and Michael Liston for very helpful suggestions.

ESSAY 9

The Only Game in Town

1. INTRODUCTION

The most frequent criticism of the method of hypothesis, or hypothetico-deductivism, is the "possibility of competitors" argument. You propose an hypothesis that entails known observational phenomena and successfully predicts new ones. Because of this you claim support for your hypothesis. If a range of different phenomena is derived (what Whewell, for example, calls *consilience*—see Essay 4), you may indeed claim high probability for your hypothesis. Now a criticism of this procedure—one typically voiced by champions of induction such as Newton and Mill—is this. There may be competing hypotheses that entail the very same phenomena. If such competitors exist, you cannot claim substantial probability for your favorite hypothesis.

Mill uses this argument to criticize what he takes to be the standard defense of the nineteenth-century wave theory of light, and in particular the hypothesis that there exists an unobservable luminiferous ether. Concerning this hypothesis he writes:

> The existence of the ether still rests on the possibility of deducing from its assumed laws a considerable number of actual phenomena. . . . Most thinkers of any degree of sobriety allow, that an hypothesis of this kind is not to be received as probably true because it accounts for all the known phenomena, since this is a condition sometimes fulfilled tolerably well by two conflicting hypotheses; while there are probably many others which are equally possible, but which, for want of anything analogous in our experience, our minds are unfitted to conceive.[1]

Mill goes on to deny that the hypothesis "is entitled to a more favorable reception" if besides accounting for known phenomena it generates new ones that are later observed.

---

1. John Stuart Mill, *A System of Logic* (London, 1959), p. 328.

Enter the "only-game-in-town" defense. Suppose your hypothesis *h* does yield a range of observable phenomena, some already known and some predicted and later confirmed. And suppose that you cannot find a plausible competitor that will also generate these phenomena.[2] Either you can find no competitor at all that will yield these phenomena, or those you can find are less (perhaps much less) plausible than *h*, that is, their probability given all the phenomena and background information is (considerably) lower than that of *h*. Now let "you" become the community at large, or better yet, the experts in the community, so that *h* becomes the "only game in town" to deal successfully with the phenomena in question. Shouldn't the fact that the experts in the community at large cannot find a plausible competitor to *h*, together with the fact that *h* does save the phenomena, count in *h*'s favor?[3]

In what follows I shall consider three different ways in which the only-game-in-town argument might be used. First, it might be claimed that it will suffice to show that *h*'s probability is high, given that it is the only game in town. Second, even if it will not show this, it will show at least that *h*'s probability has increased. Third, even if it shows neither of these things, it will still demonstrate that it is a good "research strategy" to proceed to develop and test *h*.[4] I will argue that none of these general claims can legitimately be made for the only-game-in-town argument.

2. HIGH PROBABILITY AND THE ONLY GAME IN TOWN

Let us start with the question of whether the only-game-in-town argument ensures high probability for an hypothesis. By high probability I shall mean

---

2. "You cannot find a plausible competitor" here might be understood to cover a range of cases. (a) Minimally, it means that you are not aware of any such competitor. (b) More strongly, it could mean that not only are you not aware of any, but at present you would not become aware of any if you were to think about it; you would be unable to find any if you were to search. (c) Or it could mean that you have made a search and did not find any. What I shall say is meant to hold for all these versions.

3. Whewell appeals to an only-game-in-town argument when defending his position against Mill. In response to Mill's claim that for any hypothesis that entails the phenomena there may be a conflicting one that does the same, Whewell replies "I can only say that I know of no such case in the history of Science, where the phenomena are at all numerous and complicated." And to Mill's claim that "a person of fertile imagination can always devise a hundred modes of accounting for any given fact," Whewell responds with a challenge: try it, and you will find that you cannot do it. (William Whewell, "Mr. Mill's Logic," reprinted in Robert E. Butts, *William Whewell's Theory of Scientific Method* (Pittsburgh, 1968), pp. 291–293.) Whewell, then, seems committed to the following idea: when a theory accounts for a range of data, this fact counts heavily in favor of the theory, because in such cases, as the history of science shows, there are no known competitors that will account for the same data, nor can one easily invent them.

A contemporary proponent of the only-game argument is Jerry Fodor. In his *Language of Thought* (New York, 1975), he uses such an argument to defend computational models of cognitive processes. See pp. 27ff.

4. Fodor, *op. cit.*, uses the argument in the latter way.

probability that is greater than some threshold value, say 1/2. On this proposal, if observable phenomena $O_1, \ldots, O_n$, $n \geq 1$, are derivable from hypothesis h together with background information b, and if h is the only game in town, then h's probability is high. Moreover as the number of O's derivable from h increases, where h continues to be the only game in town, then h's probability increases toward a maximal value of 1.

The only-game-in-town idea will be understood as an assumption with three parts. (i) The expert investigators are aware that hypothesis h, together with background information b, entails $O_1, \ldots, O_n$ (which, to simplify the notation, I shall frequently write as O_n). (ii) The investigators are unable to find a competing hypothesis that, together with b, also entails O_n, or else they have found only ones with a (much) lower probability on O_n & b than h has. (In what follows both types of cases will be considered.) (iii) The competitors in question are, in some sense, of the "same kind" as h. For example, suppose that h is some microtheory of physical optics postulating unobservable light corpuscles to explain observable optical phenomena. This theory may be the only game in town, even if there is another more probable *macro*theory of geometrical optics that explains the same data. The "kind" of theory the experts have in mind is a microtheory that analyzes light rays into some physical parts. The letter k will be used to refer to a condition on the kind of hypothesis sought (e.g., that it be a microtheory, that it satisfy Newtonian mechanics, or whatever).

The only-game-in-town assumption is one satisfying conditions (i) through (iii). I shall write it as $G(h, O_n, b, k)$ for "h is the only game in town of type k with respect to O_n, b, and the investigators in question." When the h, the O's, b, and k are obvious in the context I shall simply write G. Also in what follows K will mean "an hypothesis of type k (one that satisfies the k-condition, which is satisfied by h) is true."

The first suggestion for the only-game-in-town idea is this. Where $n \geq 1$, and $p(h/b)$ is not 0,

(1a) $p(h/G\&K\&O_1, \ldots, O_n\&b) > 1/2$, if $O_1, \ldots, O_n$ are derivable from h together with b. (1/2 is here being taken as the threshold value for high probability.)

According to (1a), if a set of observable phenomena is derivable from h and b, then the probability of h is greater than one-half, given the phenomena, the fact that some hypothesis of type k is true, and the fact that h is the only game in town.

Alternatively, in a weaker form, the position might be that for each hypothesis h there is some number n such that if n phenomena $O_1, \ldots, O_n$ are derivable from h, then h's probability is greater than one-half, conditional on the same assumptions as before, including the only game one, that is,

(1b) $p(h/G\&K\&O_1, \ldots, O_n\&b) > 1/2$, for some n, if $O_1, \ldots, O_n$ are derivable from h and b.

Moreover, as the number of derivable phenomena increases, h's probability tends toward 1 as a limit, that is,

(2) $\lim\limits_{n\to\infty} p(h/G\&K\&O_1, \ldots, O_n\&b) = 1$, where $O_1, \ldots, O_n$ are derivable from h and b.

(1a), (1b), and (2) reflect the idea that the only-game-in-town assumption will guarantee high probability for h. There is a weaker probability idea expressed by

(3) $p(h/G\&K\&O_1, \ldots, O_n\&b) > p(h/K\&O_1, \ldots, O_n\&b)$, for $n \geq 1$.

This asserts that at least h's probability on the O's, b, and K will increase if h is the only game in town. (K, remember, is the assumption that an hypothesis that satisfies the k-condition satisfied by h is true.)

Before we examine (1) through (3) there is one further question of interpretation. Obviously a defender of the only-game argument is not claiming that (1) through (3) hold for every function p satisfying the probability calculus. This position would be trivially false, since some probability assignments will satisfy the probability calculus but violate (1) through (3), which do not follow from that calculus. Instead I shall interpret only-gamers to be asserting that (1) through (3) hold for any "reasonable" probability function—for any reasonable scheme for assigning probabilities. Accordingly, such only-game defenders cannot be pure subjectivists. They cannot hold that any assignments of probabilities are reasonable if the probability calculus is satisfied. However, they can, if they wish, interpret probabilities as representing rationally corrected subjective degrees of belief, that is, what one's degrees of belief are or become when they are subject to various rational principles including the probability calculus. On this approach, such rational principles do not determine a unique probability function but allow subjective choices among a range of different ones.[5]

In what follows let us grant only-gamers the assumption that within the set of probability functions there is some proper subset that is "reasonable." And let us construe them to be saying that (1) through (3) hold for every probability function in this proper subset. (When discussing (1)–(3) I will attempt to choose examples involving assignments of probabilities that will generally be regarded as "reasonable.") My claim is that (1a), (1b), (2), and (3) are all false,

5. See Rudolf Carnap, *The Continuum of Inductive Methods* (Chicago, 1952).

even if construed as applying only to the set of all "reasonable" probability functions. In the next section I will consider just (1a), (1b), and (2). For the sake of argument I will assume that the weaker only-game principle (3) holds for all reasonable probability functions. In sections 4 and 5 I will show why even this weaker idea is to be rejected.

3. THREE EXAMPLES

Let me begin with an example in which there are several type-k competitors known to the experts that explain the data, one of which is considerably more probable than any of the others. Afterward cases will be suggested in which the experts can think of only one hypothesis that explains the data.

The "Twenty Lotteries" Example

b = there are twenty lotteries. Five tickets from lottery 1 will win a prize; two tickets from each of lotteries 2 through 19 will win a prize; one ticket from lottery 20 will win a prize. Each prize consists of a sum of money to be paid each day to the recipient for the rest of his life (to idealize: indefinitely for generations to come). The tickets from all the lotteries are mixed together at the outset, and John buys one ticket. Afterward the numbers are separated into the 20 respective lotteries, from which winners will be drawn as outlined. Finally, the only way a person can receive a sum of money for n consecutive days ($n > 1$) is by being a winner in one of the 20 lotteries.

h_1 = John was a winner in the first lottery.

h_2 = John was a winner in the second lottery.

> .
> .
> .

O_i = John receives a sum of money on the ith day following that in which he purchased a ticket to one of the lotteries.

k = the condition that the hypothesis give a winner of a specific lottery among the 20 lotteries (i.e., it should be of the form "x was a winner in lottery i").

K = some hypothesis giving a winner of a specific lottery is true.

$G(h_1,O_1, \ldots ,O_n,b,k)$ = with respect to the investigators h_1 is the only (type-k) game in town. That is, the investigators are aware of h_1 and believe that $O_1, \ldots ,O_n$ are derivable from h_1 and b. Moreover, they can think of no type-k competitor that entails the O's and is as probable as h_1. (We may assume that they have thought of conflicting hypotheses $h_2, \ldots ,h_{20}$ — from which, together with b, the O's are derivable. But each of these has a probability on the O's and b that is considerably less than that of h_1.)

In accordance with (3), I will assume that the fact that an hypothesis is the only game in town increases its probability. For the sake of argument suppose that in the present case it *doubles* the probability, that is,

(4) $p(h_1/G\&K\&O_n\&b) = 2 \times p(h_1/K\&O_n\&b)$, for any n.[6]

I will also assume that in this example it is reasonable to assign probabilities a priori in the standard way. In such an assignment, with the specific facts of the lottery presented in b, the probability that John is a winner in the first lottery, given $K\&O_n\&b$ — indeed given just $O_n\&b$ — is 5/42. (There are 42 winning tickets in all the lotteries together, 5 of which are from the first lottery.) That is,

(5) $p(h_1/K\&O_n\&b) = 5/42$, for any $n > 1$.[7]

From (4) and (5) it follows that

(6) $p(h_1/G\&K\&O_n\&b) = 10/42$, for any $n > 1$,

which violates (1a), (1b), and (2). The probability of h_1 does not rise above 1/2 even though h is the only (type-k) game in town with respect to the O's and b.

In this argument I have supposed (4), namely, that h_1's probability, given that it is the only game in town, is *twice* h_1's probability without that assumption. Obviously a lottery example analogous to the one just given can be presented for any generalization of (4) of the form

$$p(h/G\&K\&O_n\&b) = m \times p(h/K\&O_n\&b)$$

where m is any number greater than 1. With a suitable choice of a lottery, the probability of a specific lottery hypothesis will be and will remain less than 1/2, despite the fact that this hypothesis is the only game in town, thus violating (1a), (1b), and (2).

---

6. This will require compensating changes in probabilities of competitors. Where h_i is some type-k competitor of h_1, if (4) is satisfied in the twenty lotteries case, the following condition on competitors will have to be satisfied, for all n:

$$\sum_{i=2}^{20} p(h_i/G(h_1)\&K\&O_n\&b) = \sum_{i=2}^{20} p(h_i/K\&O_n\&b) - p(h_1/K\&O_n\&b)$$

7. $p(h_i/K\&O_n\&b) = 2/42$, where $2 \le i \le 19$. $p(h_{20}/K\&O_n\&b) = 1/42$. So h_1's probability on $K\&O_n\&b$ is 2.5 times greater than that of the next most probable type-k competitor.

The general point here should be obvious. It may be the case that a type-k hypothesis is (considerably) more probable than any type-k competitor the experts can think of. It may be more probable than every such competitor—regardless of whether the experts can think of all of them.[8] Yet even with the assumption that a type-k hypothesis is true (i.e., even assuming K), the probability of the hypothesis may still be low, despite the fact that it entails all the known and predicted phenomena. And this can remain true even if we suppose that the fact that this hypothesis is the only game in town increases its probability by some significant factor.

In the "twenty lotteries" case numerous hypotheses are known to the experts each of which entails the O's. What happens if only one such hypothesis h is known? Two sorts of cases might be considered: ones in which the experts can think of type-k competitors to h that explain the O's but each of which is precluded by other known facts; ones in which the experts can think of no type-k competitors to h whatever that will explain the O's. An example of each will be given.

Second Lottery Example

The background information includes these facts. There is a society in which each person owns one ticket in a single lottery. In this society certain people receive a sum of money each day. Of those who do, 10 percent do so because they have won a prize in the lottery, while the remaining 90 percent do so for other reasons. (Those who receive money each day do so only from a single source.) Let h = Bill was a winner in the lottery; O_i = Bill receives a sum of money on the ith day following that in which he purchased a ticket to the lottery; k = the condition that the hypothesis give a specific source of Bill's daily income (e.g., the lottery); K = some hypothesis giving a specific source of Bill's daily income is true. Now we ask our experts to investigate this society. With the exception of the lottery winners, those who receive a sum of money each day are very secretive concerning the source of their income, and our experts are unable to discover this source. However, they are able to discover that various hypotheses about possible sources of income are precluded, for example, inheritance, salary from work, stock dividends, bribery, and so on. And, with the exception of the lottery, our experts are unable to think of any source of daily income that is not precluded by the facts about this society they have discovered.

---

8. In the lottery example it was assumed that the experts could think of all twenty type-k hypotheses to explain O_n. But this assumption is not essential. We might have supposed that in addition to h_1 the experts could think of h_2–h_{19}, but not h_{20}, which has the lowest of all the probabilities. Still h_1 has the highest probability of all the competing hypotheses of type k they were able to think of, and its probability is not greater than 1/2, despite the fact that the experts could not think of all the type-k hypotheses.

With the situation just specified, I shall suppose that it is reasonable to assign probabilities in such a way that the probability that Bill was a winner in the lottery (h), given that he receives a sum of money for n consecutive days (O_n), given that some hypothesis identifying his daily source of income is true (K), and given the background information (b), is .1, that is, $p(h/K\&O_n\&b) =$ .1, for any $n > 1$. It is also the case that $G(h,O_n,b,k)$, that is, for the experts, h is the only type-k hypothesis in town. In this case, by contrast to the previous one, h is the only type-k hypothesis the experts can come up with to explain O_n that is not completely precluded by other facts.

In accordance with (3), we assume that the fact that an hypothesis is the only game in town increases its probability. As with the previous example, let us suppose it doubles it, so that $p(h/G\&K\&O_n\&b) = 2 \times p(h/K\&O_n\&b)$, for any n. Since $p(h/K\&O_n\&b) = .1$, for any $n > 1$, we get $p(h/G\&K\&O_n\&b) =$ .2, for any $n > 1$, which again violates (1a), (1b), and (2).

In both of the examples so far a certain hypothesis is the only game in town despite the fact that the experts can think of type-k competing hypotheses to explain O_n. In the first example, each of the competing hypotheses has a probability that, although considerably lower than that of the "only game" hypothesis, is nevertheless not zero. In the second example, each of the competing hypotheses the experts can think of has a probability of zero, given the established facts. What about a case in which the experts can think of one type-k hypothesis to explain the O's, where they can think of no competitors at all to explain the O's, even ones precluded by other facts? Here let me propose a new type of example, this time an historical one.

Maxwell's First Kinetic Theory

In 1860 James Clerk Maxwell published his first paper on kinetic theory.[9] In it he postulated that gases are composed of numerous spherical molecules that move in rapid motion and exert forces only at impact. From these assumptions and others, together with background information assuming Newtonian mechanics, Maxwell derived various observed phenomena regarding gases (e.g., phenomena involving pressure, volume, viscosity, heat conduction, and diffusion). Maxwell was searching for a *mechanical* hypothesis—one postulating bodies exerting forces subject to Newton's three laws of motion. (The condition k includes the stipulation that the hypothesis give a specific force subject to these laws.) He was aware of competing mechanical hypotheses to explain *some* of these phenomena (e.g., a kinetic theory involving point molecules, a nonkinetic theory with spherical molecules exhibiting vibratory motion but not translation). But these theories did not explain all the phe-

---

9. James Clerk Maxwell, "Illustrations of the Dynamical Theory of Gases," in W. D. Niven, ed., *Scientific Papers*, vol. I (New York, 1965), pp. 377–409.

nomena that Maxwell's did. (His was the first to provide a unified treatment of the so-called transport phenomena of heat conduction, viscosity, and diffusion.) At least in 1860 his kinetic theory was the only game in town in the sense of being the only mechanical hypothesis known to him or to any other physicist from which the gaseous phenomena in question could be derived.

Nevertheless, Maxwell—quite plausibly—did not regard the probability of his kinetic theory as very high. Even if molecules existed,[10] the probability that they conformed to some of the specific postulates of his theory (e.g., that they were spherical, that they exerted only contact forces), he did not take to be high.[11] What Maxwell did believe is this: Given the success of mechanical theories in other domains (in other writings he mentioned astronomy and electricity), and given certain considerations involving heat transfer, including Joule's earlier determination of the mechanical equivalent of heat, it was likely that *some* mechanical hypothesis was true that would explain the observed gaseous phenomena.[12] However, as he explicitly recognized, numerous mechanical models were possible. And the probability of the particular one he published in 1860 was not regarded by him as high, despite the fact that it was the only known theory to yield the phenomena in question.[13] He developed the one he did because it used particularly simple and mathematically tractable assumptions. Its being the only game in town did not suffice to make Maxwell, or anyone else at the time, believe it was likely to be true.

4. INCREASE IN PROBABILITY

I turn now to the weaker principle

(3) $p(h/G\&K\&O_1, \ldots, O_n\&b) > p(h/K\&O_1, \ldots, O_n\&b)$,
        for $n \geq 1$,

---

10. See quote from Maxwell's 1859 letter to Stokes, in Essay 5, p. 162.

11. In the same letter to Stokes mentioned in note 10, Maxwell writes that he regarded this first attempt as an "exercise in mechanics." And indeed in his second kinetic theory paper six years later he rejects the assumption that molecules are spherical and that they exert forces only at impact.

12. See Essays 7 and 8.

13. Maxwell was aware that it did not generate *all* known gaseous phenomena. For example, at the end of his paper he noted that his theory could not explain, indeed seemed inconsistent with, the experimental result that the specific heat ratio for various gases is 1.408. However, independently of this, I am suggesting that, although Maxwell regarded the probability of a mechanical explanation of gaseous phenomena as high, he did not accord that privilege to this particular version, and would not have even if he had not obtained the negative result concerning specific heats.

which has been presupposed so far. Since (3) is false if $p(h/K\&O_n\&b) = 1$, let us restrict (3) to cases in which this is not so. Will this make it reasonable? To decide let us ask why one might be tempted to assert (3). The answer might be this: we trust the experts. No doubt this is commendable, but how is (3) supposed to follow? Two proposals will be examined in this section and one in the next.

(A) The experts are so good that if they are unable to think of any competitors to some hypothesis in their area of expertise, that fact increases the probability that there are none.

Suppose that K and b imply that some type-k hypothesis is true that is compatible with b and together with b entails O_n. And suppose that h is the only type-k hypothesis the experts can think of that is compatible with b and together with it entails O_n. This is a strong only-game assumption, since it precludes the experts' thinking of less probable competitors. Let me write it as $G'(h)$. And let me use the letter N for the proposition "there are no type-k hypotheses compatible with b other than h that together with b entail O_n." Then (A) can be written as

(A) $p(N/G'(h)\&K\&O_n\&b) > p(N/K\&O_n\&b)$

That is, the fact that h is the only type-k hypothesis the experts can think of to explain O_n increases the probability that there are no others. Now since we are supposing that K and b imply that some type-k hypothesis is true that entails O_n, N together with K and b implies h. Therefore, given $K\&b$, if $G'(h)$ increases N's probability, that is, if (A) is the case, then since N, together with $K\&b$, implies h, it will follow that, given $K\&b$, $G'(h)$ will also increase h's probability. That is, the following will be true, which is a special case of the only-game principle (3):

(3)′ $p(h/G'(h)\&K\&O_n\&b) > p(h/K\&O_n\&b)$

This argument is fallacious. It assumes that if something, say e, increases the probability of an hypothesis h_1, and if h_1 implies h_2, then e must increase the probability of h_2. But this is incorrect.[14] In the preceding argument, from the fact that $G'(h)$ increases N's probability, given $K\&b$, and the fact that N (together with $K\&b$) implies h, it does not follow that $G'(h)$ increases h's probability.

---

14. To see this in a simple case, let e = I pick a 4 from an ordinary deck of cards; h_1 = I pick a 4 of hearts; h_2 = I pick a heart. Then $p(h_1/e) = 1/4 > p(h_1) = 1/52$; $p(h_2/e) = 1/4 = p(h_2)$; yet h_1 implies h_2.

Moreover, (A) is not universally true. The background information b may be such as to make the probability of N unaffected by the fact that the experts can only think of h. In the second lottery example, hypothesis h (that Bill won the lottery) is the only type-k hypothesis, compatible with b, that the experts can think of to explain O_n (his receiving a sum of money for n consecutive days). That is, $G'(h)$. Yet this fact does not increase the probability that there are no type-k hypotheses compatible with b other than h that entail O_n. Given the background information b, the probability that there are no other such type-k competitors is zero, irrespective of whether the experts can think of any.

> (B) The experts are so good that if there is an hypothesis in their area of expertise that they are unable to think of from which to derive a given set of phenomena, this fact decreases the probability of that hypothesis on those phenomena.

Let us suppose, as we did in (A), that h is the only type-k hypothesis the experts can think of that is compatible with b and that with b entails O_n, that is, $G'(h)$. Let U be the set containing h and all type-k competitors to h that with b entail O_n. Assume this set contains hypotheses $h_1, \ldots, h_m$ in addition to h. Suppose that $K\&O_n\&b$ is such that the probability is 1 that some member of the set U is true. Since the experts are unable to think of $h_1, \ldots, h_m$ from which to derive O_n, they are also unable to think of the disjunction of these, and therefore by (B), $p(h_1 \vee \ldots \vee h_m/G'(h)\&K\&O_n\&b) < p(h_1 \vee \ldots \vee h_m/K\&O_n\&b)$. But given that the probability is 1 that some member of the set U is true, and given that $h_1, \ldots, h_m$ are all competitors of h, it follows that $p(h/K\&O_n\&b) + p(h_1 \vee \ldots \vee h_m/K\&O_n\&b) = 1$, and also that $p(h/G'(h)\&K\&O_n\&b) + p(h_1 \vee \ldots \vee h_m/G'(h)\&K\&O_n\&b) = 1$. Therefore,

$$(3)' \quad p(h/G'(h)\&K\&O_n\&b) > p(h/K\&O_n\&b)$$

which is the version of principle (3) in which the only-game assumption is the strong one that h is the only type-k hypothesis the experts are able to think of to explain O_n.

The problem with this is that (B) is not true in general. Let us consider first objective probabilities. One reason the experts may be unable to think of some hypothesis is that its probability is very small. (The experts don't clutter their minds with very unlikely hypotheses.) In the twenty lotteries case, suppose that, for this reason, the experts are unable to think of h_{20}—that John was a winner in the twentieth lottery—to explain his winnings. Despite this fact, given b (which indicates that of the forty-two winning tickets only one is from lottery 20) the objective a priori probability of h_{20} is 1/42. The fact that the experts are unable to think of this hypothesis would not decrease its probability on the background information b. Assuming the twenty lotteries are fair ones, 1/42 represents the standard objective a priori probability assignable to h_{20}, no matter what the experts can or cannot think of.[15]

What if probabilities are construed more subjectively? Let h be some hypothesis that the experts are unable to think of to explain O_n. Let the subjective probability of h represent the rationally corrected degree of belief of someone other than these experts, say that of a relative newcomer to the field. This newcomer thinks of some hypothesis h to explain O_n, although the recognized experts are unable to come up with h. To be rationally corrected should the newcomer's degree of belief in h be decreased by the fact that the experts are unable to think of h to explain O_n? Not necessarily.

There are a variety of reasons why the experts may have been unable to come up with some hypothesis h to explain O_n which should not decrease one's degree of belief in h. For example, the experts have not thought about the problem long or hard enough; they were trying to work out some competing set of assumptions, which took a good deal of time and prevented them from thinking of h; they were not attempting to unify these particular phenomena (e.g., transport phenomena); h contains concepts very different from those the experts are used to employing, although they are not concepts the use of which decreases h's probability; h is just very difficult to think of. Maxwell might have offered a number of these reasons to explain why physicists before him were unable to come up with the particular theory he did.[16] He would not have regarded the fact that they were unable to think of his hypotheses as a reason to decrease his degree of belief in them.

Reasons of the sort just noted indicate conditions that may have prevented the experts from thinking of a given hypothesis to explain certain phenomena. If those conditions did obtain and did prevent the experts from thinking of h to explain O_n, I shall call them *disturbing conditions* for the experts with

---

15. Or, to take a case in which probabilities are construed as relative frequencies, suppose that when symptoms S are present a patient has disease d in 70 percent of the cases, so that $p(\text{disease } d/\text{symptoms } S) = .7$. But suppose the experts are unaware of disease d (it has not yet been identified as a disease). The fact that the experts are unaware of disease d, and therefore are unable to think of this hypothesis to explain symptoms S, does not decrease the probability that a patient has d, given that he has S — where this probability is construed objectively as a frequency. In this case the experts are unable to think of hypothesis h not because h's probability is very small, but because h invokes a cause with which the experts are completely unfamiliar. On a frequency view, h's probability need not be affected by what the experts can or cannot think of.

Later I will consider how a frequency theory might take into account what the experts think. But even then (3) will not be true in general.

16. For example, before statistical concepts were introduced into physics by Maxwell (and Clausius), the experts in the physics community were unable to come up with certain statistical hypotheses about molecules employed by Maxwell in 1860. But this fact did not decrease Maxwell's degree of belief in such hypotheses. He would have claimed that the reason the experts were unable to think of them is that they contain statistical ideas that were foreign to the physics establishment. And he would have rejected the idea that statistical hypotheses are more likely to be false than nonstatistical ones.

respect to h and O_n. These conditions are of two kinds. Some (as we have seen) do not decrease the probability of the hypothesis itself. I will call these *neutral* disturbing conditions.[17] Other conditions, "negative" disturbing ones, do decrease the probability of the hypothesis.

What would a negative disturbing condition be? To take a nonscientific example, suppose that the police investigating a murder are unable to come up with the hypothesis that Detective Robinson (one of the police investigators) committed the murder. The reason they are unable to think of this hypothesis is that police detectives rarely commit murders, especially those they are investigating. Assuming that this fact decreases the probability that Detective Robinson committed the murder, we have here a negative disturbing condition. It prevents the experts from thinking of the hypothesis in question and it decreases the probability of that hypothesis.

If negative disturbing conditions are present, or if the probability is high that they are, will an only-game argument work? As before, we let U be the set that contains not only an hypothesis h that with b entails O_n, but also all the type-k competitors to h that with b entail O_n. Suppose that given $K\&O_n\&b$ the probability is 1 that some member of U is true. Suppose that the experts can only think of h to explain O_n; they cannot think of $h_1, \ldots ,h_m$, the remaining members of U. And suppose that the probability is high that negative disturbing conditions, and not just neutral ones, obtain for these experts with respect to the competitors $h_1, \ldots ,h_m$. Given these suppositions, the probability of each of the competitors $h_1, \ldots ,h_m$ is decreased. Can we now use the argument at the beginning of (B) to show that the only-game principle (3)' holds?[18]

Before we draw such a conclusion two points must be noted. First, these suppositions are special. They cannot be made in general when some hypothesis is the only game in town. That is, (a) $K\&O_n\&b$ will not in general make the probability 1 that some member of the set U is true. (K implies only that some type-k hypothesis is true, but U does not necessarily contain all the type-k hypotheses, even all those that entail O_n.) (b) The probability will not always be high that negative disturbing conditions are present. In the Maxwell case we noted only neutral disturbing conditions, not negative ones.

Second, and most important, if negative disturbing conditions are present, then what does the work in this argument is not the only-game assumption but the presence of the negative disturbing conditions. Let

F = certain conditions obtain, not in $O_n\&b$, that decrease the probabili-

---

17. Probability here can be construed either objectively or subjectively; in which case we can also distinguish between objective and subjective disturbing conditions. But the latter distinction will not be important in what follows in determining whether the only-game principle (3)' holds.

18. We need to assume the existence of type-k competitors to h that entail O_n. Otherwise the present argument cannot be invoked.

ty of each type-k competitor to h that entails O_n, and these conditions prevented the experts from thinking of these competitors to explain O_n.

F reports the existence of negative disturbing conditions for each of the type-k competitors to h that entail O_n. Now in the formulas in the argument near the beginning of (B), replace $G'(h)$—the only-game assumption—with F. The argument goes through, and we obtain

(3)'' $p(h/F\&K\&O_n\&b) > p(h/K\&O_n\&b)$

Moreover, if we retain $G'(h)$, then the argument does not go through, since in its original form it assumes the principle (B), which is not true in general. But (3)'' is not an only-game principle. It does not say that h's being the only game in town increases its probability. Indeed, what makes (3)'' derivable is not really all of F but only part of it. Let

F_A = certain conditions obtain, not in $O_n\&b$, that decrease the probability of each type-k competitor to h that entails O_n.

Then, again assuming that on $K\&O_n\&b$ the probability is 1 that some member of U is true, we can derive

$p(h/F_A\&K\&O_n\&b) > p(h/K\&O_n\&b)$

This says that the existence of certain conditions not contained in $O_n\&b$ that decrease the probability of each type-k competitor to h that entails O_n increases h's probability on $K\&O_n\&b$. But this is not an only-game principle. It is not the fact that the experts are unable to think of any type-k competitors to h that increases h's probability. (This is neither necessary nor sufficient for doing so.) Rather it is the fact that certain conditions obtain—empirical facts such as that police detectives rarely commit the murders they investigate—that count against each of the type-k competitors. In short, an increase in h's probability occurs not because it is the only game in town, but because of the existence of empirical facts that decrease the probability of h's competitors.

5. THE SUCCESS OF THE EXPERTS

(C) In their area of expertise the experts are quite successful in finding hypotheses that are true.

To relate this to the only-game assumption (3), let us suppose that in general when an hypothesis in their area of expertise is the only game in town for the experts it turns out to be correct r percent of the time. Call this information $S(r)$, for "the success rate of the experts' only-game hypotheses $= r$."[19] To get at an idea behind (C) that might generate (3), let us suppose that the probability of h, given that it is the only game in town for the experts, is determined solely by r, the success rate of the experts' only-game hypotheses. We might write:

(7) $p(h/G\&K\&O_n\&b\&S(r)) = r$

On this idea, the information $S(r)$ giving the success rate for the experts' only-game hypotheses completely determines the probability of h, independently of the information in $K\&O_n\&b$. Now suppose that the experts' success rate r for only-game hypotheses is quite high, say .7. And suppose that a particular hypothesis h, although it is the only game in town for the experts, has a probability on $K\&O_n\&b\&S(r)$—but not G—that is less than .7. (This is its probability without the assumption that it is the only game in town.) Then

(8) $p(h/G\&K\&O_n\&b\&S(.7)) > p(h/K\&O_n\&b\&S(.7))$

which is in accord with the principle (3). (To make it look exactly like (3) we could incorporate the success rate information $S(.7)$ into the background information b.)

However, if we proceed in this manner, it is obvious that principle (3) will not always be satisfied. Suppose that some hypothesis h is the only game in town for the experts, but instead of having a low probability it has a high one, indeed higher than the experts' success rate r. Then, using (7) above we would have to conclude that $p(h/G\&K\&O_n\&b\&S(r)) < p(h/K\&O_n\&b\&S(r))$, in violation of principle (3).[20]

---

19. There are various options here. The broadest one is to consider the success rate of *all* only-game hypotheses for the experts in their area of expertise, whether or not such hypotheses are similar to the particular only-game hypothesis being considered. For example, if the experts are physicists, we look at their success rate for only-game hypotheses in physics generally, even though the specific hypothesis in question pertains to optics. More narrowly, we could focus on their success rate with respect to only-game hypotheses bearing some similarity to the one in question, say from the same field. If we have reliable statistics in the latter sort of case, I shall assume that the narrower concept of success rate is to be used.

20. Admittedly, (7) is a strong principle, urging that the success rate of the experts completely determines h's probability. We might modify this by taking the probability in (7) to be some weighted mean of this success rate and the value of the probability of h without the only-game assumption, that is, the value of $p(h/K\&O_n\&b\&S(r))$. If the latter probability $= s$, then we replace (7) with (7)' $p(h/G\&K\&O_n\&b\&S(r)) = w(r,s)$, where $w(r,s)$ is some weighted mean of r and s. This still won't guarantee (3) in general. Suppose $r = s$, that is, the experts' success rate for only-game hypotheses is the same as the probability of hypothesis h on $K\&O_n\&b\&S(r)$. Then, using (7)', if h is the only game in town, we can derive (9) $p(h/G\&K\&O_n\&b\&S(r)) =$

I am not here objecting to the idea of taking into account the success rate of the experts with regard to only-game hypotheses and of relativizing the probability of h to this information. If we do so, then when the success rate of the experts with regard to only-game hypotheses is higher than the probability of h, the only-game-in-town principle will be satisfied: h's probability will be increased by the fact that it is the only game in town. On the other hand, when the success rate of the experts with regard to only-game hypotheses is less than or equal to the probability of h, principle (3) will not be satisfied; h's probability will not be increased by the fact that it is the only game in town. And we cannot in general assume that the success rate of the experts with regard to only-game hypotheses will be higher than the probability of particular only-game hypotheses.

Indeed, in many cases we expect them to be the same. To see this let us recall the "twenty lotteries" example. Suppose such lotteries are run very often, and that each time, in explaining why some particular person receives a sum of money each day, the experts recognize that the hypothesis that such a person was a winner of the first lottery is the most probable of the type-k competitors. (Its a priori probability is 5/42.) Furthermore, suppose that — as we might indeed expect to happen — in the long run such type-k only-game hypotheses turn out to be true 5/42nds of the time. Accordingly, the success rate of the experts = 5/42 = the probability of the only-game hypothesis h_1 (that John won lottery 1). Therefore $p(h_1/G\&K\&O_n\&b\&S(5/42)) = p(h_1/K\&O_n\&b\&S(5/42))$, in violation of principle (3).

I suggest that such a case is not untypical; indeed, it is an ideal one for illustrating the success of the experts. When the lottery experts claim that the probability that John won the first lottery = 5/42, they fully expect nature to cooperate in such cases. That is, they expect that in general, in the past as well as in the future, analogous hypotheses for analogous lotteries will come out true approximately 5/42nds of the time. If nature does cooperate in this way with the probability assessments of the experts, their success rate with such hypotheses will match the probability of these hypotheses, and the only-game principle (3), with the success rate information built in, will not hold.

Indeed, I suggest that the best way to judge the success of the experts is by seeing to what extent their success rate for hypotheses of a given kind matches the probability of specific hypotheses of that kind. Perfect success = a perfect match. If so, then perfect success will imply propositions such as (9) of note 20 in which the only-game assumption does not increase h's probability.

$p(h/K\&O_n\&b\&S(r))$, in violation of (3). Or suppose that r = success rate = .6, $s = p(h/K\&O_n\&b\&S(r)) = .8$, and we take the weighted mean $w(r,s)$ to be a simple mean, so that $w(r,s) = .7$. Then using (7)' we get $p(h/G\&K\&O_n\&S(r)) = .7 < p(h/K\&O_n\&b\&S(r)) = .8$, again in violation of principle (3).

6. THE ONLY GAME AS A RESEARCH STRATEGY

I have argued that h's probability is not necessarily or generally increased by its being the only game in town. When it is increased by the success of only-game hypotheses, the circumstances are extraordinary. Alternatively, what may be increasing h's probability is not really its only-game status but certain empirical facts that decrease the probability of its competitors. If h's probability is not necessarily or generally increased by its being the only game in town, then when it is low to begin with, its only-game status does not necessarily give it high probability.

Suppose, then, we abandon the idea that the only game in town argument necessarily makes the probability of an hypothesis high or even increases it. Despite this, might it be construed as a reasonable research strategy? That is, can we say the following:

(R) If h is the only game in town then it is reasonable to *pursue h*.

By "pursue" h I mean to include a host of things scientists and many others typically do when they work out their ideas, including formulating h as precisely as possible, relating it to other hypotheses, applying it to new areas, drawing out consequences, and testing them. What I mean to exclude is taking some epistemic stand with respect to it, such as believing it, or believing that it is probable, or believing that it is more probable than it was before considering competitors.

I suggest that (R) is not true in general. Sometimes it will not be reasonable to pursue h even when h is the only game in town. Sometimes it will be reasonable to pursue h under this condition. But that may result not from its being the only game in town, or not primarily from this, but from other considerations. Let me note one case of each kind.

The lord of the manor has been murdered; he has strangulation marks on his neck. There are several other clues as well. The police examining all the clues note that the hypothesis that the victim was strangled by his butler would, if true, explain these clues. However, because of certain background facts about the butler (his lack of strength, his height) the police take the probability of the butler hypothesis, given all the clues and background information, to be low. Moreover, either they can think of no other hypothesis that, if true, would explain the clues, or else any others they can think of are even less probable.

What strategy should the police follow? That depends on their goal and resources. I shall suppose that their goal is "truth," that is, to find the real murderer, or at least to come up with an hypothesis that, on the basis of the evidence, the jury can accept "beyond reasonable doubt." There is already very reasonable doubt regarding the butler hypothesis, despite its being the only game in town. The police resources — money and manpower — are finite.

If they pursue the butler hypothesis—if they try to dig up more facts about the butler's past, interview his friends, and so on—this will preclude other pursuits. The police have at least two other alternatives, each of which may be more reasonable than pursuing the butler hypothesis:

1. Look for competitors to the butler hypothesis that are different from those already considered.
2. Suspend the investigation of this murder and turn to some other pressing crime that needs solving.

Given the "truth" goal—or at least the goal of presenting a convincing case to a jury—it may not be reasonable for the police to pursue the butler hypothesis, despite the fact that at the moment it is the only game in town. The analogy with scientific cases should be obvious.

Finally, for an example of a different kind consider once more Maxwell's first kinetic theory. I shall assume that it was reasonable for Maxwell to pursue his hypothesis involving spherical molecules that exert only contact forces. Moreover, I shall suppose that the probability of this hypothesis was not high on all the evidence then available, but that in 1860 this was the only game in town. Was the latter fact the only reason, or even the main one, that Maxwell pursued his theory?

Maxwell's central aim in this paper was not to present the "true" theory, or to produce evidence that would convince physicists of its truth beyond reasonable doubt. It was rather to see whether it was even possible to work out a mechanical theory of gases—one based on the assumption that gases are composed of particles subject only to principles of Newtonian mechanics. Earlier mechanical theories had been proposed by other physicists. But these had not been developed with the detail or mathematical sophistication that Maxwell desired, or applied to as many observed gaseous phenomena as Maxwell would like. He pursued the version he did—involving spherical molecules and contact forces—because it was mechanical, simple, and easily investigated, and not solely or principally because it was the only game in town.

Was its only-game status, then, *among* the reasons Maxwell pursued it? Only indirectly. There is one question about Maxwell's choice that can be answered by appeal to the only-game-in-town argument. If we had asked Maxwell why he pursued this theory rather than some other simple, manipulatable, mechanical hypothesis that explains gaseous phenomena, he probably would have replied: he can't think of any others; it is the only game in town. More generally, one may pursue an hypothesis h because it has features f (it is mechanical, simple, manipulatable, etc.). To the question: Why did you pursue this hypothesis rather than some other with features f?, an only-game response may be appropriate.

Even if this is granted, it does not follow that an hypothesis is worth considering only if it is the only game in town. It could have been reasonable for Maxwell to pursue his theory even if it had lacked this status. If one wants to know whether a mechanical theory of gases is possible from which gaseous phenomena can be derived, it is reasonable, as Maxwell did, to start with a simple, manipulatable hypothesis, even if that hypothesis is less probable than some less idealized competitor one knows about; that is, even if that hypothesis is not the only game in town.

The first example above shows that some hypothesis h's being the only game in town is not sufficient to pursue h, and hence that (R) is false. The second example shows that h's being the only game in town is not a necessary condition for pursuing it. It also shows that when h is reasonable to pursue and h is the only game in town, it does not follow that h is reasonable to pursue solely or primarily because it is the only game in town.

7. CONCLUSIONS

If some hypothesis is the only game in town, what should one do or believe about it?

1. Its being the only game in town does not give us license to conclude that the probability of the hypothesis is high or that it has increased. Nor does it necessarily follow that pursuing it is a good strategy, or, even when it is, that this is so simply or primarily because the hypothesis is the only game in town.

2. Under certain special circumstances it might be argued that an hypothesis' probability increases when it is the only game in town. One such circumstance occurs when the probability is 1 that some member of the set U is true (where U contains the only-game hypothesis h and in addition all type-k competitors to h that entail O_n); and when the probability is high that there are negative disturbing conditions with respect to each of the type-k competitors to h that entails O_n. But such circumstances do not obtain in general. Moreover, when they do, what is increasing h's probability is not its only-game status but certain empirical facts that count against each of the type-k competitors. A second special circumstance occurs when the probability of the hypothesis is exceeded by the experts' success rate for only-game hypotheses of that type. But such situations do not normally occur. If, as we generally expect, nature conforms to the probabilities the experts assign, then the experts' success rate will match the probabilities they assign. Normally, then, there will be no reason to infer from the success of the experts with regard to only-game hypotheses to an increase in the probability of such hypotheses.

3. Mill's attack on the method of hypothesis is not vitiated by an only-game argument. Mill argues that the fact that an hypothesis entails a range of phenomena — both established facts and predictions later confirmed — is not sufficient to confer high probability on it. One cannot respond by saying that if scientists are unable to find plausible competitors, then the probability of the hypothesis in question must be high or at least must have increased.*

---

*I am indebted to Don Garrett, Brad Petrie, Doren Recker, and Robert Rynasiewicz for very helpful suggestions.

PART III

Cathode Rays and the Electron

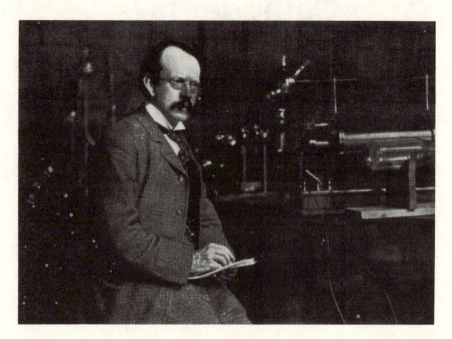

J. J. Thomson.

ESSAY 10

Introduction

"When you hear hoofbeats think horses, not zebras."

STANDARD ADVICE TO PHYSICIANS

1. HISTORICAL BACKGROUND[1]

The discharge of electricity through gases is a phenomenon known since the eighteenth century. In a standard type of experiment, a glass tube filled with air, containing positive and negative electrodes, is used. When the pressure of the air in the tube is reduced to a few millimeters of mercury and a source of high potential is connected to the positive electrode, an electrical discharge fills the space between the electrodes with a pink or reddish glow. If the pressure is reduced to about 0.1 millimeters of mercury the appearance of the glow changes, as indicated in Figure 2.

In 1855 Geissler invented a pump that allowed much lower gas pressures to be produced in the discharge tube. This permitted an important discovery to be made by Plücker in 1859. When the pressure is reduced to approximately 0.001 mm of mercury, Plücker noted that the glass near the negative electrode, or cathode, glows with a greenish phosphorescence, and that the position of the glow changes when a magnetic field is introduced. He attributed this to something emanating from the cathode that was distinct from the ordinary electrical discharge. Plücker's student Hittorf in 1869 discovered that if a solid body is placed between the cathode and the walls of the tube it casts a shadow. He concluded that rays are emitted from the cathode that travel in straight lines. There followed a series of experiments by Eugen

---

1. More complete historical accounts can be found in Isobel Falconer, "Corpuscles, Electrons and Cathode Rays: J. J. Thomson and the 'Discovery of the Electron'," *British Journal for the History of Science* 20 (1987), pp. 241-276; David L. Anderson, *The Discovery of the Electron* (New York, 1981; reprint of 1964 ed.); John Heilbron, article on J. J. Thomson in *Dictionary of Scientific Biography*, vol. 13, pp. 362-372. Stuart M. Feffer, "Arthur Schuster, J.J. Thomson, and the Discovery of the Electron," *Historical Studies in the Physical and Biological Sciences* 20 (1989), pp. 33-51. I have benefited considerably from these works.

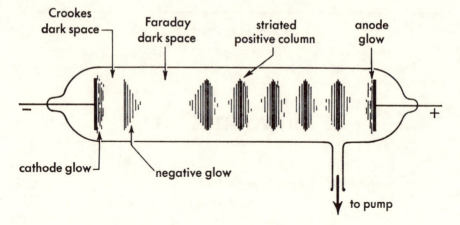

FIG. 2*

Goldstein in 1871 on a variety of different cathodes, which showed that the rays are perpendicular to the surface of the cathode; that they are emitted and generate the same effects whether the cathode is made of platinum, gold, or other metals; and that they produce chemical reactions (e.g., they cause silver salts to change color).

In 1879 the English physicist William Crookes, after conducting new experiments with a variety of cathode tubes he devised, concluded that cathode rays are molecules of the gas in the tube that have gained a negative charge when they collide with the cathode. Because of this negative charge they are strongly repelled by the negative cathode and travel at high velocity in a direction perpendicular to the cathode, striking the glass and producing fluorescence. This "charged molecules" theory could explain a number of known properties of the rays, including their rectilinear motion, the fact that they travel in a direction perpendicular to the cathode, that they are deflected by a magnetic field, and that they cause fluorescence. In response to Crookes' theory, Goldstein, as well as fellow Germans Wiedemann and Hertz, argued that the rays are not molecules, or indeed particles of any sort, but some type of ether waves, like light in certain respects but not in others. Unlike light, they are bent by a magnetic field and they are emitted only perpendicularly from a surface. But in other respects they are similar to light, for example, they travel in straight lines, they can cause glass to fluoresce, they produce a shadow if intercepted by an opaque object, and they can convey energy.

The German wave theorists produced a variety of arguments against the charged particle theory, two of which came to be regarded by particle theo-

---

*Figure 3-5 from *Introduction to Atomic and Nuclear Physics*, Fourth Edition, by Henry Semat, copyright © 1962 and renewed 1990 by Henry Semat, reprinted by permission of Saunders College Publishing, a division of Holt, Rinehart and Winston, Inc., reprinted by permission of the publisher.

rists as particularly important. First, if cathode rays are negatively charged particles, then they should be deflected not only by a magnetic field but by an electrical one as well. In a series of experiments in 1883 Hertz failed to detect any displacement of a cathode ray beam in the presence of an electrostatic field. He concluded:

> These cathode rays are electrically indifferent, and amongst known agents the phenomenon most nearly allied to them is light. The rotation of the plane of polarization of light is the nearest analog to the bending of cathode rays by a magnet.[2]

The second major problem for particle theorists arose as a result of a discovery by Hertz in 1891 that cathode rays could pass through thin layers of gold, silver, and other metals. Hertz' student Philipp Lenard extended this research, showing that cathode rays penetrate thin layers of metal and travel about half a centimeter outside the tube before the phosphorescence produced is reduced to about half its original value. Now the metal foils used were much too thick to allow molecules or atoms to pass through. (This was demonstrated experimentally, since the metal foils attached to the tube allowed no hydrogen or any other gas to accumulate on the other side.) Since atoms and molecules were considered the smallest particles, the conclusion was that cathode rays cannot be particles. By contrast, light, a wave phenomenon, was known to be capable of penetrating thin gold foils.

In 1890 the British physicist Arthur Schuster used quantitative results he had obtained with the magnetic deflection of cathode rays, together with theoretical assumptions about the maximum kinetic energy putative cathode particles might have, and information about known molecular velocities, to obtain upper and lower bounds for the ratio of mass to charge of the particles. He pointed out that the hydrogen atom in electrolysis was known to have a ratio of mass to charge that lies between the upper and lower limits he obtained for the cathode rays. So he defended Crookes' idea that cathode rays are molecules or atoms that have become negatively charged. However, unlike Crookes, he held that these negatively charged particles arise from the dissociation of neutral molecules into positive and negative parts, with the negative ones being repelled by the cathode.

In 1894, J. J. Thomson, Cavendish Professor of Experimental Physics at Cambridge, conducted experiments to measure the velocity of the cathode rays. He concluded (erroneously) that their velocity is about 200,000 meters per second, much less than the velocity of light. In 1895 the French physicist Jean Perrin arranged a cathode ray tube with a charge collector inside the tube. By showing that the collector became negatively charged when the cathode rays entered it, he concluded that cathode rays carry a negative charge. In 1897 Thomson repeated Perrin's experiment, using a somewhat different arrangement so as to avoid the objection that the rays are initially accompanied by, but not constituted of, negatively charged particles. (Thom-

---

2. H. Hertz, *Miscellaneous Papers* (London, 1896), p. 254.

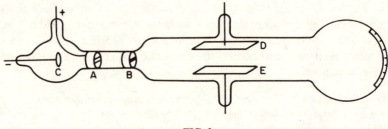

FIG. 3

son's experimental arrangement is described in Essay 11.) "This experiment," he writes, "shows that however we twist and deflect the cathode rays by magnetic forces, the negative electrification follows the same path as the rays, and that this negative electrification is indissolubly connected with the cathode rays."[3]

Next, to meet Hertz' objection to the particle theory that no electrical deflection of cathode rays had been observed, Thomson proceeded to repeat Hertz' experiment, but this time attempting to achieve a much higher exhaustion of the gas in the tube. He believed that "the cathode rays, when they pass through a gas, make it a conductor, so that the gas acting like a conductor screens off the electric force from the charged particle. . . ."[4] This effect should be reduced if the gas in the tube is more extensively evacuated.

The apparatus Thomson used is represented in Figure 3. Cathode rays travel from C through a slit in anode A, through a second slit in a metal plug B connected with the earth, through parallel aluminum plates D and E, and finally fall on the end of the tube where they produce a phosphorescent patch. At very high exhaustion, the rays were indeed observed to be deflected when the plates were connected with electrical terminals of a series of batteries.

From the results of these experiments Thomson concludes that cathode rays are negatively charged particles:

> As the cathode rays carry a charge of negative electricity, are deflected by an electrostatic force as if they were negatively electrified, and are acted on by a magnetic force in just the way in which this force would act on a negatively electrified body moving along the path of these rays, I can see no escape from the conclusion that they are charges of negative electricity carried by particles of matter.[5]

Thomson next proceeds to ask what these particles are: "Are they atoms, or molecules, or matter in a still finer state of subdivision?" (p. 302). To

---

3. J. J. Thomson, "Cathode Rays," *Philosophical Magazine* 44 (October, 1897), p. 295.
4. J. J. Thomson, "Cathode Rays," *The Electrician* 39 (May 21, 1897), p. 107.
5. Thomson, "Cathode Rays," *Philosophical Magazine*, p. 302.

answer this question, Thomson performed experiments designed to measure the ratio of the mass of these particles to the charge they carry. He used two methods, one involving the use of a cathode tube of the sort depicted in Figure 3 but without the plates D and E. Cathode rays carrying a total charge Q across some section of their beam are subjected to a uniform magnetic field of strength H and as a result are deflected in a path with radius of curvature r. The rays then strike a solid body and convert their total kinetic energy W into heating that body. Thomson derives a formula relating the mass to charge ratio m/e to the quantities Q, H, r, and W (see Essay 11). All of these quantities are measurable in ways he specifies. By experiment he shows that m/e is independent of the nature of the gas in the tube and of the metal of the cathode, and that it has a value whose order of magnitude is 10^{-7}. He notes that this is very small by comparison with 10^{-4}, the value of m/e for the hydrogen ion in electrolysis (the smallest value for m/e then known). He states that this could be due to the "smallness of m or the largeness of e, or to a combination of these two." But from Lenard's results concerning distances traveled by cathode rays after penetrating thin layers of metal, he concludes that "the carrier, then, must be small compared with ordinary molecules" (p. 310).

Finally, Thomson introduces a general explanation of the observed facts regarding cathode rays — one he considers the "most simple and straight-forward" — according to which the cathode particles are the "primordial atoms" of which all matter consists. "If these corpuscles are charged with electricity and projected from the cathode by the electric field, they would behave exactly like the cathode rays" (p. 311). The question arises concerning how a chemical atom could be stable if it were composed of such mutually repellent negatively charged corpuscles. To explain this possibility Thomson invokes a model of floating magnets, introduced by Mayer, in which magnets achieve equilibrium under mutual repulsions and a central attraction produced by the pole of a large magnet placed above the floating ones.

In December 1899, two years after his October 1897 "Cathode Rays" paper, Thomson published results of experiments with negatively charged particles produced by ultraviolet light falling on an electrified metal plate and also by heating carbon filaments in an atmosphere of hydrogen.[6] Thomson experimentally determined the value of m/e in both cases, and found it to be the same as that for cathode rays. In the case of the charged particles produced by ultraviolet light, he also determined a separate value for the charge e that is the same as that carried by the hydrogen atom in electrolysis. He regarded this as

6. J. J. Thomson, "On the Masses of the Ions in Gases at Low Pressures," *Philosophical Magazine* 48 (1899), pp. 547-567.

clear proof that the ions have a much smaller mass than ordinary atoms; so that in the convection of negative electricity at low pressures we have something smaller even than the atom, something which involves the splitting up of the atom, inasmuch as we have taken from it a part, though only a small one, of its mass. (p. 548)

Toward the end of this 1899 paper he says that he adopts the following as a "working hypothesis":

I regard the atom as containing a large number of smaller bodies which I will call corpuscles; these corpuscles are equal to each other; the mass of a corpuscle is the mass of the negative ion in a gas at low pressure, i.e. about 3×10^{-26} of a gramme. In the normal atom, this assemblage of corpuscles forms a system which is electrically neutral. Though the individual corpuscles behave like negative ions, yet when they are assembled in a neutral atom the negative effect is balanced by something which causes the space through which the corpuscles are spread to act as if it had a charge of positive electricity equal in amount to the sum of the negative charges on the corpuscles. (p. 565)

Although Thomson used the term "corpuscle," others such as FitzGerald, and by 1902 Thomson's student Rutherford,[7] appropriated the term "electron" for them. As a result of his cathode ray experiments and his hypotheses to explain them, Thomson is recognized as the discoverer of the electron.[8]

Thomson's primary interest in electrical discharge in gases beginning in 1884 did not emerge as a result of the cathode ray dispute. Rather it was sparked by the subject of vortex rings, which, as Helmholtz had shown, have a certain permanence. As noted in Essay 5, Kelvin and Maxwell had proposed a model of the atom as a vortex ring, which had advantages over elastic sphere and action-at-a-distance models. In 1882 Thomson won the Adams prize for an essay on this topic. His first work on electrical discharge was guided by this theory which, he believed, had implications for the dissociation of molecules. But the theory was not a fruitful one, and by 1890 Thomson abandoned this model. Falconer has argued that the cathode ray controversy between German and English physicists became important in England only in 1896 following Roentgen's 1895 discovery of x-rays, which are produced when cathode rays strike a target. This discovery led Thomson to develop a successful quantitative theory of gaseous discharge and, according to Falconer, hav-

---

7. See E. Rutherford, "The Existence of Bodies Smaller than Atoms," in *The Collected Papers of Lord Rutherford* (London, 1962), vol. 1, pp. 403–409.

8. The term *electron* was introduced by Dr. Johnstone Stoney in 1891, and was also employed by Joseph Larmor and H. A. Lorentz. But these physicists were referring to particles or charges or both that could be positive as well as negative, and not to the negative particles that comprise cathode rays.

ing produced this Thomson then turned to "such extraneous problems as the nature of cathode rays which x-rays had thrust into prominence."[9]

2. METHODOLOGICAL ISSUES

Let me ask more specifically about the kind of reasoning Thomson was employing in 1897, the year generally chosen as the one in which Thomson discovered the electron. Whatever its nature, Heilbron has claimed that the argument Thomson was offering in 1897 was faulty, since it claimed "far more for the 'corpuscle' than the data authorized."[10] He notes that "few physicists in 1897 were prepared to believe on this basis that the world was made of corpuscles." In discussing the evidence, Falconer states that "Thomson was prone to ambitious theoretical conjecture based on very little experimental data,"[11] and that he made a "bold, unsubstantiated leap."

Both Heilbron and Falconer are referring to a particular set of claims Thomson made about the particles comprising cathode rays (the "corpuscles"). These claims are as follows:

1. Cathode particles are much smaller than atoms and molecules.
2. They are constituents of atoms.
3. They are the only constituents of atoms.

Does Thomson present an argument for these claims, and if so, how should it be understood? In the light of methodological discussions of historical episodes considered earlier in this book, as well as of Thomson's own methodological remarks in various places, three possible interpretations will be noted.

---

9. Falconer, *op. cit.*, p. 253. In addition, both Falconer and Feffer (*op. cit.*) have argued that Thomson's "corpuscles" were not discrete particles with empty spaces between them but certain configurations in an all-pervading ether. This idea was derived originally from the view of atoms as vortex rings in the ether; in 1895 Thomson altered this by supposing the atom to consist of a system of motions akin to those produced by "a number of gyrostats all spinning in one way round the outwardly drawn normals to their surface" ("The Relation between the Atom and the Charge of Electricity Carried by it," *Philosophical Magazine* 40 [1895], p. 513). Feffer claims that "the corpuscles that Thomson discovered in 1897 were the gyrostats he had spoken of in the final weeks of 1895" (p. 58). Thomson does not mention this conception explicitly in his 1897 papers on cathode rays. Indeed, in his May 21, 1897 paper, p. 108, he writes that "the atoms of the ordinary elements are made up of corpuscles and holes, the holes being predominant."

10. Heilbron, *op. cit.*, p. 367.

11. Falconer, *op. cit.*, p. 270.

Interpretation 1

It might be thought that Thomson is using a form of the method of hypothesis, or hypothetico-deductive reasoning, to infer the truth or probability of his claims (1) through (3). Such an interpretation is suggested by various passages in his 1897 works. For example, in his "Cathode Rays" paper in *The Electrician* he writes:

> Let us trace the consequence of supposing that the atoms of the elements are aggregations of very small particles, all similar to each other; we shall call such particles corpuscles, so that the atoms of the ordinary elements are made up of corpuscles and holes, the holes being predominant. Let us suppose that at the cathode some of the molecules of the gas get split up into these corpuscles, and that these, charged with negative electricity, and moving at a high velocity form the cathode rays. (pp. 108–109)

Thomson goes on to show how these suppositions generate certain observed phenomena, in particular Lenard's results and the result that the magnetic deflection of the cathode rays is the same whatever the nature of the gas (p. 109).

The argument is repeated almost *verbatim* in a book published in 1898, but based on lectures given at Princeton in October 1896.[12] In his October 1897 "Cathode Rays" paper, the argument appears again, this time formulated in terms of explanation:

> The explanation which seems to me to account in the most simple and straightforward manner for the facts is founded on a view of the chemical elements which has been favourably entertained by many chemists. . . . (p. 311)

There follows a description of the theory and of how it accounts for various known properties of cathode rays.

On this interpretation, then, from the fact that assumptions (1) through (3) yield, or explain, a range of known properties of cathode rays, Thomson argues to the truth or probability of (1) through (3). Accordingly, those who (following the tradition of Newton and Mill) reject the method of hypothesis will fault Thomson's reasoning. No matter how many phenomena Thomson can derive or explain from his theory, critics of this method will object that he cannot infer the truth or probability of his theory in this manner. They will point out that some competing theory may also have these features.

Indeed, FitzGerald does exactly that in the same May 21, 1897, issue of *The Electrician* in which Thomson's paper appears. He writes:

---

12. J. J. Thomson, *The Discharge of Electricity Through Gases* (Cambridge, Mass., 1898), pp. 198–199.

In fact, there seems an *embarras de richesse* in the way of possible explanations of the transparency of media to cathode rays without supposing that we are in the presence of a possible method of transmutation of matter.[13]

One hypothesis FitzGerald suggests is that cathode rays are composed of (what FitzGerald calls) *free electrons*. He writes:

> This is somewhat like Prof. J. J. Thomson's hypothesis, except that it does not assume the electron to be a constituent part of an atom, nor that we are dissociating atoms, nor consequently that we are on the track of the alchemists. (p. 104)

If Thomson were employing h-d reasoning in the case of cathode rays, it would be contrary to an antipathy he expresses toward such reasoning in the kinetic theory. For example, in 1883 in a work on vortex rings, he begins by noting that the vortex theory, like the kinetic theory, explains various properties of matter. However, he claims, the former is based on known principles of hydrodynamics as well as on independently establishable facts concerning the stability of vortex rings. By contrast, the kinetic theory postulates intermolecular forces subject to "arbitrary" laws, that is, those whose only justification is that they yield known phenomena.[14] In this regard his views were similar to those of Maxwell (the first Cavendish Professor) who, when considering the vortex theory, writes:

> But the greatest recommendation of this theory, from a philosophical point of view, is that its success in explaining phenomena does not depend on the ingenuity with which its contrivers "save appearances," by introducing first one hypothetical force and then another.[15]

Interpretation 2

An alternative way to construe what Thomson is doing is to deny that he is inferring the truth or probability of hypotheses (1) through (3). How could this be? Recall our earlier discussion of Maxwell's first kinetic theory. Maxwell was in a position to give reasons to believe *some* of the basic assumptions of his theory (e.g., that gases are composed of invisible particles in motion). But in the case of other such assumptions (e.g., that the gas particles are spherical, that they exert only contact forces) he was not in such a position.

---

13. G. FitzGerald, "Dissociation of Atoms," *The Electrician* 39 (May 21, 1897), p. 104.

14. J. J. Thomson, *A Treatise on the Motion of Vortex Rings* (London, 1883), pp. 1–2. For a discussion of this and other aspects of Thomson's methodological views, see D. R. Topper, "'To Reason by Means of Images': J. J. Thomson and the Mechanical Picture of Nature," *Annals of Science* 37 (1980), pp. 31–57.

15. W. D. Niven, ed., *The Scientific Papers of James Clerk Maxwell* (New York, 1965), vol. II, p. 471.

Nevertheless, he did have good reasons for considering or pursuing such hypotheses. More generally, I spoke of reasons for considering an hypothesis that will not always be reasons for believing it to be true or probable.

It might be suggested that Thomson's situation is akin to Maxwell's. Thomson presents reasons for believing *some* of the assumptions of his theory (e.g., that cathode rays are composed of negatively charged particles). But he is not in a position to offer reasons for believing others (e.g., that these negatively charged particles are constituents of atoms). Instead he provides only reasons for considering or pursuing such assumptions.

In a later work (1907) Thomson himself expresses a general approach to physics that might be appealed to in support of this interpretation:

> From the point of view of the physicist, a theory of matter is a policy rather than a creed; its object is to connect or co-ordinate apparently diverse phenomena, and above all to suggest, stimulate and direct experiment. It ought to furnish a compass which, if followed, will lead the observer further and further into previously unexplored regions.[16]

Thomson expresses this viewpoint in other writings as well, where it is formulated as a defense of the use of physical *models* in science. He distinguishes mathematical and physical theories:

> Now, theories of physics are of two types, the one mathematical, the other physical. In the mathematical type the various physical quantities are represented by algebraic symbols, the laws of physics by equations between these symbols; the consequences of the laws are developed by attempting to solve these equations by the methods of pure mathematics. No attempt is made to connect this analysis with a mental picture of the physical processes occurring in the problem. . . . In the physical type of theory an attempt is made to form an idea of something concrete, a model, for example, which will supply us with a mental picture of what may be taking place in the physical phenomena under consideration.[17]

Theories of the physical sort, which Thomson also calls models, are "expressed in terms of concrete quantities of which we have experience . . . . and not merely in terms of algebraic symbols" (p. 21). Now, writes Thomson,

> The usual objection raised against the physical method is that the model may have other properties besides those for which it was designed, and thus may imply more than the facts justify. This, to my mind, is a point in favour of the model, for it suggests further research. (p. 19)

---

16. J. J. Thomson, *The Corpuscular Theory of Matter* (New York, 1907), p. 1.

17. J. J. Thomson, *Tendencies of Recent Investigations in the Field of Physics* (London, 1930), pp. 15–16.

And, echoing his 1907 work, Thomson writes that those who employ such models "regard a theory as a tool and not a creed, as an instrument for directing research, and not as something which it is heresy to doubt . . . " (p. 23).

Although these passages appear in a work of 1930, they reflect ideas Thomson seems to have had throughout his career. For example, in 1893 — before his cathode ray results — he distinguishes physical from purely mathematical methods when he uses Faraday's idea of tubes of force to illustrate properties of the electric field:

> The physical method has all the advantages in vividness which arise from the use of concrete quantities instead of abstract symbols to represent the state of the electric field; it is more easily wielded, and is thus more suitable for obtaining rapidly the main features of any problem . . . . It is no doubt true that these physical theories are liable to imply more than is justified by the analytical theory they are used to illustrate. This however is not important if we remember that the object of such theories is suggestion and not demonstration.[18]

Thomson does recognize that "either Experiment or rigorous Analysis must always be the final Court of Appeal." But he claims that "it is the province of these physical theories to supply cases to be tried in such a court" (p. vii).

On the present interpretation, then, Thomson's claim that atoms are composed of negatively charged corpuscles is, or is part of, a *physical* theory (or model) of matter, rather than a mathematical one. As such, it is not presented as something to be believed (as a "creed"), but something to be explored, something to direct research. Accordingly, arguments "for" the theory are not ones showing why it should be believed, but only why it should be pursued. FitzGerald, at the end of his paper, seems to be suggesting that this is a reasonable way to construe Thomson's arguments:

> In conclusion, I may express a hope that Prof. J. J. Thomson is quite right in his by no means impossible hypothesis. It would be the beginning of great advances in science, and the results it would be likely to lead to in the near future might easily eclipse most of the other great discoveries of the nineteenth century, and be a magnificent scientific contribution to this Jubilee year.[19]

Interpretation 3

The third interpretation of Thomson's procedure is to claim that he did intend to provide reasons to think his theory true or probable, and not merely

---

18. J. J. Thomson, *Notes on Recent Researches in Electricity and Magnetism* (Oxford, 1893), pp. vi–vii.

19. FitzGerald, *op. cit.*, p. 104.

reasons to pursue it, but that he was not using the method of hypothesis. How could this be?

Thomson was employing explanatory reasoning, but it is possible that crucial steps in the reasoning had (what in this volume I have called) "independent warrant." Or at least Thomson may have taken them to have such warrant. Here is a possible reconstruction of Thomson's reasoning in favor of assumption (2), that cathode particles are constituent parts of all atoms:

1. Cathode rays are composed of negatively charged particles emitted from the cathode. (Thomson considered this to be demonstrated by his magnetic and electrical deflection experiments.)
2. Cathode particles come from some matter present in the tube in the vicinity of the cathode.
3. Cathode particles are smaller in size than atoms. (Thomson argued for this from the absorption experiments of Lenard.)[20]

---

20. Heilbron represents Thomson's reasoning in 1897 as follows: " . . . from its large e/m [i.e., small m/e] he inferred its small mass (by assuming that its charge was of the order of the electrolytic unit); from its small mass he inferred (what scarcely follows) its small size; from its small size, its penetrability, and an answer to Lenard. . . . " (*op. cit.*, p. 367). This does not strike me as an accurate representation of Thomson's reasoning. In his October 1897 paper Thomson writes that "the smallness of m/e may be due to the smallness of m or to the largeness of e, or to a combination of these two" (p. 310). He then argues that Lenard's results show that the carriers of the charges in the cathode rays are small in size compared to ordinary molecules. Lenard showed that after penetrating a thin layer of metal a cathode ray travels about half a centimeter through air at atmospheric pressure before the brightness of the phosphorescence produced falls to about half its value. Thomson regarded this distance as comparable to the mean free path of the cathode particle, and noted that the mean free path of a molecule of air at this pressure is about 10^{-5} cm. From the very considerable difference in mean free paths, and assuming the larger the mean free path the smaller the particle, Thomson concludes that the cathode particle "must be small compared with ordinary molecules." Accordingly, from "penetrability" he infers small size (not the reverse, as Heilbron suggests). Then, although this is not needed for the argument I reconstruct above, either from small size he infers small mass, rather than the reverse, as Heilbron again suggests. Or else from the fact that corpuscles are much smaller than atoms and molecules, together with the assumption that atoms are composed of such corpuscles, he infers the comparative small mass of corpuscles.

Finally, contrary to Heilbron, he does not assume (at least not in his October 1897 paper) that the charge of the corpuscle is of the order of the electrolytic unit. Instead he writes that "there seems to me to be some evidence that the charges carried by the corpuscles in the atom are large compared with those carried by the ions of an electrolyte" (p. 312). Accordingly, he concludes that "the smallness of the value of m/e is, I think, due to the largeness of e as well as the smallness of m" (*ibid.*). As I noted in section 1 above, two years later, in 1899, with new experiments on negative electrification produced by ultraviolet light, Thomson revised his conclusion, claiming that "e is the same in magnitude as the charge carried by the hydrogen atom in the electrolysis of solutions" (*Philosophical Magazine* 48 (1899), p. 548).

4. But all (gross) matter is composed of atoms. (By 1897 atomic theory was widely accepted.)

5. Now (given 4) the "most simple and straightforward" explanation of 2 and 3 is that the cathode particles are constituents of the atoms comprising the gas present in the tube in the vicinity of the cathode.

6. But cathode particles with the same m/e are found in all cathode ray experiments whatever gas is present at or near the cathode.

7. So (from 5 and 6), probably cathode particles are constituents of all atoms.

Look at step 2. It is invoked to explain the origin of those particles assumed in step 1. The idea is that the presence of the particles at the cathode is most naturally explained as coming from some matter that is present (by contrast to being created anew), and since they emerge from the cathode, it is natural to explain their presence by assuming that they emerge from matter at or near the cathode (rather than, say, outside the tube). Thomson might have supposed that such assumptions are quite reasonable because the situation is similar to what experience has shown in macro cases that have been observed. (If, for example, water droplets are emerging from some source, one observes the presence of water in the vicinity of the source or the presence of substances combining to produce water.) Thomson, like many British physicists of the late nineteenth century who championed mechanical theories, believed that micro processes are subject to the same principles as those for macro ones.[21] The idea, then, is that step 2 involves not simply an explanatory claim, but one that gains some independent warrant from similar or analogous cases that have been observed. Thomson does not cite any such cases, but it is possible that he has such in mind when he speaks of his explanations as accounting for the facts "in the most simple and straightforward manner." One of the things that makes them simple and straightforward is that they invoke assumptions known to hold in similar cases.

Another explanatory step is 5, which is invoked to explain why 2 and 3 hold. Cathode particles come from matter present in the vicinity of the cathode, and they are smaller than atoms, because they are constituents of the atoms present in the gas in the vicinity of the cathode. According to FitzGerald this step is the most problematic. He would say that the previous steps, even if accepted, are all compatible with the idea that cathode particles although present in the matter in the tube are "free" and not constituents of atoms. Thomson does not even consider this possibility but defends his assumption by citing a view of the constitution of chemical elements "favourably entertained by many chemists," according to which "atoms of the

---

21. See Falconer, *op. cit.*, Topper, *op. cit.*

different chemical elements are different aggregations of atoms of the same kind."[22] He notes that Prout's version of this, in which atoms of different elements are hydrogen atoms, is not acceptable. But he claims that this does not preclude other elements. And he points out that the assumption of the divisibility of atoms has been supported recently by studies by Norman Lockyer on stellar spectra. (Lockyer observed that the same elements can exhibit different spectra under varying conditions, and took this as some reason in favor of the subatomic hypothesis.)

In addition to whatever independent warrant Thomson took Lockyer's studies to provide, his thinking was very likely more centrally tied to two related ideas. The first, and more general, one is the program of reductionism in physics to which Thomson was committed—a program to reduce matter to smaller and more fundamental parts of which it is composed.[23] He may well have regarded the success of this program with respect to various phenomena as making it plausible to suppose that if there are particles smaller than atoms that emerge from matter itself composed of atoms, then these particles are constituents of the atoms. One of these phenomena, with which Thomson was thoroughly familiar, is molecular dissociation. The second, more specific idea that may have supplied some independent warrant for Thomson's assumption is an analogy with this phenomenon. When ordinary table salt, for example, is dissolved in water there is separation ("dissociation") of the salt molecule into negatively charged atoms of chlorine and positively charged atoms of sodium. If an electric current is passed through the solution, the (ionized) sodium atoms move toward the cathode, the chlorine atoms toward the anode. The assumption is that atoms that emerge at different electrodes during electrolysis were originally parts of the salt molecule, rather than "free." Although Thomson does not cite this or any other specific example, he very clearly has the general idea of dissociation in mind when he develops his theory.[24] It is possible that examples such as this provide analogies that are at least part of the basis for his claim that the explanation that the corpuscles

---

22. "Cathode Rays," October, 1897, p. 311.

23. See Heilbron, *op. cit.* and Topper, *op. cit.*

24. In his October 1897 paper (p. 311) he speaks of the molecules of the gas being dissociated in the neighborhood of the cathode, and being split up "not into the ordinary chemical atoms, but into these primordial atoms." And in his 1899 paper in the *Philosophical Magazine* he explicitly notes the similarity between ordinary molecular dissociation and the "corpuscular" situation: "Electrification of a gas I regard as due to the splitting up of some of the atoms of the gas, resulting in the detachment of a corpuscle from some of the atoms. The detached corpuscles behave like negative ions, each carrying a constant negative charge . . . , while the part of the atom left behind behaves like a positive ion with the unit positive charge and a mass large compared with that of the negative ion" (p. 565). Perhaps it was this analogy that prevented Thomson from considering the possibility that the corpuscles come from the cathode itself.

come from the dissociation of atoms comprising the gas in the tube is the most simple and straightforward one.[25]

Philosophers of science have tended to speak of the simplicity of a set of hypotheses in terms of the number of independent assumptions or entities introduced or the complexity of the mathematical formulations. But another way in which hypotheses can be simple and straightforward is by introducing causes, or properties, or whatever that are similar to known, familiar ones. This is the basis for the adage quoted at the beginning of the essay. If one hears hoofbeats, the simplest and most straightforward explanation is that they are being produced by horses, not zebras, because hoofbeats — at least in situations familiar to us — are usually those of horses, not zebras. Indeed, this comports with Thomson's idea that a "physical" theory (as opposed to a "mathematical" one) is "expressed in terms of concrete quantities of which we have experience" (*Tendencies*, p. 21). He means that such a theory introduces physical ideas that are similar or analogous to ones that have been observed. The present interpretation of Thomson's reasoning is based on the idea that such similarities with observed cases can provide independent warrant for the physical conception introduced by the theory. It is reasonable to believe the theory, then, not simply because it can explain a range of phenomena, but because of this *and* the fact that the physical ideas it introduces have independent warrant.

If this is Thomson's thinking, then his reasoning is akin to that of the wave theorists of light who, as we saw in Part I, to explain the observed motion of light invoke the explanatory assumption that light consists either of waves or of particles. Such an assumption receives independent warrant from the fact that (as Lloyd puts it) "nature affords numerous examples of each of these modes of propagated movement." The advantage of construing his reasoning in this manner, rather than as hypothetico-deductive reasoning, is that the former can, at least in principle, be justified probabilistically (as we saw in our discussion in essays in Part I). By contrast, pure hypothetico-deductive reasoning to the truth or probability of an hypothesis is illegitimate. Because

---

25. By 1901, when Thomson is more confident in his beliefs, he takes the fact that cathode particles come from matter inside the tube, together with facts about their mass and charge, to clearly show that they are atomic constituents: "These particles occurred in the cathode rays inside a discharge tube, so that we have obtained from the matter inside such a tube particles having a much smaller mass than that of the atom of hydrogen, the smallest mass hitherto recognised. These negatively electrified particles, which I have called corpuscles, have the same electric charge and the same mass whatever be the nature of the gas inside the tube or whatever the nature of the electrodes; the charge and mass are invariable. They therefore form an invariable constituent of the atoms or molecules of all gases, and presumably of all liquids and solids." Thomson, "The Existence of Bodies Smaller than Atoms," *Proceedings of the Royal Institution* 16 (1901), p. 577.

of this, and because of the fact that Thomson never explicitly advocates h-d reasoning and even seems to repudiate it at one point, and because there are plausible alternatives, I am inclined to construe Thomson's reasoning in the case of hypotheses (1) through (3) as conforming to interpretation 2 or 3 or both rather than to 1. However, if we do interpret it in accordance with interpretation 3, that is, as based on both explanatory steps and independent warrant, we must construe much of the independent warrant as implicit.

Will understanding Thomson to be arguing in accordance with either 2 or 3 vitiate criticism of the reasoning made by Heilbron and Falconer? Yes, if we adopt 2, not necessarily if 3 is the correct interpretation. If Thomson was simply presenting reasons to pursue hypotheses (1) through (3) that were not intended as reasons to believe them, the fact that they go well beyond what the data authorize is not by itself a sufficient reason to drop (1) through (3) from consideration. On the other hand, if Thomson was presenting reasons to believe them, then the situation is not so clear. It seems fair to say that in 1897 he had good reasons (deriving from Lenard's results) in favor of believing hypothesis (1) — that cathode particles are much smaller than atoms and molecules (see footnote 20). Based on the sort of argument reconstructed above, assuming he had in mind independent warrant of the kinds mentioned, he had *some*, but not as strong, reasons in favor of believing hypothesis (2) — that cathode particles are constituents of atoms. (With respect to step 5 in the previous reconstruction, although there are similarities or analogies with observed cases of molecular dissociation, there are obvious dissimilarities as well.) But he had few if any reasons in favor of believing hypothesis (3) — that cathode particles are the only constituents of atoms.

Accordingly, a charitable, though (in virtue of his own professed methodology) by no means an unreasonable, way to construe Thomson's procedure is this. Since reasons for believing hypothesis (3) were not presented, this hypothesis was being proposed solely in the manner suggested by interpretation 2. Thomson was not inferring the truth or probability of the claim that atoms consist only of "corpuscles" but simply proposing it for consideration. It is, or suggests, a physical representation of matter that deserves study. So construed, the fact that, as Heilbron puts it, Thomson's theory claimed "far more for the 'corpuscle' than the data authorized" does not detract from Thomson's procedure. Indeed, as noted earlier, Thomson himself would regard this as a "point in favour of the model, for it suggests further research" (*Tendencies*, p. 19). By contrast, hypothesis (1) was being proposed in the manner suggested by interpretation 3. Reasons for believing (1) and not simply for considering it were proposed. Similarly, in the case of hypothesis (2) Thomson was offering some reasons for believing it, though not ones that he took to be as strong as those for hypothesis (1). To be sure, in each of these cases he was presenting reasons to consider the hypothesis. But with (1) and (2) these also constitute at least some justification for belief. Thomson's "leap" to the electron (to use Falconer's term), although bold, was not entirely unsubstantiated in the case of two of the central electron assumptions. Given his methodological and physical remarks, it is plausible to suggest that he combined explanatory reasoning with independent warrant based on similarities or analogies with familiar phenomena. Hearing (faint) hoofbeats, Thomson thought of (small) horses.

Thomson's hypotheses (1) through (3) are not the only ones he proposes in his paper of October 1897. Indeed, he does not begin with these at all but simply with the claim that cathode rays are not waves in the ether but are composed of negatively charged particles. His first concern is to conclusively establish this hypothesis and thereby refute the wave theory of the German physicists. (He is not simply providing reasons to consider the particle theory.) He proceeds to do so by conducting a series of experiments and obtaining results which, he believes, experimentally confirm the particle theory. How do they do so? More generally, what is the relationship between Thomson's theory and his experimental results? Are they derived from the theory? I believe they are not. But then how could they provide support for that theory? Although philosophers of science have devoted much attention to the relationship between theories and (what they call) "observation," the connection between theory and experiment is much less explored. These issues are addressed in the next essay.

ESSAY 11

Theory, Experiment, and Cathode Rays

"Of course, if you can predict the consequences of your own experiments before they commence, your research is very likely to be boring."

SOLOMON SNYDER, *Brainstorming*

How are theories related to the experiments to which they lead? Are the latter always derived from the former? If so, how? If not, why not? How, if at all, can theories be derived from experiments? In what follows these questions will be explored by reference to J. J. Thomson's cathode ray experiments leading to the discovery of the electron, and implications will be noted for several current topics in the philosophy of science.

1. J. J. THOMSON'S FIRST CATHODE RAY EXPERIMENT

In October 1897 J. J. Thomson published a famous paper on cathode rays in which he reports a series of experiments that, he argues, confirm the theory that cathode rays are negatively charged particles rather than ether waves.[1] Prior to Thomson's experiments various facts about cathode rays were known by physicists. These included that such rays are emitted from the cathode in a discharge tube through which an electric current passes when the pressure of the gas in the tube is reduced; that the direction of the rays is perpendicular to that of the emitting surface of the cathode; that the rays travel in straight lines perpendicular to the surface of the cathode; that they cause the glass of the tube to fluoresce; that they also cause fluorescence in zinc sulfide screens; that they are deflected by a magnetic field; that the rays can produce a tempera-

---

1. J. J. Thomson, "Cathode Rays," *Philosophical Magazine* 44 (1897), pp. 293–316. Earlier that year, on May 21, 1897, Thomson published a preliminary version in *The Electrician*, vol. 39 (1897), pp. 104–108.

ture rise in a thin foil on which they are focused; and that they produce these effects whether the cathode is made of platinum, gold, or other metals. These known facts prompted two conflicting theories about the nature of cathode rays. One, defended by Wiedemann, Goldstein, and Hertz in Germany, claimed that cathode rays are some form of electromagnetic waves. The other, defended by the English physicists Crookes and Schuster, held that they are negatively charged particles.[2]

Thomson begins his paper by noting this dispute between the English and the German physicists, and indicating that the experiments to be discussed in his paper were "made to test some of the consequences of the electrified-particle theory."[3] The first consequence is this:

> If these rays are negatively electrified particles, then when they enter an enclosure they ought to carry into it a charge of negative electricity.[4]

He notes that the French physicist Jean Perrin argued by means of an experiment that this consequence in fact obtains. Thomson describes Perrin's experiment in which a charge collector was placed inside an anode within the cathode ray tube. This collector was connected to an electroscope. When the cathode rays entered the charge collector in the anode the electroscope received a charge of negative electricity. However, when the cathode rays were deflected by a magnet so as to avoid the anode the electroscope remained uncharged. This proves, Thomson agrees, that something negatively charged is emitted from the cathode and is deflected by a magnet, but it does not prove that this something is cathode rays. It may be that the electrified substance that causes the electroscope to become charged is something temporarily associated with the cathode rays but is distinct from them. (He cites the analogy of a rifle ball and the flash when the rifle is fired, which are distinct but associated.)

To avoid this objection Thomson reports that he repeated Perrin's experiment with a somewhat different apparatus. It involves a bulb connected with a cathode ray tube. Two coaxial cylinders with slits in them are placed in the bulb. (See Fig. 4.) The cathode rays from the cathode A travel into the bulb through a slit in a metal plug in the neck of the cathode ray tube. The path of the cathode rays is traced by the phosphorescence they produce on the glass. When the cathode rays are deflected by a magnet so as to enter the holes in the cylinders, an electrometer attached to the inner cylinder shows a large charge of negative electricity. When the cathode rays do not enter the holes in the

---

2. See Essay 10.

3. Thomson, *op. cit.*, p. 294.

4. *Ibid.* Whether Thomson thought of these particles as discrete bodies in empty space or as particular configurations in an all-pervading ether is another matter. For a defense of the latter viewpoint, see the references cited in Essay 10, note 9.

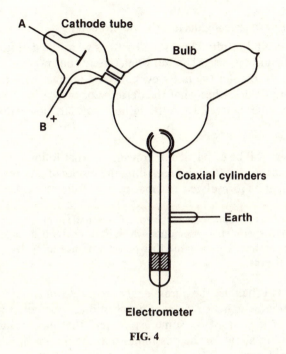

FIG. 4

cylinders, the electric charge sent to the electrometer is small and irregular. Thomson concludes that this experiment shows that however the cathode rays are deflected by magnetic forces "the negative electrification follows the same path as the rays, and . . . this negative electrification is indissolubly connected with the cathode rays."[5]

This is not the only experiment on cathode rays, or even the most famous one, that Thomson reports. But before considering any others, let me note some general points about this experiment and introduce some terminology in the next two sections.

2. EXPERIMENTAL RESULT CLAIMS

Thomson's description of his first experiment involves reference to

1. An apparatus: the cathode ray tube, bulb, magnet, and coaxial cylinders.
2. An interaction between the "substance" under study and the apparatus: Thomson describes how the rays from the cathode tube enter the bulb and are deflected by a magnet into the inner coaxial cylinder.

---

5. Thomson, *op. cit.*, p. 295.

3. A detector or measuring device: the electrometer.

4. An experimental result: Thomson describes what the detector or measuring device indicates (large charge) when the cathode rays are deflected by a magnet so as to enter the inner cylinder and interact with the measuring device. And he describes what the detector or measuring device indicates (small, irregular charge) when the cathode rays are not deflected into the inner cylinder.

The last item will be of particular concern in what follows. Let me portray it in a more general way. A claim regarding the results of an experiment of the sort above might be formulated schematically as follows:

> *Experimental result claim:* When "substance" S is made to interact in such and such a way with an experimental apparatus, which is also described, changes indicating so and so are produced in some specified detector or measuring device(s) associated with the apparatus.

In what follows I shall use the phrase *experimental result claim* to refer to any such proposition, whether or not that proposition is true, and whether or not an assertion of it is based on some experiment that has actually been performed. I want to allow for the possibility that the proposition is asserted by someone who is making a prediction about an untried experiment. And I want to allow the possibility that what is claimed is in fact false.

An experimental result claim may be formulated quite fully by giving a detailed description of the apparatus, the interaction, the detector or measuring device, and what the latter indicates. Or it may be made with a minimum of details about each (the way Thomson presents Perrin's experimental results). Not all experiments involve what might reasonably be called a substance, apparatus, interaction, and detector or measuring device. However, a significant number of them do, especially in particle physics, and what I shall say is meant to be applicable to these.

It is not my claim that the results of experiments involving an apparatus, interaction, and measuring device must always be formulated with explicit reference to these items. For example, one might describe the results of Thomson's first experiment by saying simply that in the experiment cathode rays carried a negative charge no matter how they were deflected by a magnetic field. However, an advantage of the type of experimental result claim described schematically above over the one just given is that by providing the sort of information in question it gives scientists, particularly those unaware of these items, a better chance of performing the experiment for themselves and determining whether the experimental result obtains. In what follows, then, when I use the phrase "experimental result claim" I shall be referring only to ones of this sort. This is not to say that the apparatus, the interaction, the detector or measuring device, and what the latter indicates, are the only aspects of an experiment worth mentioning.[6] My aim is to focus on one type of experimental claim frequently made. By giving the result of the experiment, such a claim, if substantiated, can provide a basis for inferences to theoretical assumptions of the theory. Moreover, by presenting information about the apparatus and so on, the possibility of substantiating the claim is enhanced.

An experimental result claim may be such that neither the theory being tested, nor some conflicting theory with which it is being compared, is presupposed by the manner in which it is given. Thomson's first experimental results were presented without supposing that cathode rays are either particles or waves. What Thomson reported was roughly this:

> (1) When cathode rays from the cathode ray tube are deflected by a magnet in the bulb in such a way as to enter the inner coaxial cylinder, a large charge of negative electricity is sent to the electrometer; when the cathode rays are not deflected by a magnet, or are deflected in such a way as not to enter the inner cylinder, the electric charge sent to the electrometer is small and irregular.

These experimental results, he believed, would be obtained by anyone repeating the experiment, whether that person subscribed to the particle or the wave theory of cathode rays. No doubt Thomson's experimental results can be described in terms presupposing the particle theory, by saying that when the negatively charged particles are emitted from the cathode and are deflected by a magnet then . . . . But in what follows I shall assume that they need not be reported in such ways. An advantage in a neutral presentation is that the experimenter can hope to gain agreement by both partisans and opponents of his theory, as well as by those uncommitted, that, whatever their theoretical views, at least the result expressed in the experimental claim does obtain.

Just as the "substance" and its interaction with the apparatus can be described in different ways, so can what is indicated by the detector or measuring device. In his first experimental result Thomson reported that the electrometer indicated a large electric charge when the cathode rays were deflected into the inner cylinder. Much more guardedly, he could have described the result by saying that when cathode rays were deflected into the inner cylinder the electrometer indicated the presence of something that was not there in such abundance when the rays were not so deflected. Or, in a stronger vein, he could have said that what is indicated by the electrometer is

---

6. Hacking, for example, notes seven "elements in laboratory experimentation," including the question(s) being raised about the subject matter, background theories being assumed, the materiel (apparatus, detector), the data and data processing, and so forth. Ian Hacking, "On the Stability of the Laboratory Sciences," *Journal of Philosophy* 85 (1988), pp. 507–514; see pp. 508–511.

that the cathode rays that are deflected into the inner cylinder carry a negative charge. In general, there will be several nonequivalent ways to formulate experimental results, some of which presuppose the theory, some of which involve bolder inferences than others concerning what the detector or measuring device indicates.

An experimental result claim may report the result of a particular experiment actually performed one or more times. For example, sometimes Thomson uses the past tense to historically record what did in fact take place in particular experiments he conducted.[7] By contrast, even though based on particular experiments that were carried out, an experimental result claim may be expressed in a more general way. Thomson frequently uses tenseless verbs to report what in general happens in such experiments.[8] The latter might be construed as inductive generalizations from other more specific claims that are historical reports of actual experiments conducted. In what follows I shall allow both types of experimental result claims.

3. THEORETICAL CONSEQUENCES

Thomson's theory, which he is testing by means of his first experiment, is simply that cathode rays are negatively charged particles, not waves. The first consequence he draws is that

> (2) When cathode rays enter an enclosure they carry into it a charge of negative electricity.

This consequence, he thinks, is proved by Perrin's simpler experiment. But that experiment does not show something stronger, that is, that

> (3) When cathode rays enter an enclosure then, *no matter how they are deflected by a magnetic force in that enclosure*, they carry a negative charge.

It is this stronger consequence that Thomson seeks to test by means of his first experiment. I shall call (2) and (3) *theoretical consequences* of Thomson's theory. He does not deduce them by producing a derivation. He simply claims that they follow from the assumption that cathode rays are negatively

---

7. "When the cathode rays . . . did not fall on the slit, the electrical charge sent to the electrometer . . . was small and irregular; when, however, the rays were bent by a magnet so as to fall on the slit there was a large charge of negative electricity sent to the electrometer." Thomson, *op. cit.*, p. 294.

8. "When the rays are turned by the magnet so as to pass through the slit in the inner cylinder, the deflection of the electrometer connected with this cylinder increases up to a certain value, and then remains stationary although the rays continue to pour into the cylinder." Thomson, *op. cit.*, p. 295.

charged particles. Perhaps Thomson's thinking can be reconstructed by means of a simple argument containing the following two premises, the second of which is a "background" assumption:

> Cathode rays are negatively charged particles. When negatively charged particles enter an enclosure they carry their charge with them no matter how they are deflected in that enclosure by a magnetic force.

(3) follows immediately.

More generally, a proposition will be called a theoretical consequence of a scientist's theory if it follows from the theory together possibly with other auxiliary assumptions the scientist is making when he proposes the theory. Do experimental result claims figure among the theoretical consequences? This question will be taken up later. For the moment let me simply note that (2) and (3) are different from what I have called experimental result claims. No measuring device or detector is invoked and no information given concerning how it is placed in the apparatus or of changes in it that would indicate the presence of negative electricity. To be sure, the very idea of cathode rays carries implicit reference to a cathode tube in which they are produced. And (2) and (3) mention an enclosure. But cathode tubes and enclosures are of quite different sorts, and no description is given of ones that might be appropriate to use or of how, or indeed whether, they are connected. I have admitted that experimental result claims will not always present a wealth of details concerning the apparatus, interaction, and measuring device. But (2) and (3) are just too incomplete in this regard. One could draw the theoretical consequences (2) and (3) from Thomson's charged particle theory of cathode rays with little if any idea how to set up an experiment to test those consequences.

Let me turn to theoretical consequences for which Thomson actually produces derivations. Having satisfied himself that cathode rays are negatively charged particles, he writes:

> The question next arises, what are these particles? Are they atoms, or molecules, or matter in a still finer state of subdivision? To throw some light on this point, I have made a series of measurements of the ratio of the mass of these particles to the charge carried by it.[9]

At this point Thomson introduces some quantitative assumptions into his theory. The first is

(4) $$Ne = Q$$

where N is the number of particles in some beam of cathode rays passing

---

9. Thomson, *op. cit.*, p. 302.

across any section of the beam in unit time; e is the charge on an individual particle, assumed to be the same for each; Q is the quantity of electricity carried by these N particles. The theoretical assumption (4) is simply that the total quantity of electricity (the total charge) carried by the N particles is equal to the charge carried by each times the number of particles.

Next Thomson writes an expression for the total kinetic theory of the particles

(5) $$1/2Nmv^2 = W$$

W = total kinetic energy of the particles; $1/2mv^2$ = kinetic energy of a given particle. He assumes that when the cathode rays strike a solid body all of the kinetic energy of the cathode particles will be converted into heat. So if we can measure the increase in the temperature of the target body when the cathode rays hit it, we can determine the kinetic energy W experimentally. (However, at this point he offers no indication of how such an experiment is to be carried out.)

Finally, Thomson assumes that if a cathode particle is subjected to a magnetic force, the magnetic force on the particle is equal to the centripetal force for circular motion. He writes this as

(6) $$mv/e = Hr = I$$

where m = mass of particle, v = velocity, e = charge on particle, H = strength of magnetic field, r = radius of curvature of particle, and I is short for Hr. (To express the idea that the magnetic force = centripetal force for circular motion he could have written $Hev = mv^2/r$, which is equivalent to (6).)

Now from (4), (5), and (6) he constructs a simple derivation of

(7) $$m/e = I^2Q/2W$$

(7) is a theoretical consequence. However, Thomson's aim is not to test (7) experimentally, but simply to determine values for I, Q, and W experimentally. This, together with (7), will then yield a value for m/e, the ratio of mass to charge of the cathode particles. Thomson clearly believes that m/e should be a constant, that is, it should have the same value for different gases, different types of cathodes, and so on. This may be considered a further assumption of his particle theory. From this assumption, together with (7), it is possible to derive

(8) $$I^2Q/2W = \text{constant}$$

which is a theoretical consequence of his theory that Thomson will test experimentally.

(8) is based on the following idea: cathode rays, which carry a total quantity of charge Q across some section of their beam, are being subjected to a uniform magnetic field whose strength is H, and as a result are deflected in a path whose radius of curvature is r (where I by definition is Hr). The rays are then to strike a solid body and convert their total kinetic energy W into heating that body. ((8) expresses a relationship between the physical quantities just mentioned.) This idea might or might not suggest some particular experimental apparatus and measuring devices to someone who understands it. Whether it does so or not, it is statable—indeed Thomson so stated it—without telling us what kind of apparatus is to be used (what sort of cathode ray tube), how a uniform magnetic field is to be created and measured, how the total charge Q, the total kinetic energy W, and the radius of curvature r of the rays are to measured. As with the earlier theoretical consequences (2) and (3), one could draw consequence (8) from Thomson's theoretical assumptions without knowing how to test it experimentally, or indeed, whether it is testable.

Having drawn the theoretical consequence (7) and, at least implicitly, (8), Thomson now proceeds to describe the experiments that he performed to measure the quantities in question, and thus to determine a value for m/e, and a test for (8). He describes three different types of cathode ray tubes he employed. In one, for example, the rays are emitted from the cathode and fall on the anode, which is a metal plug with a horizontal slit. The cathode rays pass through this slit, travel to the far end of the tube, strike coaxial cables in which slits are cut, and pass into the inside of the inner cylinder. This cylinder is connected to an electrometer whose deflection measures the quantity of electricity carried by the cathode rays into that cylinder. Thomson proceeds to describe the specific devices in the apparatus used to measure the rise in temperature produced by the cathode rays (and thus the kinetic energy carried by the rays), the magnitude of the magnetic field, and the radius of curvature of the rays. Finally, he indicates in a table the results of the measurements of these quantities when various different gases are present in the tube. Part of Thomson's table for the tube in question looks like this:

	Value of W/Q	I	m/e
Air	4.6×10^{11}	230	$.57 \times 10^{-7}$
Air	1.8×10^{12}	350	$.34 \times 10^{-7}$
Air	6.1×10^{11}	230	$.43 \times 10^{-7}$
Hydrogen	6.0×10^{12}	205	$.35 \times 10^{-7}$
CO_2	8.4×10^{11}	260	$.40 \times 10^{-7}$

The values obtained for m/e, based on the measurements recorded for this tube, range from $.32 \times 10^{-7}$ to $.57 \times 10^{-7}$. Thomson's experimental results in this series of experiments can be formulated (schematically) in the following "historical"

(9) *Experimental result claim* (from Thomson's third series of experiments): When cathode rays from a cathode ray tube of such and such a kind were deflected by a magnetic field produced in a way that is specified, then measurements of the quantities W/Q and I taken using devices of the sort Thomson describes yielded results given in the preceding table.

A more general, ahistorical experimental result claim is this:

(10) When cathode rays from a cathode ray tube are deflected by a magnetic field produced in such and such a way, then measurements of the quantities W/Q and I made using devices of the sort Thomson describes indicate that m/e has a value whose order of magnitude is 10^{-7}.

Now, to be sure, (9) and (10) presuppose the particle theory of cathode rays. W = the kinetic energy of the charged particles, and m/e is the ratio of mass to charge of these particles. However, these experimental results could just as well have been recorded using *increase in temperature* produced by cathode rays (instead of kinetic energy), and using $I^2Q/2W$ instead of m/e. In any case, one might well formulate and accept Thomson's experimental result claims without necessarily being committed to the theory that cathode rays are negatively charged particles whose ratio of mass to charge is a constant.

4. RELATIONSHIPS BETWEEN THEORY, THEORETICAL CONSEQUENCES, AND EXPERIMENTAL RESULT CLAIMS: THESES 1 AND 2

I shall propose seven theses concerning relationships that frequently obtain between theories, theoretical consequences, and experimental result claims. Each will be illustrated by reference to the Thomson example, which I take to be typical of a range of theories in physics that postulate some unobservable substance and that involve for their confirmation interactions between the substance, an experimental apparatus, and measuring devices.

Thesis 1: There are theories a scientist tests by determining the truth of experimental result claims few if any of which the scientist derives or could derive from his theory.

From his theory Thomson does not deduce experimental result claims such as (1), (9), and (10) above and then proceed to test them by performing experiments. Nor could he, for the simple reason that his theory that cathode rays are negatively charged particles remains silent on the question of experimental apparatus and measuring device. From the fact that cathode rays are negatively charged particles that can be deflected by a magnetic force it does not follow that in the particular experimental set-up described by Thomson in his first experiment the cathode rays will send a large charge of negative electricity to the electrometer. Much more is needed than Thomson's theory to derive this result.

To this the obvious response is to agree, but insist that Thomson did, or at least could, derive his experimental result claims not from his theory alone but from this together with other assumptions he was making, including ones about the specific experimental apparatus he used to perform the experiments. With respect to this response, I offer

> *Thesis 2:* (a) There are theories that a scientist tests by determining the truth of experimental result claims few if any of which are in fact derived by the scientist prior to the experiment from that theory plus other assumptions the scientist is making, including ones about the specific experimental apparatus. (b) There are theories a scientist tests by determining the truth of experimental result claims many (including some of the most important) of which are not deriv*able* from that theory together with other assumptions the scientist is making or is willing to make prior to the experiment.

Thomson does not derive *any* of his experimental result claims as predictions from his theory plus auxiliary assumptions. He does not start with the charged particle theory of cathode rays and assumptions about the experimental apparatus and from these generate predictions about what the experimental results will be when the experiments are performed. To this the response might be that the manner of presenting the results in a publication (in the "context of justification") does not necessarily reflect the original order of thought (in the "context of discovery"). So let me defend the idea of thesis 2 that even here many (including some of the most important) of the experimental result claims are not in fact derived theoretically because prior to performing the experiment they are not deriv*able* in this manner.[10] There are two reasons for this.

First, theories are frequently not rich enough even if conjoined with other assumptions one is willing to make to yield the quite specific information that can appear in experimental result claims. This is evident particularly when the latter supply values for various quantities introduced by the theory. In such cases these values, if obtainable at all, are obtainable only by actually per-

---

10. Putnam criticizes Popper for claiming that predictions in the form of "basic sentences" are deducible from theories. By contrast, Putnam claims, "theories do not imply predictions; it is only the conjunction of a theory with certain 'auxiliary statements' . . . that, in general, implies a prediction." Hilary Putnam, *Mathematics, Matter, and Method* (Cambridge, England, 1979), p. 258. If the predictions we are considering are experimental result claims, then Putnam is supporting thesis 1. What I am now claiming is something stronger, namely, that many experimental result claims made in testing a theory are neither derived nor derivable as predictions from the theory, even if you add auxiliary assumptions the scientist is willing to make.

forming the experiment. This is most obvious in historical experimental claims such as (9). Even if in advance of his experiment Thomson had known what particular magnitudes of the magnetic field strength would be used, neither the theory itself nor any assumptions he was willing to make prior to the experiment would furnish specific values for W (kinetic energy measured as heat), Q (total charge carried in unit time), and I (magnetic field strength times radius of curvature of the rays)—for a given magnetic field strength. These values, which generate the numbers in the first two columns in the table given earlier, were neither derived nor derivable from Thomson's theory of cathode rays plus auxiliary assumptions he was willing to make about the experimental set-up. They were obtained solely from the experiment itself.

The same is true even when we consider a more general, ahistorical experimental claim such as (10) that assigns a value to a quantity. Thomson's theory by itself does not yield the ratio of mass to charge of the cathode particles. It generates only (7)—which relates that ratio to a ratio of measurable quantities—and (8)—which indicates that the latter ratio is a constant. But his theory does not furnish a value for that constant, something left for experiment to determine. Even if Thomson had combined his theory with assumptions describing the experimental apparatus and measuring device he used he would not have been able to derive the experimental result (10).

There is a second important reason for thesis 2(b). Although there may be assumptions which, together with the theory, will yield the experimental result, the scientist may be unaware of them or unwilling to make them. Before Thomson's experiments, a major objection to the charged particle theory of cathode rays (an objection raised by the German wave theorists) was that if cathode rays are charged particles, they should be deflected not only by a magnetic field but by an electrical one as well. However, prior to Thomson's work no such deflection could be produced in cathode ray tubes. Thomson reports that he repeated the experiments of the German physicists, particularly of Hertz.[11] And he too observed no electrostatic deflection of the rays. Finally, he got the idea to conduct the experiments by removing most of the gas in the tube. Commenting on this years later, Thomson points out that at the time during which the experiments were conducted it was very difficult to rid the cathode tube of gas condensed on its walls.[12] From his description of the experiment it is reasonable to suppose that prior to performing the experiments with cathode tubes containing reduced density gases, Thomson would not have drawn the inference that in the tubes he was actually to use there would be electrical deflection of the rays. His attitude was most probably:

---

11. For a recent discussion of Hertz' experiment, see Giora Hon, "H. Hertz: 'The Electrostatic and Electromagnetic Properties of the Cathode Rays Are Either Nil or Very Feeble.' A Case Study of an Experimental Error," *Studies in the History and Philosophy of Science* 18 (1987), pp. 367–382.

12. J. J. Thomson, *Recollections and Reflections* (New York, 1937), pp. 334–335.

let's perform the experiments and see what happens. Perhaps he was willing to assume that if the cathode tube was sufficiently evacuated then the cathode rays would be deflected by an electrostatic force.[13] But to derive the experimental result from this he would also need to have assumed that the cathode tube in his experiments was sufficiently evacuated. And this assumption he was unwilling to make until after the experiments had been performed.

More generally, a scientist may propose to test an hypothesis by means of an experiment. Before actually performing the experiment he may be unwilling to infer an experimental result. To do so would require assumptions about the efficacy of the experimental set-up that the scientist is completely unsure of, and in any case, does not need to make, until the experiment is performed. He may be completely unsure of the assumptions because he has had to design the apparatus *ab initio*, or modify some existing apparatus, or use some existing apparatus in a new way or in an uncharted area. For these reasons, before conducting the experiment and obtaining the results he is unwilling to assume that the apparatus will work or is appropriate to test the hypothesis in question.

Nor can the derivability idea rejected in thesis 2(b) be revived if we replace deductive derivation by a weaker inductive or probabilistic one. The two reasons given in the case of deduction — the limited power of the theory and the uncertainty regarding the experimental set-up — operate here as well. Thomson's theory together with assumptions he was willing to make did not provide the basis for an inductive argument to the claim that in his electrostatic experiment cathode rays would *probably* be deflected in the apparatus in question. Even this weaker thesis would require assumptions Thomson was willing to make only after the experiment was performed. To be sure, before the experiment Thomson might well have made the modal assumption that *it is possible that* the tube was sufficiently evacuated. If so, then in advance of the experiment he could have concluded that it is possible that cathode rays will be deflected by an electric field produced in this apparatus. But the latter is too weak to be what I have called an experimental result claim. It is not what the scientist aims to establish by means of his experiment. Nor does its establishment confirm the theory being tested.

This is not to deny the existence of theories for which the scientist makes assumptions in advance about an experimental set-up, from which, together with this theory, he derives genuine experimental predictions. He may have

---

13. In 1893, before his 1897 experiments, Thomson speculated that the absence of electrical deflection in Hertz' experiment "may be because the gas through which the discharge is passing acts as a conductor and screens off the electric force." J. J. Thomson, *Notes on Recent Researches in Electricity and Magnetism* (Oxford, 1893), p. 121. See Isobel Falconer, "Corpuscles, Electrons, and Cathode Rays: J. J. Thomson and the 'Discovery of the Electron'," *British Journal for the History of Science* 20 (1987), p. 248. So prior to the experiment Thomson probably believed that with sufficient evacuation deflection would be produced.

considerable confidence in the efficacy of an experimental arrangement, and the theory may be sufficiently rich, so that a specific experimental result with the apparatus, interaction, and measuring device is predicted in advance. And of course there are experimental results known before the theory that may be derivable from the theory together with assumptions the scientist is willing to make, even if he does not in fact derive them. My claim is only that there are theories with respect to which most if not all experimental result claims made in testing those theories are not in fact derived in this way; and that, for the reasons I have given, many, including some of the most important ones, are not so derivable. Among experimental results regarded by the scientist as the most important for testing his theory are (a) results obtained by altering previous experimental arrangements to meet possible objections (as with Thomson's (1)), and (b) results unlike those that prompted the theory in the first place (e.g., Thomson's (9) and (10)). With (a) we have the idea of an improvement of experimental conditions. With (b) we have the Whewellian idea of consilience (see Essay 4). Both cases include experimental results not derived or derivable from the theory plus auxiliary assumptions.

Finally, in Thomson's case and others I am not denying that it is possible to add assumptions to the theory from which, together with the originals, experimental results such as (1) and (9) are derivable. For example, to Thomson's assumptions we could add ones giving specific values for $I^2Q/2W$ for each of the gases to be tested. From these (together with additional assumptions about the experimental arrangement) Thomson could have derived the experimental result (9) giving the m/e ratios. But this is a trivial logical exercise. Thomson did not in fact do this for two good reasons. Prior to the experiment he had no grounds at all for assuming any such specific values for $I^2Q/2W$ for each of the gases to be tested. He was in no position to make any such additional assumptions. Nor, secondly, did he need to, since the experiment itself would determine the specific values. A theory not rich enough to yield values for $I^2Q/2W$, and hence for m/e, need not be enriched to do so prior to an experiment if (i) there is no basis for doing so prior to the experiment and (ii) the experiment itself will determine these values.

5. THESES 3, 4, AND 5

If there are theories a scientist tests by determining the truth of experimental result claims, few if any of which are derived from the theory even with other assumptions, what is the origin of such claims? The answer is provided by

Thesis 3: There are theories a scientist tests by determining the truth of experimental result claims most if not all of which are made by observing the results of the experiments rather than in advance of those experiments by derivation from theoretical and experimental assumptions.

Thomson made his experimental result claims (1), (9), (10), and the rest not by first deriving them as predictions from his theory but by performing the experiments, observing the results, and then formulating his experimental claims. Thomson may have used his theory in expressing some of the latter. Instead of writing (1) in terms of the deflection of cathode rays, he could have used his theoretical assumption that cathode rays are negatively charged particles and described the result by speaking of the deflection of such particles. If so, we could say that Thomson obtained his experimental result claim — so formulated — by inference from his experiment together with an assumption from his theory. Accordingly, it is not being denied that experimental result claims are inferred. But in the cases in question, this inference is made after the experiment from what is observed in that experiment together possibly with other assumptions, including theoretical ones. It is not made prior to the experiment solely on the basis of the theory and auxiliary assumptions.

All this might be granted. Still it might be supposed that any theory will yield information about an experimental arrangement for testing it, even if it does not entail what will happen using such an arrangement (i.e., it does not entail an experimental result claim). This supposition is too strong. Thomson's charged particle theory does not contain information about an experimental arrangement for testing it. Thomson had to think up his own experiments. No doubt he was influenced in his thinking by arrangements used by other physicists, although these were different in important respects from his.[14] My point is only that whether the experimental arrangements were entirely new or some modifications of others, they were not contained in the theory itself.

Let me use the expression *experimental arrangement claim (with respect to a theory T)* for a claim that such and such an experimental arrangement is a sufficient one for testing (some part of) *T*. For example: an experimental arrangement consisting of a cathode tube, bulb, coaxial cylinders, and electroscope as depicted in Figure 4 is sufficient for testing theoretical consequences (2) and (3). Unlike what I have been calling an experimental result claim, such a proposition does not state experimental *results* (it does not say what changes are produced in the detectors or measuring devices or what these indicate). My thesis about such claims is this:

Thesis 4: There are theories the testing of which involves the establishment of experimental arrangement claims such that (a) few if any of these claims are derived or derivable from the theory; (b) before an experiment is performed the scientist is not assuming the truth or high probability of an experimental arrangement claim, nor does he need to do so; (c) such a claim is established only after the experiment is performed.

---

14. For example, in Perrin's experiment of 1895, unlike Thomson's first experiment reported above, the charge collector was placed inside rather than outside the cathode ray tube.

From his theory Thomson did not derive the claim that the experimental arrangement used to test for electrical deflection is sufficient for that purpose; nor is such a claim derivable. Before the experiment was performed Thomson did not assume that this experimental arrangement was sufficient to test for electrical deflection; he was quite unsure of that. Nor did he need to make such an assumption, since the experiment itself would establish that.

Suppose that an experimental *arrangement* claim is established after the experiment is performed. It might be suggested that the scientist now proceeds to derive an experimental *result* claim from his theory together with the newly established experimental arrangement claim and possibly other auxiliary assumptions that were not inferred from observing the experiment. At this point, it might be supposed, the scientist is sure enough about the efficacy of the experimental apparatus to derive his experimental results from his theory. In response I offer

> *Thesis 5:* (a) In general, after the experiment, experimental result claims made by a scientist testing a theory are not in fact derived by that scientist from the theory plus experimental arrangement claims the scientist is then willing to make together with other assumptions that were not inferred from observing the experiment; (b) after the experiment even if an experimental result claim is so deriv*able* there is no need to derive it.

I have admitted that, where experimental results are stated using assumptions from the theory, Thomson inferred such results from what he observed in the experiment together with assumptions from the theory. My present claim is simply that after the experiment he did not in fact derive his experimental result claims (either deductively or inductively) from his theory together with experimental arrangement claims and other assumptions that were not themselves inferred from observing the experiment. Even if they were so deriv*able* there was no point in deriving them. After the experiment there was no need to derive such claims for purposes of prediction. It was too late for that. Nor, as I shall argue in sections 6 and 8, was there any need to derive them in order to test the theory.

6. THESES 6 AND 7

If there are theories from which experimental result and arrangement claims are not in general derived, what is derived? In such cases the following obtains.

> *Thesis 6:* What the scientist does derive from his theory are theoretical consequences that for the most part are considerably more general than experimental result or arrangement claims and make little if any reference to an experimental apparatus, interaction, or measuring device.

The first consequence Thomson draws from his theory is that when cathode rays enter an enclosure they will carry into it a charge of negative electricity. This says nothing about any specific kind of cathode tube or enclosure, how to get the cathode rays into the enclosure, or how to determine whether they carry a charge when they are in an enclosure. That is, there is no mention of any experimental apparatus, how the substance in question interacts with such an apparatus, or how the effect produced is to be detected or measured. At the same time it is a more general claim than that of the experimental result (1), which does contain such information. It is more general because it makes a claim that is not restricted to the type of experimental apparatus described in (1).

Again the theoretical consequences (7) and (8) are based on the idea that cathode rays will be deflected in their paths by a magnetic field, and if allowed to strike a solid body will convert their kinetic energy into heating that body. But this idea makes no mention of any particular kind of experimental apparatus or how the quantities involved are to be measured—ideas made explicit in the experimental result (9) when schemas in the latter are properly filled in. Yet (7) and (8) are more general than (9) since they are not restricted to the type of experimental arrangement described in a completed version of (9).

One disadvantage in deriving theoretical consequences such as (2) and (3) instead of an experimental result claim such as (1) is that in doing so one may have no idea how to test them experimentally. However, there are obvious advantages. One is generality. With theoretical consequences (2) and (3) Thomson has derived something that tells us what cathode rays generally do when they enter an enclosure, not just in some particular experimental set-up. Moreover, at least in certain cases, a theoretical consequence may not be as readily subject to experimental refutation as is some corresponding experimental result claim. One of Thomson's theoretical consequences is that cathode rays will be deflected by an electric field (under certain circumstances, which he does not specify). This consequence he does not take to be refuted by the more specific experimental results obtained by Hertz and by himself in earlier experiments. Due to unspecificity in its conditions, a theoretical consequence may be more resilient than a corresponding experimental claim in the face of negative experimental results. To be sure, complete resilience with respect to negative experimental results is unacceptable. But some is advantageous.

Philosophers have frequently cited the predictive power of a theory as one of its main assets. I am claiming that there are theories from which what is predicted, even with the addition of auxiliary assumptions, are not experimental result claims but more general propositions making little reference to experimental arrangements. An example has been used that I think is typical of a range of theories in physics, postulating an unobserved substance capable of interacting with an experimental apparatus and measuring device. The appendix contains brief discussions of two other cases of this sort, both of which involve later discoveries of properties of the electron.

Even if an experimental result claim is not derived as a prediction from a theory, there is an inference in the other direction. Let me use the term *theoretical claim* very generally to refer to any proposition attributing properties to entities postulated by the theory, whether or not that proposition is included among the initial assumptions or the theoretical consequences of the theory. My final thesis is this:

> *Thesis 7:* (a) In general, the scientist makes an inference from experimental results to a theoretical claim. This inference is not deductive but involves both explanatory reasoning and inductive generalization; (b) if such an inference is justified (or to the extent that it is), the experimental results constitute evidence for, or confirm, the theoretical claim.

After describing his first experiment and its results, Thomson writes:

> Thus this experiment shows that however we twist and deflect the cathode rays by magnetic forces, the negative electrification follows the same path as the rays, and that this negative electrification is indissolubly connected with the cathode rays.[15]

This is more or less theoretical consequence (3) above. And Thomson is inferring it from his experimental results and claiming that these results confirm that consequence. Although he does not spell out the steps of this inference, the following seems to me a plausible reconstruction:

1. *Experimental result.* When the cathode rays from a cathode ray tube depicted in Figure 4 are deflected by a magnet in the bulb in such a way as to enter the inner coaxial cylinder, a large charge of negative electricity is sent to the electrometer. When the cathode rays are not so deflected the electric charge sent to the electrometer is small and irregular.[16]

2. *Explanatory step.* The fact that cathode rays carry a negative charge into the inner cylinder is the most likely explanation of the large negative charge sent to the electrometer when cathode rays enter the cylinder and of the small irregular charge when they do not enter the cylinder.

3. So probably cathode rays carry a negative charge when they are deflected by a magnet in such a way as to enter the inner cylinder of the apparatus depicted in Figure 4.

---

15. Thomson, *op. cit.*, p. 295.

16. This experimental claim, which is formulated in a timeless manner, could itself be construed as an inductive generalization of more particular experimental claims that historically report the results of experiments performed (see section 2).

4. *Inductive generalization to theoretical consequence.* Therefore, probably, however one twists and deflects the cathode rays by magnetic forces, the negative electricity follows the path of the rays.

The second step involves an assumption concerning the explanation of the observed effect on the measuring device. (This assumption, to be justified, should receive independent warrant from similarities with other observed cases.) The final step involves generalizations concerning various angles at which the cathode rays are deflected (not just those conducted in the experiment) and concerning the types of situations in which the deflection occurs (not just with the apparatus described). Accordingly, one might accept Thomson's experimental results in step 1 as correct, but refuse to draw an inference from this to the theoretical consequence 4. One might find some reason to reject the claim in step 2 that the cathode rays' carrying a negative charge into the cylinder is the most likely explanation of the charge sent to the electrometer. Or one might find some reason to reject the inductive generalization to other angles and other arrangements in step 4. (Perhaps experiments at other angles and with different arrangements are known to yield different results.) If so, one can challenge the claim that Thomson's experimental results as reported in step 1 confirm the theoretical consequence in step 4.

In the example just given the theoretical claim inferred is a theoretical consequence of the theory. But this need not be the case. From an experimental result, or set of them, a scientist may make an inference to a new theoretical claim that was not an assumption or a theoretical consequence of the original theory. This is precisely what Thomson does toward the end of his paper when, from the results of his experiments giving the m/e ratios, and from the results of Lenard's experiments concerning distances traveled by cathode rays outside the tube, he infers that cathode particles are much smaller than molecules. The latter, then, becomes a new part of a more fully developed theory.

I turn next to implications of the foregoing theses for several issues in the philosophy of science.

7. HYPOTHETICO-DEDUCTIVISM

According to this viewpoint, the scientist thinks up some hypotheses comprising a theory from which, together with auxiliary assumptions, he or she derives conclusions. The theory is tested by determining the truth of these conclusions. It is confirmed particularly if the latter include predictions whose truth is first determined after they are derived from the theory. Accordingly, we have the following:

First h-d testing thesis: Every scientific theory is tested by a scientist by determining the truth of propositions each of which the scientist derives from the theory plus auxiliary assumptions, and some of which are predictions.

This thesis is to be understood as implying that the only claims the scientist uses to test the theory are those he or she derives from that theory. This comports with the h-d idea of confirmation: to test a theory, that is, to provide confirmation or disconfirmation for it, one derives conclusions from it and determines whether they are true or false.

So understood, the first h-d testing thesis must be rejected. Thomson's establishment of his experimental result claim (10), giving an experimentally determined order of magnitude for the ratio of mass to charge of cathode particles, provided an important test for the theory that cathode rays are negatively charged particles. Yet Thomson did not derive (10) from his theory together with auxiliary assumptions he was willing to make; nor were his theory and auxiliary assumptions sufficiently rich to make (10) derivable.

More generally, there are theories that a scientist tests by determining the truth of experimental result claims few if any of which he derives, from that theory plus auxiliary assumptions, either as predictions (thesis 2) or after they already have been experimentally tested (thesis 5). Moreover, for reasons I gave in defense of thesis 2, many of the most important experimental result claims a scientist makes in testing his theory may not be deriv*able* as predictions. And, as I maintained in thesis 5, after the experiment even if an experimental result claim is derivable there is no need to derive it. What makes an experimental result claim such as (10) capable of testing a theory is not the existence of a deductive connection between it and the theory. Rather it is the fact that an inference involving explanatory reasoning and inductive generalization is justified from that experimental result to the theory (thesis 7).

In response, an h-d theorist might urge a weaker testing thesis that does not require that all propositions whose establishment tests the theory be derived or derivable from the theory:

Second h-d testing thesis: Every scientific theory is tested by a scientist by determining the truth of propositions *some* of which (including predictions) the scientist derives from the theory plus auxiliary assumptions.

This will permit experimental result claims to be used to test a theory even if they are not derived from it. So far as it goes, the second h-d testing thesis is reasonable. Thomson did test his theory that cathode rays are negatively charged particles by determining the truth of proposition (3)—that when cathode rays enter an enclosure, no matter how they are deflected by a magnetic field in that enclosure, they carry a negative charge. And he derived (3) from his theory. More generally, a scientist does test a theory by determining the truth of theoretical consequences. The problem here is not with what the second testing thesis asserts, but with what it omits.

For one thing, it does not say how the establishment of other propositions — such as (10) — that are not derived or derivable from the theory can test the theory. Moreover, neither the second nor the first thesis does full justice to what some would regard as essential to the h-d position. This is the idea that not all consequences of a theory are suitable for testing, but only those that are "observational." It is by establishing these consequences that scientists provide empirical tests for a theory. Admittedly, the sense of observational in question is not sharply defined and has been the focus of much debate. However, perhaps it is fair to ascribe at least the following two features to observational claims of h-d theorists.

First, "observational" claims are contrasted with "theoretical" ones. The latter presuppose the theory, the former do not. Observational claims are, or can be, formulated independently of the theory in a manner that does not presuppose the entities or processes postulated by the theory. Second, "observational" claims wear their methods of testing on their sleeves. They contain within themselves information on how to test them. Or at least any scientist who understood an observational claim would thereby know how to confirm or disconfirm it whether he or she subscribed to, or even understood, the theory from which it is derived.

These two features are most apparent in certain logical positivist presentations of the h-d viewpoint. Here there is an explicit division of terms and sentences into "theoretical" and "observational," and the claim is that the theory is tested by, and only by, determining the truth of observational sentences which are deduced from theoretical ones together with so-called correspondence rules that contain both theoretical and observational terms. The observational sentences are theory neutral, and one knows how to test them in virtue of knowing the meanings of the terms they employ. However, the two-vocabulary approach of the logical positivists need not be defended to emphasize the present "observability" idea. We have

> *Third h-d testing thesis:* Every scientific theory is tested by a scientist by determining the truth of observational claims each (or some) of which (including predictions) the scientist derives from the theory plus auxiliary assumptions.

The stronger claim will require "each," the weaker one only "some."

Now this third thesis, in either its strong or weak version, is dubious, if the two features of observability are kept in mind. From his charged particle theory Thomson derives (8), the establishment of which does test the theory. Yet (8) presupposes the theoretical assumption that cathode rays are particles that carry a negative charge. Moreover, theoretical consequence (8) (as well as ones such as (2) and (3)) is not such that an understanding of what it means guarantees, or even makes likely, a knowledge of how to confirm or disconfirm it. In short, consequences that Thomson derives from his theory and which test that theory do not have the two observational features above.

By contrast, these two features are present, or at least are more likely to be present, in experimental result claims, such as (1) and (9). Such claims are, or at least can be, formulated without presupposing the theory. And more than is typically the case with theoretical consequences, they wear their method of testing on their sleeves. They contain within themselves at least some description of an apparatus and measuring device used in confirming or disconfirming them. Having understood such statements one is in a better position to know how they are to be tested than is generally the case with theoretical consequences. And, as I have stated, Thomson did test his theory by determining the truth of such experimental result claims. Yet in no case did he derive one from the theory plus auxiliary assumptions.

In short, the third h-d testing thesis is objectionable because there are theories tested by (a) determining the truth of claims each of which is derived from the theory, but none of which is "observational" in the required sense, and (b) determining the truth of claims each of which is "observational," but none of which is derived from the theory.

Hypothetico-deductivists who want to pick out a special class of consequences for testing might propose substituting "testable" for "observational" in the third testing thesis. On this view, the h-d theorist requires the derivation of *testable* propositions from a theory, whether or not such propositions are construed as observational. If testable means (or includes) capable of being tested by experiments, then (some) theoretical consequences will be testable, and of course they will be derived from the theory. Thomson's theoretical consequence (8) is testable by the experiment he designed, and it is derived from his theory plus auxiliary assumptions. Won't this suffice for the h-d theorist?

This proposal will, in effect, reduce the third h-d testing thesis to the first or second. That is, the term *testable* in the claim that every scientific theory is tested by a scientist by determining the truth of testable propositions, and so on, is redundant. Moreover, those who emphasize the observationality of the consequences tested will not accept this substitution. On the present account of testability, a scientist may derive a testable consequence from a theory (i) without knowing how to test it, and (ii) without even knowing whether it is testable. Thus from his theory Thomson derives the theoretical consequence (7), $m/e = I^2Q/2W$, which relates the mass to charge ratio of the cathode particles to certain measurable quantities. This consequence is testable, but since Thomson had no independent way to determine the mass to charge ratio, he did not know how to test it, or indeed whether it is testable. However, when an h-d theorist speaks of a scientist deriving observational consequences from a theory, I take it he is not speaking of propositions for which (i) and (ii) hold. As understood by the h-d theorists in question, observational consequences are supposed to carry their method of testing with them. If so, then a scientist may test a theory without deriving any such propositions from the theory.

A second h-d reply is to admit that even if an experimental result claim introduced by a scientist is not derived from the theory together with additional assumptions the scientist is actually making, it is derivable from the theory plus assumptions the scientist could *in principle* make. What is the force of "in principle" here? If it means that given any theoretical consequence C and any experimental result claim E compatible with it there is always some assumption A such that E is derivable from C and A, then the claim is a trivial logical one. (Let $A =$ if C then E.) If it means that the scientist is always willing or in a position to make some further assumption A and derive from this and theoretical consequence C some experimental result that will test C, then the claim is not trivial, but not true in general either. The scientist may have no idea how to test a given theoretical consequence experimentally. So he or she may be in no position to make assumptions about some experimental set-up that would test the consequence. Even if the scientist has an idea about some possible experimental arrangement, he or she may be unwilling to make assumptions about it from which to derive experimental predictions. The scientist may be completely unsure about the efficacy of the experimental apparatus until the experiment is performed. And, in such a case, one does not need to make any such assumption, since the experiment itself will provide an answer.

According to one version of hypothetico-deductivism that has become fairly standard, testing a theory experimentally requires (1) deriving observational conclusions from it, (2) establishing these conclusions by experiments, and (3) making nondeductive inferences from the established conclusions to the theory. According to the view I defend, testing a theory experimentally requires (1)′ deriving theoretical consequences from it, (2)′ establishing the truth of experimental result claims by experiment, and (3)′ making nondeductive inferences from experimental result claims to the theoretical consequences. Contrary to the h-d position, I am claiming that the propositions derived in (1)′ are frequently not the same as those established in (2)′. The former by contrast to the latter are not observational in a sense propounded by h-d theorists. Accordingly, while testing a theory experimentally does require establishing the truth of observational claims, I reject the view that it requires the derivation of such claims from the theory.

Hypothetico-deductivists stress the idea that the scientist must think up, devise, or invent the fundamental theoretical assumptions of the theory. Generally these are not derived or inferred from anything else. What h-d proponents fail to note is that the same can be said with respect to testing the theory by means of experiments: *generally the scientist must think up, devise, invent some experiment to test theoretical consequences.* What experiments to perform — what apparatus and measuring instruments to use and how to do so (i.e., what experimental arrangement claims to make) — is frequently not given, or presupposed, or even suggested by the theory (thesis 4).[17] Before running an experiment the scientist obviously thinks up the experimental arrangement. But prior to the experiment, instead of making a categorical experimental arrangement claim he may make a weaker modal one of the form "it is possible that this arrangement is sufficient for testing T." Whether categorical or modal, his claim is not usually derived from the theory. And, for the reasons given in the discussion of thesis 2, frequently the results of the experiments, formulated as experimental claims, are not derived, or indeed derivable, from the theory even with the addition of auxiliary assumptions about the experimental arrangement the scientist is willing to make.

One final point. Falsificationist versions of the h-d viewpoint, such as Popper's, stress the idea that an hypothesis is experimentally falsified by deriving observational conclusions from it which turn out to be false when experiments are conducted. A typical response — due to Duhem and Quine — is to say that falsification of an hypothesis is difficult if not impossible because the observational conclusion is typically inferred from the hypothesis together with auxiliary assumptions. But there is an equally important reason for difficulty in falsification by experiment. What is inferred from the hypothesis plus auxiliary assumptions is typically not a specific experimental result claim but a less specific theoretical one that may at least implicitly contain clauses such as "in appropriate circumstances" or "if sufficiently evacuated." Thomson drew the theoretical consequence that cathode rays are deflected by an electric field (in appropriate circumstances). He did not regard this consequence as falsified by the experimental results obtained by Hertz and himself in which there was no electrical deflection of cathode rays. He simply questioned whether the circumstances of the experiment were appropriate. Since the experimental claim that cathode rays will be deflected by an electric field in the sort of experimental set-up devised by Hertz was not something he derived from his theory plus assumptions, the falsification of the latter claim by experiment was not sufficient to refute the theory.

8. CONFIRMATION

Suppose there are some experimental results e that bear on a theoretical hypothesis h. In deciding whether, or how much, to believe h, given e, scientists often seek new empirical information, including possibly new experimental results. To determine whether, or to what extent, to believe the wave theory of cathode rays, rather than the charged particle theory, in the light of Hertz'

---

17. Indeed, it may not be known by the scientist who derives the consequence. In 1860 James Clerk Maxwell derived his distribution law of molecular velocities from assumptions of kinetic theory. Yet an experimental test for that law was devised only in the 1920s with molecular beam experiments. See Essay 6.

negative results, Thomson sought to perform new experiments in which the cathode tube was more completely evacuated. Why did he do so? This can be understood by appeal to thesis 7, but not, as we shall see, by invoking certain standard philosophical accounts of confirmation or evidence.

In deciding whether, or to what extent, to believe an hypothesis h, given e, one may attempt to construct an inference from e to h. According to thesis 7, a typical inference from an experimental result to a theoretical proposition involves both explanatory reasoning and inductive generalization. But each of these steps may require that additional experimental results be obtained. For example, to get from Hertz' experimental results in which no electrical deflection was observed to the theoretical claim that cathode rays are waves, not charged particles, one argues that the fact that cathode rays are not negatively charged particles but waves in the ether is the most likely explanation of why no electrical deflection was detected in Hertz' experiments. But to determine whether this explanatory claim is reasonable, Thomson wanted to consider an alternative explanation, namely, that the cathode tube was not sufficiently evacuated, as a result of which the electric field intensity was too small to produce detectable deflection. To evaluate the plausibility of this alternative explanation Thomson constructed new experiments in which the cathode tube used was more completely evacuated.

Now the concept of confirmation or evidence is related to that of belief. If e confirms or is evidence for h, that can and ought to have an effect on whether, or to what extent, to believe h, given e.[18] Moreover, I have claimed (thesis 7) that if (or to the extent that) an inference involving explanatory and inductive reasoning is justified from an experimental result e to a theoretical claim h, e is evidence for, or confirms, h. Yet typical philosophical accounts of confirmation provide inadequate motivation for seeking additional empirical information beyond e in determining whether such an inference is justified and hence whether e confirms h. In what follows I shall mention theories of two general sorts. The first, which will take up most of the discussion, includes theories according to which confirmation is completely decidable by a priori calculation. The second is subjective Bayesianism.

On the a priori view, to determine whether, or to what extent, an experimental result e confirms an hypothesis h one simply performs some logical or mathematical computations.[19] Now suppose we have obtained some informa-

---

18. See Peter Achinstein, *The Nature of Explanation* (New York, 1983), ch. 10.

19. For example, according to a simple version of hypothetico-deductivism, e confirms h if and only if e is deductively derivable from h. On Hempel's satisfaction theory, e confirms h if e entails the development of h for the individuals mentioned in e. (Carl G. Hempel, "Studies in the Logic of Confirmation," reprinted in Peter Achinstein, ed., *The Concept of Evidence* (Oxford, 1983), pp. 10–43.) On Glymour's more sophisticated bootstrap version of this, e confirms h with respect to a theory T if and only if using T it is possible to derive from e an instance of h, and the

tion e and we are considering hypothesis h. If confirmation is solely a matter of such a priori calculation, then no new empirical information is needed — no new experimental results — to determine whether (or to what extent) e does, or does not, confirm h. So far, then, there is no reason to obtain any new information. Do a priori theories provide any such reason?

An idea frequently associated with such theories is the requirement of total evidence. According to Carnap,

> In the application of inductive logic to a given knowledge situation, the total evidence available must be taken as a basis for determining the degree of confirmation.[20]

By "total evidence available" Carnap means facts that have been observed (rather than ones that are observable but have not yet been observed). Suppose that the degree of confirmation that e confers upon h is r. Then, writes Carnap:

> If e expresses the total knowledge of [person] X at the time t, that is to say, his total knowledge of the results of his observations, then X is justified at this time to believe h to the degree r. . . . (p. 211)

The latter version of the total evidence requirement is the one of concern to me here. It supplies a sufficient condition for being justified in having a (degree of) belief in some proposition. This version furnishes a motivation for taking into account some piece of information, provided that it is part of the scientist's total observational knowledge. But if it is not — if it is information the scientist has not yet obtained — the requirement of total evidence offers no reason to search for it. If e reflects the scientist's total observational knowledge at time t, and if e confirms h (to degree r), then by the above principle at time t the scientist is justified in believing h (to degree r), no matter what else may be true. At some later time t' if the scientist has obtained new information he or she may no longer be justified in this belief. But the principle itself gives the scientist no reason to obtain new information. It simply allows basing beliefs on, and only on, all the observational knowledge the scientist has.

---

derivation is such as not to guarantee an instance of h no matter what e is chosen. (Clark Glymour, "Relevant Evidence," reprinted in Achinstein, *op. cit.*, pp. 124–144.) According to Carnap's probabilistic version, e confirms h to degree r if and only if the ratio of the sum of the measures of the state descriptions that entail h&e to the sum of the measures of those that entail e is equal to r; and e confirms h if the degree to which e confirms h is greater than h's prior degree of confirmation. (Rudolf Carnap, *Logical Foundations of Probability* (Chicago, 1962).) In all these cases a priori computation settles the issue of confirmation.

20. Carnap, *op. cit.*, p. 211.

In short, on standard a priori theories of confirmation you do not need new empirical information to determine whether, or to what extent, some old empirical information *e* confirms an hypothesis *h*. And if *e* is your total (relevant) empirical information at time *t*, then you do not need any new empirical information to determine how justified you are at time *t* in believing *h*. So why seek any new information? The only reason I can see standard a priori theories offering is this: new information may change the (degree of) confirmation of *h*, and therefore change the extent to which you are justified *at some later time t'* in believing *h*.

I do not regard this *mere possibility* as a sufficient reason to pursue new information, since it is also possible that new information may leave the (degree of) confirmation of *h* unchanged. Perhaps the following is really being supposed. Let the degree of confirmation of *h*, given *e*, be *r*, and assume that *e* itself provides a reason to think that some new evidence will be forthcoming that will change *h*'s degree of confirmation. Then we should try to pursue that new evidence. The problem with this supposition is that it is self-contradictory. If *e* itself provides a reason to think that new evidence will be forthcoming that makes *h*'s degree of confirmation unequal to *r*, then this should contradict the assumption with which we began, that is, that *h*'s degree of confirmation, given *e*, is *r*.

Now let us return to Thomson's response to the absence of electrical deflection of the cathode rays in experiments of the sort conducted by Hertz and by Thomson himself before his later experiments. Instead of taking these experimental results to constitute a justification to believe that cathode rays are waves, not charged particles, Thomson proceeds to seek new information by performing a new experiment. Can this strategy be defended?

It can if we abandon the view that confirmation is always decidable a priori, or abandon the previous version of the requirement of total evidence, or both. First, we might say that whether some information *e* confirms or disconfirms an hypothesis *h* is not always settleable by a priori calculation. Indeed, this is perfectly compatible with the type of inference involving explanatory reasoning and inductive generalization considered in the discussion of thesis 7. To ascertain whether Hertz' and Thomson's earlier experimental results confirm the wave hypothesis one may want to consider whether the most likely explanation for the lack of electrical deflection with the apparatus in question is that cathode rays are waves, not charged particles, and whether the lack of electrical deflection with this apparatus can be generalized to other experimental arrangements in which the cathode tube is more extensively evacuated. To draw either the explanatory inference or the inductive generalization to other experimental arrangements, new empirical information may be sought concerning what happens when more gas is removed from the cathode ray tube. If so, then to determine whether Hertz' and Thomson's earlier experiments confirm the wave hypothesis, additional empirical information is relevant. On this proposal, Thomson sought such new information to justify his (empirical) claim that Hertz' experimental results do not confirm the wave hypothesis. More generally, a scientist will seek new empirical information if that will help to show whether some current information confirms an hypothesis. Here, then, is one motivation for seeking new information that helps to explain why Thomson performed a new experiment.

Second, we might deny that if e confirms h (to degree r) and if e represents a scientist's total evidence, then necessarily the scientist is justified in believing h (to degree r). We may deny this if we think the scientist should have obtained additional information. Even if Thomson were to agree that Hertz' experiments confirm the hypothesis that cathode rays are waves, not particles, and even if these experiments had constituted Thomson's total relevant available evidence before 1897, Thomson might have argued that he was not justified in believing that hypothesis. The reason is that the available experimental evidence, even if confirmatory, is too meager or incomplete to justify a belief. Here, then, is a second motivation for seeking new information that if valid helps to explain why Thomson performed a new experiment.[21]

In fact I believe that both proposals are reasonable: confirmation is not always decidable by a priori calculation, and Carnap's version of the requirement of total evidence is false. I shall not pursue these matters further here, except to note one advantage in abandoning a completely a priori view of confirmation. A priori accounts of confirmation fail to explain, or indeed even to mention, the fact that confirmation of a scientific hypothesis is frequently *controversial*. To be sure, scientists may disagree over the experimental result claims themselves—whether the results they report were actually obtained or are repeatable. But this is not the controversy I mean. Two scientists may agree about the experimental results—as did Hertz and Thomson about the absence of electrical deflection of the cathode rays in experiments of the sort conducted by Hertz. Yet they may, and frequently do, disagree over whether these results confirm or disconfirm a given hypothesis. But if confirmation is solely a matter of a priori computation, then—where scientists agree on the experimental claims—why should there be much if any controversy over whether an hypothesis is confirmed? Just perform the computation and settle the issue!

Frequently, however, it is not a computation that settles the dispute. Rather

---

21. An a priorist might respond by saying that although the absence of deflection (A) does not by itself disconfirm the particle theory (P), this together with the assumption that the gas in the tube is sufficiently evacuated (E) does. And that A and E disconfirm P is an a priori fact. Accordingly, Thomson performed a new experiment to determine the truth of E so that he would know whether there is evidence that a priori disconfirms P. But this response makes little sense in the light of the requirement of total evidence. If A together with all the other relevant evidence Thomson has does not disconfirm P, then Thomson should not disbelieve P on the basis of A. Moreover, if all other available information together tends to confirm P, then Thomson should believe P on the basis of this evidence. Thomson should base his beliefs on evidence he has, not on (possible) evidence he does not have.

appeal is also made to some empirical claim. In determining whether Hertz' experimental results *e* disconfirmed the particle hypothesis *h* Thomson decides to find out whether (i) cathode rays will be deflected when the tube is much more completely evacuated. There is disagreement between Hertz and Thomson because Hertz is committed to the view that (i) is false, while Thomson suspends belief about (i) until his new experiment is performed. If in this case the claim that *e* disconfirms *h* is construed as empirical, rather than a priori, we can understand the dispute between Thomson and Hertz, and why Thomson seeks a new experiment rather than an a priori argument purporting to show that *e* does not disconfirm *h*.

Finally, let me turn briefly to a very different approach to confirmation, namely, subjective Bayesianism. According to this, *e* confirms *h* for a particular person if *e* increases *h*'s subjective probability for that person. Suppose, for example, that in 1897, before new experiments on electrical deflection had been performed, a typical wave theorist's subjective probability associated with the particle theory was considerably lower than Thomson's. On the subjective viewpoint, Thomson sought to perform the new experiment with a more evacuated tube because whatever its outcome it would bring his and his opponents' degrees of belief in the particle theory closer. If deflection occurred, an opponent's degree of belief in the particle theory would become higher and closer to what Thomson's would be. If deflection did not occur, Thomson's degree of belief in the particle theory would become lower, and closer to what an opponent's would be. And, on this approach, whatever can be done to achieve (more) intersubjective agreement in science is of value. So Thomson performed the new experiment to obtain an empirical result that would cause changes in degrees of subjective belief in such a way as to produce more intersubjective agreement.

Granted that Thomson did want more agreement, why did he choose to achieve this by conducting a new experiment? If intersubjective agreement was paramount, then without performing any new experiment he could simply have altered his own degree of belief in the particle theory to match that of the wave theorist (just as one alters one's beliefs on discovering them to be incoherent). He might have chosen to follow the cherished principle: go along to get along. Or he might have tried to use this principle to convince the wave theorist to change his beliefs.[22]

A subjectivist may respond that what Thomson wanted was not simply to

---

22. This can be formulated in terms of the usual conditionalization principle accepted by Bayesians. Let $p_h(t_1)$ (P) be Hertz' degree of belief in P (particle theory) at time t_1. Suppose this is equal to .3. Now suppose that Hertz is moved by the "go along to get along" principle and is motivated to change his beliefs when there is disagreement and appeal is made to this principle, so that the conditional probability $p_h(t_1)$ (P/there is disagreement at t_2 with particle theorists and appeals are made to Hertz to go along) = .7. By the conditionalization principle $p_h(t_2)$ (P) = .7.

obtain intersubjective agreement but to do so by empirical means, in this case, by obtaining new experimental results. But the question is why Thomson would want to do so by those means rather than others that might have been simpler to achieve. If Thomson's main concern in seeking more information was to produce more intersubjective agreement, this might well have been accomplished without performing any experiment at all.

The proposal I have been making is that Thomson's primary motive in performing the new experiment was not to get more intersubjective agreement, but to determine whether Hertz' and his earlier experiments did, as Hertz claimed, confirm the wave theory and disconfirm the particle theory. Contrary to subjective Bayesians, I am saying that this is an objective, not a subjective, question. Contrary to a priori theorists, I am claiming that Thomson settled the question empirically, not a priori. If the question is an objective empirical one, then, by contrast to the subjective viewpoint, the *only* thing Thomson could do in settling it was to obtain new empirical information of a sort provided by an experiment. Moreover, if he could settle the issue in this fashion, he could get intersubjective agreement as a byproduct.

9. DATA AND PHENOMENA

Recently Bogen and Woodward have claimed that a distinction between data and phenomena needs to be recognized.[23] This distinction is important, they claim, because, by contrast to what is frequently assumed, what is *observed* are data, not phenomena; and what is *explained* are phenomena, not data. For example, when the melting point of lead is determined by experiment, a series of temperature measurements is made, not just one measurement. The particular thermometer readings, which form a scatter, constitute the data. These readings are what is observed. From this scatter in the data some "true" melting point is inferred or estimated using a theory of statistical inference. This true melting point (327°C), or the fact that lead melts at this temperature, is a *phenomenon*, not a datum or a part of the data. Moreover, it is not something that is observed. Rather it is inferred from various data that are observed. However, it is something that a scientist will try to explain. By contrast, the specific set of thermometer readings obtained—the scatter—is not something a scientist will attempt to explain, since it depends not only on the nature of lead but on a confluence of factors pertaining to the mechanism of the particular thermometer and how and when it was applied and read.

Suppose we think of those experimental result claims that have been established by experiments as data, and the theoretical claims one infers from them

---

23. James Bogen and James Woodward, "Saving the Phenomena," *Philosophical Review* 97 (1988), pp. 303–352.

(in the manner of thesis 7) as phenomena. Then, if Bogen and Woodward are right, we can understand why theses 1 through 7 of earlier sections hold. Those experimental result (as well as arrangement) claims that have been established (the data) are not in general derived or derivable from a theory — theses 1, 2, 4, and 5. (No theory of lead, or of solids, will yield the particular scatter of thermometer readings obtained in an experiment.) Rather they (as well as experimental arrangement claims) emerge by observation from the experiment itself (theses 3 and 4). What is derivable (or more generally explainable) from the theory are the theoretical consequences (the phenomena) — thesis 6. However, these theoretical consequences are not observed. Rather they are nondeductively inferred from the experimental results (the data) that are observed — thesis 7.

I reject this facile explanation of my earlier theses. To begin with, what I have been calling (established) experimental result claims include some that Bogen and Woodward would clearly call data, but many others that I think they would not. Among the former is (9) of section 3, which contains specific sets of values Thomson actually obtained for W/Q and I in his third set of experiments. Bogen and Woodward, I take it, would include (9) among the data, just as they do in the case of some particular temperature measurements obtained for lead. However, my (established) experimental result claims also include many more general, ahistorical claims, such as (10), which contain no recorded "data points" and seem different from what Bogen and Woodward classify as part of the data. Indeed, they are more like what these authors call phenomena, being inferred from various recorded "data points." Yet (10), no less than (9), is not derivable from Thomson's theory. Accordingly, while the Bogen and Woodward idea might explain why some experimental claims are not derivable from the theory being tested, there are many others for which it will not provide such an explanation.

Moreover, some of their assertions about what they regard as phenomena and data I find dubious. For example, they say that phenomena are not observable. The deflection of cathode rays by a magnetic field (or the fact that cathode rays are so deflected) is the sort of thing they would call a phenomenon. Yet it can readily be observed. To be sure, it is observed by observing immediate effects such as the fluorescence. But there are contexts in which it is perfectly correct to speak of observing the deflection of cathode rays by a magnetic field.[24] Bogen and Woodward also say that data, although observable, are not generally explained. Now if to "explain the data" means to answer some explanatory questions about them,[25] then I suggest that Bogen and Woodward are correct in some cases and incorrect in others. For example, one question about the data obtained by Thomson in the m/e experiments is

24. See Peter Achinstein, *Concepts of Science* (Baltimore, 1968).
25. See Achinstein, *The Nature of Explanation*.

this: Why are the specific values of W/Q and I in the first row of Thomson's table 4.6×10^{11} and 230, respectively? Clearly Thomson does not explain this. But another question about Thomson's data is this: Why are the specific values for I, Q, and W obtained in these experiments such that $I^2Q/2W$ is approximately constant? Clearly Thomson does explain this by reference to his charged particle theory of cathode rays.

The concept of "data" is context dependent. Whether some body of information constitutes data depends on what, in the circumstances, can be taken for granted or can be taken as having been established. For example, for both the wave and particle theorists of cathode rays, the following would have been considered data, in virtue of having been established to the satisfaction of both sides: cathode rays are emitted in a cathode ray tube; they travel in straight lines; they produce fluorescence in glass; they are deflected by a magnetic field. Admittedly each of these claims—which Bogen and Woodward would call phenomena—were inferred from other things. But once established to the satisfaction of all sides, they now function as data for further inferences. If data comprise only what is not and never was inferred but "immediately perceived without inference," then many of the items Bogen and Woodward classify as data—including measurement results—will need reclassification.

10. CONCLUSIONS

1. There are theories a scientist tests by determining the truth of experimental result claims few if any of which, prior to the experiment, are derived by the scientist from the theory together with auxiliary assumptions. Because of the limited power of the theory and uncertainties about the experimental set-up, many such claims are not even derivable in principle. Instead they emerge by observation of the results of the experiment. What is derived from the theory prior to the experiment are consequences that typically are much more general than experimental result claims and make little or no reference to an experimental apparatus.

2. Confirming a theory may involve establishing the truth of experimental result claims. But, contrary to hypothetico-deductivism, it does not require the derivation of such claims from the theory. What suffices is the derivation of more general and experimentally "silent" theoretical consequences, and an inference in the opposite direction from experimental results to these theoretical consequences. The latter inference is not deductive, but involves both explanatory reasoning to theoretical causes of the experimental result and an inductive generalization to the more general conditions expressed in the theoretical consequence. Because of such reasoning, contrary to a priori accounts,

whether some experimental result confirms a theory is not in general settle-able by a priori calculation.

APPENDIX

Here I shall briefly note two famous cases involving theoretical predictions that were experimentally confirmed. The question is whether experimental result claims were derived from the theory. The first case is mentioned by Popper as "the most beautiful instance" of a theoretical prediction of an observable effect: de Broglie's prediction of the wave character of electrons first confirmed experimentally by Davisson and Germer.[26]

De Broglie's basic idea is that every particle of matter has an associated wave whose wavelength λ is related to its mass m and velocity v by the formula $\lambda = h/mv$, where h = Planck's constant. He applies this idea to electrons that acquire a velocity v under the action of a difference of potential P. The kinetic energy of any such electron is $1/2mv^2 = eP$, where e = the charge of an electron. Solving for v and substituting the result in the formula $\lambda = h/mv$ yields $\lambda = h/2meP$. Substituting known values for h, m, and e, he obtains $\lambda = 12 \times 24/P \times 10^{-8}$ cm, where P is in volts. De Broglie notes that for electrons under the action of a difference of potential of at least some tens of volts the associated wavelengths will be of the order of 10^{-8} cm, which is also the order of magnitude of wavelengths of x-rays. But, he points out, x-rays are known to be diffracted by crystals. So he concludes, "we may fairly expect to obtain a scattering of this [electron] wave by crystals, in complete analogy to the Laue phenomenon [involving scattering of x-rays by crystals]."[27] The argument to the conclusion that electrons can be diffracted by crystals in-volves deductive steps and a crucial analogical one. But what is inferred is a value for the electron wavelength as a function of potential difference and the claim that electrons can (probably) be diffracted by crystals, neither of which is an experimental result claim. De Broglie goes on to mention that Davisson and Germer devised an experiment to show electron diffraction and confirm the quantitative prediction about electron wavelengths. But he does not de-rive experimental results from his theory, which indeed was worked out before de Broglie knew of these experiments.

My second example involves a case that recent philosophers and historians of science have focused on, Millikan's oil drop experiment. Millikan writes that one of his aims in conducting this experiment is to present confirming

26. Karl Popper, *Logic of Scientific Discovery* (London, 1959), pp. 107–108.

27. Louis V. de Broglie, "The Undulatory Aspects of the Electron," Nobel prize address, Stockholm, 1929, reprinted in Henry A. Boorse and Lloyd Motz, eds., *The World of the Atom*, vol. 2 (New York, 1966), pp. 1048–1059; quotation on p. 1057.

evidence for the theory that "all electrical charges, however produced, are exact multiples of one definite, elementary electrical charge, or in other words, that an electrical charge instead of being spread uniformly over the charged surface has a definite granular structure. . . . "[28]

Millikan begins by describing his experimental apparatus, which consists of an atomizer that sprays fine oil droplets into a space between two parallel plates. An oil droplet will fall under the influence of gravity, but because of air resistance will soon reach a terminal velocity v_1 that can be determined by measuring the time and distance of the fall. Next the plates are charged so as to drive the droplet upward with a force given by $Fe_n - mg$, where F is the magnitude of the electric field between the plates, e_n is the charge on the droplet, m is the mass of the droplet, and g is the gravitational constant. The electrical field produces an upward terminal velocity v_2 for the droplet, which can be determined by measuring the time and distance of the rise. Millikan describes the experimental apparatus in detail, as well as the method of observing the droplets and the times of their fall and rise.

He then proceeds to derive the following formula:

$$(11) \qquad e_n = \frac{4}{3}\left(\frac{9\mu}{2}\right)^{3/2}\left[\frac{1}{g(\sigma-\rho)}\right]^{1/2}\frac{(v_1 + v_2)v_1^{1/2}}{F}$$

All the quantities on the right side of equation (11) are measurable in the oil drop experiment. (μ = coefficient of viscosity of the medium through which the droplet moves; ρ = density of this medium; σ = density of the drop.) The experiment is then run and various values of v_1 and v_2 are determined experimentally. Millikan then uses equation (11) to obtain values for e_n, the charge on the oil droplet.

His most important experimental result claim might be formulated (schematically) as follows:

(12) When oil drops in the experimental arrangement described by Millikan are allowed to fall in a gravitational field between the plates and then are pushed upward by an electric field, the charge on the drops, as determined from measurements of various quantities, are all whole multiples of an elementary charge whose mean value is 4.917×10^{10}.

In advance of the experiment Millikan did not derive this claim from the theory that electric charges are whole multiples of an elementary charge, or even from this theory together with (11) above. Nor indeed is (12) so derivable. Rather, he inferred (12) from observing the results of the experiment by

---

28. R. A. Millikan, "The Isolation of an Ion, a Precision Measurement of Its Charge, and the Correction of Stokes's Law," *The Physical Review* 32 (1911), pp. 349–397; quotation on p. 350.

making use of (11) to compute e_n from other quantities measured in the experiment.

What about (11)? Did Millikan derive it from the theory, and is it an experimental result claim? My answer to both questions is no. To derive (11), Millikan uses Stokes' law and a number of assumptions from classical mechanics and electrostatics, but not the assumption that charges are "atomic" rather than continuous. Furthermore, (11) is not an experimental result claim. Even if one adds to (11) information about the experimental arrangement and the results of measurement of all the measurable quantities on the right side, (11) would not be inferable, since no independent way of measuring e_n is given. Although (11) itself is not an experimental result claim, nor a theoretical consequence of the "atomistic" theory being tested, it is nevertheless used by Millikan in establishing his experimental result claim (12).

In brief, then, the theoretical prediction that charges come in whole multiples of an elementary charge is confirmed by establishing the experimental result claim (12), using the derived formula (11). (12) is not derived or derivable from the theory, even if assumption (11) is added. Instead Millikan infers it, using (11), by observing the results of the experiments.*

---

*I am indebted to Robert Rynasiewicz for critical comments.

Index